ROYAL COMMISSION ON THE PRESS

CHAIRMAN: PROFESSOR O R McGREGOR

Industrial Relations in the National Newspaper Industry

A REPORT BY THE
ADVISORY CONCILIATION AND ARBITRATION SERVICE

Research Series 1

Presented to Parliament by Command of Her Majesty
December 1976

LONDON
HER MAJESTY'S STATIONERY OFFICE
£5 net

Cmnd. 6680

ISBN 0 10 166800 7

ELIZABETH R.

ELIZABETH THE SECOND, by the Grace of God of the United Kingdom of Great Britain and Northern Ireland and of Our other Realms and Territories QUEEN, Head of the Commonwealth, Defender of the Faith, to

    Our Trusty and Well-beloved Sir Morris Finer, Knight, one of the Justices of Our High Court of Justice;

    Our Right Trusty and Well-beloved Henry Cecil John, Baron Hunt, Commander of Our Most Excellent Order of the British Empire, Companion of Our Distinguished Service Order;

    Our Trusty and Well-beloved:

    John Eilian Jones, Esquire, Officer of Our Most Excellent Order of the British Empire;

    Eirlys Rhiwen Cadwaladr Roberts, Officer of Our Most Excellent Order of the British Empire;

    Elizabeth Anderson;

    David Basnett, Esquire;

    Geoffrey George Goodman, Esquire;

    Malcolm Horsman, Esquire;

    Paul Bede Johnson, Esquire;

    Oliver Ross McGregor, Esquire;

    Ian Francis Richardson, Esquire,

                                                                     Greeting!

WHEREAS We have deemed it expedient that a Commission should forthwith issue to inquire into the factors affecting the maintenance of the independence, diversity and editorial standards of newspapers and periodicals, and the public's freedom of choice of newspapers and periodicals, nationally, regionally and locally, with particular reference to:

(a) the economics of newspaper and periodical publishing and distribution;

(b) the interaction of the newspaper and periodical interests held by the companies concerned with their other interests and holdings, within and outside the communications industry;

(c) management and labour practices and relations in the newspaper and periodical industry;

(d) conditions and security of employment in the newspaper and periodical industry;

(e) the distribution and concentration of ownership of the newspaper and periodical industry, and the adequacy of existing law in relation thereto;

(f) the responsibilities, constitution and functioning of the Press Council;

and to make recommendations;

NOW KNOW YE That We, reposing great trust and confidence in your knowledge and ability, have authorised and appointed, and do by these

Presents authorise and appoint you the said Sir Morris Finer (Chairman); Henry Cecil John, Baron Hunt; John Eilian Jones; Eirlys Rhiwen Cadwaladr Roberts; Elizabeth Anderson; David Basnett; Geoffrey George Goodman; Malcolm Horsman; Paul Bede Johnson; Oliver Ross McGregor and Ian Francis Richardson, to be Our Commissioners for the purposes of the said inquiry:

AND for the better effecting the purposes of this Our Commission We do by these Presents give and grant unto you, or any four or more of you, full power to call before you such persons as you shall judge likely to afford you any information upon the subject of this Our Commission; to call for information in writing; and also to call for, have access to and examine all such books, documents, registers and records as may afford you the fullest information on the subject and to inquire of and concerning the premises by all other lawful ways and means whatsoever:

AND We do by these Presents authorise and empower you, or any of you, to visit and personally inspect such places as you may deem it expedient so to inspect for the more effectual carrying out of the purposes aforesaid:

AND We do by these Presents will and ordain that this Our Commission shall continue in full force and virtue, and that you, Our said Commissioners, or any four or more of you may from time to time proceed in the execution thereof, and of every matter and thing therein contained, although the same be not continued from time to time by adjournment:

AND We do further ordain that you, or any four or more of you, have liberty to report your proceedings under this Our Commission from time to time if you shall judge it expedient so to do:

AND Our further will and pleasure is that you do, with as little delay as possible, report to Us your opinion upon the matters herein submitted for your consideration.

GIVEN at Our Court at Saint James's the Sixteenth day of July, 1974; In the Twenty-third Year of Our Reign.

By Her Majesty's Command.

ROY JENKINS.

ELIZABETH R.

ELIZABETH THE SECOND, by the Grace of God of the United Kingdom of Great Britain and Northern Ireland and of Our other Realms and Territories QUEEN, Head of the Commonwealth, Defender of the Faith, To all to whom these Presents shall come,

Greeting!

WHEREAS by Warrant under Our Royal Sign Manual bearing date the Sixteenth day of July, 1974, the Royal Commission on The Press was constituted:

AND WHEREAS We have deemed it expedient to appoint further members:

NOW KNOW YE that We reposing great confidence in the knowledge and ability of Our Trusty and Well-beloved George Sidney Bishop, Esquire, Companion of Our Most Honourable Order of the Bath, Officer of Our Most Excellent Order of the British Empire; Roger Richard Edward Chorley, Esquire, (commonly called The Honourable Roger Richard Edward Chorley) and Zangwill Aubrey Silberston, Esquire, have authorised and appointed and do by these Presents authorise and appoint the said George Sidney Bishop, Roger Richard Edward Chorley and Zangwill Aubrey Silberston to be Members of the said Commission.

GIVEN at Our Court at Balmoral the Sixteenth day of August, 1974; In the Twenty-third Year of Our Reign.

By Her Majesty's Command.

MERLYN REES.

ELIZABETH R.

ELIZABETH THE SECOND, by the Grace of God of the United Kingdom of Great Britain and Northern Ireland and of Our other Realms and Territories QUEEN, Head of the Commonwealth, Defender of the Faith, To Our Trusty and Well-beloved Oliver Ross McGregor, Esquire.

Greeting!

WHEREAS by Warrant under Our Royal Sign Manual bearing date the Sixteenth day of July, 1974, the Royal Commission on The Press was constituted:

NOW KNOW YE that We, reposing great confidence in your knowledge and ability, have authorised and appointed, and do by these Presents authorise and appoint, you the said Oliver Ross McGregor, to be Chairman of the said Commission in the room of Our Trusty and Well-beloved Sir Morris Finer, Knight, deceased.

GIVEN at Our Court at Saint James's the Seventh day of March, 1975; In the Twenty-fourth Year of Our Reign.

By Her Majesty's Command.

ROY JENKINS.

ROYAL COMMISSION ON THE PRESS

RESULTS OF RESEARCH CARRIED OUT FOR THE COMMISSION

To the Queen's Most Excellent Majesty

MAY IT PLEASE YOUR MAJESTY

We, the undersigned Commissioners, having been appointed by Royal Warrant "to inquire into the factors affecting the maintenance of the independence, diversity and editorial standards of newspapers and periodicals, and the public's freedom of choice of newspapers and periodicals, nationally, regionally and locally, with particular reference to:

(*a*) the economics of newspaper and periodical publishing and distribution;

(*b*) the interaction of the newspaper and periodical interests held by the companies concerned with their other interests and holdings, within and outside the communications industry;

(*c*) management and labour practices and relations in the newspaper and periodical industry;

(*d*) conditions and security of employment in the newspaper and periodical industry;

(*e*) the distribution and concentration of ownership of the newspaper and periodical industry, and the adequacy of existing law in relation thereto;

(*f*) the responsibilities, constitution and functioning of the Press Council;

and to make recommendations":

HUMBLY SUBMIT TO YOUR MAJESTY THE FOLLOWING REPORT.

1. In May 1975, we invited the Advisory, Conciliation and Arbitration Service (ACAS) to undertake on our behalf a study of industrial relations in the newspaper industry. This was one part of the programme of research which we commissioned into various aspects of the press.

2. The terms of reference of their enquiry were

"To examine and report to the Royal Commission on the Press in the light of the terms of reference of the Royal Commission on the Press on the present industrial relations institutions, procedures and practices in the newspaper and periodical industry, with particular reference to the national newspaper industry; and on any improvements in those matters that appear necessary or desirable."

ACAS submitted their report on industrial relations in the national newspaper industry to us in October 1976. They are reporting to us separately on industrial relations in the provincial newspaper industry.

3. This is the first time that such a comprehensive study of this major subject has been carried out. We believe that it will add to public understanding of industrial relations procedures and problems in the national newspaper industry. It may also help the efforts which are now being undertaken to resolve those problems and which have already produced most encouraging agreements. We have decided to publish forthwith the report which follows so that it will be publicly available while important developments are taking place. Other volumes of research results will be published later.

4. We make no comment on the content of the report at this stage. The Royal Commission took no part in framing the conclusions and proposals of the report: they are entirely those of ACAS. We shall revert to the subject of industrial relations in the national and in the provincial newspaper industry in our final report. We should, however, like to place on record our gratitude to the officials of ACAS, especially Mr Peter Carr, Mr Richard Hillier, Mr Frank McGettigan and Mr Neil Donald, for the ability, thoroughness and speed with which they have conducted the enquiries; and to all those organisations and individuals on both sides of the industry whose helpful co-operation with the Royal Commission in setting up this study and with ACAS in carrying it out has been indispensible.

ALL OF WHICH WE HUMBLY SUBMIT TO YOUR MAJESTY

O R McGregor (*Chairman*)
John Hunt
Eirlys Roberts
Elizabeth Anderson
David Basnett
Geoffrey Goodman
Malcolm Horsman
Paul Johnson
John Eilian Jones
Ian Richardson
George Bishop
Roger Chorley
Aubrey Silberston
L C B Gower

Paul McQuail (*Secretary*)

Francis Golding (*Assistant Secretary*)

Nicholas Hartley (*Assistant Secretary*)

Professor O R McGregor
Chairman
Royal Commission on the Press

In May 1975 the Council of the Advisory, Conciliation and Arbitration Service undertook to inquire into and report on industrial relations in the newspaper and periodical industry for the Royal Commission on the Press. The inquiries are now complete and, with the approval of the Council, I have pleasure in submitting to the Royal Commission the following report on the National Newspaper Industry.

14 October 1976

D R F Turner
Secretary to the Council

MEMBERS OF ACAS COUNCIL

Mr J E Mortimer (*Chairman*)
Professor H A Clegg
Mr H G DeVille
Mr L F Edmondson
Mr H L Farrimond
Professor L C Hunter
Mr J L Jones, MBE
Mr G F Smith, CBE
Mr T A Swinden, CBE
Mrs D E C Wedderburn

Contents

		Page
PART A	**Introduction**	
Chapter 1	ACAS Involvement and Background	1
Chapter 2	The Early Assessment and Programme of Inquiries	5
PART B	**The Industry and its Labour Force**	
Chapter 3	The Industry and the Technology	10
Chapter 4	The Labour Force	27
Chapter 5	Terms and Conditions of Employment	43
PART C	**Management and Union Organisation**	
Chapter 6	Management Organisation within Houses	63
Chapter 7	The NPA	70
Chapter 8	Chapel Organisation	80
Chapter 9	Union Organisation	94
PART D	**Industrial Relations Procedures and Practices**	
Chapter 10	The Negotiation of Pay and Conditions	111
Chapter 11	Disputes and Disputes Procedures	121
Chapter 12	Disciplinary, Redundancy, Work Organisation and other Procedures and Practices	129
Chapter 13	Consultation, Communication and Disclosure	135
Chapter 14	Industrial Relations Training	142
PART E	**Special Cases**	
Chapter 15	Industrial Relations in the Manchester Establishments	148
Chapter 16	Editorial Staff	158
PART F	**Conclusions**	
Chapter 17	Developments since the 1962 Royal Commission	171
Chapter 18	The Case for Change	175
Chapter 19	Conclusions	183
Chapter 20	Summary of Conclusions	204

TERMS OF REFERENCE FOR THE ACAS STUDY

To examine and report in the light of the terms of reference of the Royal Commission on the Press on the present industrial relations institutions, procedures and practices in the newspaper and periodical industry, with particular reference to the national newspaper industry; and on any improvements in those matters that appear necessary or desirable.

Abbreviations

ACAS	—	Advisory, Conciliation and Arbitration Service
ADM	—	Annual Delegate Meeting
ASLP	—	Amalgamated Society of Lithographic Printers
ATAES	—	Art, Technical, Administrative, Executive and Sales (SOGAT)
AUEW	—	Amalgamated Union of Engineering Workers
BDC	—	Biennial Delegate Conference
BFMP	—	British Federation of Master Printers
BPIF	—	British Printing Industries' Federation
CAEJ	—	Communauté d' Associations d' Editeurs des Journaux de la CEE
CLB	—	Central London Branch (NUJ)
COHSE	—	Confederation of Health Service Employees
CRB	—	Circulation Representatives' Branch (SOGAT)
CWS	—	Co-operative Wholesale Society
DE	—	Department of Employment
EETPU	—	Electrical, Electronic, Telecommunications and Plumbing Union
ET & O	—	Executives Technicians and Overseers (NGA)
FHC	—	Federated House Chapel
FIEJ	—	Federation International d' Editeurs des Journaux
FOC	—	Father of the Chapel
GMWU	—	General and Municipal Workers' Union
HMSO	—	Her Majesty's Stationery Office
IFOC	—	Imperial Father of the Chapel
IGF	—	International Graphical Federation
IOJ	—	Institute of Journalists
IPC	—	International Publishing Corporation
IRE	—	Industrial Relations Executive (NPA)
JSB	—	Joint Supervisory Board
JSC	—	Joint Standing Committee

JHC	—	Joint House Committee
LCB	—	London Central Branch (SOGAT)
LLC	—	London Labour Committee (NPA)
LMB	—	London Machine Branch (NATSOPA)
LSC	—	London Society of Compositors
LTS	—	London Typographical Society
MC & TS	—	Monotype Casters' and Typefounders' Society
MGN	—	Mirror Group Newspapers
MMC	—	Manchester Managers' Committee (NPA)
MOC	—	Mother of the Chapel
NAR	—	Non-Automatic Replacement
NATSOPA	—	National Society of Operative Printers, Graphical and Media Personnel
NBPI	—	National Board for Price and Incomes
NCTJ	—	National Council for the Training of Journalists
NEC	—	National Executive Committee
NGA	—	National Graphical Association
NGN	—	News Group Newspapers
NPA	—	Newspaper Publishers' Association
NS	—	Newspaper Society
NUJ	—	National Union of Journalists
NUP & PW	—	National Union of Printing and Paper Workers
NUSMWCH & DE	—	National Union of Sheet Metal Workers, Coppersmiths, Heating and Domestic Engineers
NUPB & PW	—	National Union of Printers, Bookbinders and Paper Workers
P & KTF	—	Printing and Kindred Trades' Federation
PMB	—	Printing Machine Branch (SOGAT)
PMMTS	—	Printing Machine Managers' Trade Society
PPITB	—	Printing and Publishing Industry Training Board
RIRMA	—	Revisers, Ink and Roller Makers and Auxiliaries (NATSOPA)
SDNS	—	Scottish Daily Newspaper Society
SGA	—	Scottish Graphical Association
SLADE	—	Society of Lithographic Artists, Designers, Engravers and Process Workers
SNPA	—	Scottish Newspaper Publishers' Association
SOGAT	—	Society of Graphical and Allied Trades
TA	—	Typographical Association
TA & E	—	Technical Administrative and Executive (NATSOPA)
TUC	—	Trades Union Congress
TUCPIC	—	Trades Union Congress Printing Industry Committee
UCATT	—	Union of Construction, Allied Trades and Technicians

Part A: Introduction

CHAPTER 1: ACAS INVOLVEMENT AND BACKGROUND

1. On 16 July 1974 the Government appointed the Royal Commission on the Press to "inquire into the factors affecting the maintenance of the independence, diversity and editorial standards, of newspapers and periodicals and the public's freedom of choice of newspapers and periodicals nationally, regionally and locally... and to make recommendations". Among the factors to which the Royal Commission was enjoined to make specific reference was the state of management and labour practices and relations in the newspaper and periodical industry. In Spring 1975 the Royal Commission invited ACAS to undertake, on its behalf, a study of industrial relations in the newspaper industry. In proffering the invitation the Royal Commission emphasised the central importance it placed on any study of industrial relations taking full account of the context provided by the wide issues set out in the Commission's terms of reference (see Appendix 1).

2. On 28 May 1975 the ACAS Council formally agreed to accept the Royal Commission's invitation though the exact terms under which the inquiry was to proceed were not immediately settled and operational work by the inquiry section of ACAS did not start until the beginning of September 1975. The terms of reference for the ACAS study, reproduced at the beginning of this report, required us to pay particular attention to the national newspaper industry. Because of this and because of the request by the Government to the Royal Commission on 19 September 1975 that an urgent study of the immediate difficulties facing national newspapers be carried out, the early stages of our work concentrated on industrial relations in national newspapers: our inquiries into industrial relations in the provincial press started several months later.

3. In response to our terms of reference we have produced two reports, one dealing with the "national" and one with the "provincial" newspaper industry. The reasons for this are partly practical—both the inquiry process and the ultimate reports have been made more manageable—but are mainly concerned with the many distinctive industrial relations features of each of these industries. However, it is not an assumption of our work in this area that national and provincial printing and publishing for industrial relations purposes can be entirely separated. On the contrary, whilst it is true that national newspapers and provincial newspapers are covered by different employers' associations and have certain distinctive characteristics, the industrial relations situation in the national press is related in important respects to that existing in the provinces. To begin with, the institutions are often the same. The unions are organised on a national basis and agreements between them and structural developments in one part of

the country have an impact everywhere else. Individual branches may span the national and provincial newspaper industries as well as general printing. Similarly, the employers operate in both London and the provinces. Apart from the substantial holdings some "Fleet Street" employers have in the periodical field, they also control a large segment of the provincial newspaper industry. Between them Associated Newspapers, the Thomson Organisation, S. Pearson and Son, News International, The Guardian and Manchester Evening News (MEN), Beaverbrook Newspapers and Reed International in 1974 owned 55 provincial daily and Sunday newspapers, and 213 weekly or bi-weekly newspapers.

4. Second, the labour market within which the national newspapers function is conditioned by the situation obtaining in printing generally. Apprenticeship rules, the state of employment in the general printing trade, and the service qualifications insisted upon by unions before an employee can seek entry into a national newspaper, each affect directly or indirectly national and provincial newspapers and their employees and the printing industry generally.

5. For these and other reasons it is unwise completely to compartmentalise the national and provincial newspaper industries. However, as this report and our report on the provincial newspaper industry will show, the product markets in which national and provincial newspapers operate differ radically and, with other factors, have led to characteristic industrial relations procedures and practices. At a simpler level the size of national newspapers in terms of numbers of employees and the concentration of employment in or around Fleet Street in London and in a few establishments in Manchester has no parallel in the provincial newspaper industry. It also seems to be the case that where organisations have interests in periodicals and provincial newspapers as well as in national newspapers, the national newspaper sectors of their businesses develop their own industrial relations policies independently. Whilst such diversified organisations might be economically more stable and this might affect general management approach to industrial relations in national newspapers, we found no evidence to support the latter suggestion during our inquiries.

Scope of the National Newspaper Industry

6. For the purposes of this report the term "national newspaper industry" is used to encompass those newspapers governed by agreements between the Newspaper Publishers' Association (NPA) and the printing unions, the three main newspapers in the Mirror Group, and the *Morning Star*. This means that the two London evening newspapers, and several other fairly specialised publications are included. Mirror Group Newspapers (MGN) is included because its publications have a national circulation, and were until recently (see Chapter 7) formally covered by NPA agreements. Above all, however, the Mirror Group is an integral part of the Fleet Street industrial relations scene and whether or not formally covered by NPA agreements both affects and is affected by the activities of "NPA" newspapers. To a lesser extent the same is true of the *Morning Star*.

7. Our inquiries aimed to cover nine daily and two London evening newspapers, the *Morning Advertiser*, and seven Sunday newspapers (see Chapter 3). However, some of the statistics and commentary in the report relate to a rather different base. This is because, first, national newspaper houses produce publications such as *Sporting Life*, *Reveille* (MGN) and *The Times Education, Higher*

Educational and *Literary Supplements* (Times Newspapers Limited). Whilst on a strict definition of a national newspaper these publications were outside the scope of our inquiry, in practical terms it was unavoidable that they were sometimes included. The information available to us did not always distinguish between these publications and the national newspapers in whose premises they were produced. Second, whilst we included the *Morning Star* and *Morning Advertiser* in our general inquiry, we recognised from the outset that their size, circulation, content, objectives and even technology* distinguished them from the rest of the industry. The data at our disposal, particularly on the terms and conditions of employment, do not always cover these two publications. Third, for a number of reasons (see paragraph 23) statistical material from the "core group" of nine major national newspaper houses was not always comprehensive. We have used in different parts of the report the definition of the national newspaper industry within this framework which seemed appropriate to the subject under discussion and in relation to which full information was available. The effect of such definitional variations is marginal (for example, the total number of staff employed on the *Morning Advertiser* and *Morning Star* is less than two per cent of the total employed in the industry generally), and does not detract from our conclusions.

The Report

8. There are two particular aspects of the organisation of the report which require some explanation. The first is that we have dealt separately with industrial relations in the Manchester establishments of the national newspapers. A principal reason for this is that in several important respects industrial relations procedures and practices in the Manchester establishments contrast strongly with those in their Fleet Street counterparts. There are, for example, significant differences in the administration of the casual system of employment, payments systems, the organisation of the parties, and the operation of the disputes procedures. It is also true that union and management representatives in Manchester, whilst recognising that they are affected by developments (for example, in technology) in the industry as a whole, have a sense of separate identity and feel that in industrial relations they have conducted their affairs more effectively than unions and management representatives in London. Whilst the rest of the report does refer to aspects of the Manchester situation where appropriate most of the discussion relates to Fleet Street establishments and Chapter 15 attempts to bring together the main features of industrial relations in Manchester.

9. Secondly, we have also largely dealt with industrial relations in the editorial field separately, though again the main body of the report does refer to matters concerning journalists where not to do so would leave an important gap in the narrative. The reason for this treatment is that although the employment situations of production workers and editorial staff are inextricably linked and this is reflected in inter-union co-operation and in other ways, traditionally journalists have had distinctive objectives, procedures, terms and conditions of employment, and problems. One of the most important problems has been concerned with the closed shop but we make no proposals about it in the report:

---

* Both publications are printed on web-offset machinery.

the Royal Commission, in outlining the areas it wished us to cover, considered that it would be more appropriate to deal with this particular question in its own final report.

10. The first draft of this report was completed by the beginning of June 1976, following which, on the basis of the draft, we held limited consultations within the industry. Since June significant developments have taken place in the industrial relations field, particularly at industry level, and these have been broadly in the direction of our recommendations to the Royal Commission (see Chapter 19). We welcome these developments and have been encouraged by some of the parties to believe that our report has been, and is being, helpful in bringing them about. Much remains to be done and the developments that have occurred need to be sustained and consolidated.

CHAPTER 2: THE EARLY ASSESSMENT AND PROGRAMME OF INQUIRIES

Some Preliminary Considerations

11. The British national newspaper industry has many unusual features. It is one of the world's largest such industries; it is heavily concentrated in 16 production establishments in two cities; the production facilities of the constituent firms of the industry are often closely interlinked (see Chapters 3 and 15); about a third of the Fleet Street's labour force is shared between the constituent houses; and the industry's performance and future survival gives as much cause for political as for economic concern.

12. It has had an ambivalent reputation for efficiency. On the one hand, each of the houses produces a unique product each day and between them distribute daily between 15 (dailies) and 21 (Sundays) million newspapers throughout Britain. On the other, the industry has often been criticised, and indeed has been self-critical, for its slowness to innovate and for its manning levels. At the time of the 1962 Royal Commission on the Press it was estimated that manpower in newspaper offices could be reduced by up to about a third without affecting production (see Chapter 17) and the current estimate by houses is that, outside composing rooms, staff reductions of 6–30% would still be possible. Though these figures have been and no doubt will continue to be controversial, there is a measure of agreement that manning can be reduced within existing technology (see Chapter 17).

13. In industrial relations terms, too, national newspapers have unusual characteristics which sometimes reflect and are reinforced by the production and market environment. From a trade union point of view, the industry is one of the most tightly organised in the country. Not only is trade union membership high, and universal in production areas (see Chapters 8 and 9), but the degree of production control exercised at the workplace by chapels has few, if any, equals in Britain. The way in which unions have developed in the industry, the development of collective bargaining, and the apparent extent of conflict combine with other factors to produce a unique industrial relations situation.

14. With these features it is inevitable that industrial relations within national newspapers should have attracted widespread interest over a number of years All the more so in a period in which the industry is facing economic difficulties; in which imminent technological change threatens to disturb traditional job demarcation lines; and in which reductions in production manpower of about a third have been posited (Royal Commission on the Press: Interim Report: page 10). Change on this scale would put pressure on any industrial relations system and at the outset of our inquiry it was unclear how the system would respond. The full response is still uncertain, though there have been important developments as this report will indicate.

15. During our preliminary inquiries both employer and union representatives expressed concern about industrial relations in Fleet Street. Employers' representatives were particularly worried about the level and conduct of disputes and about bargaining practices within houses, and union representatives complained about the lack of cohesion between employers and about consultative deficiencies. Both sides were, of course, extremely concerned about the industry's

viability, about whether houses would be able to implement appropriate remedial measures, and about the loss of job opportunities. This report will have more to say on these matters in subsequent chapters. Here it is enough to note that fears about the short-term and medium-term situation predominated during our preliminary inquiries, that while there was some agreement about nagging day-to-day industrial relations problems there was no consensus about solutions to them (or about the facts in relation to some of them), and that the development of industrial relations in Fleet Street was widely considered to have been strongly influenced by the product market for newspapers.

16. As expressed by management and union representatives the "product market" argument in essence is that the daily production cycle, the intense competition between newspapers, and the disproportionately heavy losses that can be incurred as the result of relatively minor disputes encourage fragmented bargaining, encourage short-term attitudes on the part of employers to dispute settlement, and impose strains on co-operation between employers. As the *Observer* has pointed out, even in the current situation of acute economic difficulty "it is still a matter of fine balance for an employer to decide whether to give in to a claim, because in straightforward cost benefit terms it often seems foolish to resist a minor claim and accept all the costs of lost production, when the cost of settling is—initially at least—comparatively small."* The argument was put with equal cogency to the 1962 Royal Commission on the Press which did not accept this "traditional management defence" as the complete explanation of the "... ineffectiveness of the employers' collective organisation."† Nevertheless, that the product market does strongly influence industrial relations and has to be realistically assessed in framing proposals for change in this field is a proposition that has weighed heavily with us during our inquiries.

17. We were supported in this by independent work in this area. A recently published study‡ examined the relative movement of pay within and between newspaper offices in Fleet Street in 1961–70 and attempted to test the significance of the possible factors influencing such relativities. It found that there were substantial differences in earnings between newspaper offices; that there were similarities in the size of the occupational earnings differentials in different offices; that differentials had narrowed; that changes in earnings followed common trends in several offices and that there were a large number and variety of components of pay. The study thought that there might be a relationship between the rank order of earnings and the changes in earnings and the introduction of new technology; and that the location of maintenance workers in the production process and the size of department might be significant. The principal positive finding was, however, that the product market was the most important factor influencing the pay characteristics observed. There was a positive relationship between differences and changes in earnings and differences and changes in page sizes. Moreover, workers employed on newspapers which were direct substitutes for each other had very similar earnings. The attitudes and goals of chapels, trade unions and managements had also influenced the narrowing of differentials, the common trend of earnings and the variety of pay components.

---

* *Observer's* evidence to the Royal Commission on the Press.
† Royal Commission on the Press 1961–62. Page 40.
‡ *Industrial Relations in Fleet Street*. Mr Keith Sisson (Blackwell 1975). This is a valuable study which was useful to us in framing our inquiries.

18. Reinforcing the influence of the product market, and reinforced by it, are the chapels. The chapel remains a self-governing association within the workshop and differs from most other forms of workshop organisation whose "... sole reason for existence lies in it being part of the wider association of a trade union."* The distinction is of vital importance because for industrial relations reforms to become effective they must come to terms with the *status quo* concept that operates at chapel level. Changes cannot take place without the chapel's consent and its independence within the workshop, allied to the sensitivity of the product, means that it cannot easily be overridden. It seemed to us during our preliminary study that previous official inquiries had given insufficient attention to the position of the chapel.

19. Three other factors influenced our approach to the inquiries and to this report. First, the Royal Commission in outlining the areas it wanted us to consider has said that it requires a descriptive account of such matters as the organisation, structure, attitudes and policies of the parties; procedures and practices of job regulation; and the economic, technological and organisational effects of change. We have tried to fulfil this remit.

20. Second, whilst the prospect of technological change is throwing up many urgent problems and whilst we do make comment about these and the way they are being handled, we have tried to look beyond technological change at problems that will exist after current photo-composition plans for the composing rooms have been implemented, and particularly at those concerned with bargaining procedures; payments systems; and management, trade union and chapel organisation.

21. Third, it was clear from the beginning that the national newspaper industry is composed of very different enterprises. Whilst it is true that each house produces a newspaper(s) using basically similar techniques, that they operate in close physical and economic contact with each other, that in the industrial relations field the decisions made by one house may have repercussions on others, and that in principle union policies apply across Fleet Street, in practice there are quite substantial differences between houses (and newspapers within houses) that materially affect industrial relations within them, both in the short and long-term. The type of newspaper—morning, Sunday or evening—can influence the industrial relations climate (see, for example, paragraph 193); and the size of houses is another important variable. Industrial relations procedures and practices are likely to be and are, different in houses with 4–6,000 regular employees than in houses with a few hundred employees. The economic and market situation of houses varies considerably and influences their approach to pay negotiations and to whether, and if so what, technological changes should be introduced into the composing rooms. Whether a newspaper is a "quality" or "popular"† affects the proportion of composition to total costs and has a bearing on the financial return from photo-composition. We designed our inquiries not only to explore the industrial relations problems that houses have in common, but also the differences in the house by house situation.

---

* A J M Sykes. *Trade Union Workshop Organisation in the Printing Industry—The Chapel*.
† Throughout the report we have used the conventional terminology to refer to groups of newspapers (see Chapter 3).

The ACAS Inquiries

22. The first phase of our inquiries from September until the end of October 1975 was concerned with seeking the co-operation and views of the eleven newspaper houses and the national officers of the principal unions involved, with assessing the work that had already been done in this area,* meeting other interested individuals and representatives of other organisations linked with industry, and with deciding the matters that our detailed inquiries should aim to elucidate and planning the detailed inquiries themselves.

23. The detailed inquiries, which were activated at the end of October/beginning of November 1975, consisted of:

(a) the retrieval of written and statistical information from individual newspaper houses on employment, earnings, other terms and conditions of employment, management and chapel organisation, industrial relations training, industrial relations policies and procedures, and the operation of those procedures. Each house, other than the *Morning Star* and *Morning Advertiser*, was asked to complete the extensive checklist of information we required by the beginning of January 1976. Two events helped prevent this happening. First, as the result of the Government's request to the Royal Commission to produce an interim report in January 1976, the Royal Commission itself decided to undertake a substantial survey in November/December 1975. Though our own survey of employment and production workers' earnings was largely absorbed into the Royal Commission's Survey†, houses found they were unable to meet both our, and the Royal Commission's, time limit and the former was therefore extended by the Royal Commission. Second, in the new year because of industrial relations developments within the industry (see Chapter 17) further burdens of work fell upon houses that had, of necessity, to have priority. Nevertheless, returns began to be made in March 1976 and eight of the nine houses have supplied us with much of the information we requested;‡

(b) the conduct of detailed studies within each of the eleven houses consisting of structured and semi-structured interviews with fathers of chapels (FOCs) and their colleagues and with managers at all levels,§ and of further retrieval of documentary material at house level. The aims of the in-house studies were to extend our knowledge in most of the areas for inquiry identified in the preliminary stages; to enable broad inter-house comparisons to be made to see whether the experience and approach of individual newspaper houses provided lessons that could be of benefit to the national newspaper industry generally; to explore the views of chapel and management representatives on a

---

*A full bibliography on industrial relations in the newspaper industry has been compiled by G Bowen Thomas, Suzanne Ledwith and J Irvine and published in 1975 by the PPITB.

† Since we and the Royal Commission consulted closely about the design of this part of the survey and it covered matters in which we had an interest, the returns have been available to us. We refer to it throughout the report as the Labour Survey.

‡ We are satisfied that the fact that these returns were not complete has not affected our conclusions.

§ ie including overseers and their assistants. We use the archaic-sounding term "overseers" in this report because even where houses have formally adopted other titles to describe supervisory grades, it remains in common usage among FOCs and managers.

number of matters and, in particular, on future bargaining arrangements; and to provide an opportunity for chapel and management representatives to make to us any other representations they thought desirable. In total we met about 250 chapel representatives from about 150 chapels (including imperial chapels: see Chapter 9) covering about 20,000 Fleet Street employees (ie the vast majority of journalists and clerical staff, and about 75 per cent of production staff); and a similar number of managers. The in-house studies were conducted largely in December 1975 and January 1976;

(c) a series of meetings in Manchester in February 1976 with appropriate management and union representatives concerned with the three major Manchester establishments of the national newspapers;

(d) detailed discussions with the main parties throughout, and special examinations of NPA and union organisation, and industrial relations training. Houses gave us permission to examine records relating to training at the Printing and Publishing Industry Training Board (PPITB) and/or provided us with information on this subject themselves. On union membership and organisation we conducted a special survey of union branches, through national union offices. Unions also supplied us with certain material relating **to** casual employment in the industry;

(e) a short comparative study of industrial relations in the newspaper industries of three European countries (see Appendix 2).

24. We would like to thank all those houses, trade unions, the NPA and other organisations and individuals who gave us so much help in the course of our work.

Part B: The Industry and its Labour Force

CHAPTER 3: THE INDUSTRY AND THE TECHNOLOGY

The Companies

25. National newspaper ownership is heavily concentrated in the hands of a comparatively small number of large publishing groups. The industry nevertheless contains companies with considerable differences in type and size of organisation and product. As might be expected, these differences influence the management and organisation of each company. Of the eleven companies producing nineteen daily, evening and Sunday newspapers covered by our inquiries Beaverbrook Newspapers and News Group are directly controlled by individual proprietors, and Associated Newspapers, Times Newspapers, and the *Daily Telegraph* (including the *Sunday Telegraph*) are controlled either by individuals or families. The *Observer* and *Guardian* are controlled by trusts, the *Morning Star* by a co-operative,* and the *Morning Advertiser* (a daily trade journal) by the Society of Licensed Victuallers. The *Financial Times* is a wholly-owned subsidiary of the Pearson Longman Group, and Mirror Group Newspapers is owned by Reed International, following a merger with the International Publishing Corporation in 1970.

Performance

26. There are difficulties in assessing the economic performance of each newspaper title. First, many are part, or subsidiary companies, of larger groups. Second, many of the groups to which they belong have a broad span of other business activities, including holdings in regional daily and evening newspapers, independent television, and local radio. Third, newspaper titles extensively use common services (buildings, equipment and labour) and problems can arise on the apportionment of costs between titles for such services. Nevertheless, using the companies' own figures, since 1970 the Sunday quality newspapers† have made losses of some £4,500,000 and have been in profit only in 1972 and 1973; the daily quality newspapers‡ have made profits of just under £4,000,000 but in 1974 and 1975 have made losses of £4,400,000; the popular daily and evening newspapers§ have made profits of £26,400,000 (which takes into account losses of just over £1 million in 1973 and 1974); and the popular Sunday newspapers‖ have made profits of £13,700,000 (including losses of £6,000,000 in 1974)¶.

---

* The People's Press Printing Society Ltd.
† *Sunday Times, Observer, Sunday Telegraph.*
‡ *Daily Telegraph, Guardian, Financial Times, The Times.*
§ *Daily Express, Daily Mail, Daily Mirror, Daily Sketch, Sun, Evening Standard, Evening News.*
‖ *News of the World, Sunday Express, Sunday Mirror, Sunday People.*
¶ Derived from Royal Commission on the Press *Interim Report* (page 99). Profit and loss are before interest, related publishing activities, extraordinary items and taxation.

27. A combination of factors have resulted in the erosion of the industry's general market position recently. These have included inflation and its effect, together with the downward floating of sterling, of sharply increasing the price of newsprint by some 120% between 1970 and 1975. (Newsprint represents between 28 and 33% of the operating expenditures of each house.) At the same time circulation has declined (although circulation revenue has increased as a result of higher cover prices), advertisement volume has dropped and revenue has generally remained static, and fixed costs (such as telephone charges, postage and rates) have increased.

28. Several aspects of these figures are relevant in considering industrial relations in the industry. First they indicate the difference in the economic position of the quality and popular newspapers particularly over the last two years, as well as the difference between Sunday and weekday newspapers. In 1975 only five (four of them daily newspapers) of the 17 newspapers made profits. A second point is that the economic situation has deteriorated rapidly since 1973. In 1973 the quality newspapers made an aggregate profit of £2·9 million. In 1974 this became a loss of £2·8 million, and in 1975 a loss of £6·8 million. The popular and evening newspapers similarly moved from substantial profit in 1972 into a loss making position in 1974. They recovered ground in 1975 largely owing to cover price increases: the popular newspapers are less reliant on the contribution of advertising revenue to profits and can more easily recoup falls in advertising revenue with cover price increases.

29. Third, the position for 1976 does not look much brighter. Newspapers' forecasts are that the 1975 losses made by quality newspapers will decline only marginally and that the 1975 profits of popular daily and London evening newspapers will fall by over a third. The financial strains on newspapers over the past two or three years and the outlook for the future have concentrated attention within the industry on the level of employment, the possibility of making savings by introducing photocomposition, and, partly as a consequence, on industrial relations procedures and practices.

30. Finally, though the economic state of the industry has stimulated a reappraisal of industrial relations, the process began fairly slowly. One reason for this is that employee representatives were unwilling to believe that the situation was as critical as some newspapers had stated. That profitability is not the sole or primary goal of many proprietors is a belief still widely held. Certainly, the relationship of profits to turnover in the industry has not generally been very favourable to the investor in the last few years. Employees and their representatives have required to be convinced that the economic difficulties facing national newspapers were real and this has taken some time.

Competition and its General Effects

31. Exceptionally fierce competition, both for readers and advertisers, is a dominant feature of newspaper business and editorial activity, and strongly influences the conduct of industrial relations in the industry. The high level of fixed costs is an important factor governing competition in the industry. The 1970 NBPI report* found that the effect of high cost levels was to give an advantage to the newspaper which can operate at a high level of output, enabling it to spread its costs more widely. Because the achievement of a higher circulation and consequent economies of scale raises these costs, the result, the report noted "is that the

---
* See Appendix 17(a), paragraph 15.

break-even point at which the weaker paper can begin to make a profit is raised to successively higher levels . . . In short . . . the strong may become stronger and the weak weaker".

32. The attitudes of the printing trade unions and their members' circumstances have been affected by inter-house competition. The number of newspapers that have ceased publication or been affected by plant closures and redundancies has created a general feeling of instability*. Since the war, nine† national daily and Sunday newspapers have closed, although one new Sunday newspaper the *Sunday Telegraph* (1961), has been introduced, together with the colour supplements of the *Daily Telegraph, Sunday Times* and *Observer* (although they are not printed in London). Substantial staff reductions have also been recently effected by the *Observer* (in 1975) and by Beaverbrook Newspapers Ltd, with both the closure of the Albion Street, Glasgow printing plant of the *Scottish Daily* and *Sunday Express* and the *Evening Citizen*, and the relocation of the *Evening Standard* into the Fleet Street premises. An ongoing reduction of staffing has been carried through in varying degrees by most newspaper houses since 1968 with the introduction of, and revisions to, comprehensive agreements (see Chapter 5).

33. A large influx of newspaper workers into the industry occurred with the ending of newsprint rationing and the increases in page size in 1956. A number of trade union officials associate many of the industry's current problems with this period. They feel that in the circumstances applying at the time, of intense competition both within the newspaper industry and between the industry and television, and of high newspaper demand and profitability, proprietors had unwisely and even deliberately caused staffing levels to rise excessively. This was seen by some of those within the industry as part of the competitive process: an attempt, by forcing costs up, to weaken rival newspapers.

The Current Position

34. The location of the production establishments of national newspapers is shown in Appendix 3, Table 1. A number of relocations have been carried out by newspaper houses since 1970. Apart from that mentioned in paragraph 32, the *Scottish Daily* and *Sunday Express* are now printed at Beaverbrook Newspapers' Manchester plant. Other relocations include the transfer of *The Times* and its supplements to the New Printing House Square site in Gray's Inn Road, the move of the *Observer* into adjacent premises in Queen Victoria Street, the centralisation of the Associated Newspapers Group's operations upon Carmelite Street, and the move in late 1976 of the *Guardian*'s news departments and setting of time-critical material to Farringdon Road.

35. The duplication of printing centres in London and Manchester, and rationalisation in the utilisation of printing plant by developing shared and sub-contracted services and facilities are matters that have exercised managements

---

* In the foreword to a survey conducted for the P & KTF in 1972 its President stated that "the future of the newspaper industry . . . (and) the national newspaper industry in particular . . . has been a matter of grave concern to the unions in the printing and kindred trades during virtually the whole of the post-war period". It was felt that the provincial press had achieved a state of reasonable stability, although the effects of local commercial radio on advertising revenue did give rise to concern. (National Newspaper Industry, P & KTF Survey conducted by the Labour Research Department.)

† *Daily Dispatch* (1955), *Sunday Chronicle* (1955), *News Chronicle* (1960), *Star* (1960), *Empire News* (1960), *Sunday Graphic* (1960), *Sunday Dispatch* (1961), *Sunday Citizen* (1967), and *Daily Sketch* (1971).

recently. While, as Appendix 3, Table 1 indicates, there are a number of instances of competing newspapers using shared facilities, not all such schemes have materialised. In 1973 the *Financial Times*, the *Daily Telegraph*, Times Newspapers and the *Guardian* established a joint working party to discuss a jointly-run production facility, based on the New Printing House Square site. The scheme foundered despite the economies of scale and the possibilities of freeing capital through the sale of some of the existing prime commercial sites owned by the houses.

36. Negotiations have also taken place between the *Guardian* and the *Observer* on sharing the latter's plant at Printing House Square, although it proved impossible to agree acceptable terms. Evidence about the difficulties facing national newspapers in relocating outside London with the advantage of cost savings in distribution, premises and labour* has been submitted to the Royal Commission on the Press. Following the decision of *The Times* to move to premises in Gray's Inn Road in 1969, the *Observer* Board attempted to find another contract printer. While there was spare press capacity at the *Financial Times*, it could only cope with half the Saturday night print order. The *Observer* planned to complete the print order in Leeds, but negotiations with the printing unions on this were not successful. According to the *Observer* the larger unions were "not prepared to see any part of this Saturday night print, which they regard as very valuable to their members, leave London, and refused any co-operation."

37. Other alleged examples of the influence of printing unions on proposed relocation plans by houses have been put to us during our inquiries. The approach taken by the unions to such matters has been governed by both a desire to maintain existing (and future) employment opportunities and to ensure the preservation of the London branches' spheres of influence, and by concern over the progressive decline of the printing industry in London generally.

Employment

38. The number employed by national newspapers (see Appendix 3, Table 2) has declined steadily from 41,590 in September 1970 to 37,367 in March 1975 (10%)†. There has been a much greater decline in numbers employed by popular newspapers during the period (13%) than in those employed by the qualities (2%). Between March and October 1975 we estimate that the numbers employed in the industry dropped by a further two per cent.

39. While the British printing industry generally experienced a shortage of labour in the early 1960s, since 1969 there has been a decline in numbers employed by 7·7%, and a growth in those unemployed by 60·8% (see Appendix 3, Tables 3 and 4). London has been particularly affected by the contraction of the general printing industry, and this has in turn influenced the attitudes of the London printing trade union branches, and in a direct sense, the national newspaper industry (see Chapter 4, paragraph 86, et seq).

40. The effects of these closures and redundancies on the membership of the NGA London Region and NATSOPA Machine Branch is illustrated in Appendix 3, Tables 5 and 6. It has been noted that in 1971 about 600 NATSOPA

---

* In a report on the London printing industry produced by the NGA, it is noted that among the reasons for the decline in London is "the difference in wage rates and manning practices between London and the Provinces". (*The London Printing Industry—Problems of Change*. Supplement to the London Region *Annual Report* 1974.)

† The figures are based on those submitted by houses to the PPITB. The PPITB defines an "employee" as anyone working for at least two-thirds of the normal working week.

machine branch members and more than 1,000 SOGAT London Central Branch (LCB) members were reported to be looking for work.* The position since 1974 has worsened considerably. The action taken by unions to counter this situation is discussed more fully in Chapters 4 and 5 but included from the termination of apprentice recruitment, the limitation on numbers of shifts worked, and the extension of union organisation to previously unorganised firms to establish new employment opportunities. The introduction of new technology has not yet been a major contributory element to the numbers of unemployed printing union members in London, apart from those of SLADE. SLADE's London membership has twice the annual average total of unemployment of its provincial membership, despite the fact that membership in London is less than a third of the total nationally. Much of SLADE's unemployed membership is in the photo-engraving section, and results from the development of litho printing methods.

41. It is with the knowledge of these largely external influences that the printing trade unions have faced national newspaper managements seeking to achieve cost reductions and most recently, planning in many cases to introduce new, labour-saving equipment in the composing, process and platemaking areas.

The Existing Technology

42. The method of composition currently used in all national newspaper offices is referred to as "hot metal", all matter being produced from metal types and slugs and imposed in chases for moulding and stereotype plate making, as opposed to the "cold type" process where the matter is produced on a phototype setter for subsequent "cut and paste" prior to plate making. The location of occupations and the union memberships associated with them in London offices is shown in Table 1. The general process is described below.

Composing and Reading

43. Editorial and advertising copy is sent from the relevant departments to the composing room. Copy is also received and transmitted by wireroom staff (NGA), who may also in some offices be interchangeable with telephoto staff (NGA), and who receive and transmit pictures, advertisements, and pages using facsimile equipment. The printing of photographic negatives is carried out by photoprinters (NATSOPA).

44. Keyboards specifically designed for a typesetting operation and operated by NGA linotype operators are used for either casting lines of type in single metal slugs or producing a paper tape. The tape operates the caster which produces either single characters or lines made up from single characters (Monotype machines). Teletype setting (used, for example at the *Guardian*†), produces type on line casting machines operated remotely. The servicing, preparation and supply of metal to the machines and other ancillary duties are undertaken by linotype engineers (AUEW) and linotype assistants (NATSOPA).

---

* *Industrial Relations in Fleet Street*. ibid, page 76.
† This section, particularly as it refers to occupation and union membership, is concerned with London offices. There are, however, some differences between London and Manchester discussed in Chapter 9, paragraph 318, et seq.
† The *Guardian*, however, plans to phase out teletype setting.

TABLE 1

LOCATION OF OCCUPATIONS AND UNION MEMBERSHIPS IN THE PRODUCTION PROCESS

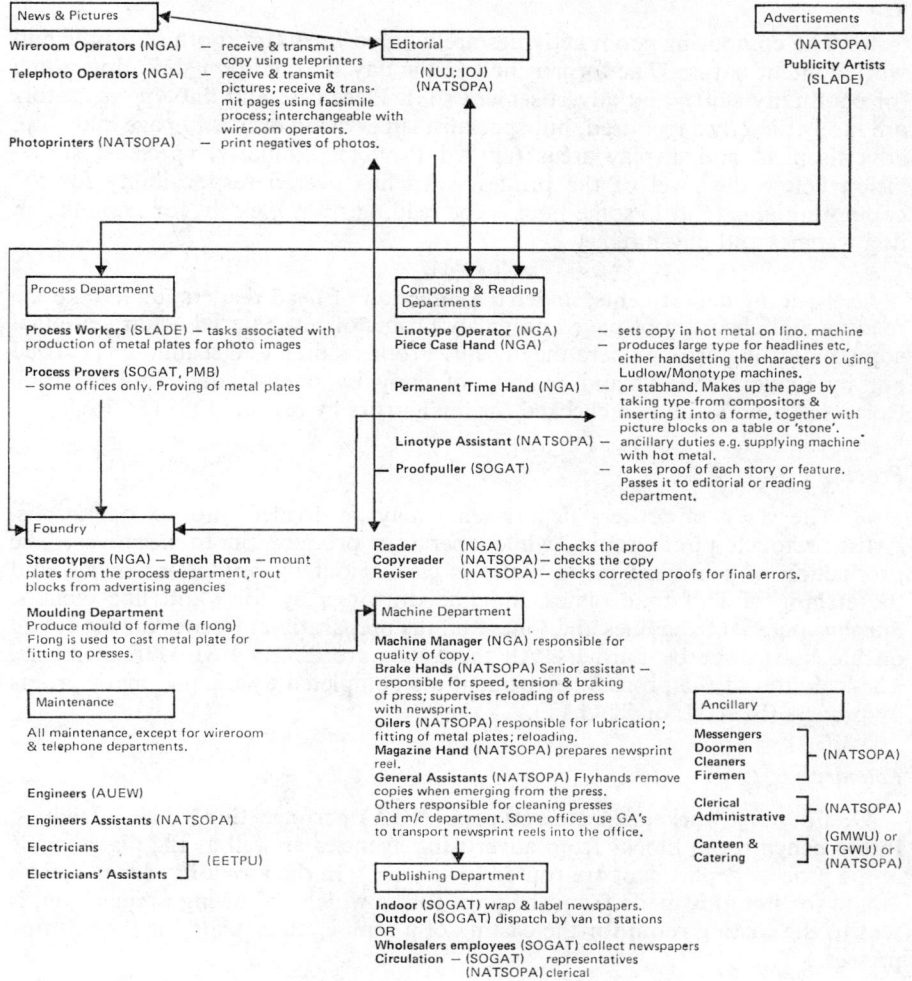

Source: ACAS Inquiries

45. The production of large type by machine (Ludlow or Monotype), and handsetting of tables, headline display and advertisements is carried out by piece case hands (NGA) and occasionally linotype operators are involved. The make-up of lines of type and the handling of pictures and line blocks and advertisement material into page form is the work of permanent time hands (sometimes known as stab hands) (NGA). The table on which this work is done is known as the stone. Proofs are taken by proof pullers or pressmen (SOGAT), and are passed to the reading department for checking and subsequently to the editorial department for revision.

46. The composing room activities are worked in shifts*, both of a time and work content nature. The former include the day shift, edition shift, dog watch (or continuity shift), and advertisement shift. Piece case and linotype operators are rarely directly supervised, but specialist supervision occurs in page make-up, advertisement and display areas (eg Ad Printer). Similarly, specialist supervision below the level of the printer, who has overall responsibility for the composing area (and in some houses the reading room), exists, for example, on dog watches and dayshifts.

47. Reading departments, under the direction of head readers, undertake the reading and checking of page and galley proofs of set material against original copy, indicating errors where they occur. Proof reading and scanning is carried out by readers (NGA) and reading of copy by copy-readers (NATSOPA). Corrected proofs are then checked for final errors by revisers (NATSOPA).

Process

48. The work of process departments may be divided into six operations. Artists retouch photographs, while operators produce photo negatives. The production of sensitised metal plates is carried out by printers-on-metal, and the etching of half tone plates and line drawings by tone and line etchers. Surplus material from lines and tones and the preparation of plates for mounting on blocks is done by finishers. All these jobs are done by SLADE members. The activities of the process department are completed by the pulling of proofs by provers (SLADE or SOGAT).

Foundry

49. Foundry workers or stereotypers (NGA) perform three main activities. In the bench room blocks from advertising agencies as well as the plates made in the process department are routed (or planed). In the moulding department a mould (or flong) is made from the page forme which, following preparation, is sent to the casting room for the casting of a semi-circular plate for the printing presses.

Machine

50. Apart from the *Morning Advertiser* and the *Morning Star* which are printed on web-offset equipment†, all national newspaper houses use rotary

---

* Referred to as "ships" in many houses.
† As are the *Daily Record* and *Sunday Mail* in Scotland.

letterpress machinery. Machine managers or minders (NGA)* are responsible for the quality of copy and are in charge of the presses. Brake hands (NATSOPA) are responsible for the correct running of the machines, adjusting speed, tension and braking, and reloading (or sheeting) with newsprint. The brake hand is the most senior of the machine assistants, who include oilers (NATSOPA), magazine hands (NATSOPA), fly hands and general assistants (NATSOPA). The oiler lubricates the press, fits and removes plates, and assists in webbing and re-webbing the press. The magazine hand prepares the newsprint reel, the transport of reels generally being handled by general assistants or day reel gangs. The fly hand assists the oiler in transporting and removing plates, assists in the reloading of the press and removes copies from the press and waste. General assistants are responsible for cleaning the presses and the machine room.

51. Fly hands also work at both ends of Igranic conveyors which transport copies from the folders to the publishing room. Where counterstackers are used to make up copies into quires, fly hands take quires from the conveyor and manually stack them into bundles. Machine minders are present to screen waste.

Publishing

52. The publishing function involves the receipt, wrapping, labelling and despatch of bundles of newspapers. All publishing room work after copies have been stacked into bundles is carried out by members of SOGAT. Most indoor work is assisted by mechanised equipment, activities being divided into lines for each distribution point. Outdoor work involves the loading of bundles onto vans and lorries for transport to railway terminals or collection by wholesalers' employees.

Maintenance and ancillary

53. Maintenance, apart from in wirerooms and telephoto areas (NGA) is carried out by electricians and their assistants (EETPU), and by engineers (AUEW) and their assistants (NATSOPA). Some offices also employ carpenters, painters and bricklayers (UCATT) and heating engineers (NUSMWCH & DE). Messengers, cleaners, commissionaires and firemen are members of NATSOPA, as are some canteen workers, although others are in membership of the GMWU.

Industrial Relations and The New Technology

54. Our inquiries have been carried out in an atmosphere of impending technological change that is unprecendented in the national newspaper industry. The Interim Report of the Royal Commission on the Press† was prepared at a time when Beaverbrook Newspapers, Mirror Group Newspapers (MGN), the *Financial Times*, the *Daily Telegraph* and the *Guardian* and MEN Ltd had already announced plans for technological changes. The Interim Report described the techniques covered by the generic term "new technology" and the plans of the national newspapers at that time. Since then, Times Newspapers has announced its plans for the future.

---

* Apart from the different circumstances in the machine room at the *News of the World* and the *Sun*, described in Chapter 9, paragraph 317.
† ibid pp 46–54.

55. The formation of the Joint Standing Committee (JSC) has now provided a national focus for the introduction of the new technology (see Chapter 17). The Royal Commission's Interim Report recommended that Government loans to individual houses be conditional on their plans being "consistent with the guidelines established for the industry" by the JSC. It urged that all houses "adopt industry-wide, rather than piecemeal solutions" to their problems, including that of introducing new technology. The question of manning under the old technology as well as the reductions in manpower involved with the new is also under discussion. In the words of the Interim Report, management should seek to make reductions in production costs by "introducing a new technology in the composing room and related areas, and seeking agreement with the unions on new methods and lower manning levels, especially in departments not directly affected by technological changes such as the machine and publishing rooms, as well as in clerical and ancillary areas". The *Financial Times* development plan, for example, proposes considerable manning reductions in the warehouse and machine room.*.

56. The agreement that there will be no compulsory redundancy arising from the introduction of new technology and methods except when both sides agree that a newspaper is in a desperate financial position or in other mutually agreed circumstances†, eased the way to the setting up of three working parties to discuss voluntary redundancy terms, pensions and decasualisation. The conclusions of these working parties will affect both staff displaced directly by the new technology and those from other areas where manning reductions may be agreed. The agreements reached within the pensions and redundancy working parties, however, will have a direct bearing on in-house negotiations on the introduction of the new technology and, many of these negotiations were delayed until the JSC reached agreement.

57. It is intended that the JSC will supervise the introduction of new technology and methods, but it is difficult to predict to what extent guidelines produced by the committee will affect the in-house implementation of plans. There were discussions between some houses (Times Newspapers, the *Financial Times*, the *Daily Telegraph* and the *Guardian* and *MEN*) during 1974 and 1975 over the possibility of shared printing using the latest composing technology, but the houses have now gone their separate ways and have announced plans which they feel are tailor-made to their own requirements‡. The different time-scales of the various plans, and the absence of SLADE from the JSC might mean that negotiations on certain issues will have to be settled outside the new national machinery. The danger that has been recognised is that those in the field early may make agreements that set the pattern for the rest of Fleet Street without those concerned throughout the industry having been properly consulted.

58. By June 1976, five§ of the national newspaper houses had announced plans for introducing the new technology and another, Associated Newspapers,

---

* This is not to say, however, that the machine and publishing areas will remain untouched by technological progress. Beaverbrook Newspapers, for example, have recently installed a new foundry, machine and publishing rooms for a total reported cost of £9 million.
† Joint Industry Statement, 5 December 1975.
‡ According to the *Financial Times*, "it emerged from these discussions that the requirements for change which other newspapers have differed at this stage so much one from another that it was not possible to reach a joint position on a sufficient scale".
§ MGN, Beaverbrook Newspapers, *Financial Times*, *The Times* and *Guardian*. (The *Guardian* has no immediate plans to introduce photocomposition in London. Its non-time critical material is set in Manchester where photocomposition is already in use.)

was actively investigating the possibilities in this area. Only four houses, NGN, the *Observer*, the *Morning Advertiser*, and the *Morning Star*, did not have plans for technological changes. The haste to introduce new techniques may have been more apparent than real; Beaverbrook Newspapers, for example, was actively investigating computerised photocomposition in 1969. The plans as announced so far can be grouped into two main categories depending on whether they envisage direct editorial input into the computerised photo-typesetting system. Beaverbrook Newspapers' and MGN's plans do not include such direct editorial input, while those of the *Financial Times*, the *Daily Telegraph* and Times Newspapers do*. The two types of system, the "production-type" and the "original input" (or "on-line"), differ basically in their immediate effects on traditional departmental demarcation lines. Tables 2 and 3 show the difference between the two systems diagrammatically and we outline the various plans below as well as some possible problem areas.

59. **Mirror Group Newspapers** plans basically to introduce a photo-typesetting system, including graphics, which will incorporate the capability of full page composition and pattern plate operation to convert the photocomposed page to a letterpress forme. The company's approach has been to follow traditional demarcation lines as far as possible. Thus it is still possible to define editorial, composing, process and foundry areas in the proposed structure, although the actual work done in each area will be changed to a greater or lesser extent.

60. MGN has proposed that its five publications should share an integrated composing room and a single reading room; the Group estimated that the new composing room would require 153 staff, as opposed to the current total of 370 in London plus the 59 working in the graphics area as a whole in Manchester. The staff in the new composing room will, for the most part, be employed on text input keyboards keying into the system copy sent from the copy desk along a conveyor and it is the design of these keyboards which perhaps best demonstrates MGN's approach to the new technology. The system will have two types of keyboard; the QWERTY 46-key standard typewriter design and a 90-key "linotype" keyboard. The latter machines have been ordered at extra expense so that the skill and experience of existing linotype operators can be used with a minimum of re-training. Piece-case hands and timehands will be trained to use the standard QWERTY keyboard. The "linotype" keyboard is undoubtedly less productive than the QWERTY type, but the Group obviously thinks that the advantages involved compensate for any loss in potential productivity.

61. MGN's system also defines the work of the process department. The negative of the page produced by the photo-composer will be printed on to a magnesium plate and powderlessly etched into relief; this process has many similarities to the existing blockmaking work carried out in Fleet Street newspapers. The resultant "pattern plate" is then used as a mould in the foundry for the production of the plate for printing by letterpress, as at present. Thus, the work of the stereo department, although modified, is clearly defined.

62. **Beaverbrook Newspapers'** plans follow similar lines to MGN's for much the same reasons. In the words of its Managing Director† the company adopted

---

* Beaverbrook Newspapers, however, does plan to allow direct editorial access at a later stage (see paragraph 62).
† "New technology and the print industry", *Campaign* 4 June 1976.

TABLE 2
PHOTOCOMPOSITION: PRODUCTION—TYPE SYSTEM (SIMPLIFIED)

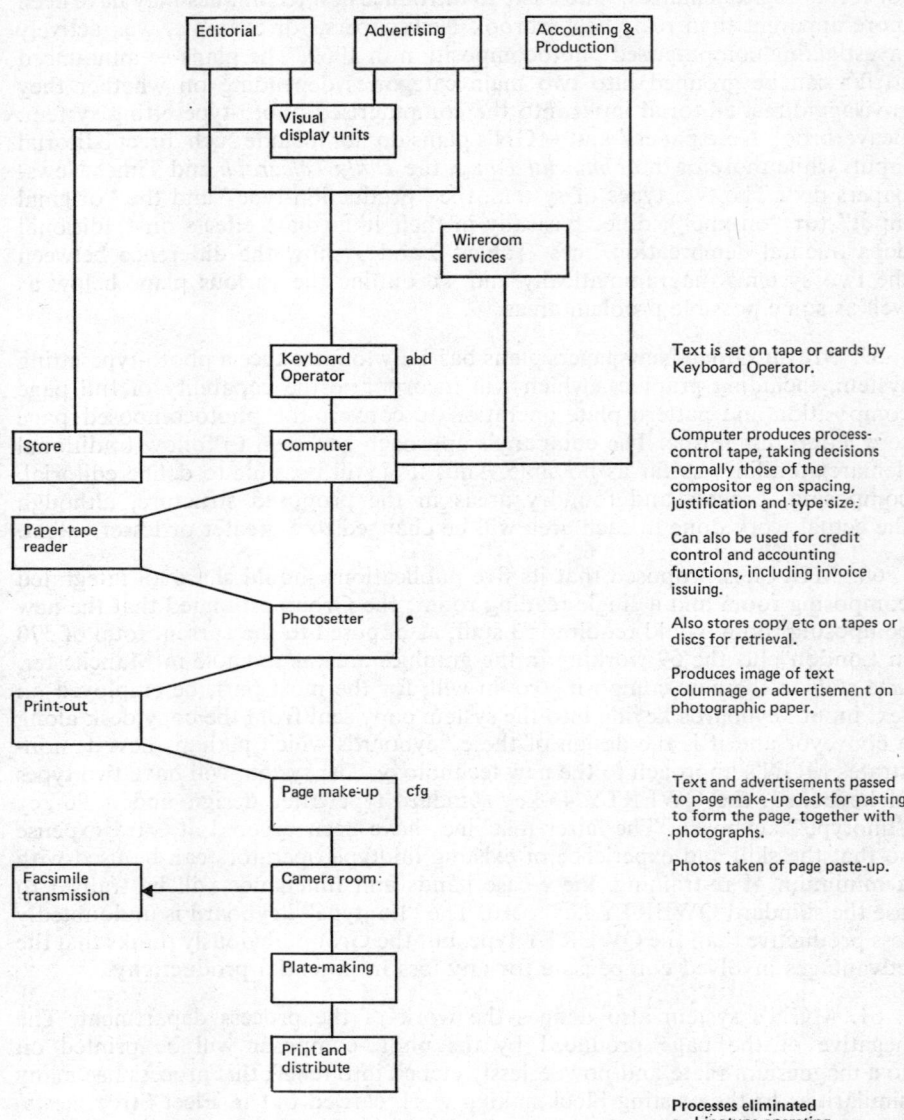

Text is set on tape or cards by Keyboard Operator.

Computer produces process-control tape, taking decisions normally those of the compositor eg on spacing, justification and type size.

Can also be used for credit control and accounting functions, including invoice issuing.

Also stores copy etc on tapes or discs for retrieval.

Produces image of text columnage or advertisement on photographic paper.

Text and advertisements passed to page make-up desk for pasting to form the page, together with photographs.

Photos taken of page paste-up.

Processes eliminated
a Linotype operating
b Headlining, ruling, Ludlow and Monotype operating
c Page make-up of type
d Metal preparation
e Proofpulling
f Copyreading
g Revising

Source: ACAS Inquiries

TABLE 3

PHOTOCOMPOSITION: ORIGINAL INPUT (OR ON-LINE) SYSTEM (SIMPLIFIED)

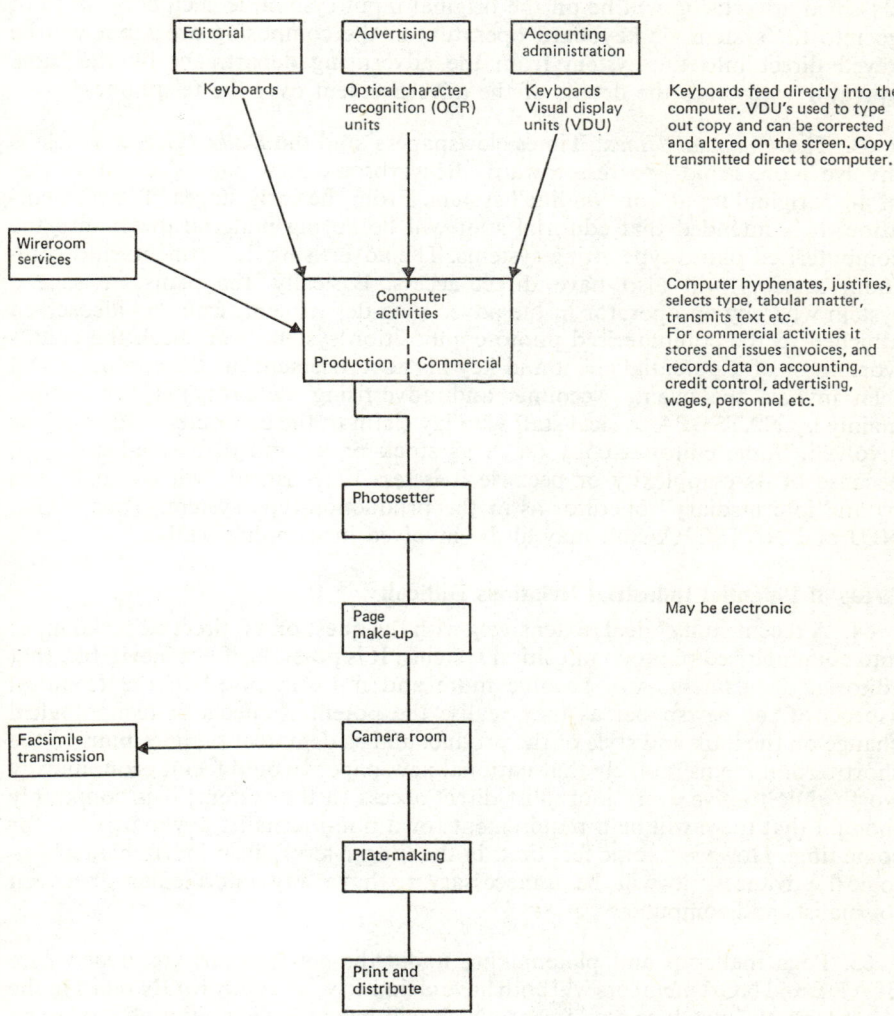

Source: ACAS Inquiries

"the system most likely to be acceptable to the men who have to do the job, particularly of course to those members of the NGA whose primary responsibility it will be . . . . . . (The) system maintains the existing job structure within the organisation". He went on, however, to say that "subsequently the original production-type will be changed into an original input system, going through several intermediate steps in the process". The Group intends the editorial departments to have a "gradually developing system of their own" which will eventually be used for the input and up-dating of all editorial matter. In addition, classified advertising will be on the original input system, ie such copy will not go into the system via keyboard operators in the composing areas but will be keyed direct into the system from the advertising department by the same operator who takes the details of the advertisement over the telephone.

63. The *Financial Times*', Times Newspapers' and the *Daily Telegraph*'s plans involve more rapid progress towards Beaverbrook Newspapers' eventual aim of an "original input" or "on line" system. From the early stages of implementation, it is intended that editorial staff will be keying material direct into the computerised photo-typesetting systems. The advertising departments and wire-room services will also have direct access. Basically, the plans envisage a system whereby an operator in the advertising department, using a videoscreen attached to the computerised photo-composition system, can check the credit-worthiness of a potential client and key his advertisement in; the computer will then invoice the client. Accounts and advertising departments are staffed mainly by NATSOPA clerical staff who lay claim to the computer operator jobs involved. Some editorial copy (such as stock prices and display advertising), because of its complexity or because it is less time-critical, will be dealt with by an "intermediary" operator as in the production-type system. Thus NGA, NUJ and NATSOPA staff may all be involved in manning VDUs.

Areas of Potential Industrial Relations Difficulty

64. A recent study* deals extensively with the question of direct editorial input into computerised photocomposition systems. It is possible, if not inevitable, that editorial departments will become more and more involved in the technical aspects of the newspaper as they realise the potential effects of technological change on the look and style of the product and as demarcation lines blur. In the short term it seems unlikely that national newspapers would feel it economically worthwhile to give every journalist direct access to the system; it is commonly thought that there will be a requirement for a non-journalist keyboard staff for some time. However, some feel that, in the longer term given inevitable technological advances, it will be unnecessary to have any intermediary between journalists and computer.

65. Page make-up and platemaking under the new systems are areas where SLADE and NGA members will both have claims to work. Only MGN plans in the short term to introduce equipment which will have the capability of producing complete newspaper pages electronically†. The Group's pilot introduction of

---

* "New Technology and the Press: a Study of Experience in the United States." Rex Winsbury for the Action Society Press Group and the Royal Commission on the Press (HMSO 1975).

† Equipment with the capability and suitable for use by other national newspapers is currently under development.

photocomposition with *Reveille*, however, involves the "cut and paste" techniques which are included in the plans of the other companies. Page make-up work under the hot metal system is carried out by NGA timehands using type produced by linotype operators and headlines produced by piece-case hands as well as photographic blocks produced by SLADE process workers. The timehands lock these various components into a forme which is used by the stereo department to make the mould from which the metal plate for printing is cast. In all the planned systems except MGN's the text set by the photosetter is passed to the page make-up desk, where "cut and paste" techniques are used to produce a whole page.

66. The page paste-up is photographed, and the negative is used for making a soft photosensitive plastic plate, known as a polymer plate. The process used to make this plate has similarities with the block-making work currently carried out by SLADE members, in that it involves the creation of a raised printing surface by hardening parts of the plastic through the page negative and washing the rest away in a bath. It is possible to use the plate in two ways: either as a direct printing plate which is bent and fastened to the press printing cylinder or as a "pattern plate" (or mould) from which a metal plate is cast as in existing technology. The latter system maintains a division between the "process department" producing the pattern plate and the foundry casting the metal plate for printing. Only the *Financial Times* has stated that it intends using photopolymer plates for direct printing. The *Daily Telegraph* is seeking a photopolymer plate suitable to its needs, and Times Newspapers have not decided which system to use. MGN and Beaverbrook Newspapers, in line with their attempts not to disturb departmental demarcation lines, intend to use the pattern plate system.

67. An agreement was made in September 1974 between the NGA and SLADE covering the use of photopolymer plates within provincial newspapers using rotary letterpress machines. It was agreed that SLADE members would make photopolymer plates used as pattern plates from which NGA members cast stereos or duplicates. Photopolymer plates used for direct printing would be made by NGA members.

68. A number of other groups of workers will be affected by the introduction of computerised photocomposition. SOGAT Printing Machine Branch (PMB) members' and NATSOPA copyreaders' jobs as presently defined will disappear. Under the existing technology, maintenance of linotype machines is carried out by the AUEW engineers and their NATSOPA assistants. Other equipment maintenance is carried out by EETPU members, AUEW engineers and their NATSOPA assistants and NGA T and E members. Most of the new equipment will be electronic, and the question of who is qualified to maintain it has already arisen. The influx of computers will necessitate specialist knowledge in their use and maintenance being utilised.

69. These areas of potential demarcation problems were the prime cause of the *Financial Times*' management producing a novel suggestion for in-house trade union organisation once the technological changes began to be introduced. The company suggested an "experiment in joint organisation", a joint technology

section, in the "absence of any mutually acceptable demarcation arrangements" (see Chapter 17). The *Financial Times* saw the "joint technology section" as having three main functions. First, it would negotiate with the company and implement jointly a scheme for allocating existing employees covered by the section to jobs defined in the new technology. The scheme would be based on an objective assessment of each individual's ability, and would disregard previous lines of demarcation between unions. Second, it would negotiate a "mutually acceptable logical salary structure" for all employees represented by the sections; remuneration would be based on skill, responsibility and effort factors and would ignore the occupational background of individuals. Third, it would, jointly with the company, arrange training programmes to equip its members for their new tasks. Such a section, it was thought, could also negotiate with the company on questions such as re-training, re-deployment and redundancy compensation.

The New Technology and the Manchester Establishments*

70. Those companies which produce in both London and Manchester have considered the future of their Manchester print in their development plans. The *Guardian* and MEN, the *Daily Telegraph* and MGN have all announced plans which reduce or eliminate composing in Manchester by the use of electronic transmission of "facsimile" pages by land-line from London to Manchester†. The original plans of MGN and the *Daily Telegraph*, which proposed that no composing at all would be carried out in Manchester caused much consternation among composing staff working on both newspapers at Thomson Withy Grove, whose numbers would be drastically cut. Editorial staff cuts were also proposed as the editorial control of Northern editions was switched to London‡. MGN has subsequently modified its plans and now proposes to phase out hot-metal composing in Manchester over the next few years.

Union Attitudes to the New Technology

71. Not surprisingly, in view of the negotiations still to take place within the JSC and at house level, national, branch and chapel officials have been guarded in their public pronouncements on the new technology. Some comments have been made, however, which reveal the unions' general attitudes. The "new" technology is no longer new in the provincial newspaper industry but its introduction into national newspapers creates a different set of problems. Where houses plan to reduce total staffs the question of job rights and demarcation takes on far greater significance than might otherwise be the case. Increasing unemployment among the London branches of the printing unions increases the pressure on chapels to resist de-manning proposals whether these are associated with the new technology or not§.

72. The implications of the new technology are undoubtedly most serious for the NGA. Recognising this, the union has given a national officer the task of monitoring the introduction of new technology and assessing the implications

---

* See also Chapter 15.

† The facsimile process is by no means a new one; the *Guardian* and *MEN* pioneered its development in the 1950s.

‡ Although the *Guardian* sets all time-critical material in London, non-time critical material will continue to be composed in Manchester and matted to London.

§ See paragraph 425.

for the NGA. The union's London Region has a fund which has enabled members to see the new techniques in action both in this country and abroad. The two main areas of concern of the union were outlined by its General Secretary in an editorial in the union journal*. The first is a fear that some national newspapers were "rushing into new technology with all the verve and suicidal tendencies of a kamikaze pilot"†, with little feeling for the individuals involved and with the mistaken view that the technology will provide a panacea for the industry's ills. The General Secretary thought that the "gradual" approach to the introduction of new techniques taken in the provincial press was an example which national newspapers should follow. He pointed out that the changes planned for the immediate future by Beaverbrook Newspapers had been operating in the provinces since the late 1950s, whereas those of the *Financial Times* involve "something entirely different . . . which is more a question of the unions agreeing about what happens over demarcation and jurisdiction"†. He also emphasised his view that it was unrealistic to expect new technology to sweep away at a stroke all the existing demarcation lines, and that the only realistic way to implement new techniques was to introduce them on the basis of existing demarcation lines.

73. Similar concern is expressed by SLADE. The union has claimed‡ that the print unions were being asked "to accept fewer jobs now on the gamble that a smaller number of jobs can be saved for much longer in the future". It is argued that if newspapers use manpower cuts to sharpen their competitive edge the constant circulation battle would result in more newspapers going out of business. The union believes that it is right to "use every effort to preserve as many jobs as possible" and while not "seeking to steal the work of other unions" SLADE would be safeguarding work which was currently theirs. It is hoped that this will provide "a basis for the maximum possible unity among the unions". While there is a feeling within SLADE that it will gain in importance within national newspapers because of the "photographic" nature of the new techniques, the union's unemployment problem over the last ten years has been considerably aggravated by new technology including that introduced into provincial newspaper houses§. New technology involving a planographic process has eliminated the production of advertising blocks for newspapers undertaken by commercial photo-engraving companies.

74. The general secretaries of SOGAT and NATSOPA have given a qualified welcome to the new technology. While accepting its inevitability and of manpower reductions, the two unions, with the NGA, have argued strongly for fair treatment of those who have to leave the industry. The General Secretary of NATSOPA has given four reasons why new technology should be introduced‖. These are, first, to keep the majority of the union's members in secure and well-paid jobs; second, "to maintain the viability of all existing titles in the interests . . . of a free press"; third, "to ensure that retired members 'receive pensions to maintain them in decent standards and dignity after a lifetime of service to the

---

* *Print*, April 1976.
† Oral evidence by the NGA to the Royal Commission on the Press, 2 April 1976.
‡ SLADE Journal, December 1975.
§ See also Chapter 9, paragraph 367 et seq.
‖ *Journal and Graphic Review* June 1976.

industry' "; and fourth, "to ensure that in any case of voluntary redundancy, the member is adequately compensated".

75. The NUJ has been examining the implications of technological changes for editorial staff. The union's two main areas of concern are the immediate redundancies among editorial staff in Manchester because of the various development plans and the role of editorial staff within the computerised photocomposition systems. The debate within the union has been reflected in a series of articles in the union's journal which have gone beyond what might be seen as the sectional interests of the NUJ. For example, the union's General Secretary urged that all the unions within the industry take note of the American experience of the new technology: "For the unions generally the most disturbing outcome of the technological revolution in America has been the production of newspapers by unorganised, non-union workforces"*. In December 1975, the NUJ's NEC invited the other printing unions to participate in an investigation into the likely impact of new techniques on national newspaper production.

76. The NUJ has been urged to participate positively in the introduction of new techniques especially bearing in mind the adverse effects on the quality of the product which had occurred in some American newspapers as a consequence of new technology†. Editorial staff would find that they became increasingly involved in the production process, and indeed, that the distinctions between production and editorial departments would inevitably blur. In America, it has been found that the videoscreen has begun to change the nature of editorial jobs by providing the journalist with a device, like a typewriter, on which a story can be composed and edited; he can feed the story into the system and help with page make-up. With these resources, it will become increasingly difficult to differentiate between NGA and NUJ jobs.

77. The industrial relations implications of the introduction of new technology into national newspapers are complex. Elsewhere, we have discussed possible implications for payments systems (in particular the appropriateness of the London Scale of Prices (see Chapter 5)); for bargaining procedures; and for union and chapel structures. The JSC is discussing terms for voluntary redundancy and improved pension arrangements; the unions have accepted manning reductions as inevitable but wish to gain the best possible terms for those leaving the industry. In an atmosphere where jobs are under pressure, however, demarcation and jurisdiction issues become more difficult to resolve, and these are the areas likely to cause greatest problems in the short term. The national newspapers seem to have adopted differing approaches to the question. The plans of the *Times*, *Financial Times* and *Daily Telegraph* seem to involve more thoroughgoing changes in departmental demarcation lines than do those of Beaverbrook Newspapers and MGN.

---

* *Journalist*, January 1976.
† *Journalist*, April 1976. Mr R Winsbury.

CHAPTER 4: THE LABOUR FORCE
General Characteristics
78. About 35,500 people work in the national newspaper industry as it has been defined for the purposes of the ACAS inquiry. The characteristics of the labour force and the patterns of working of production staff have developed from the requirements of the industry and the attempts of the unions to reduce the uncertainties of employment within it. In the medium term the fortunes of newspapers have fluctuated and in the short term pagination has varied: the need therefore was for a labour force the size of which could be related easily to the economic circumstances of individual newspapers so that unit labour costs could as far as possible be stabilised. From the unions' point of view, the overriding objectives were to protect employment in the industry from outside incursion, to maximise (and at least retain) their individual claims on jobs within the industry, and, especially latterly, to ensure that job opportunities were fairly distributed among their own members. These objectives have given rise to strict controls on entry into the industry, fine definition of demarcation lines, the often fierce struggles over job "ownership", and the increasing regulation by unions of working patterns of members.

79. The structure of the labour force in the industry is complex and is not only the result of the interplay of forces acting upon the industry but also in its turn influences attitudes (for example to technological change) and events within it. The first point to note is that there are at least two, possibly three, fairly distinct major groups of employees: production*, clerical and editorial staff. These groups, particularly the first and last-named, have substantially different characteristics. Journalists have a lower average age, a different eductional background, and often have qualifications giving them potentially wider fields of alternative employment. In addition the route into journalism in the national newspaper industry differs from the paths followed by production and clerical workers. Clerical workers, too, tend to have a lower average age than production workers and are more mobile (ie are more likely to move in and out of the industry) than either production workers or journalists.

80. The second point is that within these broad groupings there are important sub-divisions. The most obvious is the regular/casual distinction used both in relation to production workers and journalists (see Chapter 16). The variety of definitions available as to what is a regular, a regular casual, and a casual casual employee can be confusing. For the purposes of the ACAS survey a "regular casual" was defined as an employee who normally works on a regular basis for less than the full number of shifts to which full-time production employees in the appropriate occupational category are conditioned by their contracts of employment. A casual casual worker on this definition is one who does not work on a regular basis for an employer. However, newspaper houses sometimes adopt different definitions and may classify as full-time regular employees those who work three or four shifts regularly. Moreover, a regular casual is sometimes defined not simply in terms of the regularity of his employment pattern in a particular house but in relation to the status of his employment. An employee normally working less than the full number of

---
* Throughout the report we use the term "production" employees to cover not only staff directly engaged on physically producing newspapers, but also engineers, electricians and similar maintenance and ancillary staff.

TABLE 4
REGULAR FULL-TIME PRODUCTION WORKERS EMPLOYED IN LONDON BY TYPE OF WORK AND NEWSPAPER CATEGORY

Type of Work	Regular Full-time Production workers employed by:-						Total	
	Popular Dailies	Popular Sundays	Populars Combined	Quality Dailies	Quality Sundays	Qualities Combined	Numbers	%
Linotype Operators	256	32	102	254	75	0	719 } 1,836	15.0
Time Hands	250	61	155	270	78	0	814 }	
Piececase	112	17	81	76	17	0	303 }	
Readers	133	19	59	145	36	0	392 } 944	7.7
Revisers/Copyreaders	182	20	90	200	60	0	552 }	
Proof Pullers	37	4	37	65	10	0	153 } 340	2.8
Linotype Assistants	46	5	58	53	13	0	175 }	
Monocasters	0	0	1	10	1	0	12 }	
Process Workers	41	0	188	13	12	88	342 } 378	3.1
Process Provers	3	0	23	1	0	9	36 }	
Stereotypers	230	14	180	92	23	59	598	4.9
Machine Managers	120	0	220	71	10	0	421 } 2,497	20.4
Machine Assistants	773	0	1,171	130	2	0	2,076 }	
Publishing (In)	1,737 }	13	83	324	9	0	2,166	17.7
Publishing (Out)								
Engineers	37	0	454	38	36	126	691 } 1,244	10.2
Engineers' Assistants	26	0	403	13	14	97	553 }	
Electricians	47 }	0	460	32	15	131	685	5.6
Electricians' Assistants								
Phototechnicians	4	0	64	1	2	23	94	0.8
Telegraphists	2 }	0	113	19	12	24 }	170	1.4
Wire Room								
RIRMA	99	2	573	58	62	297	1,091	8.9
Others	0	0	31	145	0	3	179	1.5
Total — Numbers	4,135	187	4,546	2,010	487	857	12,222	—
%	33.8	1.5	37.2	16.5	4.0	7.0	—	100

Source: Labour Survey

1. Full-time regular refers to production workers who are regularly employed by one house for 5 shifts per week on a daily newspaper or for 4 shifts per week, one of which includes a Saturday.

The Royal Commission on the Press define "other regulars" as "production workers who are (a) contracted to appear in any one house for 4 shifts per week none of which is a Saturday; (b) contracted to appear in one house for less than 4 shifts per week, one of which may be Saturday".

shifts to which full-time employees are conditioned by their contracts of employment, but who is entitled to be covered by appropriate pension schemes, sick pay, and holiday arrangements would, in the eyes of some newspaper houses, be regarded as a regular casual. Another employee regularly working a similar shift pattern, but not necessarily contracted to do so, who is not entitled to be covered by all these fringe benefits would be regarded by the same houses in London as a casual casual employee*. Further complications can arise because an employee can work regularly for one newspaper and be employed as a casual casual on one or other of the shifts for which he is not contracted to work on a regular basis.

81. The Royal Commission on the Press, in its interim report†, separated production employees into three classifications, full-time regular, other regular and casual, on the basis of the number of shifts employees are contracted to work (see footnote to Table 4). For the sake of easy comparison we use the same categorisation in Table 4 and in Appendix 4, Table 2. However, the delineation is less useful in describing the types of casual on the books of each union branch: it is not invariably apparent from the records available whether a casual is, or is not, contracted to work on a regular basis. In the description of the casual system which follows, the unions' own terms are used.

Regular Production Staff

82. There were some 12,200‡ full-time regular employees working in the industry in London in October 1975. About a third of them worked exclusively for a popular week-day newspaper and nearly three quarters worked for the popular week-day and Sunday newspapers. Relatively few (just under 700, or six per cent) are exclusively employed by a Sunday newspaper, whether popular or quality. These publications rely heavily on dual working employees (i.e. those who regularly work on both week-day and Sunday newspapers) and on regular casual and casual casual employees. Among the popular newspapers over half the full-time regular employees are employed on this dual-working basis. The proportion is much lower for the quality newspapers (i.e. about a quarter) partly because of the existence within this group of a "solo" Sunday and week-day newspaper (the *Observer* and the *Financial Times*).

83. Table 4 shows the numbers of full-time regular production workers in London by occupational category and type of newspaper. In addition to the full-time regular production staff a number of employees are regularly employed on a part-time basis. The exact number of these cannot be calculated because, whilst each house knows the number of shifts each such employee is contracted to work for it, it does not record the name of any other house for whom the employee may work. There is no central register enabling the pattern of working between houses of each part-time regular employee to be recorded because

---

* In the Manchester establishments of the national newspapers the terms "regular casual" and "casual casual" are not in common usage: the distinction there is simply between "regular" and "casual" employees (see Chapter 15).

† Royal Commission on the Press Interim Report 1976. Cmnd 6433, page 106.

‡ These and subsequent figures in this Chapter exclude the *Morning Advertiser* and *Morning Star*. Between them these two newspapers employ some 500 production, clerical, and editorial staff.

there has been no need for one. Nevertheless the number is known to be substantial. The Labour Survey indicated that there might be as many as 4,600 regular part-time employees who work on a Saturday. The bulk of these (about 97%) work in the publishing and machine rooms. During our inquiries we have sought from newspaper houses details about each regular part-time employee at work to enable precise numbers and working patterns to be established but it has not proved possible to collect a full record along these lines.

84. From information supplied by seven houses the general pattern of regular part-time working does, nevertheless, emerge. First, over half the regular part-time employees worked for any one house on a Saturday night only. In total two-thirds of regular part-time employees worked on a Saturday night, though nine per cent of them worked more than one shift for any one house (see Appendix 4 Table 2).

85. Second, of the 39% of such employees not working on a Saturday night, three quarters worked for three or four shifts. These figures are consistent with a fairly extensive three-and-one (i.e. three week-day and one Saturday shift) and four-and-one pattern of working and it is probable that a high proportion of the 29% of regular part-time employees working three or four shifts excluding a Saturday night for one or other of the newspaper houses also worked for another house on a Saturday night. Even so it is clear that many of those who worked regularly on a Saturday-night-only basis either had no other regular engagement or were full-time regular staff whose regular employment was with another house*.

Casual Production Staff

86. The casual system of employment is one of the distinctive features of the national newspaper industry. There are several reasons for its growth. The main advantages from the employers' and unions' points of view are outlined in paragraph 78. In addition, given the relatively high levels of pay within the industry (see Chapter 5) it provided a means by which employees in the general printing trades could supplement their earnings particularly on a Saturday night. Third, in periods of unemployment it provided employment opportunities for otherwise out-of-work union members. Each of these reasons for the growth and continued existence of the casual system is an obstacle in the way of its modification.

87. Whilst casual working in national newspapers occurs in the reading and stereo departments, the machine and publishing departments are the main areas where casual employees work. Three unions—the NGA, NATSOPA, and SOGAT—have appreciable numbers of casual employees within their ranks and SOGAT has more than the other two combined (see paragraph 95). The Labour Survey indicated that in October 1975 around 2,000 production workers in London obtained casual work on a Saturday night. Since not all casual casuals obtain a Saturday night working the total number of workers seeking "casual" employment on a Saturday night must be something in excess

---
* The LCB of SOGAT prohibits any employee from working on a weekday and Sunday newspaper in the same house.

of this figure. However, a proportion of those seeking work on a Saturday night on a casual basis have regular jobs elsewhere (e.g. NATSOPA permit holders). The number of men with no regular contractual arrangement with any national newspaper in London who are registered with one or other of the unions as requiring casual employment is around 2,200.

88. The extent of casual casual working varies considerably not only between departments, as has been mentioned, but also between categories of newspapers, individual newspapers, and over time. Appendix 4 Table 1 shows that in October 1975 a weekly average of 7,298 casual shifts were worked in London and about 63% of them were worked in publishing rooms (with a further 25% in machine rooms). Just over half the shifts were worked on the popular daily newspapers, one-fifth on the popular Sunday newspapers and the remainder on the quality daily and Sunday newspapers. About 28% of casual shifts were worked on a Sunday newspaper, normally on a Saturday night and an average of 14% of all casual shifts were worked on each other weekday.

89. The average number of weekly shifts worked in April 1975 differs by only three per cent from the October 1975 figure and disguises the seasonal variation in the demand for casual staff to stand in for regular staff who are on holiday. Appendix 4 Table 3 and its accompanying graph, compiled from NATSOPA statistics*, illustrate this variation well. The peak demand for casual staff from the NATSOPA Machine Branch calls office occurred in September 1975 (with a weekly average of over 1,700 calls made on the office) and the month of lowest average demand was January 1975 (just over 700 calls). The graph does in fact show two marked peaks (during the Summer and at Christmas) and two troughs (around January and November) in the demand for casual staff†, though the last peak may largely be the result of the different recording procedures adopted at the end of 1975: the 1974 pattern does not have, for calls made on the NATSOPA office, the same Christmas peak. Nevertheless, the sharp fluctuations in the demand for casual staff could have important implications for the way in which the attempts to modify the casual system of employment are implemented.

90. Appendix 4 Table 3 and the graph also show that the general trends in the demand for casual NATSOPA staff during 1975 were the same in daily and Sunday newspapers. Appendix 4 graphs A and B bear out the same point but show in a rather different way the demand for casual casual employees from the NATSOPA Machine Branch and the SOGAT LCB calls offices between April and June and between September and November 1975. The graphs illustrate the preponderance of SOGAT calls in relation to NATSOPA

---

* Caution should be exercised in making use of this Table and graph. First, it does not show for most of 1975 the number of shifts filled by red toppers and permit holders (see paragraph 94) reporting directly to the appropriate chapel representative. Second, the basis on which the statistics were compiled was changed at the end of 1975 to include the latter figures.

† Not surprisingly these peaks and troughs correspond with peaks and troughs in the number of "short workings"—occasions when for one reason or another a casual employee was required under the terms of the relevant agreement but was not available. The weekly average of short workings in the month of peak demand for casuals (September) was also at a peak of 235. In the "trough" of January it was 22.

calls*; re-emphasise the significance of Saturday night working (38% of all calls made on both union call offices in May 1975); and highlight the daily pattern in the demand for casual employees. Appendix 4 Table 4 explores this further by setting out the daily average number of calls made on the NATSOPA and SOGAT calls offices in each period. It is clear that the demand for casual staff begins to rise on Thursdays until it tails off after the Saturday maximum†.

91. The extent to which casuals are called into an office obviously depends on the size of the house, the circulation of its newspaper(s), whether it produces daily or Sunday newspapers or both, and its internal employment policies. There is considerable variation in the demand for casual casual staff between offices. In 1975, for example, well over half the calls made on the NATSOPA calls office came from two houses, whilst from some other houses the number of calls made as a proportion of the total was negligible.

Types of Casual Employee

92. Each union uses its own terminology and has rules with differing emphases in connection with casual employees. The main categories used by unions and the numbers in each category at the end of 1975 are outlined below and Appendix 4(a) reproduces the relevant union rules relating to casual employment.

93. The NGA at the end 1975 had nearly 450 "casual" members distributed as follows:

Grass hands. These are linotype operators who work during the week in the general trade and on Saturday night in Fleet Street on a Sunday national newspaper. At present, and since the *Observer* redundancies in 1975, there are 40 grass hands and the number is strictly controlled by the union, having been 44 between 1961 (when the *Sunday Telegraph* was introduced) and 1975.

Stereotypers. Some 230 stereotypers worked as casuals at the end of 1975 (108 of whom had a regular Saturday night engagement). Until fairly recently there were no limitations on the working hours of stereotypers and in 1975 there were some who worked six shifts a week, five for a daily newspaper and one for a Sunday newspaper. Towards the latter part of 1975, however, a special delegate meeting of the NGA decided that from October 1975 stereotypers should not be entitled to work more than five shifts each week. Some 70–80 stereotypers were thought likely to be affected by this decision, the reason for which was the growth in unemployment among this group of workers. In the year ending in November 1975 over 22,000 calls for stereotypers were made, an average per member of about two each week.

Machine minders. Since 1966–67 it has been the policy of the NGA to allocate "casual" machine minders to fixed regular casual engagements and most machine minder casual members do not therefore obtain their work

---

* For example, in May 1975 the total number of SOGAT weekday calls was over three times the number of calls made on the NATSOPA office and the number of Saturday calls was over five times the NATSOPA figure.

† Appendix 3 Table 3 also shows that the average daily demand for SOGAT casual employees was significantly higher in the latter period than the former, whilst for NATSOPA the reverse was true.

directly through the London Region office. Some 140–150 machine managers have regular casual engagements on solo Sunday newspapers and midweek shifts in morning or evening newspapers. These employees do not sign the "call" book at the London office and may not work more than one Saturday and three mid-week shifts each week. Currently, a maximum of around 65 machine minder casuals may sign the call book to indicate their availability for work though the daily average is around 30. Only 25 machine minders have no regular commitments at all. The shift in emphasis from casual casual to regular casual working among the group has come about through the negotiation of comprehensive agreements. In 1967 the average number of casuals signing the call book was about four times higher than it is at present. Of the 167 machine managers classified by the NGA as casuals, 120 had regular engagements to work on a Saturday night. In 1974–75 3,100 casual calls were made for machine managers.

Readers. Between 15 and 30 readers may be employed casually on a Saturday. At other times the number employed on a casual basis is eight.

94. NATSOPA's London branches between them have some 1,850 members who are employed, or entitled to seek employment, as casuals. There are four main categories of NATSOPA casual employees:

"Red toppers". So called because their cards are completed in red ink, these are Machine Branch members with twenty or more years' membership. They have the right directly to approach, and be approached by, FOCs for work. The numbers and proportions of casual staff (not just red toppers: see below) directly called in by FOCs is substantial. In December 1975 over half the total number of calls required were directly filled by FOCs though the proportion was generally lower where the total demand was highest. There are about 300 "red toppers", a figure which has been increasing because of redundancies. In effect, a "red topper" has priority for casual work and even if he becomes a regular full-time employee of a house, retains his status in the event of a subsequent redundancy.

Other machine assistants. There are just over 300 casuals who obtain their work through the NATSOPA call office. These are men who have no fixed pattern of working and who have not the membership qualifications, and therefore the privileges of the "red toppers".

Permit holders. Some regular employees who have up to four shifts regular employment and who have held red cards, want to obtain casual work to make up the total number of working hours permitted under the rules. Since, on taking up regular employment, such an employee is required to surrender his red card to the appropriate chapel, a special permit must be issued to enable him to seek casual work. About 1,200 men hold such permits though the total number of shifts sought by permit holders to span the gap between their regular commitments and their total allowable earnings is unavailable.

RIRMA. The Branch has an average of 36 members who work on a casual basis on a Saturday night in the reading and editorial rooms.

95. SOGAT has two main types of member who work on a non-regular basis in London. The LCB rules (see Appendix 4(*a*)) define a regular employee as one who works "five days, five nights or three and one". No such employee may work for another employer or do more than eight hours' overtime, except when sanctioned by the Branch Secretary. The purpose of these provisions is to maximise the employment opportunities for those seeking casual employment:

> **Jobbers or jobbing hands.** These are the equivalent of the NATSOPA "red toppers" in that they may apply direct to an FOC for casual employment. The basis of most jobbing hands employment is a regular Saturday night working and most of the 2,000 or so jobbers have a regular pattern of work through the week. Only about fifty of them seek work through the LCB call office. The number of jobbing hands is strictly controlled and, apart from an increase in 1970 of about 200, has been so since the mid-1960s.
>
> **LCB casual casuals.** Nearly 1,400 SOGAT LCB members are listed as casual casuals. The Branch policy is to try to distribute work evenly between those making themselves available to work. Saturday-night working is much sought after and the Branch has laid down that a casual casual must have worked three nights or four days in the week to qualify for Saturday night employment.

96. The only other substantial area of casual working is among journalists. The extent and form of non-regular employment among journalists is outlined in Chapter 16. SLADE does not have members employed as casuals in the national newspaper industry but temporary workings which must be of a minimum length of one week do occur.

Job Controls.

97. Fleet Street has been for many years a much sought after source of employment for print workers. The main reason is that the levels of earnings have been significantly higher than those obtaining outside the national newspaper industry (though this has been less marked in recent years: see Chapter 5). To protect jobs and earnings the unions have developed a range of controls on entry into the industry and on access to full-time regular employment within their respective spheres.

98. The job entry controls rest on apprenticeship qualifications, length of union membership conditions or both. Whilst the NGA, for example, does not insist that all its members should have served an apprenticeship*, the vast bulk are required to have done so†. Moreover, securing an apprenticeship qualification does not entitle a member of the NGA's London Region to work in a national newspaper house: at least two years' experience in the general printing industry is a necessary pre-condition for this. SLADE process members

---

* ie an apprenticeship condition might exclude actual or potential members among computer operators, programmers, systems analysts, etc.

† Until 4 August 1975 the apprenticeship period was five or six years (depending on when the apprentice left school). Since then it has been reduced, by agreement with the BPIF and NS, to four years (with provision for three and a half years if the apprentice passes the appropriate tests).

have had to undergo a five year apprenticeship though the proposal that the period be reduced to four years from 31 July 1976 is under active consideration. Within the London Branch of SLADE no special conditions apply to entry in the national newspaper industry: any unemployed member of the Branch has priority on vacancies occurring in Fleet Street and only in the unlikely circumstance that there are no unemployed London Branch members are other Branches notified of vacancies.

99. SOGAT and NATSOPA do not have general apprenticeship rules governing entry into the printing industry and, therefore, into the national newspaper industry. The LCB of SOGAT and the LMB of NATSOPA do, however, operate regulations that specifically or in practical application impose restrictions on entry into Fleet Street jobs. No LMB member can be transferred into national newspaper employment with less than four years' membership in the general printing sector (see Appendix 4(a)) and entry to the newspaper section of the LCB is based on length of LCB membership. Currently, an individual needs to be a member of the Branch for about twenty years before he can obtain a regular job in Fleet Street, though he can be employed as a casual*.

100. The AUEW and EETPU also have entry controls. For example, not only are the bulk of the AUEW members in Fleet Street newspaper houses time-served craftsmen but a time-served craftsman may have to wait a considerable time before securing a regular job (there is no casual working). The Fleet Street Branch maintains a vacancy book and any vacancies arising are normally allocated by seniority of position in the book†. At the beginning of 1976 there were some 400 names in the vacancy book.

101. The demand for jobs in Fleet Street and the controls on entry have several important effects. First, there are very few apprentices in national newspaper houses. The jointly administered apprenticeship scheme for electricians' apprentices is the only such scheme that still operates in Fleet Street and even this has an average intake of not more than two or three apprentices each year.

102. Second, the average age of regular production employees, in particular, is relatively high. Our attention was drawn to this by several union and management representatives and the Labour Survey showed that the median ages of different occupational groups in different houses in London and Manchester in October 1975 was almost invariably above 40 years, often above 50 years, and sometimes above 60 years‡. 6·5% of full-time and other regular production employees in London were over age 65 (21·5% over age 60) as were 4% (16·7%) in Manchester. The percentages over 65 years were particularly high in the publishing rooms.

---

* However, since Saturday night working is so much in demand a casual casual must have worked either three nights or four days during the week to qualify for a Saturday night working permit.
† This is not an invariable rule. Where workers with special skills are required the question of seniority in the vacancy books may be disregarded.
‡ Royal Commission on the Press. *Interim Report*. Cmnd 6433, Table F.5, page 112.

103. Three points were made by union and management representatives about the age profile. One was that since regular employment in a national newspaper house is often seen as the apex of an employee's career in the printing industry in London and Manchester there was little likelihood of a substantial lowering of the age of entry. It was estimated that for indoor SOGAT publishing room staff the average age of entry into a regular job might be around 40 years (the range of median ages of such staff between houses in London is 53·3 years to 58·4 years). Another point was that the existence of a significant proportion of production staff over 65 years old was a legacy of the pension arrangements in the industry, which for many years were poor or non-existent; even today there are reservations about the pension arrangements within the industry (see Chapter 5). Finally, in a number of production jobs, particularly those with a high physical content, it was said that the high average age of staff was causing, or could potentially cause, a problem of job allocation, because of the difficulty older men may have with heavy work.

104. The same factors that engender job entry waiting lists tend to ensure that once a production worker obtains a regular job in the national newspaper industry he stays in it for the rest of his working life. The median length of service of full-time and other regular production staff in London in October 1975 was twelve years* and our in-house inquiries showed that the extent of voluntary termination of employment was in normal circumstances very low, often too low to encourage houses to monitor the situation†.

105. The third effect of the demand for jobs in Fleet Street has been to reinforce the casual system of employment. Those in the appropriate London and Manchester branches who work outside the national newspaper sector look continually at ways of securing jobs in newspaper houses. Casual employment is the first step towards a regular job and the termination of the casual system would diminish entry opportunities.

106. The stability of the regular labour force within newspaper houses is not simply the result of relatively high pay within the industry; it is assisted by the union rules governing transfer between jobs. In practical terms it is virtually impossible to transfer from one house to another.

Administration of the Casual System

107. The placing of some 4,000 casuals (i.e. including red toppers and permit holders) in employment each week is a fairly big job. At the end of 1975 about 1,600 casuals were being slotted into jobs by the "calls office" that operates within each of the main unions with members who work on a casual basis: the NGA, NATSOPA and SOGAT. The rest were able to seek work for themselves direct from FOCs.

108. In all areas of production manning levels are tightly defined by agreement. The usual pattern is for manning levels to be fixed or standardised up

---

* Royal Commission on the Press Interim Report *ibid*, page 62.
† In one house which does keep figures on labour turnover (defined as the number of leavers over the average staffing level), turnover was just over half of one per cent in July 1975 and the estimate for the year was less than ten per cent.

to pagination levels agreed between each chapel and the employer and for manning to increase thereafter. The relationship between the average pagination of the newspaper and the point after which standard manning levels cease to apply determines the extent to which casual staff are employed. One newspaper, for example, never has a pagination lower than 24 pages and rarely more than 32 pages; the fact that agreements are based on a standard manning level of 32 pages means that the use of casual staff is confined, for the most part, to sickness and holiday cover. In other houses too, there has been some pressure from chapels, and some inclination on the part of some managers, to eliminate the use of casual staff except for sickness and holidays.

109. The administration of the casual system of employment at chapel level is linked with the chapel functions in relation to holiday rotas and, in many cases, the recording of absentees. The chapel officers in consultation with the appropriate overseer/manager determine the holiday rota for staff and may record absence from work and handle sick pay arrangements. Once given the pagination requirements, the chapel officers know whether, and if so how many, casual staff are required. They may then consult their own register of casual staff entitled to seek work directly from chapels and telephone the required number of such staff according to their seniority on the chapel list or they may contact the Branch (Region) calls office.

110. The procedure adopted at each of the calls offices is basically similar. The SOGAT office receives calls both from Fleet Street and the general printing industry and between about 8 am (general printing) and 9 pm (stand-by) calls are received by telephone from FOCs. Unemployed members report to the calls office and wait there for work. The NGA call books at the London Regional Office are open from 9 am to 3.30 pm and members looking for casual work usually sign in at about lunch time. NATSOPA operates a similar system. In each newspaper office the NATSOPA FOCs receive notification from management of the following weeks' planned pagination, generally on a Wednesday, and from this they determine as far in advance as possible the allocation of work for "red-toppers" and inform the calls office of the availability of work for casual casuals. The NATSOPA calls book should be signed each day by unemployed members* and any member not signing the call book is considered employed.

111. When a call is made by an FOC to the Branch a card is issued by the calls office to a member seeking work which authorises him to present himself at the newspaper office making the call. The casual worker must show his card to the authorised chapel official before starting work. The call card is passed by the appropriate chapel official to the cashier so that payment can be made at the end of the shift. Chapels are required to keep records of calls that are made to the call office and since the end of 1975 the NATSOPA regulations have been tightened in this respect: chapel returns to the LMB must show the number of calls filled by the FOC without recourse to the Branch calls office. This provision enables an assessment to be made of the number of casual shifts worked by red-top casuals and permit holders.

---

* Subject to the qualification in paragraph 94.

112. Each union with members who work on a casual basis attempts to ensure that the work available is fairly shared between those seeking it*. A number of rules are designed to further this aim. For example, NATSOPA's rules require the Branch Secretary to draw up a list of members signing the call book each week, the order of names (on the basis of which casual work is allocated) being determined by the number of times each member has signed the call book during the previous week. A member working a night shift is not allowed to sign the call book the next day, (or in the case of a Saturday night, the following Monday) and one working a day shift must miss signing the call book once†. SOGAT has very similar, though somewhat more complex, rules (see Appendix 4(a), rule 37) and the NGA simply provides that "calls will be allocated by the London Regional Office on the basis of sharing available work amongst those members available."

113. The administration of the casual system of employment puts a work load on some chapels that has led to chapel officers being wholly engaged on chapel duties in this respect (see Chapter 8). At Branch level, too, the unions allocate significant resources to their "labour exchange" functions, and there is some feeling that the service provided by the Branches is insufficiently recognised by newspaper houses. The LCB of SOGAT employs three call-room staff who are supported by the general staff of the Branch as a whole and NATSOPA's machine branch (and RIRMA) call-room is similarly staffed by two personnel (and sometimes three). The total administrative cost to the union of operating the casual system is estimated by NATSOPA to be in the region of £45,000 a year, and the union has from time to time claimed that the newspaper houses should reimburse this cost. On the basis used by NATSOPA for the calculation of the cost of operating its calls office the total cost to the unions of operating the system as a whole is over £100,000 a year.

Problems of the Casual System of Employment

114. There are two sets of problems associated with the use of casual staff. The first concerns the position of the casual staff themselves and the second the administrative and other problems created for newspaper houses and unions by casual working.

115. Casual casual staff are in a very insecure situation. They are not contracted to work on a regular basis and may have no non-contracted regular pattern of work. They have to sign in regularly at the appropriate calls office (see

---

* There is also some attempt by chapels to ensure that there is no "ghosting" which would, in a situation of fairly heavy unemployment, increase chapel earnings at the expense of diminishing job opportunities for casual staff. From our discussions with management and chapel representatives it would seem that "ghosting" as a deliberate practice is now relatively rare. Union branches certainly disapprove of it.

† In 1974 an interesting situation arose concerning the allocation of calls to redundant members which illustrates the problem of controlling the casual system from the union point of view. The LMB decided that any member accepting voluntary redundancy should, for those workings for which redundancy had been accepted, seek his work at the Branch Office and that such work would be allocated after the allocation to other unattached members seeking casual employment. However, it came to be realised that this provision could deter older members from accepting voluntary redundancy and force younger members, who might then be allocated red cards, into casual employment. These would then have the right to seek work independently at other offices and the calls available at the calls office would be correspondingly reduced. They would be reduced, it was thought, to a greater extent than would be the case if older red card holders were placed in the same position, because older members were more often satisfied with two or three workings each week. The decision of the Branch was modified.

paragraph 110) and bear their own travelling expenses for doing so* even though they may receive no work. Stand-by casuals† can be in a still worse position; they may have to wait until 10 pm before they know whether or not they will be working and, again, if they are not called on to work they receive no pay. During the ACAS inquiries many adverse comments were made about this "terrible" system which resulted in unemployed union members "wasting their lives away in the call-room".

116. The uncertainties about day-to-day employment are augmented by longer-term insecurity. The tendency in recent years has been to try to reduce manning levels and the use of casual staff. Whilst at least one recent set of agreements within a house has in some cases resulted in increased use of casual staff to take the place of retiring or voluntarily departing regular staff, the effect is thought to be temporary, and other agreements in other houses have led to significantly lower numbers of casual employees. For example, the number of casual staff working at the *Evening Standard* has dropped significantly, partly as the result of the non-publication of the newspaper on a Saturday and the integration of the *Evening Standard* into the Daily Express offices in Fleet Street, and partly for other reasons. Beaverbrook Newspapers also provides an interesting example of the effects of long term planning within newspaper houses on the levels of casual working. For a number of years regular publishing staff leaving the *Daily Express* for one reason or another were replaced by casual employees in the expectation that planned mechanisation would lead to manning reductions and that these could be more easily accommodated by shedding casual labour. The *Sunday Express* management and publishing chapel have also concluded a mechanisation agreement which similarly has had much more effect on casual working than regular employment. In these and other cases casual employment has been used as an integral part of the planning process. The opportunities for casual work have been extended only as a precursor to a substantial reduction in such opportunities.

117. Not only can casual staff be distinguished from regular staff by the insecurity of their employment pattern, but also the content of their work and their remuneration may differ. Invariably casual casual staff are required to undertake the lowest grade of work available. In the machine room NATSOPA casual staff are employed as fly hands or broom hands (see Chapter 5) and in the publishing room as wrapper hands. Where regular staff working on the higher grades in the machine or publishing rooms are absent from work, other lower grade regular staff temporarily replace them; so that casual casual staff always do the lowest grade, and often least well-paid jobs. Moreover, we have heard suggestions during our inquiries that casual casual staff sometimes work longer hours than their counterparts who work on a regular basis because the latter may take full advantage of the possibilities for finishing work early.

118. The pay of casual staff varies in comparison to the pay of regular staff doing comparable work. In some cases casuals receive the same pay as their

---

* There are strict rules against a casual signing the call book on behalf of another casual.
† At the beginning of each shift the FOC or other authorised chapel officer checks the manning requirement against the number of men reporting for work and, in the event of a shortfall may telephone through to a "pool" of men standing by to meet this eventuality. The *Sun* NATSOPA machine chapel office has, for example, been used as a base for stand-by casuals to wait for work at night.

regular counterparts* and in others they receive less, perhaps even the NPA "book" rate. Even in the same house casuals in different departments may be paid according to varying principles. During our inquiries we found that in one house NATSOPA casuals in the machine room received a nightly rate of one-fifth of the appropriate comprehensive weekly wage and SOGAT casuals in the warehouse received one-sixth of the comprehensive wage. Whilst the reason for the latter situation was unclear to those immediately concerned, it is possible that it was related to the fact that a small proportion of the "casuals" in the warehouse were regular five-night employees working the sixth night of production on the newspaper each week. In another house, NATSOPA casuals working in the machine room received £1:40 a night less than their regular staff. This was because certain fringe payments were made to the chapel (which determined their allocation) and these did not include payments for casual workers†.

119. Despite the disadvantages of the system for casual employees it obviously has its advantages. Whilst no precise figures are available it has been estimated that the turnover of casuals on the NATSOPA LMB calls office lists is about 50% (ie about half of those on the lists obtain permanent employment, usually in the general printing industry, during the year and are replaced as casuals by incoming unemployed members). However, there is less turnover among those who have been longest on the list, and the Branch tends to operate a policy of offering permanent job opportunities that arise in general printing to those who have been casuals for a relatively short time. This is because many casuals prefer to work casually in Fleet Street than to have permanent, lower-paid, employment elsewhere. From time to time this has created difficulties for the Branch. In 1974, for example, it expressed its deep concern that so many unattached members were persistently refusing to accept regular vacancies in the general printing industry. It was unfair, in the Branch's view, that members of 15 years standing should be waiting to get onto the NPA register whilst fairly new members were flouting Branch policies. A decision was taken that if newer unattached members refused to accept regular employment becoming available in general print they would not be allocated work in Fleet Street.

120. The problems caused by the casual system of employment for managements and unions are less concrete than those faced by the casual employees themselves, but, in the view of many of those involved in the system, are more threatening to the future of the industry as a whole.

121. The most common allegation is that casual casual staff do not have the same degree of commitment to the success of the industry or to any particular house within it as the regular employees. This is thought to be partly because not all casual casual staff depend entirely, or even mainly, on the industry for their

---

* In all cases, however, casuals receive an additional payment of one-twelfth of the appropriate house (comprehensive) rate, in lieu of an annual holiday entitlement of four weeks (there has been a union/NPA agreement on this matter since 1972). Although the general aim of this provision is to ensure comparability of treatment between regulars and casuals in this field it does not always succeed in doing so: regular employees sometimes work under house agreements that entitle them to more than the four weeks holiday.

† A further difficulty for casual staff, indirectly related to earnings, is the question of taxation. Each casual casual employee is responsible for keeping his own record of earnings for submission to the tax authorities. Given the variability of earnings and work patterns it is not hard for the casual employee to lose track of what he has earned and to underestimate it. This can, and has, we understand, led to cases in which substantial liabilities in respect of past unpaid tax have been incurred by individual casual employees.

livelihood; and partly because success is often equated with change, and change often means fewer job opportunities for casual staff, with the consequence that the latter prefer the status quo. There is also the evident point that any house intent on developing company "loyalty" and "identification" finds this difficult with an itinerant work force. Indeed, the casual casual has very little, if any, direct contact with the house management within whose general area he is working. The casual employee reports to the appropriate chapel officer at the start of his shift, is usually allocated work by him, and does not usually need to receive instructions from managers during his work.

122. On a more practical plane some managers said during our inquiries that casual casual staff were less familiar with the machinery and operating systems within individual houses and that therefore inefficient working was encouraged. Inefficiency was further promoted, it was said, by the advanced age of some casual staff in relation to regular employees, and by some of the attitudes of some regular employees fostered by the existence of the casual system. For example, it was alleged that in some cases regular employees used the casual system to facilitate half-night working, absenteeism, and excessive "blow" patterns. We even heard it said that the combination of relatively high earnings for Saturday night casual work and the complex administrative problems inherent in the casual system had in the past led to corrupt practices. On this point, however, we were assured by both managers and union officers that it is difficult for an individual to improperly obtain and use a union authorisation to undertake casual work.

123. It is hard to find any quantifiable evidence to support or refute the supposed disadvantages of the system for managements and unions. It is true, however, that the burdens of the system have become heavy enough to warrant a serious attempt by publishers and unions to dispense with, or at least drastically to modify it. This is not the first time the system has come under review but the current examination of the system by the working party jointly set up by the unions and the national newspaper houses (see Chapter 17) is a fundamental attempt progressively to decasualise the industry.

124. The activities of the working party have so far concentrated on collecting relevant information about the use of casual employees and on exploring ways in which the labour force can be entirely regularised. With such a complex situation it would be unreasonable to expect detailed agreement on how to decasualise to be reached rapidly. A number of problems have arisen. The principal point of difference has been whether decasualisation should be linked with the establishment of optimum manning levels (the view of the newspaper publishers) or whether these matters, as the unions think, should be dealt with separately. The newspaper publishers first considered a self-funding scheme to "buy out" casual staff whilst at the same time reducing manning requirements. But, because this might prove unfair to some regular staff, at the beginning of April 1976 they eventually proposed, among other things, that a scheme be devised enabling manning reductions to be agreed department by department, that within the new manning levels regular staff be offered the option of redundancy on agreed terms, and that for every two regular staff taking this option one casual employee would be regularised. The unions found these proposals unacceptable.

125. Other proposals that have been put forward by the publishers include the elimination of additional shift working by regular staff, the arrangement

of holiday rotas to minimise the need for casual working, and the fixing of manning levels to include provision for holiday and sickness cover. Reference has already been made to the heavy incidence of casual working during the summer months (see paragraph 89). In 1974, whilst casual casuals seeking work from the NATSOPA calls office received an average of five workings a week between March and October the average was only two-and-a-half to three workings a week in the remaining five months. If the demand for casual staff were even throughout the year it should be easier to arrive at a regular manning requirement. Some action has been taken in this connection. The NATSOPA Machine Branch, for example, decided in April 1976 that chapels should ensure that local holiday rotas ensured an even spread of holiday leave throughout the year. Even if the general peaks in demand for casual staff could be eliminated, there would still be surges in demand for casual labour to meet exceptional circumstances (for example, to cope with distribution problems occasionally created through the non-running of train services).

Non-Production Staff

126. About 22% of employees in the industry are managers, overseers and non-production staff. These are, of course, largely regular full-time staff and constitute about 28% of all such employees, and just under half the total of full-time regular production staff in London and Manchester. Appendix 4, Table 5, shows the distribution of non-production staff between popular and quality newspaper houses and between broad occupational categories. Around half of such staff, of which the bulk are NATSOPA members, are doing clerical or secretarial work. In houses producing more than one newspaper title, clerical and senior management staff are usually employed on a house, rather than a title, basis as far as their terms and conditions of employment are concerned.

Women

127. In no national newspaper house are women employed in either the origination, machining or publishing areas of the production process. Female employees are concentrated mainly in the clerical, advertising and administrative areas, where they form about half the total workforce, being organised by the NATSOPA clerical section. The only other sizeable group of women employees are cleaners organised by NATSOPA RIRMA. Women are also employed in canteens (organised either by GMWU, TGWU or NATSOPA), as journalists, and as publicity artists (SLADE). In four large houses the proportion of women employed expressed as a percentage of their total workforces was 6·8, 6·7, 10·7 and 9·5%. The proportion of women employees compared to the total of non-production employees in these houses was 23·3, 34·0, 30·3 and 28·8% respectively.

CHAPTER 5: TERMS AND CONDITIONS OF EMPLOYMENT

128. A major criticism of industrial relations within national newspapers has concerned the alleged confusion of payments structures and earnings patterns that the current bargaining arrangements have produced, and the on-going differentials and other problems that exist as a consequence. The inter-relationships of the terms and conditions of employment of different occupational groups in different houses can be seen both as an image of the bargaining process and as a measure of the criticisms that have been made. In examining the terms and conditions of employment of employees within the industry our aim was to throw light on the operation of collective bargaining especially since 1970; to elucidate the working of current payments systems and, as far as possible, to see to what extent previous research held good.

Production Workers
Earnings Patterns

129. The information on earnings at our disposal consisted of the average earnings of twenty-four grades of production workers across Fleet Street as a whole for 1961, 1964, 1967, 1970, 1971 and 1972* and the average earnings of twenty-three grades of production workers† within individual houses in April and October 1975. Houses also provided us with information on the distribution of earnings within individual employee groups and the earnings of particular groups over a number of years.

130. Appendix 5, Table 1, shows the movement of average weekly earnings between 1961 and 1975 for twenty-one occupational groups and the ranking of the weekly averages. The earnings of all groups have, of course, moved more rapidly in the last three years than in any other comparable period since 1961 but they have moved significantly faster for some groups which have as a result improved their ranking. Linotype operators who were third in the earnings rankings in Fleet Street in 1961 are now generally first and time hands have moved from tenth to fourth place. Electricians have made a similar improvement and stereotypers have dropped from second to sixth place. Just over half the groups maintained a fairly stable position in the hierachy (ie did not move more than three places) and, since 1970, only three groups changed their position appreciably. Over the whole period machine managers have consistently earned more, on average, than machine assistants and the latter, in turn, have invariably earned marginally more than publishing room staff. Stereotypers earned more on average throughout the period than process workers and for all except one year (ie 1964) for which information is available readers earned less than time hands, though the figures were usually close. Readers always earned more than revisers who always earned more than copyreaders.

131. In 1975, as in the period 1961–1970‡, there were great variations in the earnings of similar categories of full-time production workers in different

---

* Derived from the NPA annual earnings survey (see Chapter 7). The figures give separate data for four grades of machine assistants. In our Tables, however, to match the figures for 1975 we have developed a single weighted average for machine assistants thus effectively reducing the twenty-four items of information for each of these years to twenty-one.
† Derived from the Labour Survey.
‡ See K Sisson: "Industrial Relations in Fleet Street", *ibid*.

houses. In many cases the earnings of such workers on the production shift in the highest-paying houses were half as much again as the earnings of those in the lowest paying houses, and sometimes about twice as much. Appendix 5, Table 2, illustrates this point for April 1975. Even within the same house, where more than one publication is produced, the earnings of similar full-time production employees exclusively employed on one or other of the newspapers always differed and sometimes considerably. For example, in one house the earnings of linotype operators on one newspaper title exceeded those of similar employees on another title by over a quarter and in another house the difference was over 50%. In those cases where a largely separate labour force works on each newspaper title within the house it is possible to speak in general terms of higher and lower-paying house titles, but only in the sense that a *majority* of occupational groups working on one title may be earning more, or less, than their counterparts on other title(s) in the house; the relationship is not consistent for all occupational groups. In one house, composing room employees for one title earned substantially more than those working on another title but the position was reversed for machine room staff. This not an uncommon feature of intra-house earnings comparisons.

132. Comparisons of earnings of similar types of production staff employed on newspapers in similar categories do not reveal a clearer picture. Appendix 5, Table 3 shows the range of earnings within popular and quality newspapers, respectively, by occupational category, and within these two general categories we have examined a further breakdown on a daily/Sunday/evening basis. The closest alignment of earnings in April 1975 occurred between the evening newspapers but even here there were substantial earnings variations between, for example, the linotype operators and piece case hands. On the popular daily newspapers differentials varied from 2% to over 100% and similar variations were evident in the earnings of employees of the popular Sunday newspapers. The earnings of similar employees of the popular and quality Sunday newspapers, respectively, were also far from uniform, with particularly wide differentials among composing room and foundry employees.

133. The comparison of departmental average earnings within houses is more valid in the national newspaper industry than in many others. This is because of the pooling* of earnings within chapel boundaries and the equal distribution of earnings, with some relatively minor exceptions, between chapel members in the same grade. Such equal distribution applies not only to employees on fixed hourly rates but also to linotype operators and piece case hands who work on a piecework system (see paragraph 146). We sought from houses information about the distribution of earnings within occupational groups. In no case was there any significant scatter of earnings.

---

* The operation of chapel pools has from time to time created difficulties. One particularly interesting case concerned a chapel and management in Manchester in 1973–74. An individual chapel member brought an action against Thomson Withy Grove Ltd to recover money to which he claimed he was individually entitled but which had been paid into a pool account (the Bump Saturday Fund) and distributed by the chapel on a basis which included some sick chapel members. One of the several questions at issue was whether the Bump Saturday Fund was controlled by management or the chapel. Judge Franks found that the fund was controlled solely by the chapel which had a right, which it had used, to decide on the distribution of money from the Fund by ballot.

Earnings Components

134. The earnings of production workers are generally composed of the NPA basic rate or a house basic or comprehensive rate (see paragraph 139) plus a number of extras which may be fixed or variable. Where there is a comprehensive rate this itself usually has a number of components. Appendix 5, Table 4, gives a number of examples of how total wages are made up for a selected group of employees. The NPA basic rate forms only a small proportion of total weekly pay and other payments are concerned with consolidated or equated overtime and other variable payments, productivity payments related to changes in manning levels or in work content, etc. When the NPA rate rises the percentage increase applies to many, if not all, the components of pay. Thus whilst the size of the NPA rate may be relatively insignificant in relation to the level of earnings within houses, the size of the *increase* in NPA rates is much more significant and, indeed, particularly in the last two or three years the increases in pay resulting from NPA/union negotiations are the only substantial increases many employees have received.

135. That the relationship between the level of NPA basic rates and earnings within houses has become more distant is illustrated by Appendix 5, Tables 5 to 7. Table 5 shows the general movement of NPA rates since 1960 and the basic rate of publishing staff throughout that period; Table 6 the NPA basic rates in detail since 1970; and Table 7 the relationship between the earnings of ten selected occupational groups and the appropriate NPA basic rate since 1961. At the beginning of the period the average weekly earnings of the ten groups in Fleet Street ranged from about one-and-a-half to two-and-a-half times the relevant rates. At the end of the period earnings ranged from about three times to three-and-a-half times the basic rates, with the stereotypers at the top of the range. The gap between NPA rates and earnings widened appreciably faster in the three-year period to April 1975. These changes in the relationship between NPA rates and average earnings are evidence of the growing importance since 1960 of in-house bargaining and of the associated influence of the variable payments referred to in paragraph 134.

136. NPA rates have more than doubled since 1960. Apart from the award and subsequent consolidation into basic rates of cost of living bonuses in the 1960s and early 1970s, and of threshold payments in the 1970s, NPA pay increases have been expressed in percentage terms (see Appendix 5, Table 5). The variations in the percentage increases to different groups have been limited. In the same period earnings have trebled or quadrupled. The indications are, however, that in the last year or two the rate of earnings growth has slowed more sharply than in manufacturing industry generally and that a tighter hold has been exercised by houses on payments unrelated to manning or other changes resulting in savings to the house. In one house we were told that in the early 1970s the house budgeted for an annual wage drift* of around 14%. This has been substantially reduced. In other houses, too, there is evidence that earnings increases unrelated to productivity savings have lessened. Indeed, the effect of pagination reductions has had a restraining, if not a negative, effect on earnings. Appendix 5, Table 2, shows that between

---

* Defined as increases in the wage bill unrelated to the NPA increases or other formal agreements.

April and October 1975 the average earnings of many major groups in Fleet Street rose only marginally and in several cases were static or fell slightly.

137. Appendix 5, Table 8 and the accompanying graphs show the movement of NPA rates for publishing room staff against the movement of basic rates for all manufacturing industries, and compare the movements of earnings in Fleet Street (using publishing room earnings as the standard) with movements in all manufacturing industries since 1961. Both comparisons show that pay in Fleet Street has been increasing more slowly than in manufacturing industry generally in recent years, and especially since 1971. Of course earnings levels in Fleet Street remain significantly higher than in manufacturing industry generally (ie 39% higher in April 1975 on the basis of the figures in Appendix 5, Table 8, compared with 65% in 1970), but two points must be borne in mind. First, night-work is more extensive in the newspaper industry and, second, whilst average earnings are high, at the lower end of the scale there are significant numbers of people earning below the national average earnings figure.

138. A further interesting feature of Appendix 5, Table 8, is that NPA basic rates have increased more slowly than basic rates in all manufacturing industries since 1964-65. This, too, can be seen to reflect the growing importance of house agreements over the last decade.

Payments Systems
Comprehensive Agreements

139. Comprehensive agreements were introduced for two main reasons. They were intended to reduce the level of overtime working and to secure a reduction in manning levels by sharing the savings from any reductions between managements and chapels. The national agreements which provided the guidelines for in-house negotiations were made between the NPA and the LCB of SOGAT in 1963 and between the NPA and NATSOPA in 1966. Both agreements specified the percentage share of the savings that should go, respectively, to managements and chapels as reductions in manning levels were agreed locally.* It was also an objective of the comprehensive agreements to reduce or eliminate the number of variable elements in pay (but see paragraph 145), and it was hoped in some quarters that the system of payment by task would disappear.

140. The spread of comprehensive agreements was assisted by the need on the management side to reduce the increase in costs and on the union side to frame agreements that would during periods of incomes policy come under the broad "productivity" heading. Whilst there were some very early comprehensive agreements the comprehensive process did not achieve any great momentum until 1968-69 and, taking eight of the houses for which information is available, two-thirds of the agreements now current in London were negotiated after 1970. In 1975 at least six new comprehensive agreements were negotiated in Fleet Street though the frequency with which such new

---
* In the former case the first ten per cent of any saving was to go to the management and the rest was to be equally divided; and in the latter case savings were to be shared on a straight 50/50 basis.

agreements are made has obviously tended to fall as the number of groups not covered by comprehensive agreements has diminished. Linotype operators and piece case hands are the most significant groups still outside any comprehensive arrangements, probably because their earnings are relatively high (see paragraph 130) as the result of the working of their piecework system (see paragraph 146).

141. Several important aspects of the early productivity agreements were recognised from the beginning. First, the term "comprehensive" can be misleading. Not only does each agreement, as the NBPI recognised*, cover a relatively small proportion of the labour force in each newspaper/house but it is not invariably the case that comprehensive payments are made in exchange for tightly defined quotas of work. A fairly common provision is that staffing levels for various sizes of newspaper are defined and that the comprehensive rates shall be the only charge made upon the house in respect of all "normal" issues of the newspaper. In other cases the specific purpose of the comprehensive agreement is "to provide a comprehensive service . . . to standards and work loadings which have been mutually agreed and recorded between the chapel and departmental management". The precise formulation of the agreements and the extent of common ground on what work is included within the terms of the agreements can influence their success or failure. In some arrangements in some houses the jobs included in the comprehensive schemes are outlined in some detail but this is not usually so and there are arguments both ways about the desirability of this. Many managers we interviewed felt that comprehensive agreements had had limited success in securing an all-in service for a regular wage, and were critical of the fact that each time there is a change in the work load, however small, or a change in working practices not necessarily resulting in harder work, reviews of comprehensive agreements are sought.

142. Second, the agreements were seen by the houses only as a beginning in an attempt to achieve more efficient working. Arguments about the division of savings were to some extent a diversion from the central aim, from the houses' point of view, of improving efficiency. The original concept of roughly equal division of savings from the introduction of comprehensive arrangements has not, of course, lasted. The respective shares of chapel and management have varied, with the largest share normally accruing to the chapel (eg 60/40, and less tidy ratios such as $62\frac{1}{2}/37\frac{1}{2}$, have not been uncommon). In terms of the reduced manning requirement, the financial savings from any agreement could usually be calculated fairly accurately, but it was recognised to be true initially that the physical potential for reduced manning was a matter for enlightened guesswork. What normally happened was that departmental overseers and managers estimated on the basis of their experience the reduction in manning that the relevant chapel would be likely to accept. There was, and is, little, if any, work or method study.

143. In some houses, however, comprehensive agreements have contained references to these techniques. For example, in one house the parties agreed, subject to a guarantee of job security, "jointly to explore the use of method study techniques in the interests of operating effectiveness". In other houses

---

* NPBI Report 141 "Costs and Revenue of National Newspapers" 1970. Cmnd 4277, page 14.

it was jointly agreed to conduct a method study in the composing room. In a third case, whilst agreements do not specifically refer to method study, they do accept that comprehensive working "is the first step towards increased productive efficiency ... (and) ... in the light of experience gained, further examinations will be undertaken with the help and co-operation of the chapel ...". Other houses sometimes have more general references in their agreements, for example, to co-operation after consultation "in the introduction of new materials, equipment and methods".*

144. The third point about comprehensive agreements that was recognised was that they tended to reward the inefficient disproportionately and perhaps even to stimulate a more restrictive approach to working practices. This point was made as strongly during our inquiries by chapel as by management representatives and difficulties have frequently arisen where internal differentials have been upset because, for example, a chapel is considered to have negotiated a bogus productivity deal or one that has been possible only because of excessively loose manning accepted by management in earlier negotiations.

145. The introduction of comprehensive agreements has by no means meant the disappearance of all variable payments. Apart from variable overtime payments which under certain circumstances may still be made to employees covered by comprehensive agreements (see paragraph 170) the most common variable payment is related to the pagination of the newspaper concerned. Pagination payments may be made to production employees in all parts of the newspaper and are usually calculated on a six-monthly or annual "valuation" of the relevant agreement. The most usual practice is for pages produced in excess of a given total in the period covered and/or pages produced in excess of a daily (weekly) total to be valued and paid for in a review at the end of the period. When pagination declines as it has done since 1973 it can lead to fairly substantial falls in earnings levels which can and have produced industrial relations difficulties. In one case, for example, we were told by a senior manager that cuts in bonus payments brought about by pagination reductions have been "impossible to get through the chapels". This situation has been reflected in other houses so that pagination payments have tended to rise as pagination rose but not to fall as it declined. It is partly for this reason that there is some feeling among managements against the regular review of comprehensive agreements (see Chapter 10). It is argued that the aim of chapels is often to eliminate all variable payments made during the review period by incorporating them into the guaranteed payments in the agreement and to use this as the new base from which to seek supplementary extraneous payments in the next period of the agreement. It is certainly true that comprehensive agreements vary in the degree of their comprehensiveness. In some cases virtually the whole of the components of total earnings are covered by the comprehensive arrangements whereas in others the proportion can be as low as 70%

---

* Despite the occasional reference or allusion to method study it appears to have been used only rarely and even then not necessarily with lasting effect. In one case in which method study was carried out the chapel representatives were left with the impression that no changes were required and that work was organised perfectly efficiently. In other instances the results were more successful. In one composing room in 1969 a joint management/chapel work study committee was established to find possible savings of money and manpower which could be used as the basis for a productivity agreement. The committee's detailed work, which had been preceded by work study courses for the chapel members concerned, lasted for three weeks and took the form of an activity sampling exercise. As a result a comprehensive agreement was developed which still in essence applies.

Piecework Systems

146. Within Fleet Street composing rooms linotype operators and piece case hands are paid on the basis of the national agreement commonly referred to as London Piece Scale or the London Scale of Prices (LSP). The LSP is a complex scale or series of scales which set out the minimum payment for lines of various lengths of various sizes of type. Each piece case and linotype operator keeps a record of the work he performs and makes a nightly return to the piecework tracker or other appropriate management representative. Earnings of pieceworkers, though calculated individually, are pooled and divided equally each week amongst each group respectively.

147. Though the LSP is at the core of the system, each newspaper may and has developed its own variant of the scale. Often the setting payment made within a house is a multiple of the LSP rate. For example, in one house the basic setting charge for standard size type is twice the LSP figure. The multiple is different (and larger) for smaller type sizes. Other variations include the provision that the whole of an advertisement or article is paid for at the highest rate for any piece of moveable type it contains. Most items that have to be set within a newspaper have been priced either by the LSP or in-house negotiations. New charges do not often have to be set, though arguments develop about the need for minor readjustments, and when there is a need for a new job to be priced the LSP often only provides general guidance. Disputes do sometimes occur about a charge which has been made (dockets are usually checked on a random basis by the production cost clerk or similar employee) though these are normally quickly settled between chapel and printer*.

148. Other variable payments to pieceworkers include normal payments for overtime, payments for "slip" editions†, and payments for colour printing, etc. Such payments can substantially boost the earnings of pieceworkers. Earnings may also be affected by interruptions in the work flow caused perhaps by machine breakdowns. A variety of payments is made in these circumstances ranging from flat-rate payments for any substantial delay to a variable lineage payment for shorter work interruptions. An example of the latter situation would be where an operator is required to change machines or the size of type on which he is working.

149. Three things should be said at this stage about the piecework system in the composing rooms. First, it is disliked by some managers because it is said that it can be distorted and produces a relatively high rate of earnings growth which stimulates a reaction from work groups outside the composing room both in the production and editorial field; because it does not relate money rewards in any sensible way to effort involved‡; and because it can be difficult to interpret. On the other hand other managers favour it because, while it has faults, it ensures that work is done quickly and encourages the maintenance of relatively low staffing levels. Second, the system can produce disparities in the

---

* Where the charges are relatively well-defined, disputes have nevertheless arisen about the amount of setting that is required to be done (eg the point at which editorial changes require the complete resetting of a page). The LSP states that if more than an agreed percentage of a page or article is reset to meet editorial needs the whole of it is charged as newly-set.

† ie when an edition goes to press and is stopped to introduce some late change or addition.

‡ In one case the system has been described as "not so much a payment-by-results scheme but a payment-for-what-would-have-been-the-results-had-the-work-been-done-(scheme)".

earnings of the different groups of employees within the composing rooms and this can cause, and has caused, friction. Third, the prospect of technological change in many composing rooms is forcing a reappraisal of payments systems therein (see Chapter 17).

Payments Structures and Differentials

150. No national newspaper house has a formal pay structure covering all production employees. All houses are, however, constrained by prevalent ideas about the appropriate differentials that should exist between broad groups of employees. Previous paragraphs have pointed to the similarities and changes in earnings rankings over the last fifteen years and there has also been a tendency for differentials between groups of workers within houses to narrow. Despite this there are certain fairly consistent concepts about in-house pay relationships. It is, for example, fairly generally recognised that NGA composing room employees will tend to be at the top of the earnings ladder and that other NGA grades as well as electricians and engineers will be somewhere near the top; that machine assistants will come significantly below this level; and that publishing room and ancillary workers will come somewhere near the bottom (with the former earning significantly more in absolute terms than the latter, and fairly closely aligned with the machine assistants' earnings).

151. Within this loose framework, which is not invariably accepted as desirable, several more specific pay relationships exist or are sought after. The notion most tenaciously adhered to by many chapel representatives, and sometimes conceded by managements, is that the differential that should exist between the pay of NGA employees and NATSOPA assistants should be $12\frac{1}{2}\%$, or, as some NGA chapel representatives would have it, not less than $12\frac{1}{2}\%$. The formal birth of this idea occurred in 1970 when following a dispute concerning the *Daily/Sunday Mirror* the parties agreed after assistance from the TUC that the comprehensive rate for grade 1 machine assistants should be fixed at $87\frac{1}{2}\%$ of the machine minders' rate*.

152. Several points should be made about this. First, the idea that this differential should exist has spread outside the machine rooms to the reading rooms (readers and revisers/copyreaders) and to the service areas (linotype and other engineers and their assistants). During our inquiries we asked chapel representatives which other groups, if any, were used by the chapel as points of reference when determining pay claims or seeking to maintain differentials. Apart from allusions to earnings of similar employees on other newspapers both outside and within the house, the inter-occupational comparisons made by comparable chapels in different houses were similar. The NATSOPA and NGA machine chapels compared their rates with each other to try to ensure that the differential was not greater/less than $87\frac{1}{2}$:100. The machine managers sometimes looked to the time hands' rates as a basis of comparison; the NATSOPA and NGA reading room staff similarly made internal reading room comparisons usually on the same basis as those made in the machine

---

* The differential is embodied in the Joint Pressroom Agreement (see Chapter 8) signed in November 1970 which says that "... the NATSOPA grade 1 rate shall be $87\frac{1}{2}\%$ of the machine minders' rate and ... this differential will be maintained unless negotiations at national level establish some different percentage differential or some other method of wage calculation".

room, as did the SLADE process workers and the SOGAT process provers. Both readers' and process workers' chapels tend also to make comparisons with composing room earnings. In one case, for example, where the pay increases given to the two groups concerned are kept in close though not inflexible relationship to each other, the readers have an observer present during the time hands' negotiations and vice-versa. In all houses both groups are members of the appropriate imperial chapel and the imperial father is present at all negotiations, a situation which tends to prevent obvious anomalies occurring*. Within the composing rooms, whilst no fixed differentials apply, there is a feeling that the earnings of linotype operators and piece case hands are unjustifiably ahead of other skilled groups. Between engineers and their assistants chapel representatives felt that at least/not more than a $12\frac{1}{2}\%$ differential should exist.

153. The second point about the $12\frac{1}{2}\%$ differential is that though it is often sought, especially by NATSOPA chapels, it is far from universally achieved and is not often formally or in practice recognised by managements (or NGA FOCs) as a fixed relationship†. Between the groups of employees mentioned above whose chapel representatives sought this differential the actual relationship of comprehensive rates range from 73% to 91%.

154. The third point is that even where a fixed percentage differential does formally or by custom and practice tend to be maintained between the basic or comprehensive rates of different work groups the relationship does not invariably carry over into earnings. Finally, there is no agreement at national level or any percentage relationship between the pay of different groups implicit in the nationally-agreed rates that embodies the concept of the $100:87\frac{1}{2}$ differential.

155. Appendix 5, Tables 9 and 10 illustrate these points. In none of the groups where one might expect an $87\frac{1}{2}\%$ relationship does one appear in NPA rates in 1970 or 1975. The brakehands' rates ranged in 1975 from 77% to 89% of the machine managers' rate (the Tables use the middle of the brakehands' and machine managers' rates given in the national agreements but whatever the combination used the $87\frac{1}{2}\%$ relationship does not appear), and the readers; revisers; copyholders ratio was 100: 77: 75. With the exceptions outlined in paragraph 157 the relationship between the NPA rates of different groups has remained very stable between 1970 and 1975 and, indeed, since 1960‡, a feature which, given the form of national pay awards over the last fifteen years, is to be expected (see paragraph 136).

156. As far as earnings are concerned, the picture is mixed. In just over half the occupational categories selected as the basis for Appendix 5, Table 10 the differences in inter-occupational average earnings differentials are within five per cent of the corresponding percentage differentials in NPA rates. Differences in the percentage earnings/rates differentials between the remaining categories is often fairly wide and in some cases, particularly where stereotypers are concerned, differentials are reversed. For example, the NPA rates for

---

* See Chapter 10. The same point can be made to a lesser extent in relation to stereotypers and to telecommunications and electronics employees.
† This is so even in the machine rooms of the Mirror Group, outside the *Daily Mirror/Sunday Mirror* where the Joint Pressroom Agreement operates.
‡ Appendix 5, Table 11 illustrates this.

stereotypers in 1975 were 12% lower than the readers' rates*, but the average earnings of stereotypers in Fleet Street were some seven per cent higher. A similar situation existed between stereotypers and, respectively, process workers and machine managers.

157. The exceptions referred to in paragraph 155 are the engineers and electricians. These two groups have significantly improved their NPA rates in relation to other groups between 1970 and 1975 (ie by between four and five per cent). It is also in this area that another fixed pay relationship is commonly recognised. For many years it has been accepted that the hourly rates of electricians and mechanical engineers should be the same. The principle became more firmly embedded as the result of an adjudication in December 1971 on a complex dispute at the *Daily Telegraph* concerning the relationship between the earnings of electricians and engineers where their shift rotas varied†. The NPA rates for engineers and electricians are identical and differences in earnings are accounted for by differences in hours worked. Time hands and readers also have the same NPA rates and this parity is reflected in in-house concepts of what readers'/time hands' differentials should be, despite actual earnings differences. Readers' and time hands' NPA rates are practically the same as those of engineers and electricians, and the rates of indoor and outdoor publishing staff are identical, a situation which is fairly well reflected in the average earnings figures (see Appendix 5, Table 1).

158. It does seem, then, that there are certain very broad concepts of the ranking of jobs in Fleet Street and these have practical application in each house. In negotiating in-house agreements managements have to be careful not to transgress too far on differentials between closely related groups. The more commonly recognised and firmly-established the differential the harder negotiations can be. In seeking to negotiate manning reductions managements have often had to reach parallel agreements with related chapels to prevent the differential changing too far‡. Whilst there is no formal articulation of rates between departments, the way in which rate comparisons can be made through departments, with the possible exception of the publishing rooms, can be discerned. Pay structures within departments do exist formally and the situation in several production areas outside the composing room is outlined below:

> **Machine Rooms.** There are four general grades of machine assistants in the NPA agreements: brake hands, magazine hands, oilers, and general assistants (from the highest to the lowest paid). This grading structure has been followed in most houses though there has been a tendency to reduce the number of grades. In one house, for example, the four grades (brake, magazine, oil, and fly hand) have been reduced to two and a

---

* The normal working hours of stereotypers as specified by the national agreements are fewer than for readers and this may be a justification for the rate differential.

† In addition to making his finding on the specific parity question referred to him, the referee, Professor H A Clegg, also criticised the negotiating arrangements that had contributed to the dispute. Entirely separate negotiations with each union were, it was argued, inappropriate and "... the only solution (was) for a single negotiation with both unions ...". No changes in the negotiating procedure in this respect have, however, taken place.

‡ Problems can also arise where, within the terms of an existing agreement, one chapel manages to close the differential gap between its members and the members of a chapel between whom a pay relationship exists. For example, in one house in 1974 the NATSOPA reading room members by frequently receiving short-working payments disturbed readers'/readers' assistants differentials.

differential of nearly £3 separates the grades. In other cases there are three machine assistant grades. Even where there are four the monetary difference between the top and the bottom grade may be relatively narrow (in one case it was only £1·43 at the end of 1975). In some quarters it is felt that the number of assistants' grades could be reduced further, perhaps even to a single grade. Those managers and chapel representatives, during our inquiries, who did not favour this idea thought that the removal of a differential would reduce the incentive for the brake hand to do more responsible work, cause friction (because a casual operator could immediately earn as much as an experienced regular brake hand), and entail the loss of a disciplinary measure. Occasionally a man can be downgraded temporarily for disciplinary reasons, such as unauthorised absence.*

159. The question of the machine minders'/brake hands' differential has already been discussed, but two related issues were raised by NATSOPA representatives. The first concerned the differential at the "waste end" of the machine room (ie removing bad copies before transit to the publishing room). Here NATSOPA and NGA operators do the same work but an extra payment is made to the NGA staff. The second issue is the larger one of promotion from brake hand to machine minder. The promotion barrier at this point (except at News Group Newspapers†) has been much debated in the industry, as to a lesser extent has the barrier between engineers and their NATSOPA assistants. The criticism is that the barrier is unjustified by any skill differences as experience in News Group Newspapers and the provincial newspaper industry would seem to corroborate. The justification is that in the context of industrial relations in Fleet Street it is as fair for the NGA to build walls around the jobs which are traditionally its own as it is for other unions to protect their traditional job rights. It is enough here to say that whilst there is a certain amount of resignation, the situation in the machine rooms in this respect creates strong resentment.

Publishing Rooms. The payments structures in publishing rooms again are fairly straight-forward. Taking one typical example, the night publishing staff are grouped into two operating grades with additional payments to drivers, and a number of separate rates for pay clerks, back number

---

* It is the chapel which decides by rota (see Chapter 8) who will do what job but the length of time it can take for a man to progress from the lowest grade of machine room assistant to brake hand can be considerable. In one house, the progression was from fly hand, waste hand, printed waste hand, broom hand, stripping, reel supply, oiling, magazine hand, to brake hand, and we were told that the high average age of machine assistants makes it unlikely that all members can progress through all grades. At the moment it takes about 12 years to move from fly to oil hand.

† News Group Newspapers is unique in Fleet Street in employing NATSOPA Machine minders. Historically, *News of the World* minders had always been NATSOPA members. When the *Sun* moved into the *News of the World* plant in Bouverie Street there was conflict between the NGA, whose members had been machine minders on the old *Sun*, and NATSOPA which felt that the "custom of the house" should be applied and that all machine minders' jobs in Bouverie Street should be filled by NATSOPA members. In the event a compromise was reached: all the old *Sun* machine minders were retained on the new *Sun* but vacancies were filled by NATSOPA members until there was an even balance. Thereafter vacancies were filled alternately to maintain the balance. NATSOPA brake hands who are promoted to machine minder remain NATSOPA members though the chapel arrangements (see Chapter 8) make this a rather academic point. *News of the World* machine minders' jobs continue to be filled entirely by NATSOPA members; some are brake hands on the *Sun* during the week.

clerks, etc. In another case, the two basic rates applicable to day staff are supplemented on a Saturday night and separate rates apply to bench hands, machine operators and wrapper hands (from lowest to highest paid) and the drivers' rates are linked to those of the machine operators. On one newspaper there is a single production rate to which is added five or six "merit" payments for responsibility, the smallest payable to the postal clerks and the highest to the chief clerk. There are a number of small variants on these patterns and, as in the machine room and elsewhere, the rates may be affected by pagination and other variable payments. The payments structure in the publishing rooms seems to give rise to few difficulties and the biggest changes that have come about or which seem likely to occur in future arise from the integration of publishing rooms in duel newspaper houses. Internal publishing room differentials are less controversial than in, for example, the machine room partly because SOGAT is the only union with members in the area.

Process Departments. Employees in these departments comprise camera operators, printers on metal, etchers, finishers and retouchers. There is often some movement between jobs but this creates no problems because the staff usually receive the same basic rate and the same pagination and colour payments. Process provers (SOGAT) receive a rate related to that of other process workers (in October 1975 earnings of the former were 91% of the earnings of the latter but the percentage relationship between basic rates is normally somewhat less favourable to process provers) but because of the close links between the two groups (see Chapter 8) few difficulties seem to arise.

Reading Rooms. The grading structure in the reading rooms is uncomplicated, and we heard during our inquiries no complaints that, within the existing technology, it did not effectively meet the requirements of the job. The only nagging problem is the relationship between readers' and other rates, a problem reflecting that in the machine rooms. The national agreement shows two rates below the readers' rate for, respectively, revisers* (the highest) and copyreaders, and this tripartite grade structure is generally embodied in house agreements, and reflected in earnings throughout Fleet Street. Another parallel with the machine room is the line between NGA readers and NATSOPA assistants. In theory, this line is not as rigid because through the NGA readers' examination† assistants have been promoted in the past and could be in future. However, the employment situation has effectively ended the prospects of holding readers' examinations for the present, and in practice the line is as rigid as that in the machine room and the disatisfaction it causes as great.

(d) Other Terms and Conditions of Employment

Sickness Arrangements

160. A wide range of schemes to protect the earnings of regular employees absent from work through sickness or injury exists in the national newspaper

---

* The NPA rate for revisers is, incidentally, the same as that for linotype assistants, a parity which further links the rates in the composing room and related areas.

† According to the rules of the NGA, (rule 17) allows "the London Region, in their discretion, . . . following a successful examination of the candidate, (may) recommend the admission to full membership of suitable revisers and copyholders who have had six years' continuous experience of revising and/or copyholding provided that such applicants are not less than 21 years of age".

industry. Within individual houses a number of schemes usually operate (for example, in one house eleven separate arrangements for sickness pay have evolved) and the benefits they provide and their dates of implementation vary according to the priority accorded to such arrangements by the chapels negotiating them and the policy of the house involved. In some cases there is no sickness or injury scheme as such but the local agreement provides that absence due to sickness up to a prescribed level shall be covered by the remaining employees and, provided that a casual is not employed to replace the sick absentee, full or part wages are paid to the latter.

161. Separate sickness and injury schemes with significantly different provisions tend to operate for, respectively, production, clerical and editorial staff. Qualifying periods before benefits can be claimed, the periods during which benefits are payable, and the amount of benefit differ considerably between categories of employees within individual houses, sometimes between production workers in different occupational groups in the same house, and, of course, between houses.

162. Two points emerge from our examination of sick pay schemes which are generally applicable. First, there have been improvements in sickness schemes in the last five or six years. Several of them have been implemented or reviewed since 1970. Second, there is no ostensible common policy in relation to sickness benefits. At least one house tries to follow the general policy that employees should not suffer substantial decline in their basic earnings during a reasonable period of sickness and that they should not gain financially from sickness. Another scheme's objective is to provide "a measure of security for permanent staff employees" who are sick. The principle behind a third scheme is that by the third week of sickness, when earnings related state benefit becomes payable, the average married man without children should receive about the same net income from all sources as when he is working. There is no NPA agreement or guideline on sickness pay arrangements.

163. A further point is that whilst most schemes are directly funded by the newspaper houses some are contributory and are managed by committees composed of chapel and management representatives. Not all employees are covered by formal sickness pay arrangements implemented by houses. Sometimes chapels do not participate in the relevant house scheme because they prefer to finance and operate schemes of their own. In other cases certain types of staff—for example, regular casuals and staff who have opted not to join the appropriate company pension scheme—are ineligible for membership of the relevant sickness scheme.

Pensions

164. The Government Actuary has recently analysed the pension arrangements within nine newspaper houses.* One of the conclusions of the Actuary was that, in contrast to private industry as a whole, the twenty-two schemes within these houses between them ensured that almost all regular employees are eligible to join a scheme.

* Government Actuary's Survey of Pension Arrangements for Employees of National Newspapers: Royal Commission on the Press Interim Report 1976. Cmnd 6433, page 68.

165. There are only two comments we wish to add here to what the Actuary has said. For the purposes of this report, our definition of the national newspaper industry is rather wider than the Actuary's. If the wider definition is taken it is not the case that in all houses almost all regular employees can join a pension scheme. In the current situation it is also relevant to note that whilst in the preponderant number of schemes currently open to new members (ie 15 out of 18 schemes) benefits are payable on the relatively favourable basis of a fraction (from one eightieth to one hundredth) of final pensionable salary for each year of pensionable employment, this does not necessarily mean that most employees are in a happy situation with regard to their immediate pension prospects. This is because many of the existing schemes are comparatively new and employees have not yet been able to build up substantial pension rights. This is, indeed, a problem to which the newspaper houses and the printing unions have been giving careful joint consideration since the end of 1975 (see Chapter 17).

Hours and Shifts

166. It is often said by FOCs and managers that the great variety of working conditions within a newspaper establishment leads to many differences in hours and shift patterns, at least for production staff, which tend to encourage chapel bargaining: only the chapel and managers immediately concerned, it is argued, can understand the detailed considerations behind the configurations of the shift patterns of any particular group of employees.

167. The NPA agreements lay down, for each category of employee, the number of weekly working hours. The exact formulation of the "working hours" clauses vary. In some cases the agreements specify the maximum number of hours exclusive of mealtimes that an employee shall work at "ordinary rates". In other industries it is simply stated that the hours of working "shall be . . . . based . . . . (on) . . . . .x hours". However phrased, there is certainly a view held by some management representatives that houses should not deviate from what they consider to be the "standard" hours specified in the national agreements. It is recognised, however, that there are such "deviations". Our inquiries showed that, for example, in October 1975 the normal weekly contractual working hours of composing room staff ranged between houses from 30 to $37\frac{1}{2}$ (the latter figure, if one includes half-an-hour per shift for meal times, is that in the national agreement). In most categories of production staff there were differences between the normal contractual working hours applying within houses and those specified in the national agreements, though the differences were limited to a minority of houses.

168. It is relevant to make the point here that the contractual working hours of employees often bear a tenuous relationship to actual working hours. This is because most production work in a newspaper is essentially task-orientated and once the newspaper has been produced (or, on day work, the necessary cleaning, for example, has been done) there is no advantage in employees waiting around until their contractual finishing time before going home. Apart from regular "early cuts", a system whereby individuals by rota may leave work early, it is usually the case that production shift times last, by tacit or explicit agreement, until the end of the normal night's work.

169. This means that employees may become accustomed to finishing work earlier than their constractual finishing time. When the "custom and practice" hours have to be exceeded for one reason or another the question of the payment for the "extra" hours sometimes arises even though such hours may fall within the contractual working period. For example, in one case weekly contracted hours for a group of production workers are 40 (ie ten hours a night inclusive of meal times for four nights a week) and the contracted shift is from 20.00 pm to 06.00 am. The normal working night, however, is from 21.00 pm to 04.30 or 05.00 am and, whilst the chapel agrees to cover all contracted hours, if these employees are required to work beyond 05.00 am they receive overtime payments.

170. Overtime payments may also be paid for work performed not only within contracted hours outside custom and practice hours but also within the latter. Where this happens the term "overtime" can be misleading. The payment is actually made in exchange for members of a chapel performing work considered to be outside the terms of their comprehensive agreement or the commonly understood boundary of their normal job. Or the payment may be made where managers require members of a chapel to do their normal work differently or with fewer men. For example, in one situation night machine assistants claimed a payment in return for clearing ink spillage that they argued they were not required to do as a normal part of their work; and in another situation an extra payment was sought because men were unable to use their normal working thoroughfare and had therefore to carry materials further than usual. In both these and many other cases arguments ensued between managers and chapel representatives on whether extra money or "simultaneous overtime" should be paid. At the root of the arguments was not only the question about what the relevant clause(s) in the relevant agreement meant but also the broad issue of the purpose of comprehensive agreements.

171. The payment for overtime is usually, but not invariably, based on the NPA minimum rate for the employee group concerned. This can cause difficulties because of the gap between the NPA rates and those embodied in comprehensive agreements. It can happen that time-and-a-half the NPA rate is less than the hourly comprehensive rate, and that without a specific clause in the relevant comprehensive agreement or some compensating adjustment it is not easy to persuade men to undertake overtime when production difficulties require it. There has been some recent pressure within houses for the overtime rate to be based on the comprehensive hourly rate.*

172. The extent of overtime, especially in the current economic climate, is not great. In most houses overtime payments are carefully monitored and departmental and other managers have to account in detail for any overtime payments they make. Sometimes overtime is virtually non-existent in production areas and

---

* In some cases the situation is complicated by the fact that piece rates apply (ie for piece case hands and linotype operators in the composing rooms). For the latter employees the provision in the national agreement is that overtime premium shall be charged at the difference between one and a half times the permanent time hands' rate and ordinary hourly rates (defined in the agreement). In house agreements the position can be more involved. The number of overtime hours paid to such an employee may be related to the edition to the end of which he continues to work. Payment is at a standard premium and if an operator's piecework earnings do not reach a given level during overtime periods he may claim guaranteed "cover" or waiting time rates on an agreed formula.

management policy is specifically directed to ensure that this is so. In other cases late working occurs only when there is a machine breakdown or industrial action. In one machine room such late runs occurred on an average of only about twelve times a year. In another house in October 1975 overtime payments for fifteen groups of machine room employees, with one exception, averaged between under one per cent and about seven per cent of average weekly earnings. The exception was a group of machine assistants whose overtime earnings represented an average of eleven per cent of their weekly earnings. Again, in another house overtime payments to production workers as a whole totalled just over four per cent of total wages paid to production workers.

173. For some chapels there is provision for guaranteed overtime. In one foundry (not covered by a comprehensive agreement) all employees receive regularly and automatically three hours overtime for machine preparation and two employees (determined by rota) receive an extra three hours for coming to work earlier than their colleagues. In the same foundry "late" overtime is paid for work after 1 am and is never less than about three hours. Overtime payments are also made for pagination beyond a certain level, page changes and double-set working.* Overtime arrangements of this kind are mirrored elsewhere but they are the exception not the rule. One of the objectives of comprehensive agreements was to eliminate such overtime payments and absorb them into an equated wage.

174. It is the policy not only of managements but also unions to limit overtime working and this is reflected in rules and agreements. The composing room and reading room agreements for NGA members prohibit overtime working beyond eight hours (12 hours for readers on evening newspapers), and the rules of each of the print unions contain overtime and/or working hours provisions. The LCB of SOGAT forbids its members in regular employment to work more than eight hours overtime a week (and limits "jobbing" hours to 56 a week); the London Region of the NGA limits each of its members to a maximum of 17 hours' overtime in any week and 56 in any four-week period; NATSOPA's weekly limit is nine hours for men engaged on nightwork on a newspaper†; and SLADE, whilst it does not specify a weekly limit in its rules‡, requires members to inform the appropriate chapel representative of overtime hours worked. Chapels have to record overtime hours and make monthly returns to the branch. Members exceeding the monthly limit consistent with the NPA agreement without the branch committee's permission can be fined up to £25. The engineers and electricians have agreed the general principle with the NPA that "the working of excess overtime is to be deprecated" and attempts are made to ensure that time-off-in-lieu is taken by members who have to work overtime, though difficulties have sometimes arisen where the taking of time-off-in-lieu has been prevented by local circumstances.

The Blow System

175. The term "blow system" is widely used to cover situations in which manning arrangements permit some members of a production department to be

---
* One machine is usually sufficient for producing plates but occasionally a second is required. It has been agreed in this case that there should in these circumstances be an extra overtime payment rather than a casual call.

† The regulation is actually more complex than this.

‡ But the NPA agreement lays down a limit of 15 hours for each member per fortnight except in emergencies.

absent for some part of their shift. The system is widely felt by managers, by the standards normally applicable in industry generally, to be unjustifiable in its present form and a contributory factor to the current economic position of national newspapers. It is given some formal recognition in the national agreements. The agreement between the NPA and the LCB of SOGAT records, for example, that " . . . the proprietors agree that 'blow times' may be allowed in addition to the mealtime". The agreement also provides that the number of blows shall be determined by management and that they "must be for periods and at times to suit the convenience of the work by mutual arrangement with the chapel".

176. Blow systems usually operate at their most formal in the publishing and machine rooms and in the foundries. The blow patterns, however, vary somewhat between and within houses. In one house, for example, the blow system for one publishing chapel is one-for-one and for another chapel is two-for-one.* Groups of staff break for rest periods on a rota system on this basis. In another house half the publishing room arrive some hours after the starting time observed by the other half and replace them. This is a practice known to management and reluctantly accepted.

177. Not infrequently the blow system is formally embodied in agreements between chapels and houses. In one publishing room agreement, for example, it is provided that blows "shall be organised by the chapel, with the approval of the publisher and accommodation for that facility is contained within the staffing arrangements (herein) defined . . . ". The agreement does not, however, define the pattern of blows. In some areas manning levels are negotiated which allow the chapels to operate their own blow system informally.

178. The justification for the system is that rest periods are necessary in arduous working conditions. In the machine rooms, for example, chapel representatives argued that the noise levels and other physical conditions could not be supported for lengthy periods. Against that managers said to us that machine room conditions had shown some improvement (ink mists have been considerably reduced, for example). In the main, however, managers have become accustomed to the blow system. What causes particular concern is the situation that sometimes occurs in which unauthorised absence takes place. According to some managers half-night working is not uncommon, though houses have tried to combat it, fearing that it could eventually lead to working one night on and one night off. There have been cases where fairly severe disciplinary action has been taken against employees found absent from work without permission.

Annual Holidays

179. The general provision in the national agreements is that production workers should receive a minimum of four weeks annual holiday. As might be expected there is rather more uniformity on the practice within houses on this issue than on other matters. Nevertheless, there are houses in which some categories of full-time employees receive under the terms of their house agreements more than four and up to six weeks' annual leave. In at least one case, as part of a bargain involving the introduction of new equipment, annual holiday entitlement was temporarily increased, as a precursor to a shorter working week.

---

* ie one period of work for an equivalent period of "blow" and two periods of work for one period of "blow", respectively.

Clerical and Management Staff

Clerical Staff

180. Whilst clerical staff, in common with production staff, are divided departmentally and occupationally, they differ from production staff in one important respect: they are covered by a single union. This means that the possibilities of achieving a common, jointly agreed, salary structure across the whole of the clerical area in each house have been greater. Against this, of course, must be set the fact that clerical staff are potentially more mobile than production staff and internal rates must be more sensitive to rates in outside industry.

181. The fact that the chances of securing comprehensive salary structures for clerical staff are relatively good and that the need for such structures is widely perceived among managers and FOCs does not mean that they exist universally in Fleet Street. The picture is very mixed. Just over half the houses have clerical agreements that cover all or nearly all their clerical staff, though in at least one house there is provision for departmental pay supplements to be negotiated on productivity grounds.

182. Several of the all-embracing agreements have been negotiated fairly recently (ie in 1975). One of the earlier agreements which took effect in 1972 contains provisions that are fairly typical of this type of agreement, with one exception. It introduced a new job-evaluated salary structure providing for six grades of clerical staff. The lower grades have a minimum rate, a five-point annual incremental scale, an allowance for merit payments and a maximum salary. The top grade is an inclusive grade and employees on it are not entitled to overtime pay or service increments but there is no limit on the merit pay such staff may receive and therefore no maximum salary. The job evaluation system by which employees are allocated to particular grades is jointly operated by the management and the union and incorporates an appeals procedure.

183. In those houses where there is no comprehensive clerical agreement there have been some attempts to improve the existing situation. In general such houses have a series of individual departmental agreements which often contain no grading clauses other than a general reference to or slight elaboration on the NPA agreement*. In addition to basic pay there may be provision for service increments, merit increases, night rate and shift rates extras, and a variety of other house payments. Anomalies can, and do, arise and disparities in earnings of comparable staff in the same house have developed in some cases. In one house attempts were made, beginning in 1970, to introduce a more rational pay structure. A joint union/management job evaluation exercise was conducted but was discontinued in 1973 because agreement could not be reached on the monetary aspects of the proposed grading structure. In another house, the question of the introduction of a house agreement for clerical staff has been under consideration for some time. A job-evaluation exercise was conducted by management consultants and a draft agreement was drawn up covering a wide range of matters including negotiating, grievance and recruitment procedures, non-automatic replacement of staff, staff flexibility and joint efficiency studies. However, for a variety of reasons final agreement was not reached, and there has been

---

* This agreement simply divides staff into junior and senior clerks, shorthand-typists, and shorthand-typists/telephonists.

unrest, including stoppages of work and other action, among some of those involved.

184. Many of the agreements applying to clerical staff contain consultative clauses and provisions relating to productivity and flexible working. One agreement, for example, provides for "full integration and flexibility of working arrangements of all clerical staff covered ... between publications, locations and jobs within the areas covered by this agreement". Another states that the planning of improvements requires method study, work measurement and similar techniques. Whilst there are reservations (see Chapter 13) about the effectiveness of some of the consultative procedures, the broad impression given by managers and FOCs has been that the provisions relating to joint procedures and method study have worked reasonably well, as have the agreements covering all clerical staff. Nevertheless, problems of internal differentials do arise as well as problems of differentials between clerical and production staff. It appears from our inquiries that clerical workers' representatives make comparisons between earnings levels of production workers and their own an explicit part of their in-house claims more frequently than production workers make explicit earnings comparisons between each other.

Managerial and Supervisory Staff

185. We have not examined in any detail the earnings of managerial staff generally. Our impression is that within whatever general framework houses have developed for the regulation of managerial salaries there is considerable latitude for individual variation. There is, however, one area in relation to managerial terms and conditions of employment that has had important industrial relations effects. The erosion of the pay and conditions "lead" of overseers and their assistants has given rise to a good deal of concern on their part and was often mentioned during our inquiries.

186. The most common pay "system" for overseers and assistant overseers is for the salary of each such employee to be linked by way of a fixed percentage differential with the pay of his superior or of the production workers he supervises. The percentages by which overseers' and their assistants' pay exceeds that of their subordinates varies normally between five and fifteen per cent. Several difficulties arise. First, the exact formula for determining the production workers' pay to which that of overseers is related can affect the absolute amount of the differential. In one case, the overseers' pay is related to the highest-paid significant (in terms of numbers) group they supervise. In others the overseers may not be entitled to variable payments that may be made to the workers they supervise. This can mean that the differential falls to low levels or even disappears. Second, where overseers' pay is linked to that of production workers it can happen that the differentials between overseers and more senior managers can become very narrow. Third, the fixed differential system between overseers and production workers can lead to odd relationships between the pay of overseers in different departments.

187. Overseers are perhaps still more concerned about the loss of some of their relative material advantages in other directions. As holidays, sickness arrangements, and pension provisions have improved for production employees they

feel that their fringe benefits have not improved correspondingly and, in at least one case, have worsened. We have been told by both managers and FOCs of the difficulties sometimes experienced partly because of the limited financial advantages, in filling vacancies for overseers and their deputies. Dissatisfaction among supervisory grades with the terms and conditions of employment and with their status in houses has in some instances led to the creation of management associations (see Chapter 8).

Part C: Management and Union Organisation

CHAPTER 6: MANAGEMENT ORGANISATION IN INDUSTRIAL RELATIONS

188. A recent study has concluded that since 1970 the general quality of management in the national newspaper industry has considerably improved, especially with respect to financial management and cost reduction policies; and that the improvement has been partly due to outside recruitment, and to reorganisation and development of existing staff*. In at least one house improvements predated 1970 and were stimulated by the EIU report in 1966 and it seems more generally true that there has been a growth since then in the status of the industrial relations function within houses.

Board Involvement in Industrial Relations

189. In three of the larger houses all the main departmental activities, including industrial relations, are represented at board level (Appendix 6, Table 1 shows a typified diagram of this kind of board and top management structure). Most other houses have a smaller board membership with individual directors each having responsibility for several facets of business activity. The general manager often has responsibility at board level for industrial relations between the house and its production and clerical employees (see Appendix 6, Table 2). Though only three houses had directors with specific industrial relations responsibilities, job titles are not invariably an accurate guide to job content: many general managers devote most, if not all, their time to industrial relations matters. Moreover, the responsibilities for industrial relations of board members, both in relation to day-to-day matters and to longer term formulation of policies which have industrial relations implications, sometimes overlap both potentially and actually. This can provide fertile ground for internal conflict and such conflict, where in a number of houses it has occurred, is widely recognised by managers to have been played upon by FOCs.

190. The EIU report noted in 1966 that the most striking feature of the national newspaper industry "... and possibly its greatest problem, (was) its dominance by a small number of individualist proprietors with their own personal interests and philosophy of management". The "proprietorial" influence is criticised in the industrial relations field because, it is argued, proprietors do not invariably regard profitability as their main objective, at least in the short term, and this influences their attitude to industrial relations. Where proprietors insist on production targets being met even if this means surrendering to a claim managers think to be unjustified, and where they personally intervene in disputes

---

* *Report* prepared by PA Management Consultants Ltd for the Royal Commission on the Press. A summary appears in the Royal Commission's Interim Report page 81.

at a quite early stage, the task of management in seeking to operate a consistent policy can be made more difficult.

191. The ownership of substantial portions of the industry is still in the hands of individual proprietors (see Chapter 3), but the criticisms made of the proprietorial style of management can also be made of those houses where, strictly, ownership is widely dispersed. Where managing directors or other managers of comparable status behave in the same way as proprietors the industrial relations effects can be the same. The proprietorial influence on industrial relations is difficult to quantify. In some houses, the proprietor or most senior executive is said never to intervene inappropriately; in others we were given examples by junior managers, and by FOCs, of cases where it was alleged that those normally responsible for dealing with an industrial relations matter were overruled arbitrarily by senior management or the proprietor. Whatever the truth of the allegations it was certainly the case that those thus overruled were left with the feeling that the "proprietorial intervention" had been made without proper regard to the possible industrial relations consequences, especially in relation to the loss of management authority and credibility.

192. The proprietorial influence is also said to prevent the adoption of long-term industrial relations policies both within houses and within the industry as a whole (see, for example, Chapter 7). Few houses have comprehensive, written policies of this kind, though the economic situation and the need to introduce new technology have stimulated rather more policy co-ordination within houses in recent years. There are several factors other than the possible proprietorial influence that have inhibited comprehensive policy development. The long period of relative stability of production processes, the pressure on managers to make short-term expedient settlements which may pull against long-term policy aims, the burden of work on key managers simply in dealing with routine matters, and the narrowness of the experience of some managers have also tended to contribute to the present situation.

Management below Board level: Senior Production Management

193. Appendix 6, Table 3 sets out in simplified form a typical production management structure in the industry. The number of production management layers below Board level partly depends on the size and the number of newspaper titles of each house. Senior production managers are generally responsible for machinery, processes, technical development policy, and for day-to-day administration in these areas. Many, in addition, have a major responsibility for industrial relations. Whilst most senior production managers are on call for 24 hours a day, their normal working hours are during non-production shifts. At night a relatively small staff of night production managers takes over. This relative absence of senior managers at night is in some houses a deliberate attempt to develop middle management. It was, nevertheless, often criticised by FOCs during our inquiries because it added to delay in management decision-taking on matters which, though apparently fairly minor, were important in the immediate work situation.*

---

* In the two London evening newspapers, senior production managers and labour relations managers are present during production shifts. Industrial relations in these cases were described by a number of managers as being "more explosive" than on daily and Sunday newspapers, although this has less to do with the presence of senior managers on production shifts than with the characteristics of production (a high level of inter-title competition, more concentrated and continuous working in production areas, a high number of edition changes and consequently shorter production runs).

194. Production managers below the level of senior production manager in those houses producing more than one title often have responsibilities on a title basis. Most managers at this level and below have employment backgrounds in the national newspaper industry, and it is common to find managers with upwards of twenty years' experience with one newspaper. These managers tend to remain in their speciality, few having had any formal management training before or after their appointment.

195. Most houses have tried to follow a policy of devolving direct responsibility for industrial relations to production and other line managers. Senior production managers may become involved both directly and indirectly in the discussion of questions raised by chapels. Production managers may act in an advisory capacity to overseers/heads of departments who are directly concerned in negotiations at the lower end of the management hierarchy. Later, failing settlement, they may be the principal management negotiators, and, should the issue remain unresolved, may advise more senior management or liaise with industrial relations staff in seeking an agreement.

Other Line Management

196. The role of overseers* and production supervisors is circumscribed by the control that chapel officials exercise over labour administration matters, and by the extent of their delegated authority in industrial relations. Their function is, broadly speaking, to ensure that machinery, processes and manpower are provided and maintained to allow production to take place.† Many of the overseers contacted during the ACAS inquiries associated the introduction of comprehensive agreements with an erosion of their functions particularly in relation to work allocation and the drawing up of rotas for shiftwork, overtime and holidays (see Chapter 12).

197. The function of overseers in industrial relations has been the subject of scrutiny by some houses in recent years and has resulted in a number of houses attempting to involve overseers to a greater degree in the bargaining process. While their negotiating role is limited in that they cannot consider changes to payments or staffing levels in existing agreements, they are generally involved in an advisory capacity in any negotiations involving their own department. Overseers in the production areas of high circulation newspapers indicated to us during our inquiries that on average at least 50% of their time was spent on industrial relations or related matters, and in some houses this was as high as 80%. In offices producing titles with lower circulations, most overseers spent less than 30% of their time on industrial relations. Much of this is taken up by non-monetary problems that arise during production shifts, involving discussion and negotiation with chapel officials on matters such as production schedules, work allocation, discipline and conditions of work.

---

* Overseer is the term used to describe first-line managers except in the composing and publishing rooms where the terms "printer" and "publisher" are used. In some houses the term "overseer" has been dispensed with in favour of the term "manager" to describe anyone heading-up a production department (for example, machine room manager, process department manager, etc).

† The ratio of overseers/supervisors to operatives in production areas in London is approximately 1:14 and in Manchester 1:18. For comparative purposes, the ratio for the motor vehicle industry has been calculated at between 1:10 and 1:20, and in coalmining between 1:8 and 1:12.

198. Overseers' deputies normally have no major industrial relations responsibilities (though the senior deputy overseer in each department assumes the responsibilities of the overseer in his absence). Similarly junior overseers (or staff hands) have no industrial relations duties. Their particular responsibilities vary. In publishing rooms they may distribute wrappers, start and close down machines, and assist in the smooth running of the department; in composing rooms they may have more specialised responsibilities (see Chapter 3).

199. Overseers in production areas are almost without exception promoted from the shop floor and, apart from those in the publishing room, are drawn overwhelmingly from the craft unions (the NGA, SLADE, AUEW and EETPU). During our inquiries we were told that very occasionally overseers had been subjected to chapel pressure because they had taken actions contrary to chapel interests or because they had been recruited from outside the newspaper concerned. However, very few overseers indicated to us that they had encountered any problems as a result of union membership. Such problems that did arise usually resulted from personality conflicts between the overseer and individual chapel officials rather than from concerted attempts by the chapel to undermine the overseer. Relationships between chapel representatives and overseers were usually said to be reasonably harmonious, and in some cases FOCs represent overseers when problems arise (see paragraph 287).

Industrial Relations and Personnel Management

200. The development of industrial relations as a management function in its own right is associated in some houses with the introduction of comprehensive agreements. Such agreements facilitated pay comparisons between adjacent chapels and necessitated closer central control and co-ordination of industrial relations in different departments. Wage drift and a tighter economic situation encouraged the growth of budgetary control systems which provided those at the centre with a means of assessing and influencing bargaining activities within departments.

201. Six houses have specialist industrial relations departments although the dividing line in other houses between those with nominal responsibility for other functions and an actual ongoing commitment to industrial relations is thin. The background of the specialist industrial relations managers in the industry is shown in Appendix 6, Table 7. More than three-quarters of the 41 specialist executives for whom eight houses provided details have had no industrial experience outside the newspaper and printing industry. About a quarter had been employed only in the house for which they currently work and two-thirds had been with the house for which they currently work for ten years or more. Some have progressed from the shop floor (usually craft areas) and have held chapel or union office.

202. In the larger houses employing a number of industrial relations staff each executive may specialise in a particular production area or grouping of departments. The bulk of the industrial relations resources of houses are devoted to production staffs, although industrial relations departments are also responsible for clerical and administrative staff matters. Few have any responsibility for editorial staff whose industrial relations are handled on a

day-to-day basis normally by managing editors, editors and other directors (see Appendix 6, Table 2).

203. Industrial relations managers and production managers have close and often overlapping responsibilities. In some houses management structures acknowledge this. Industrial relations staff formally report to senior production management, or to a general manager with a major responsibility for production matters. In recent years, attempts have been made to devolve to production managers' responsibility for the conduct of labour relations within their particular fields, with industrial relations managers having in theory an advisory role. Some discrepancy exists between theory and practice, however. Major negotiations, such as the revision of comprehensive agreements, the introduction of new plant and equipment, non-replacement and redundancy, are handled at fairly senior levels in all houses. Should such negotiations become intractable or give rise to a possible dispute, they quickly transfer to the highest levels within each house. The advice of labour relations staff is nearly always sought on these major issues, and the lead in conducting negotiations is often taken by them. The line between advising production management on the conduct of negotiations and actually conducting the negotiations is a fine one and is crossed by labour relations staff with the tacit consent of those involved. The theoretically enhanced responsibility for industrial relations of production management is rarely reflected adequately in their job descriptions. A typical description refers to the manager's responsibility for "upholding agreements between the company and the press room staffs, for maintaining good labour relations within the department (and) for liaison at all times with the staff relations department to ensure good labour relations and compliance with company policy".

204. Five houses have personnel departments, sometimes in addition and closely allied to industrial relations departments. In some cases they report to an administration executive rather than to the executive primarily responsible for industrial relations. They may deal with such matters as personnel records, recruitment (of certain clerical staff), the recording and implementation of wage and salary adjustments, the development and maintenance of job grading and job evaluated salary structures for clerical staff, and training (the preparation and implementation of company training plans, and liaison with the PPITB and the NPA training committee).

205. In comparison with some other industries the personnel function in national newspapers is relatively undeveloped and has a relatively low organisational status. This is partly the result of the absence of management control over recruitment, job grading, etc. in production departments. Perhaps for the same reason personnel management tends to be concentrated in clerical and managerial areas, where there is more room for selective recruitment, career development and promotion planning. Nevertheless, we were told during our inquiries by many of those concerned with such matters that the sectional approach of unions, and sometimes managers as well, prevented the easy placement of managers in departments other than their "home" department. This was said to inhibit management development and the formation of a management team composed of individuals with broad-based experience.

Management and Budgetary Controls

206. The need to reduce costs has given impetus to the development of budgetary controls. In 1970 12 out of 17 national newspapers (excluding the *Morning Star* and *Morning Advertiser*) made profits and by 1975 the number had declined to five (see Chapter 3). Efforts to reduce costs have had important industrial relations effects. Appendix 6, Tables 4, 5 and 6, give cost figures since 1970. Newsprint is a major and growing cost (31% of all costs in 1975) but, apart from waste reduction and other limited economies, must be regarded to all intents and purposes as a fixed cost. Economies have also been attempted in better use of plant and buildings, and savings have been made, though sometimes marginal and usually after considerable industrial relations upheaval, in amalgamating and closing premises.

207. However, it is in staffing levels and wage costs that the greatest potential for cost savings lies. Wages and salaries represent an average of 63% of total costs excluding newsprint and contract printing; in production areas wage costs represent over 90% of all costs, and in editorial areas the proportion is between 50% and 60%.

208. Earlier inquiries in the national newspaper industry have concluded that its difficulties have stemmed partly from a failure to control manning costs and other forms of expenditure, and from the general inadequacy of budgetary planning. Since 1970 substantial progress has been made in developing financial control systems using regular budget variance or standard costing techniques. The control systems are sometimes quite new and are still developing.

209. All the major houses now engage in some form of annual budgeting or financial performance appraisal, with revenue forecasts forming the basis of the systems, and monthly reports on performance are normally produced. In most houses the introduction of control systems for production wage costs has been associated with and facilitated by the negotiation of comprehensive agreements. In some houses detailed analyses on a weekly basis are made by production cost controllers of actual wage agreements, thus identifying all extra costs in comparison with standard conditions.

210. Departmental heads and managers of similar status, together in some houses with junior managers and overseers, assist in the development of departmental budgets. As a matter of routine night production managers and overseers prepare nightly production reports for examination by industrial relations, accountancy and other senior management staff during the next working day. Such reports normally detail production difficulties that have occurred and any extra payments (including overtime) that have been made.

211. Within each departmental budget there is generally a margin to take account of extra payments and other contingencies, such as extra transportation costs caused by late "lifts" from the presses. The contingency margin or "adverse variance" is expected to be used sparingly. Any concession of extra payments has to be justified to senior management and the use of regular reporting procedures and the increasing sophistication of budgetary control arrangements have largely eliminated any *ad hoc* arrangements on pay between

overseers and chapels. Junior managers and overseers cannot take decisions on claims that fundamentally alter the terms and provisions of existing agreements. Overseers are generally empowered only to evaluate claims made by chapels and to concede additional payments in the form of overtime for exceptional or "one-off" situations (defined in one job description, for example, as the authority to "approve all expenses and payments to staff in connection with special work or duties outside normal working hours").

212. In composing rooms it is usual for departmental heads to be assisted in the monitoring of wage costs. This is because of the LSP (see Chapter 5) and the need to check individual earnings dockets throughout the shift. The assistants, known as piecework "trackers", ensure that claimed earnings for setting correspond to the agreed scale rates and the variations that may apply in the house. It is in the piece-working areas that, predictably, the greatest difficulties in budgetary control have been encountered. In these areas special methods have been adopted for wage cost forecasting.

213. Industrial relations management generally receive regular information on earnings from the wage administration or equivalent managers, and also are closely involved with them in an ongoing activity of analysing and costing claims made at both chapel, house and national levels. Copies of all agreements are kept centrally by industrial relations management. All comprehensive agreements are recorded, any substantive amendments being added to existing agreements in written form.

Intra-Management Communication

214. Managers contacted during the ACAS inquiries were often unaware of any overall corporate objectives and policies in industrial relations, yet had a general responsibility (as one overseer's job description stated) "to promote and engender good industrial relations at all times for the maintenance of harmony within the working environment".

215. Apart from the frequent routine bilateral contact that takes place between managers on production matters, the scale of intra-management communication on wider issues varies between houses, and is very limited in some. Some houses have adopted the concept of "briefing groups" to enable information to flow quickly from the Board to all levels of management. In one house these briefing group meetings, held by each Board director with the managers reporting to him, are backed up by written executive communications. These are circulated to all managers and FOCs as soon as practicable after Board meetings. The briefing groups have been introduced relatively recently but seem to be regarded by many managers as having considerably improved management communications.

CHAPTER 7: THE NEWSPAPER PUBLISHERS' ASSOCIATION

216. Historically, the prime functions of the Newspaper Publishers' Association (NPA) have been in the industrial relations field. Before the British Federation of Master Printers was formed in 1900, there existed a number of regional employers' associations, one of which was the London Master Printers' Association (LMPA), which covered both newspapers and general printing. In 1906 a dispute at a London firm of printers, Hampton's, led to a threat of strike action by the London Society of Compositors against all London printers, including national newspapers. Just before the strike threat was due to be implemented, the compositors were invited by a body of newspaper proprietors to a meeting at which no member of the LMPA would be present. At this meeting the Hampton's dispute was settled and the LSC in calling off its strike, agreed "to treat with the new Society of newspaper proprietors as a separate body on all trade questions affecting London newspapers, provided that no member of the said society shall be a member of the LMPA, and also undertake not to involve the society in any question or dispute affecting only other branches of compositors' work". The Newspaper Proprietors' Association Limited was incorporated on 23 July 1906.

217. The formation of the NPA was to meet the national newspaper proprietors' need for a distinct voice in labour matters. But there were other areas where the national newspapers could act in concert. Distribution was the most important of these and in 1910 the first meeting of the Daily Circulation Managers' Committee took place and the development of a joint distribution system using the growing railway network began. Other "trade association" functions have developed through the years, to the extent that the NPA is now both an employers' association and a trade association whose main formal objectives are:

(*a*) to promote and regulate relations between the members of the Association and their employees;

(*b*) to facilitate the interchange of views among members in areas of common interest and to arrange consultation with legislative, public, trade and industry bodies over matters of mutual concern;

(*c*) to take such joint action as agreed to protect, preserve and promote the interests of members;

(*d*) to provide on behalf of members services in the fields of labour relations, distribution, advertising, marketing and information, training, administration and finance, etc.

NPA Organisation and Structure

218. Subject to the approval of the NPA Council, membership of the NPA is open to publishers of newspapers with an agreed minimum national circulation. The Association currently has in membership eight of the national newspaper publishers, together with the Society of Licensed Victuallers which publishes the *Morning Advertiser*. The Morning Star Co-operative Society Ltd does not belong to the Association. The present position of Mirror Group Newspapers is that although (as IPC Newspapers Ltd) the group resigned from the NPA in March 1974, it still actively participates in a number of trade association functions (see paragraph 244).

219. The NPA is financed by annual subscriptions from its members based on wages paid in the preceding year to those employed in the mechanical and publishing departments of the newspapers which are in membership.

220. Appendix 7, Table 1 shows the NPA departmental and committee structure. The supreme body is the Council, which is made up of newspaper proprietors or representatives of similar status and which elects the chairman and vice-chairman of the Association. The Executive Committee, which is composed of members of the council of chief executive status and over which the chairman of the NPA presides, controls the day-to-day running of the organisation. The chief executive is the director who has responsibility for all NPA activities. Until 1974 there were two directors; one, the commercial director, was responsible for trade association functions and the other responsible for labour affairs. Appendix 7, Table 2 shows the numbers of staff employed in each department since 1972. In 1972 the total number of NPA staff was 34. This fell slightly then rose in 1976 to 35. The apparent stability in staffing disguises a rather more fluid internal situation. In 1973 when there was a commercial director, ten staff covered commercial and industrial relations matters. In 1976, six staff cover the general area previously covered by the ten.

221. The Daily Circulation Managers' Committee and the Circulation Managers' Committee supervise the joint distribution system which has been operating in essence since 1910. A major part of the distribution of national daily and Sunday newspapers within both the UK and overseas is operated on a joint basis. The NPA makes arrangements with British Rail and with various air companies about the joint transportation of supplies. The Circulation Executive consists of circulation managers or directors from member offices. It liaises with the above committees and sponsors action to promote the circulation and sales of national newspapers. The "Communicor" scheme was set up by the NPA to counter a shortage of newsboys and girls.

222. The advertising department of the NPA co-ordinates the joint advertising activities in which members participate. The senior advertising committee is the Advertisement Executive which is made up of member office representatives of advertisement director status. The Advertisement Executive attempts to co-ordinate and develop a joint policy on advertising. The Joint Copy Committee considers advertisement copy referred to it by newspapers and decides whether dubious advertisements should be published. A number of other committees and sub-committees monitor advertising practice, in particular in the holiday and mail order areas.

223. The marketing and external relations department provides an information and advisory service to members in matters of mutual concern to their marketing activities and to their relations with outside bodies in trade, industry and government. It assists in representing members' interests to these bodies and deals with overseas enquiries and contacts. It also helps to plan and implement jointly-agreed research and promotional programmes. Such research has ranged from examining methods of promoting the image of national newspapers as an effective advertising medium to advising on the problems of Value Added Tax. In addition, the department provides the secretariat for a number of other committees in which NPA members participate. These cover, among other things, the

measurement of readership trends and readership profiles, and the place of the press amongst the other advertising media.

224. Although Appendix 7 includes the newsprint department as part of the NPA, its staff of two form the secretariat to the UK Newsprint Users' Committee and are answerable to that body. The committee was set up in 1971, mainly to cope with the duty free quota arrangements following the UK's entry into the EEC. It represents the interests of all the national and regional press as newsprint users, and attempts to monitor and safeguard the supply of newsprint to its members.

225. The training department (see also Chapter 14 on training) co-ordinates and organises the training activities of member companies where a common need has been identified, where economies of scale are possible or where there is interest in experimental courses. The bulk of training in Fleet Street is carried out internally by the houses and the Training Committee has a representative from most member offices. The committee liaises with the PPITB. The NPA runs a number of training courses itself; recent courses have been concerned with the training of those responsible for in-house training, supervisory staff and advertisement representatives. The training department also runs monthly seminars on topics of interest to members. Subjects covered so far include health and safety in the newspaper industry and current and future legislation. The department also has under its auspices the Health and Safety Committee, set up in consequence of the Health and Safety at Work Act.

NPA Industrial Relations Activities

226. When the NPA had two directors one was responsible solely for labour affairs. For the past two years, however, responsibility for all of the Association's activities has fallen on the shoulders of the one NPA director. Despite this, much of the present director's time is taken up with labour matters. Working to him is the industrial relations department consisting of two labour advisers and their secretarial help. Much of the time of the department is taken up with servicing the two main labour committees, the Industrial Relations Executive (IRE) and the London Labour Committee (LLC) described in paragraphs 228 to 231.

227. Apart from providing agendas, organising meetings and keeping minutes of these committees, the labour advisers may be required by the IRE or LLC to collect information on particular topics from each house, perhaps by questionnaire, and to collate and analyse the returns. The NPA has in the past attempted to conduct a monthly survey of manpower and earnings but the survey has gradually become less regular and comprehensive partly because the response of offices has been incomplete and partly because pressure of work on the NPA organisation has inhibited adequate follow-up. The industrial relations department provides an advisory service and deals with queries from member offices on industrial relations matters. Such queries might, for example, concern current practice in other houses where management is faced with a house claim, or the implication of labour legislation. In addition, the labour advisers service the NPA disputes procedures (see paragraph 233) and are responsible for arranging meetings associated with the procedures. The establishment of the JSC and its various working parties (see Chapter 17) has involved further work for

the NPA director and labour advisers who form the NPA side of the joint secretariat.

228. The main NPA committee concerned wholly with labour matters is the IRE. It is composed of (currently eight) senior managers/directors responsible for industrial relations within their companies. It is normally chaired by the NPA director and one of the labour advisers acts as its secretary. There is no uniformity of job titles among the Executive Members; some have solely industrial relations responsibilities, others have an overall production/industrial relations brief. The IRE is the NPA's negotiating body for national wage agreements. The national wage negotiations are carried out by some or all of the IRE members and draft agreements are referred to the Executive Committee, or in some cases the NPA Council, for ratification. A "Strategy Group" is drawn from the Executive and was created to carry out forward planning on behalf of the Executive, especially in relation to national wage bargaining. The tendency has been, however, for the Group's work to be carried out after a claim has been made rather than in advance of it.

229. The Executive normally meets once a week (it met on 52 occasions between October 1974 and January 1976) and deals with a wide variety of topics (approximately 100 were discussed in the above period). Typical agendas nearly always include a question of interpretation or application of a national agreement. Current national negotiations and live disputes within houses form another staple part of agendas. Member houses are under no obligation, however, to report in-house disputes. In the past House Claims Procedures have operated, whereby each member office undertook to provide the NPA with details of chapel claims which were to be discussed in order to reach a joint position before the management responded in-house. The idea was to ensure that one house did not commit itself to action, or concede claims, which would have repercussions elsewhere without fully consulting all those houses involved. These procedures appear to have broken down, however, mainly because of pressures on managements for immediate response to claims. Some claims are still notified to the IRE, but most are settled in-house without reference to the Executive. The present understanding seems to be that where a claim has obvious ramifications for other NPA members, for example where it attempts to increase holidays or reduce the working week, it is notified to the IRE. This is not a rigid rule, however, and claims which do have consequences for other houses may, and do, remain unnotified.

230. The LLC is answerable to the IRE and consists of a representative from every house or title who has industrial relations responsibilities (in particular for day-to-day dealings with chapels), and who, within his own house, is responsible to his house representative on the IRE. Much of the work of the LLC concerns the detailed application of national agreements. The LLC, whose current membership is twelve, may, for example, meet the unions at London Branch or Region level to hammer out the detailed application of national agreements. Following such meetings the LLC makes recommendations for the approval of the IRE. Questions of detail on such matters as social security payments for casuals, and disputes in individual houses are also considered by the LLC. Other responsibilities of the LLC include monitoring the implications of legislation in the employment field. The Committee normally meets fortnightly.

231. Much of the time of the Executive Committee (EC) and the Council is taken up by industrial relations matters. The EC meets every month and a standard part of its agenda is the regular monthly report from the IRE. The Council gathers when necessary, with meetings being concentrated around the time of national wage negotiations. Although the IRE conducts the negotiations, the Council and/or the EC are closely involved at all times.

Disputes and the NPA Disputes Procedures

232. All national agreements made by the NPA contain disputes clauses. These make provision for the NPA to arrange "three plus three" or "five plus five" joint arbitration on a dispute (see also paragraph 444, et seq.). Such arbitrations are done by a panel made up of an equal number of union and management representatives. The latter are usually IRE members from houses other than that involved in the dispute. There is no rule about where the union representatives should be drawn from although the NPA has objected where a full-time official has been involved in-house with a dispute and has been nominated for the national procedure disputes committee set up to consider it.

233. Before the disputes committee machinery is activated NPA officials may become involved in a dispute and be asked to use their "good offices" or "best endeavours" to settle it. Although the union branch may be involved in a dispute before the NPA, when the help of NPA officials is sought meetings involving representatives of management, chapel, branch and the NPA may be held either at the office concerned or at the NPA offices. In major disputes there may well be NPA Council/senior union officer involvement. A recent example was the dispute between Beaverbrook Newspapers Ltd and its engineers at the end of 1975 which threatened the publication of all Fleet Street newspapers.

The NPA in Manchester

234. The NPA's affairs in Manchester are generally directed by the Manchester Managers' Committee (MMC) the membership of which comprises of the senior executives of the NPA member companies which produce in Manchester (although deputies are allowed to attend). The MMC has three sub-committees covering circulation, health and safety, and an "accountants sub-committee" which works out the detailed application of the national agreements to Manchester.

235. The MMC usually meets fortnightly, and its main deliberations are on industrial relations matters although the business of the sub-committees also forms part of the agenda. On labour matters, its function is similar to that of the IRE in London, with exchange of information, interpretation of agreements and discussion of house claims and disputes forming the bulk of its business. It is claimed that the flow of information between members of the MMC is freer than between NPA members in London.

236. Since NPA agreements negotiated in London cover staff employed by national newspapers in Manchester the MMC cannot negotiate locally on any major issues with the unions. Most of its dealings with the Manchester Branches concern the application of national agreements or purely local issues.

Any substantial questions raised by the unions have to be referred to the IRE in London, which receives a regular report from the MMC.

237. The staff of the NPA in Manchester consists of the Labour Secretary and his secretarial assistance. The Labour Secretary acts as secretary of the MMC and of the other committees. He attends IRE meetings in London fortnightly, and other NPA committee meetings as necessary, to keep MMC members informed of events and to represent them where Manchester issues are raised.

238. The NPA in Manchester operates its own disputes procedure, which culminates in a "six plus six" meeting between representatives of the MMC and the relevant union branch. Most disputes reaching this stage are settled there; there is said to be a mutual reluctance on the part of management and unions to allow matters to be referred to London. Manchester branches of the unions seem to be more willing to use the NPA procedure than their London counterparts.

239. The Manchester office of the NPA also contains the casual "call" office staffed by four NATSOPA members but financed by the newspaper houses (see Chapter 15). The office forms part of the NPA's lease, and its overheads are thus paid by the Association.

Relations with other Employers' Associations

240. The NPA is a member of the Confederation of British Industry as well as the FIEJ (the international organisation of press publishers' associations) and the CAEJ (the EEC organisation of press publishers' associations).

241. The only formal link between the NPA and the Newspaper Society (NS), the British Federation of Master Printers (BFMP), the Scottish Newspaper Publishers' Association (SNPA) and the Scottish Daily Newspaper Society (SDNS) is the Employers' Joint Liaison Committee (Printing and Allied Industries) which also encompasses other employers' associations in the printing industry and provides a forum for the exchange of information on industrial relations matters. It has been in existence for five years, and meets about four times a year. There have been suggestions in the past, in particular by the 1967 Court of Inquiry into the problems caused by the introduction of web offset machines in the printing industry, that the NPA, NS and BFMP give consideration to a merger. The Court felt, despite statements to the contrary from the organisations themselves, that there was enough common interest between them to warrant such a merger. We have found no current demand within the industry for a merger between the various employer organisations.

Mirror Group Newspapers and the NPA

242. The ostensible reason for the withdrawal of Mirror Group Newspapers (then IPC Newspapers Ltd) from the NPA in 1974 lay in a dispute between the company and some of its journalists, though other, more deep-seated, factors affected the decision.

243. IPC had taken a lead on journalists' pay and conditions in 1968 when it agreed to pay substantial increases to its editorial staff. This agreement was

followed by an improved national agreement. Having set the pattern of house bargaining with editorial staff, IPC, in 1973, found itself under increasing pressure from its NUJ chapels to concede pay rises in excess of those previously agreed between the NPA and the NUJ at national level. It resisted this pressure and during the ensuing dispute several million copies of the *Daily Mirror* were lost. It emerged, however, that another house had already settled at a higher figure, a disclosure which led to the vice-chairman of the house concerned apologising to the NPA and IPC for the actions of his company. In 1974 IPC's NUJ chapels, believing there was likely to be a wage freeze following the general election, put pressure on the company to negotiate a new house agreement in advance of the national negotiations. The company agreed to negotiate with its NUJ chapels within the terms of the current pay legislation, but advice to the NPA by the Pay Board led the company to refuse to negotiate in-house. Action by IPC journalists in Manchester and Glasgow led to seven million newspaper copies being lost in February 1974. IPC believed, however, that another newspaper had negotiated a salary increase with its editorial staff in excess of that agreed by the NPA. This belief, coupled with the company's wish not to deprive the country of national newspapers during a general election led IPC to withdraw from the NPA rather than to seek the active support of other NPA members in the dispute, a process which could have meant the complete cessation of publication of NPA national newspapers. It has also been suggested that the IPC management was angered by a belief that certain of its competitors had unfairly taken advantage of the non-appearance of the *Daily Mirror* during the dispute to win some of its readers.

244. The current relationship between the NPA and MGN is ambiguous. While the Group is technically not a member of the Association, with no representation on the Council or the Executive Committee, MGN executives remain on all other committees except those directly serviced by the industrial relations department. Thus the Group still participates in the "trade association" functions of the NPA, and contributes *pro rata* to its funding. On the labour relations side, the MGN/NPA relationship is further complicated by MGN's participation with the other Fleet Street employers in the talks which led to the joint submission of the unions and publishers to the Royal Commission and then to the creation of the JSC and its working parties.

Views on NPA Effectiveness
NPA Member Views

245. The IRE and LLC are seen primarily as vehicles for the exchange of information on labour matters and as bodies within which members can seek to reach a consensus on matters of common interest to counter union attempts to set one house against another. Some managements think, however, that there has been a growing reluctance on the part of NPA members to exchange information and ideas; it is thought by some that the main reason for this is increasingly sharp competition between newspapers. The growing importance of house agreements and the consequent decrease in the significance of national bargaining is also thought by some managers to contribute to the absence of a frank exchange of information within the NPA labour committees. Others think that the differences between companies, and in particular the varied labour costs/total costs ratios among them, make the task of getting a common front on labour matters difficult.

246. There is also some feeling that the IRE spends too much of its time wrestling with the day-to-day problems of the industry and not enough on long-term planning and strategy-making. The Strategy Group's role, it is felt, might be made an integral part of the Executive's working.

247. Related to these views about the tendency for the NPA to concentrate on short-term issues at the expense of longer-term strategy, are comments about the adequacy of the staffing of the industrial relations department, particularly for the purpose of providing an advisory service to members. It is felt that work on the implications for the industry of employment legislation, for example, is being inhibited because of pressure of work on the labour advisers. It is argued that the labour advisers' workload in servicing the various committees and the disputes procedures has precluded them from providing the necessary research and advisory services, despite their efforts to carry out all these tasks. In a situation of increasing workload, both actual and potential, NPA resources are felt to be overstretched.

248. Although the IRE reports regularly to the Executive Committee and to the Council, some concern has been expressed during our inquiries over what is felt to be a lack of influence by the IRE on the decisions on industrial relations matters made by these superior bodies. Some management representatives we talked to believed that collective decisions made by the Council should be binding on members.

249. Although IRE members generally saw benefits in agreeing annual wage increases nationally with all the printing trade unions some doubts were expressed as to the value of determining basic rates at national level and it was also suggested that NPA's wage bargaining role would become less important as agreements are made at house level about the introduction of new technology.

Non-Member Views

250. Paragraph 243 describes the events which led to MGN's withdrawal from the NPA. For MGN, these encapsulated much of what it considered to be wrong with the Association. Since its withdrawal, the company has made known within the industry its views on the performance and structure of the Association.

251. The major defect of the NPA, in MGN's view, is the lack of an effective Executive Committee empowered to make decisions and to adhere to them. The company had long believed that the NPA's failure to agree a coherent industrial relations policy was inhibiting it from tackling important internal labour problems. The NPA, it was felt, was absorbing valuable management resources of MGN which could be more usefully employed within the company.

252. MGN believes that the NPA's consistent failure to agree and implement joint decisions is mainly due to the proprietorial system of management control operating in most NPA companies. It is also felt that the spirit behind the recommendations in the Haley Committee Report*, that managing directors

---

* This Committee was set up by the NPA Council in June 1967, under the chairmanship of Sir William Haley, to review the constitution, organisation and finances of the NPA and make recommendations accordingly. Its main recommendations of relevance here were that the industrial relations department's advisory and research facilities be extended and that an Executive Committee, consisting of the managing director of each company, be set up to take over the routine control of the NPA leaving the Council to consider only matters of major importance to the industry.

of NPA member firms within the Executive Committee should be able to commit their companies to courses of action, has been frustrated by individual chairmen or proprietors. Thus the Group feels that the unity required to enable the NPA to play a real part in reforming industrial relations within the industry is not forthcoming, nor is likely to be.

253. MGN also has a number of detailed criticisms of the running of the commercial functions of the NPA. As a consequence of these, it believes that the two revenue-earning areas of the NPA (advertising and circulation/sales) should be hived off into a separate trade association covering all national newspapers. This would mean that the industrial relations functions would be dealt with separately.

254. While MGN, with certain conditions, would be prepared to participate in the trade association, it does not feel it likely that the company will, in the foreseeable future, form part of the industrial relations organisation. There are four other changes in the NPA organisation that the Group would like to see, however, and it would seem that if these were implemented then MGN might rejoin the Association for all purposes. They are:
  (1) the appointment of a part-time chairman supported by all members who is empowered to represent and commit all members of the NPA;
  (2) the appointment of a full-time Chief Executive supported by all members who has the right to obtain all information from member companies needed for the NPA to operate efficiently;
  (3) the appointment of a "high level marketing man" with the main task of achieving unified action by the NPA on advertising and circulation to the benefit of all members;
  (4) the establishment of a technical directorate, to monitor the introduction of new technology into Fleet Street, and to attempt to ensure consistency in labour agreements reached during this introduction.*

Trade Union Views

255. FOCs' views on the NPA are inevitably interwoven with their opinions of the usefulness or otherwise of national negotiations on pay. Their opinions are coloured by the relative significance of the NPA-agreed increases in pay for the chapel concerned. In other words, chapels for which the national agreements form most or all of the annual pay increase naturally tend to consider the negotiations, and the NPA, to be important. Those chapels which have in the past negotiated increases in-house during the year which improve substantially on the NPA increases have a greater tendency to think that the national negotiations, and thus the NPA, are an irrelevance.

256. A further distinction can be drawn between the opinions of FOCs who see their newspapers as being more successful than most others, and those within newspapers which are felt to be less successful. In the former case, some FOCs felt that their managements were (sometimes willingly) held back during negotiations by the inability of other NPA members to pay. Some FOCs on the "weaker" newspapers felt their managements were dragged along during NPA negotiations and that, without the NPA agreements, the gap between

---

* These views were formulated before the establishment of the JSC.

the rates of their companies and others in Fleet Street would rapidly widen. Similarly, some FOCs on the "stronger" newspapers were prepared to tolerate being held back in order to ensure that difference in rates between newspapers did not become too wide.

257. The views of full-time branch, regional and national officials also centre around their opinions on the usefulness of the national negotiations. It was felt by some that so long as the NPA offers during national negotiations remained at the lowest common denominator level, subsequent in-house pressures were inevitable. Given the inevitability of these pressures, some officials questioned the value of having national negotiations at all. On the other hand, some officials stressed the need for national wage agreements as a safeguard against wage rates in individual houses falling too far behind the rest of Fleet Street. Trade union officials, too, felt that the necessity of introducing new technology on a house basis might further weaken the national wage negotiations.

258. Comments were also made on disunity among NPA members. Examples were given where a collective position taken by NPA members had been rapidly undermined by individual houses settling with unions. Such cases, it was felt, served only to bring the Association into disrepute and to impair its credibility in union eyes during subsequent negotiations. Some union officials felt that although a disunited employers' association might seem to be to the unions' advantage, this was not so and said emphatically that only with a strong united employers' body could necessary reforms within the industry be brought about.

CHAPTER 8: THE CHAPELS

259. The national newspaper industry and the printing industry in general has a long history of workshop organisation. In the printing trade the chapel* form of organisation existed long before the development of printing trade unions, and though earliest notified accounts of it date from 1683 its existence almost certainly had been established for some time before this. In the early nineteenth century, chapels and their representatives were chiefly instrumental in establishing local societies and associations of printers, which in the mid-nineteenth century began to group into trade unions. This pattern of development, together with the extensive workplace functions performed by chapels, is of key importance both in explaining how industrial relations in the newspaper industry came to be as they are, and in conditioning the direction of industrial relations change. Chapter 2 outlines the emphasis we placed on inquiries at chapel level during our study. Apart from chapel attitudes to the practice of collective bargaining, our studies of chapels examined the exercise of chapel functions, chapel structure and organisation, and relations between chapels and between chapels and unions.

Chapel Functions

260. The rule books of every printing trade union†, and of the NUJ, require members employed in any office to form themselves into a chapel, and regulate administration and finance. The formation of chapels and their rules are subject to the control and approval of the appropriate Branch committees, and, once made, chapel rules are binding on all members of the chapel. Most union rule books refer only briefly to the form of constitution the chapel should seek to adopt, although NATSOPA's rules set out a code of principles which "in no circumstances can there be any departure from" (see Appendix 8(a))‡.

261. Chapel rule books rarely say anything about chapel functions except insofar as they specify the various benefits and grants that may be payable from chapel funds, the procedure for election of chapel officers, the disciplinary procedure within the chapel, the salaries to be paid to chapel officers, and the provisions applying to the convening of meetings. In practice, and this applies almost without exception in respect to production workers, the chapel is responsible for:

(a) the regulation of the workgroup and the workplace through the control and administration of work rotas, discipline and recruitment;

(b) the representation of the chapel members both individually and collectively in disputes with management, and through its officers and delegates, the representation of chapel interests at branch and national level within the union;

---

* The chapel, the common form of workshop organisation of employees and the nuclear unit of the organisation of trade unions in the printing industry, is a form of organisation that has been adopted by unions (such as the AUEW and EETPU) with members both within and outside the industry.

† We use the term "printing trade union" as a shorthand phrase for those unions whose members are engaged wholly or principally in production processes in the newspaper, periodical and general printing industries: NGA, SLADE, SOGAT, NATSOPA.

‡ The NGA, in an information handbook prepared for its FOCs, also sets out model chapel rules. The handbook includes sections on chapel organisation, legal and education matters and health, safety and welfare.

(c) the formulation and negotiation of in-house claims relating to its members;

(d) the welfare of its members (and to a degree their families), through the provision and administration of sickness schemes, the payment of grants, superannuation and death benefits, and the granting of loans and the giving of general advice and assistance;

(e) the upholding of union rules, the implementation of trade agreements, and the effective implementation of union policy decided at branch or national level.

Chapel Officers and the Exercise of Chapel Functions

262. The day-to-day executive power of the chapel resides with its officers, whose number and duties are prescribed by chapel rules. The Father (or Mother) of the Chapel (FOC) is invariably "the responsible chapel official, and in his absence, the deputy shall have the same authority". Other officers are either functional or representational including a chairman, treasurer or financial secretary, clerk or secretary and a number of committee members.

263. The number of officers is in part dependent on the size of the chapel, and also on the number of different workgroups and locations where its members are to be found. For example, it is usual for NATSOPA clerical chapels and revisers', ink and roller makers' and auxiliaries' (RIRMA) chapels to have committee members, who may represent either specific geographical areas and departments or particular sub-groups in the chapel. Similarly the NGA imperial composing chapels (see paragraph 307) have a committee made up of FOCs of the constituent local chapels. These always include the readers', piece case, time hands', and linotype operators' chapels and may also include the stereotypers' and T and E chapels.

264. The NGA Imperial FOC (IFOC) is present at, and usually takes the dominant role in, all negotiations affecting any of the local chapels, though the appropriate local FOC accompanies and assists him. Other FOCs operate in a similar way, being accompanied either by the deputy FOC, chairman, or appropriate local representative of the chapel committee. The FOC is the senior chapel representative, and is the route through which disputes between members and management must be channelled. Chapels generally have rules expressly preventing individual members approaching management on any matter unless accompanied by a chapel official.

265. FOCs tend to be experienced chapel representatives having progressed from interested chapel member to committee man, to minor chapel officer, deputy FOC and finally to FOC. Elections are normally held annually, although prior to January 1976 elections of FOCs in NATSOPA were held quarterly. During our inquiries we were told by management representatives that the quarterly elections of NATSOPA FOCs tended to cause bargaining difficulties, in that the frequency of elections imposed pressures on FOCs to gain quick results in order to maintain office.

266. Appendix 8, Tables 1 and 2 show, for chapels contacted during our inquiries, the average length of time FOCs have held office, together with the

frequency with which elections for their office are contested. Apart from the NATSOPA FOCs who at the time were still subject to quarterly election the overwhelming majority of elections for such positions in other unions are held annually. This (together, in the case of RIRMA, with the generally lower average number of members in its chapels) in part explains the somewhat lower percentages of elections that were contested in NATSOPA chapels.

267. FOCs of NUJ chapels tend on average to remain in office for shorter periods than other FOCs. This may be partly because of the employment situation of journalists. An FOC representing production workers occupies what is generally regarded by the workgroup as a position of the highest status, and (see paragraph 271) often has a man-management function. NUJ FOCs, in contrast, are employed in a work situation which is not only one in which career progression and promotion takes place but also where the degree of chapel control over the workplace is less extensive than that of many production chapels. The increased demands made on NUJ FOCs in recent years as a result of the development of house bargaining have also increased the amount of time required of them for chapel and union business. Where the NUJ FOC sees his future as a journalist, his union position can leave him less time to concentrate on his career. It does seem that there is less enthusiasm for chapel office among journalists than among other groups.

268. The amount of time FOCs and other chapel officers spend on chapel business is generally dependent on workgroup size, the type of work carried out, and the degree of usage made of casual employees. NATSOPA machine and SOGAT publishing chapels, almost without exception in multi-title houses, have at least one chapel official spending nearly all his working time on chapel business (see Appendix 8, Tables 3 and 4). It is also usual in the larger houses for the Imperial Father of the NGA composing chapel, the FOC of the NGA machine managers chapel and the FOC/MOC of the NATSOPA clerical chapel to be almost fully engaged on chapel affairs, together, in some cases, with other chapel officials.

269. Management practice on the recognition of the amount of time chapel officials are engaged on chapel business varies both within and between houses. Some chapel agreements, particularly in the machine and publishing rooms, provide in their total staffing requirements for one or more chapel officials to be supernumerary or "stood out". Even where there is no formal arrangement, chapel officials often in practice spend much of their time on chapel business and this is accepted, sometimes reluctantly, by management.

270. The number of non-working chapel officials, and the workgroups from which they are drawn, has increased considerably in recent years, a development associated by many in the industry with the introduction of comprehensive agreements. Before this it was usual for NATSOPA machine room and SOGAT publishing room chapels to have a number of full-time chapel officers dealing with the large amount of administrative work generated by the use of casual labour, and this was accepted by management as a necessary consequence of the chapels' responsibility in this field. Comprehensive agreements have in the case of production chapels formalised a sub-contracting relationship between management and the chapel, with much day-to-day man management

being carried out by the chapel through its elected officials. In the larger production chapels with a number of full-time officials the administrative process is relatively sophisticated. Some chapels have a clerk(s) permanently engaged on maintaining the various seniority lists and staffing rotas under the chapel's control, together with a financial secretary with responsibility for both the collection of union and chapel dues, and the administration of various chapel funds and benefits.

271. The role of the production chapel FOC does, then, extend considerably beyond the negotiation of terms and conditions of employment. Contact between the FOC and departmental manager and supervisory staff is frequent and concerns not only negotiable issues but also, for example, production difficulties, breakdowns, production requirements for work allocation purposes, and future pagination (in order that staffing requirements can be determined). As well as allocating work, FOCs also receive, particularly in the composing area, individual work and overtime dockets for checking prior to their being passed to the overseer for payment authorisation. Records are generally maintained by FOCs of the circumstances in which additional payments have been negotiated together with the amounts paid for future reference. In the composing area the imperial FOCs are responsible not only for members working to comprehensive arrangements, and for pieceworkers, but currently have additional duties arising from the introduction of new technology. Demands on the time of chapel officials have also increased as a result of the effects of declining pagination levels, the introduction of new machinery (eg mechanisation of the publishing areas), and the integration and rationalisation that has taken place in a number of houses.

272. Given the principal, subject to certain limitations, of equality between members of the chapel and its self-governing nature, it possesses in itself a certain momentum to extend its control of the workplace situation as far as possible. The drawing up of work allocation, overtime and shift rotas in a number of chapels contacted during our study, previously undertaken by departmental managers, became a chapel responsibility because of general dissatisfaction with what was seen as the unfairness and favouritism in the system when operated by management. Many chapels exercised sufficient collective strength to enforce extensions to workplace control in areas of man-management and work organisation.

273. During our inquiries we sought the views of chapel representatives on the current and potential responsibilities of the chapel in regulating the situation at the workplace. Most were happy with the existing situation and very few had any strong views about the extension of such responsibilities (see paragraph 452). FOCs do, nevertheless, see themselves as having managerial responsibilities. One FOC, for example, regarded it as "the chapel officer's job to get the paper out", and another saw himself as "a buffer between the overseers and the staff, with a responsibility to ensure that the work gets done".

Clerical Chapels

274. Clerical chapels are among the largest numerically in national newspapers. While it is usual to find clerical F/MOCs spending all or a considerable proportion of working time on chapel business, the incidence of other chapel officials doing so is lower than in production chapels. The

structure of clerical chapels is such that the chapel committee is generally comprised of departmental and sectional representatives; a parallel can perhaps be drawn between this form of structure and the convener and shop steward form of organisation outside the printing industry, the functions of the representatives also being similar. Clerical departments often have their own individual comprehensive agreements, rather than or in addition to having one overall chapel agreement, a factor which contributes to the lower numbers of full-time chapel officials but enhanced role of committee members in clerical chapels.

275. Though in the case of both clerical employees and journalists job allocation is predominantly a management function, some clerical chapels have in recent years encroached into this area and now organise shift, overtime and holiday rotas and work allocation, and have attempted to establish manning levels against agreed workloads. Clerical chapels generally include among their officials a "calls" or employment clerk, whose responsibility it is to administer and process vacancies and temporary positions, both by internal notice to the chapel and in liaison with the NATSOPA Clerical Branch calls office*.

The Disciplinary Function

276. Chapel rules both reinforce the chapel's collective interests and protect and uphold the authority of the FOC and chapel officials. While chapel rules allow for disciplinary action to be taken for misconduct which weakens the chapel's collective strength (such as non-attendance at chapel meetings, approaching management without the authority or presence of the FOC, and arrears of contributions), they also reinforce discipline at the workplace and the the semi-managerial role that chapel officials have (see Chapter 12).

277. The procedure for internal chapel and union discipline, together with the sanctions applied (see Appendix 8, Table 5), scarcely varies between unions. Consideration and determination of the misdemeanour is usually the responsibility of the chapel committee, with rights of appeal in the first instance to a full chapel meeting, then to the branch committee and finally to the national executive committee and delegate meeting of the union. In more serious disciplinary cases, for example where a chapel member has been a continual offender, the chapel may forward the case for decision to the branch committee. The types of misconduct dealt with through chapel disciplinary procedures of which we were told during our inquiries included persistent lateness, drunkenness, fighting, non-attendance at the allocated place of work or equipment, and the giving of false names (or "biffing") by casuals. The numbers of such offences have been, however, relatively small.

278. Many of the chapel disciplinary actions notified during the course of the ACAS study involved casual workers. The offences ranged from drunkenness, not working to the required specification or manner, to the stealing of copies. When such misconduct is proved and accepted by the chapel committee, it is usual for the offender to be sent home without pay, and later requested to

---

* There is a slightly blurred membership boundary between chapels and Branches of clerical and RIRMA employees. Thus in some chapels, for example, editorial assistants, telephone reporters or switchboard personnel may be members of the clerical chapel, while others may be members of RIRMA chapels.

attend a Branch committee meeting at which a chapel official, usually the FOC, will be present. In such cases, Branches may both fine the member concerned (usually up to £20) and "bar" him from casual work for a period of time. The discovery of the giving of false names by casual workers is generally the result of a random check by chapel officials on union cards and working permits, and is regarded and treated as a serious offence by union Branches.

Chapel Organisation and Membership

279. The catchment area of the chapel is determined principally by the physical location of the work, the type of work and the shift on which the work is performed. The historical development of the printing unions and the history of the industrial relations at the workplace itself are also, of course, important factors. Union rules require that when two (NATSOPA, SOGAT), three (SLADE), or four (NGA) members work in an office they must draw up rules for chapel administration purposes.

280. In circumstances where union members are employed in more than one establishment it is customary for them to join the appropriate chapel in each establishment, but they are deemed to be members for the purposes of nomination and election in the union concerned only of the chapel to which union dues are paid (as distinct from chapel dues). This membership provision applies only to regular casuals (in the case of NATSOPA and the NGA) or jobbing hands (in the case of SOGAT). Unattached casual workers while not qualified to join any chapel in NATSOPA or SOGAT, in the NGA must be members of the appropriate Casuals Chapel. Production chapels in London often include members with single, dual or triple chapel memberships. The representation of unattached casuals is handled in a variety of ways. All casuals are subject to chapel discipline and protected by the appropriate local chapel, but generally only regular casuals may participate in chapel affairs.

281. The type of work is, perhaps, the strongest single determinant of chapel organisation, and the need to formalise workgroup identity to provide a basis for independent bargaining is an important related factor. A further influence on the organisation of some ancillary workers' chapels is the chapel organisation of the (in most circumstances) craft workers they assist. It is general, for example, to find engineers' assistants, members of NATSOPA RIRMA, with their own chapel separate but complementary to the appropriate AUEW engineers' chapel.

282. Each London house contains chapels with one or more of the following characteristics:—
   (a) chapels representing all members of the same union branch in an integrated department (generally involving a seven-day working cover by chapel members) or at the one location. These are principally service chapels and may include those of SLADE, AUEW, EETPU, NUJ and NATSOPA clerical workers;
   (b) chapels representing all members on a newspaper title basis, such as those of NATSOPA machine and NGA machine managers;
   (c) chapels representing members working on more than one title published by the house;

(d) chapels representing members working in a number of locations, which may also include locations of subsidiary companies not involved with producing national newspapers. The reasons for this may be concerned with staff relocation or reorganisation.

283. There are some 360 chapels in Fleet Street. The size of chapels varies tremendously, ranging from one member (in some chapels of the SOGAT PMB for example) to about 800 in one NATSOPA Machine Chapel (see Appendix 8, Table 6). The number of chapels each union or branch has in any particular house rarely correlates with its membership in that house. Thus in two multi-title houses, while the RIRMA membership as a total of all union members was 8% and 10%, the number of RIRMA chapels was 25% and 23% respectively of the total. On the other hand chapels with the largest memberships, had 32%, 24% (SOGAT publishing) and 16% and 18% (NATSOPA machine) of all union members in the house, but only 9%, 12% (SOGAT) and 6% and 7% (NATSOPA machine) respectively of the total number of chapels.

284. The merger of chapels of the same union does not appear to be encouraged by most branches or regions. While NGA rules provide for there to be "in every printing office . . . an Imperial Chapel and Father of the Chapel", and that "only one chapel shall exist in any office", in practice the NGA machine managers with one exception have a separate chapel, as is commonly the case with stereo and, to a lesser degree, T & E chapels (see Chapter 9). Since 1960 the NGA has also not allowed dual working (eg 4 and 1 working) in the same house, a pattern of work regarded as likely in its view to lead to staffing reductions. Some managements said during our inquiries that this policy militated against any moves in dual or multi-title houses towards fully integrated staffing (ie single staffs for seven-day-working cover in all departments).

285. The pattern of local chapel organisation has changed relatively little largely because of the stability of the production process and work situation. During the NATSOPA and NUPB & PW combination within SOGAT (see Chapter 9) no changes of their respective chapel organisations in national newspapers were carried through (but see paragraph 325).

Growth of Clerical Chapel Boundaries

286. NATSOPA clerical chapels have in recent years attempted to extend, and in a number of houses succeeded in extending, their membership boundaries among previously unorganised staffs, particularly those employed in sales, marketing and advertising departments. The previously low level of union organisation in these areas has been attributed both to management opposition and to the difficulties of maintaining membership because of relatively high labour turnover.

Overseers and Other Managers

287. Overseers are generally members of the union whose members they supervise, or, in the case of composing and machine rooms, of the predominant craft union (ie the NGA) at the workplace. Whether or not they are members of the appropriate chapel varies both within and between houses. Some chapel

officials take the view, that once a chapel member becomes a staff hand he has divided loyalties. Generally while junior overseers may still be required to pay chapel dues, there is no participation in chapel meetings by supervisory staff above chargehand. Some chapel officials do, nevertheless, take up with management grievances notified to them by overseers although this is dependent on the relationships that exist at the workplace and the views of individual chapel officials on such activity.

288. In a number of houses NATSOPA TA and E chapels, composed of managerial and executive members, have been formed and have sought, so far unsuccessfully, recognition and negotiating rights particularly over salary structures. In most houses the NATSOPA clerical chapel organises and negotiates for all grades below the level of departmental head, although there have been a number of disputes in houses concerned with the aim of clerical chapels to extend upwards their negotiating and representational influence, and at the same time, their influence on promotion.

289. In at least two houses there are overseers' and managers' associations which have both social and representational functions, although there have been noticeable increases in emphasis on the latter function in recent years. The associations are fairly loosely-constituted bodies, meeting infrequently. The two largest (both in multi-title houses) have memberships of 165 and 175. In one house the association is recognised with rights of representation over pay and conditions, the hearing of grievances and consultation. Another house has limited its association's recognition to advisory and consultative matters only, specifically precluding "any rights to negotiate on issues that fall within the purview of any of the recognised trade unions". These bodies (and similarly NATSOPA TA and E chapels) have been formed or reactivated because of dissatisfaction with what is seen as a policy by companies of cultivating relations with FOCs to the detriment of junior management authority. Supervisors and junior managers have also felt that manual and clerical workers' terms and conditions have been disproportionately improved in comparison to their own.

Chapel Finance

290. All chapels maintain their own funds, which vary considerably both in their amount and the uses to which they are put but which, nevertheless, are an important factor in any consideration of "chapel autonomy", a phrase frequently used by chapel representatives. Production chapels generally maintain the larger funds, which in part reflects the wider role of such chapels. Apart from a chapel administration or general fund, which is used to cover the usually token emoluments (see Appendix 8, Table 7) to chapel officers, delegates' fees, postage, appeals and necessary administrative expenses, chapels may have separate funds for sickness payment, aged members, and death benefit. The general fund is commonly used in the absence of separate and specific funds for these latter purposes also.

291. Chapel subscriptions, as distinct from union subscriptions, also vary markedly (usually between 6p and 10p per week, although levies of up to 30p per week and more may be imposed: see Appendix 8, Table 8). Those chapels which

have Saturday-only members generally make provision for a smaller subscription for such members. Most chapel rules give chapel committees the power to impose a levy when the state of the individual chapel's finances warrant it, or when special circumstances, such as a member's long-term sickness or bereavement, arise. Some chapels also impose a maximum limit on the size of their funds, any surplus being either annually distributed to the membership or disposed of for charitable purposes. Total union subscriptions (ie including chapel and union dues) of up to 80p a week are not uncommon.

292. The use of NUJ chapel funds reflects the narrower role of the chapel, particularly on "social welfare" matters. Among the purposes for which such funds are increasingly being used is the hiring of professional advice, notably of a legal and financial nature. NUJ chapels vary considerably between houses in their financial arrangements, with some chapels having no funds at all. The use of professional advice is indicative both of the style of bargaining adopted by NUJ chapels and the type of problems and grievances which their membership have (see Chapter 16).

Chapel Facilities

293. Chapel facilities, whilst physically sometimes rough-and-ready, are generally acceptable. The pay of chapel officers who are "stood out" either by agreement or custom and practice is based on either the average earnings of the workgroup from which the official is drawn, or the equivalent rate of the highest grade of chapel member (more particularly in the case of NATSOPA machine and SOGAT publishing chapels). In instances where chapel officials are not "stood out", but nevertheless spend a regular proportion of their time at work on chapel business, it is usual for them to be "covered" by the workgroup for such time, and are generally paid their normal wages. Some chapel agreements additionally provide for a set number of hours at overtime rates to be paid to those chapel officials with a regular chapel work commitment.

294. In production areas there have been isolated attempts by managements to reduce the number of chapel officials spending considerable proportions of their time on chapel business. Such disagreements that have occurred on this question have partly resulted from the steady widening in the area of chapel responsibility and control, and a lack of any formal related agreement on facilities for time-off for chapel duties.

295. Similarly, few formal agreements exist between managements and chapels (except in the case of the NUJ*) on the provision of facilities for the conduct of chapel business and administration. Most large production and clerical chapels either have or share an office, have easy access to internal and external telephones, reproduction equipment and the use of notice boards. Both the circumstances in which these have been obtained and the degree to which they are furnished are related to the needs of the chapels' memberships. In some

---

* Provisions in NUJ agreements generally allow "employees who are chapel, branch or national union officials or representatives . . . every assistance in the performance of their duties". Some agreements also specify the payment to be made for such duties. Payment may, for example, be by time-off in lieu, at a negotiated rate, or at the NPA/NUJ casual rate.

instances offices have been provided following informal agreements with management while in others they appear to have been obtained almost by a form of "squatting". The facilities afforded to chapel officials are felt by many of them to be inadequate in relation to the chapel's administrative and organisational duties which are a necessary element in the effectiveness of the total production process*.

296. Arrangements for the automatic deduction of union subscriptions at source (or "check-off" arrangements) are not widespread in national newspaper houses. It is a facility that not every union branch wishes to take up, although of those that make use of it the vast proportion are NATSOPA chapels (of all three branches). Chapel dues are without exception, however, collected physically.

Chapel/Union Relationships

297. Relationships between chapels, through their representatives, and their appropriate branch or regional organisations develop in three main ways. First, chapel delegates express chapel views at branch, regional or sectional level in the union. Some branches (for example, those of SLADE, the NGA, and AUEW) regularly convene meetings of their national newspaper FOCs to exchange information, co-ordinate activities and develop policy on a wide range of items. The status and size of national newspaper printing trade union chapels allows them to play an important role in union affairs both at branch and national levels (or in the NGA's case, in its Trade Group Board). A significant number of FOCs and chapel officials also hold Branch or national committee positions in their unions.

298. Second, administrative contacts take place between chapels and Branches fairly frequently and in many cases daily. These range from matters concerned with employment (both temporary, casual and permanent), communications and interpretation of correspondence, the conduct of ballots and finance (eg subscriptions, appeals, etc), to disciplinary questions.

299. Third, there are often contacts between chapels and union full-time officers when disputes occur or when changes in working practices and methods are proposed. While all claims, whether day-to-day, related to a review of an existing agreement or to the introduction of a new agreement, are formulated and negotiated by individual chapels, all draft agreements are required to be submitted to the appropriate Branch (and additionally, in some cases, national executives) for approval. If, during the course of negotiations deadlock has been reached either chapel or management may contact the appropriate full-time officer and seek advice or assistance. The extent of such intervention depends on the views of the chapel, the personal relationships involved, the issue, and the judgement of the officer concerned. In some unions there is a reluctance on the part of chapels to involve full-time officers, and it is often managements that take the initiative in doing so during disputes. This is sometimes resented by chapels on the grounds that management by so doing are attempting to by-pass the chapel to secure agreement on less advantageous terms to the chapel than might otherwise be the case.

---

* It is fair to add that the same could be said of the office facilities of line management and, in some cases, middle and senior management.

300. In cases where industrial action is occurring or where an issue affects more than one chapel of the same branch or union in the house, Branch officers are invariably called in. The extent of full-time officer-involvement in chapel affairs is also dependent on the individual chapel's collective bargaining strength. Thus some of the small chapels, for example, those of NATSOPA RIRMA, are much more dependent on their full-time officers in this respect than is the case with the larger chapels such as those of NATSOPA machine, NGA imperial composing and SOGAT publishing.

301. Though chapels are often influential bodies within their Branches and have independent rights, granted under the rules, in certain areas the notion of blanket "chapel autonomy" is misplaced. The vetting of chapel draft agreements by Branches takes place in every union, including the NUJ whose chapel agreements are submitted to the union's wages committee. Items in draft agreements may often be amended or even rejected by Branches, although Branch decisions may be, and occasionally are, challenged by the chapel concerned through the unions' appeals machinery. Decisions of Branches on such matters are rarely defied by chapels, and certainly not after the appeals machinery has been activated.

302. Chapels are formed within the official machinery of the printing trade unions, are closely controlled in their structural development, and members may be expelled from the union if union rules or policy are not upheld. Nevertheless, they have their traditional rights, their voting strength, and often the ability to directly affect production. Their influence has grown as their work organisation functions have expanded, and as the relationship between national and house agreements has changed (a matter of particular note in any consideration of the developing role of NUJ chapels).

303. The ability of chapels to pursue local claims, or as one manager put it "to hunt on their own", is bound by a number of constraints, and these also apply to the taking of industrial action without the prior approval of full-time officers in most unions. In the case of SLADE, the NGA, and NATSOPA most FOCs contacted during the ACAS study indicated that any stoppages of work they might wish to call required the approval of the appropriate branch, and in some cases, the national executive of the union. Some unions have in fact taken action against chapel officials for the calling of unofficial disputes. It is nevertheless the case that the range of sanctions other than a full stoppage of work a chapel can employ in pursuance of a claim or grievance may be equally effective.

Joint Chapel Working Arrangements within Houses
Federated House Chapels (FHC)

304. Eight of the eleven Fleet Street houses have FHCs, and two of the multi-title houses each have two FHCs. In those houses in which there is no FHC the possibility of convening one has from time to time been mooted. In one case an FHC did exist until about 1960 but was wound up when the then FHC father gave up his post. A typical FHC is an in-house organisation to which chapels of all unions within the house may affiliate. It normally consists basically of a committee composed of chapel representatives (usually

FOCs and/or their deputies) from which FHC officers—chairman, federated FOC, deputy federated FOC, and secretary/treasurer—are elected.

305. FHCs have their own funds generated by a capitation levy payable by chapels in membership, and written rules. They may meet quarterly, annually or intermittently. The powers and negotiating functions of FHCs are strictly limited. They cannot commit any individual chapel to a decision of the FHC, and cannot "interfere with the business of individual chapels", although "if requested shall assist when necessary in organising the workers in each department" (extract from one multi-title FHC rule book). FHCs vary in their strengths and activities, but are generally weak bodies, both because of the absence from membership of some chapels and also because of the desire of each chapel to retain its own independence. At most, FHCs deal with pensions, safety, medical facilities, canteen and restaurant arrangements and matters that concern all employees equally in the house. Some FHCs have become involved in redundancy questions and have been used by managements for consultative purposes, but attempts to extend FHC activities are received with suspicion by most of the chapels whose representatives we interviewed and have generally failed.

306. An FHC rarely covers all chapels within the house or title, the reasons for non-membership varying considerably. Withdrawal from FHC membership has been occasioned, for example, by concern on the part of some chapels that FHCs have become too political; that an FHC has intervened excessively in the affairs of individual chapels; by resentment at the "one chapel, one vote" rule which in some cases was felt to give disproportionate influence to small chapels; and by dissatisfaction over FHC administration and lack of progress on matters of concern to individual chapels.

Single Union Inter-Chapel Arrangements

307. Most other formal joint working arrangements between chapels are based on a federation or grouping of chapels of the same union in each house. The most common of these is the NGA imperial composing chapel, which is usually formed of NGA composing chapels working on each newspaper title. All NGA imperial chapels include the local chapels of time hands, piece case hands, linotype operators and readers, and some also include local chapels of stereotypers and telecommunications and electronics members. The NGA's chapel rule requiring all NGA chapels in each house to form themselves into one imperial grouping is generally thought to be unworkable. There is, nevertheless, usually a close liaison between non-affiliated composing chapel officials, those of machine managers' chapels and the Imperial composing FOC in each house. This relationship has, in some houses, become formalised with the establishment of an NGA house chapel, with its own officers and committee negotiating with management on common problems such as the level of redundancy payments. Coincidental with the disclosure by managements of plans to introduce new technology in composing areas, there has also been closer working between NGA imperial composing chapels in each house (through liaison groups) to develop common policy and approaches to such matters.

308. It is also common in the larger houses, for all or most NATSOPA chapels to be affiliated to a NATSOPA Federated House Chapel. These

federations have their own officers and rules, and meet every few months or when occasions warrant it. The NATSOPA federations' attempt to achieve common policies among their chapels on matters that affect them equally and act as a medium for the exchange of information. There was a feeling among some of those we interviewed during our inquiries that the attitude of NATSOPA Branches to the formation of such federations is ambivalent, in that while their presence and development is acknowledged it is not actively encouraged as Branches are regarded as the appropriate medium through which policy development and communication between chapels should take place.

309. In some houses various SOGAT publishing chapels may be members of liaison groups or combined publishing chapels, the latter having an elected imperial father. The groupings, while similar to those of the NGA's imperial composing chapels, vary in the degree to which the IFOC is the sole or chief negotiator for the chapels in membership. The negotiating role of local SOGAT chapel FOCs is generally greater than the NGA local chapels. In SOGAT's case the IFOC is available to local FOCs as one put it, "should they need power to their elbow". Some matters of joint concern (for example, recruitment, transfer of members between chapels, promotion and items dealt with by FHCs) common to all chapels are dealt with by each combined chapel.

310. Similarly NUJ chapels in multi-title houses may form themselves into group or federated editorial chapels. These may also liaise with NUJ chapels in the Manchester and Glasgow establishments of the same house, particularly to discuss the determination and presentation of house claims. Most NUJ FOCs in London houses co-operate with one another, particularly before the drawing-up and submission of house claims, although this is an informal working arrangement not necessarily taking place through the medium of the union's branches.

Inter-Union Chapel Arrangements

311. There are two other forms of formal joint working of note. In the process departments SOGAT PMB members participate in combined chapel arrangements with SLADE. It is usual, though there are exceptions, for the chapel to negotiate one agreement covering both memberships, and for the SLADE members to allow the small number of SOGAT members full participation, including the right to hold chapel office, in all chapel affairs. SLADE publicity artists who are covered by the provisions of their own national agreement, are generally organised in chapels separate from those of the process workers. Some liaison takes place between the respective chapels in each house and joint meetings occur, but the common ground between publicity artists and members of the process departments seems limited.

312. The second form of inter-union joint working arrangement applies in MGN and NGN. The NGA machine managers and NATSOPA machine chapels of the *Sun* on the one hand and the *Daily* and *Sunday Mirrors* on the other are parties to joint pressroom agreements. While the chapels of each union consider their own positions, mandating their officers to discuss any claim before it is put to the company, there is a joint chapels negotiating committee in each house. The resultant agreements are put to the London Machine Branch

of NATSOPA and the London Region of the NGA for ratification, and any major problems are handled by the officers of the two unions jointly. The arrangements at the *Sun* are in part a result of the special NATSOPA/NGA relationship there (see footnote on page 53).

Working Relationships

313. Working relationships between members of chapels when they come into contact are almost always said to be good. Between the chapels themselves relationships are either reasonably satisfactory where the chapels have some kind of formal link as described earlier in this chapter, or they are conducted at a distance or are non-existent. Many chapels claim to function oblivious of the policies and activities of other chapels, and any contact between chapel officials occurs sporadically, either through the medium of the FHC (if the chapel is in membership) or on demarcation issues.

CHAPTER 9: TRADE UNION ORGANISATION

314. The development of trade union organisation in the national newspaper industry has been associated with a high level of skilled manual employment and, until the late 1950s, a relatively stable and highly specialised production system. This has assisted the growth of a high density of trade union membership*, the craft unions having been able to control labour supply by the establishment of pre-entry closed shops and the limitation of the number of apprentices to the general trade. The control of labour supply was later achieved by the non-craft manual unions, and, more recently, has been developed to a degree by editorial and ancillary workers in the industry.

315. The principal unions with membership in the national newspaper industry on the printing process side are the National Graphical Association (NGA), the National Society of Operative Printers, Graphical and Media Personnel (NATSOPA), the Society of Graphical and Allied Trades (SOGAT 1975), and the Society of Lithographic Artists, Designers, Engravers and Process Workers (SLADE). The National Union of Journalists (NUJ) established in 1907, organises the overwhelming majority of editorial workers (principally journalists), although the Institute of Journalists (IOJ), a professional body incorporated by Royal Charter in 1890 has a minority and sometimes a minimal, presence in most national newspaper offices.

316. Ancillary workers in administrative and clerical positions, and in general services are organised by NATSOPA, which, with the formation of a Technical, Administrative and Executive Section (TA and E) in 1969 also has in membership middle and senior management employees (eg directors, company secretaries, labour relations managers etc.). The majority of maintenance workers are members of the Amalgamated Union of Engineering Workers (AUEW Engineering Section) and the Electrical, Electronic, Telecommunications and Plumbing Union (EETPU). The former represents mechanical maintenance engineers and linotype mechanics and the latter electricians and their assistants. There are, in addition, other unions with small memberships in maintenance and service activities, including the Union of Construction, Allied Trades and Technicians (UCATT: bricklayers, carpenters and painters), the National Union of Sheet Metal Workers, Coppersmiths, Heating and Domestic Engineers (NUSMWCH and DE: heat engineering maintenance), the General and Municipal Workers' Union (GMWU: canteen and catering staffs), and the Confederation of Health Service Employees (COHSE: industrial nursing staffs).

317. The place of printing occupations in the production and ancillary processes in the London national newspaper houses, together with the union membership associated with each job, is set out in Table 1, page 17. This pattern of membership is common to all national newspaper houses in most respects, although variations do exist. The *News of the World*, for example, has for historical reasons a pressroom staffed entirely by NATSOPA members.

---

* The Printing and Kindred Trades' Federation (P & KTF) Executive recorded in their report for 1914 "the opening up of *The Times* newspaper as a Trade Union House. This paper has, from time immemorial, been worked on non-union lines, and this success completes the last link in the chain of Trade Unionism in the newspaper world, as far as London is concerned".

The *Sun* machine room, following the decision to print the title at the *News of the World* plant, also has its presses manned by NGA and NATSOPA machine managers on a numerically equal basis.

318. The Manchester printing centres of the national newspapers have a similar occupational content, although the pattern of trade union organisation differs in a number of respects from that applying in London. The principal organisational difference is the absence of SOGAT members from the production process. The work of pressmen (or proofpullers) in the composing room is an NGA function; process proving is entirely undertaken by SLADE; and all inside work in the publishing areas is organised by NATSOPA. SOGAT organises van loaders and drivers, circulation representatives and some employees working in local offices of Manchester newspapers. The NGA, through its Manchester Graphical Society branch, organises non-printer caster operatives, whereas London monotype casters are organised into the Monotype Casters' Branch of SOGAT.

319. The common division of printing trade unions into craft and non-craft types, which was ostensibly correct in the immediate post-war years, is a distinction that can no longer clearly be made. The blurring of membership boundaries has been a result of the interaction of a number of factors, including trade union amalgamation, technological change, the extension and relaxation of membership qualifications and the growth in membership by recruitment and organisation of previously unorganised workers, particularly in clerical, technical, administrative and executive occupations.

320. An understanding of the history of trade union organisation in the newspaper industry is vital to any comprehension of current attitudes on amalgamation and of inter-union relations. A summary of developments in this area up to 1939 is given in Appendix 9(*a*). Broadly, the story has been one of the gradual synthesis of local societies to form regional or national bodies mainly, but with important exceptions, along craft/non-craft lines. Since 1945 there has continued to be a considerable fall in the number of separate unions (see Appendix 9, Table 1). The first of the post-war amalgamations occurred in 1955 between the LSC and the PMMTS (to form the London Typographical Society (LTS)) thus bringing together occupational groups in London organised by the TA in the provinces. The merger was largely stimulated by the relative stagnation in membership of the two London societies compared to the growth in membership of the non-craft national printing trade unions, and by a desire to maintain the London differential and the craftsmen's strength in negotiations *vis-a-vis* that of the non-craft unions.

321. The formation of the NGA in 1964 by the merger of the LTS and the TA came about for similar reasons. The NUPB & PW had been growing in membership both through recruitment and through amalgamation with a number of smaller societies, the largest being the Monotype Casters' and Typefounders' Society (MC & TS) with 913 members. The latter merger was significant in that the MC & TS was a craft union, its members manning and maintaining several kinds of type-founding equipment. The majority of its members were employed in the general trade in London, while similar craftsmen in the provinces were

organised by the TA. Discussions on amalgamation had also been taking place between the NUPB & PW and NATSOPA, and this together with the development of new technology, was a material influence in the formation of the NGA.

322. In 1965 the Association of Correctors of the Press (ACP) and the National Union of Press Telegraphists (NUPT) joined the NGA. The membership of the ACP was confined to London, organising readers in NPA houses, as was the bulk of the NUPT's membership. In 1967 the National Society of Electrotypers and Stereotypers (NSES) joined the NGA, followed in 1968 by the Amalgamated Society of Lithographic Printers (ASLP). The ASLP was a growth union unlike the ACP, NUPT and NSES, and was of particular importance to the future strength of the NGA in allowing it a degree of control in new processes, especially in lithographic printing.

323. In January 1966 the NUPB & PW and NATSOPA merged to form SOGAT Division A and Division 1, respectively. The two divisions were to be maintained for three years in order that questions of administration, rules and finance could be determined, but a common Executive Council was formed. The merger was not a success however, and following a Rules Revision Conference in November 1968, relationships deteriorated between the two divisions, eventually leading to the re-establishment of the two separate unions, with Division A (formerly the NUPB & PW) re-emerging simply as SOGAT.

324. An important difference between the two unions lay, and remains, in the difference in their government (see paragraphs 337 and 338) and organisation. SOGAT organises workers in the printing and paper industries and in the offshoots of these industries such as fibreboard, plastic cups and containers, polythene manufacture and the manufacture of conduits and pipes from pitch, paper and asbestos. In contrast, NATSOPA was and is both a smaller organisation, with a major proportion of its membership concentrated in London and confined to a more limited industrial base in national and provincial newspapers.

325. The period of the merger between the two unions saw little, if any, change in their organisation at branch level or at chapel level, particularly in the national newspaper houses. The only membership change concerned the transfer of some 190 NATSOPA proof-pullers to the SOGAT PMB. The PMB has a skilled membership and the transfer of membership from the RIRMA Branch was in part an attempt to improve the relative status and earnings position of the proofpullers, who subsequently adopted the term "pressmen". (Pressmen are skilled craftsmen, the majority of the 3,420 working members of the PMB being employed in London in general printing, typesetting, blockmaking, litho proving and platemaking.)

326. The most recent merger of printing trade unions has been that between SOGAT and the Scottish Graphical Association (SGA) in 1975. The SGA claims within its ranks more than 90% of all those employed as craftsmen in the printing industry in Scotland, but also includes assistants and ancillary workers*. The amalgamation has been facilitated, as were the mergers

---

* Its membership includes compositors, process provers, pressmen, and machine minders, as well as printers' assistants in printing offices recognised by the SGA.

(or "fusions", the term used by SOGAT) that formed the NUPB & PW, by giving trade section status to the SGA, which is now the Scottish Graphical Division of SOGAT.

Membership and Officers

327. There has been a steady growth in total national printing trade union membership in every year since 1964, apart from 1971, as Appendix 9 Table 2 shows. The fastest growing union has been the NUJ. Between 1964 and 1974 it increased its membership by over 64%. The relatively low growth of production union membership (10% between 1964 and 1974) is in part a reflection of the high degree of union membership density in the printing industry referred to in paragraph 314, and also of the decline of employment in some areas, particularly the paper and boardmaking industry*.

328. With two exceptions, the head offices of the trade unions with memberships in the printing industry are located in the London area. The headquarters of the NGA are in Bedford, a reflection within the union of the amalgamations between the London and provincial craft societies, and also the importance of the London Region of the union, with over one-fifth of the total membership of the NGA. Of the printing unions, only the NGA has a formal research department, although it is SOGAT's intention to develop one following the relocation of its head office from South London to Hadleigh, in Essex (see also paragraphs 524 to 528). Research matters were largely the responsibility of the P & KTF until its dissolution (see paragraph 387).

329. The London memberships of the printing trade unions have declined since 1970-71 by 8% (see Appendix 9, Table 3). In Manchester the NGA and NATSOPA membership has increased by 10% since 1971. Three of the four NUJ branches with which we are concerned have shown a slight growth over the period (but there has been a vast increase in the Freelance Branch's membership). This is indicative of the consistently high level of union membership density among national newspaper journalists in contrast with their counterparts elsewhere. (This density of membership may also be partly attributed to the effectiveness of the 1965 NPA/NUJ Memorandum on journalists entry into Fleet Street detailed in paragraphs 580, et seq.)

330. The printing trade union branches in London and Manchester, together with the NUJ's Central London Branch, have between one and nine (NGA London Region) full-time Branch officers. In addition the Branches, particularly in London, have substantial numbers of administrative back-up staff (see Appendix 9, Table 3). The numbers of members serviced by each Branch officer varies between the 7,791 serviced by the RIRMA Branch officer to the much lower numbers of the London and Manchester SLADE Branch officers (981 and 650 respectively).

The Present National Structure

331. While present trade union organisation in the printing industry retains some of its original craft and non-craft divisions, the pattern of amalgamations

---

* In a pamphlet entitled "Save our Industry" (published by SOGAT in 1976), it is noted that "SOGAT as a union has been severely hit by the economic crisis in the (British paper and board-making) industry". In the period 1967-75 more than 20,500 of its members were made redundant as a result of mill closures and machines shut down.

has progressively blurred this distinction. It was possible to draw a craft-based distinction until SOGAT's fusion with the SGA, since, before then, SOGAT was overwhelmingly composed of non-apprentice-trained members (as was NATSOPA) and such craftsmen as it did contain were employed in the finishing processes, while the other unions had a predominant responsibility for the origination and printing processes.

332. The craft unions have at the same time widened their interests in membership terms to include, in the NGA's case, not only members with recognised apprenticeships in printing but also "such other persons whom the National Council shall consider it desirable . . . to admit into membership". SLADE similarly not only organises apprentice-trained members, but also has an Auxiliary Section for workers in preparatory processes to printing "whose qualifications are limited to operations not requiring the normal apprenticeship", together with Associate Membership for supervisory grades, technicians, research workers and demonstrators. In 1974 SLADE also formed the SLADE Art Union, to represent members "engaged in preparing and producing art and photographic material". This is a sector containing a highly skilled workforce closely allied to SLADE's existing membership, but in which there is little or no trade union organisation.

333. One reason for the relaxation of membership conditions is that technological change has confused and in some cases obliterated traditional jurisdictional areas and increased technical work content at the expense of craft skills. Technological change has brought demarcation disputes between unions for a number of other reasons. In the case, for example, of web-offset machinery over which major disputes occurred at Southwark Offset Ltd (part of the then International Publishing Corporation Ltd), the Manchester printing plant of the CWS and a number of other establishments. NATSOPA claimed equal rights with the NGA in minding the equipment. NATSOPA (then Division 1 of SOGAT), in this and in other situations, was presented with an opportunity to reassert its long-standing aim of achieving the status of craftsmen for its members, who had been denied advancement to "skilled" jobs traditionally taken by members of a "craft" union. Technological change has been seen by the craft unions as a threat to the employment prospects of their members, and has influenced their attitudes towards amalgamation. This was especially true of the organisations that came together as the NGA.

334. Demarcation disputes have also arisen because of the overlapping membership areas of the unions, a product of the amalgamation of craft unions, particularly in the London area, with SOGAT. The presence of London monotype casters and typefounders in SOGAT (in the Monocasters', Filmsetters' and Typefounders' Branch) with their provincial counterparts being organised by the NGA has led in recent years to a number of demarcation problems in London with the introduction of new technology. Such problems are not exclusively confined to disputes between "craft" and general unions, as some types of new equipment obviate the need for traditional methods of printing plate-founding, and have consequently blurred the jurisdictional lines of work between SLADE and the NGA (principally affecting the latter's stereotyping membership). Such difficulties arise mainly as a result of the policy common to all unions that members should have the right to "follow the job" in the event of technological change.

335. The printing unions have required a period of time to consolidate the amalgamations that have been successfully achieved. The two largest unions, the NGA and SOGAT, together with SLADE, now have very similar organisational structures. The NGA, following the series of amalgamations culminating in 1968 with that of the ASLP, embarked on a reorganisation of its structure to harmonise its constitutional position, to establish a new branch and regional structure and, most significant of all, to develop trade representation in the union through the creation of a number of trade group boards (see Appendix 9, Table 4). These include a Letterpress Trade Group Board and News Trade Group Board elected from members on both national and provincial daily newspapers. The development of this form of organisation was undertaken in the belief that further amalgamation would be resumed at a later date with the eventual aim of creating a single printing industry union. It was acknowledged that, given such an event, the need for trade representation would be essential.

336. In similar vein, SOGAT, at its 1972 Biennial Delegate Conference, adopted an organisational structure which created a number of trade sections as shown in Appendix 9, Table 5. This restructuring, as well as allowing trade representation at national level in the union (there being, for example, a Newspaper Production and Distribution Trade Section), was also adopted for the flexibility it afforded in furthering amalgamations of printing unions. It has long been SOGAT's aim (and the NUPB & PW's before it) to create a single printing industry union, and its amalgamation with the SGA was a further step in this direction. This amalgamation was greatly assisted by the new organisational structure which allowed trade section status for the SGA, the ultimate objective being the creation of a national graphical division embracing members in the Monocasters and Printing Machine Branches*.

337. SLADE has itself a sectional organisation (see Appendix 9, Table 6) with trade sections for members in gravure, lithography, engraving, photo-engraving and newspapers. The structures adopted by the NGA, SOGAT, and SLADE with their accent on trade group representation, tend to make for a decentralised form of organisation, and increase the importance of the role of the chapel in their respective structures.

338. NATSOPA, in contrast, has a more centralised form of structure and government (see Appendix 9, Table 7). Its branch structure for its national newspaper membership in London and Manchester distinguishes three main occupational groupings (ie, clerical, machine and publishing, and general assistants). Every NATSOPA branch must conduct its business "in accordance with and subject to the rules of the Society", and its "Executive Committee supervise(s) the work of all branches and branch officers". The Executive is in turn bound by decisions of the Governing Council, which normally meets biennially. The Executive Committee has, in addition to one representative from each District (a total of six representatives), and four from the clerical

---

* Referring to the negotiations on amalgamation with SLADE and the SGA at SOGAT's 1974 Biennial Delegate Conference, Mr Keys, the General Secretary, said that "we believe that the structure (the conference) agreed at the last BDC allowed for flexibility for these organisations to come into SOGAT under the SOGAT rule book as it now stands". The SGA amalgamation was successfully concluded, although the negotiations with SLADE have reportedly been broken off.

membership, nine from the London and Manchester branches. In contrast to those of NATSOPA the branches of SOGAT have considerable independence (for example, over their finances) which was itself an issue in the break-up of the merger between NATSOPA and the NUPB & PW*.

339. The largest journalists' union, the NUJ, which had 29,433 members in 1974, decided at its 1975 Annual Delegate Meeting to change its structure, the main effects being a restructuring (and reduction in numbers) of the National Executive Committee, and the creation of seven Industrial Councils (see Appendix 9, Table 8). NEC members represent a combination of geographical areas and industrial sectors. Branch members thus vote in elections for the appropriate industrial sector NEC member, and on the same basis for Industrial Council Members.

340. The changes resulted from the NUJ's 1972 conference which endorsed a proposal that the union be divided into its "natural" parts to allow for the realities of negotiation. The new Industrial Councils cover national newspapers, provincial newspapers, magazines and books, public relations, freelances, broadcasting, and Eire.

341. The NUJ has had four unsuccessful attempts at amalgamating with the much smaller Institute of Journalists (IOJ) since 1928. The most recent attempt ended in 1972 following a six-year period of experimental dual membership, during which the NUJ concerned itself with all industrial negotiations, while the IOJ dealt with professional matters with the exception of the Press Council and international affairs. Agreement had been reached on a common rule book for a proposed National Association of Journalists, and on arrangements for a Parliamentary Bill effecting the merger†. The joint delegate meeting held in 1972 to approve the proposals decided against a merger, and the two organisations since then have moved some distance apart. Indeed, relations between the two bodies have not been good since 1972.

342. The introduction of new technology into printing, and the national newspaper industry in particular, together with the most recent amalgamations of trade unions, the reaffiliation of the NGA to the TUC and changes in leadership of three of the four production unions have contributed to a relaxation of the rivalry that existed between the unions in the period 1968 to 1975. This period was also one during which the long-established P & KTF declined in effectiveness as a co-ordinating body between printing trade unions, eventually being dissolved in 1974. In addition these years gave the unions with an opportunity to consolidate previous amalgamations and mergers, and to restructure themselves, leading to the present organisational similarities between some of the unions.

The Branch Structure

343. The London branches of the printing trade unions are, without exception, the largest in numerical terms of each union. Branches with members working

---

* In SOGAT, Branches can keep up to one-third of members' contributions for local management expenses. Branches with over 1,000 members may raise a local levy to pay for the services of a full-time elected branch secretary. In NATSOPA the General Secretary is responsible for finances, Branches having cash for small expenses only. While the London and Manchester Branch officers are elected, District secretaries are appointed by the unions' EC.

† Necessary to ensure that benefits from the IOJ's charitable trusts would have continued to be available to members of the new body.

in national newspapers tend either to be predominantly concerned with national newspaper matters, or, as in the case of the NGA London Region News Department, have separate arrangements for the representation of members working in national newspapers.

344. In part because of their numerical strength, and also because of the key position held by London-based societies and trade unions in the development of the present printing trade unions, the London branches have considerable influence in the affairs of their parent bodies. This influence expresses itself not only in voting strength and policies of the national unions, but also in the presence at national level of many trade union officers who were originally officers in the London Branches of their unions. There are two further factors that have sustained the influence of the London Branches over the years. The key importance of the Branches in affecting industrial relations in the printing industry generally has tended to preserve for them a greater degree of independence and autonomy than their provincial counterparts. The second factor in sustaining their position has been the pre-eminence of London as both a printing centre and in providing high earnings opportunities and relatively favourable terms and conditions of employment. This position has been achieved in and is largely based on the national newspaper industry, employment in which has been regarded as a final stage in the career development of union members in London.

NATSOPA

345. There are three branches organising NATSOPA's London printing offices membership. These are the Machine Branch, Clerical Branch, and the RIRMA Branch. The London Branches not only cover Fleet Street, but all members within a 15-mile radius of central London.

346. The Technical Administrative and Executive Section (TA & E) has no branch structure, is an autonomous part of the union, and is the direct responsibility of the National Assistant Secretary. It has its own chapels and members in nearly all the houses in both London and Manchester. Membership is applied for directly to NATSOPA Head Office, and generally results from the promotion of clerical members to supervisory positions. While 200 members in the London Clerical Branch have transferred into the Section in recent years, there are still many managers and executives remaining in membership of clerical chapels, although they do not participate in chapel affairs. At the end of 1975 the TA & E Section included 116 members in the national newspaper industry in London, and 18 in Manchester.

347. Recognition of the TA & E chapels has not yet been universally achieved in national newspapers, despite approaches to the NPA by NATSOPA for recognition and bargaining rights. At the same time there has been some reluctance on the part of clerical chapels to establish separate Executive and Managerial chapels, partly because they wish to maintain some control over promotion prospects and career opportunities for their members.

348. In 1962 the Clerical Branch changed its recruitment boundaries to include all employees in non-mechanical areas apart from those involved in the formation and execution of policies at board level. Only senior managers

and their secretaries are thus exempted from compulsory membership, there being an *ad hoc* arrangement between the NPA and the Branch to consider contested cases. The clerical and administrative area of national newspapers is the only employment area where some expansion of trade union membership among existing employees has taken and could take place. Advertising and marketing staffs are reputed to be resistant to trade union organisation, although in some offices NATSOPA have organised such employees, particularly tele-ad sales staff.

349. The Clerical Branch has 42% of its membership working in national newspapers, with an almost equal balance between male and female members: it is the only branch in Fleet Street with a substantial number of female members. Its membership is more liable to fluctuation than that of the other branches, principally because the skills and work content of its members are not confined to the printing industry alone. The Branch has a calls office, employing three full-time staff and dealing with an average of 6,000 permanent vacancies each year. The Machine Branch, in contrast, has a much more stable membership. It has in membership the vast majority of NATSOPA casual workers, and shares with the RIRMA Branch a call office to administer and control casual working arrangements.

350. The RIRMA Branch encompasses such widely differing occupational groups as engineers' assistants, cleaners, revisers and phototechnicians. Whereas the Machine Branch has the greatest number of casual workers, the RIRMA Branch was largely decasualised with the advent of comprehensive agreements. Some casual working is done in reading and editorial areas on Saturday nights, together with some outside the national newspapers on local newspapers and publications such as the *Radio Times*. In 1976, and following its merger with NATSOPA in 1972, the London membership (*c.* 1,000) of the Sign and Display Trades Section (formerly the Sign and Display Trades Union) was merged into the RIRMA Branch. The SDTS membership outside London was merged into NATSOPA's provincial branches.

351. The London and Manchester Branches of NATSOPA have equivalent status to Districts of the union. Each of the Branch Secretaries is a permanent officer of the Society, and is elected by ballot of the Branch concerned. Candidates for such offices must have six years' membership for eligibility. The members of the Committees of London Branches are elected by biennial ballot of Branch members, with the proviso that only one member from each chapel may sit on each Committee.

352. There is also a Central Committee for co-ordinating the business and activities of the London Branches of NATSOPA. According to the union's rules, "In all matters other than purely domestic affairs of each individual Branch, the three Branches, as now established, shall function as a unit representing the London membership as a whole". There is no official co-ordination of national newspaper industrial relations matters, such as the formulation of claims, between the London and Manchester Branches of NATSOPA, although informal discussions do take place.

353. In 1975, 95% of Manchester NATSOPA Branch members worked on national newspapers (including the *Manchester Evening News*). The Branch

has three sections covering respectively machine and publishing members, readers and general assistants, and the clerical grades. Each sector elects delegates to the Central Branch Committee, which is the Branch's policy-making body and deals with matters affecting all three sectors. The Branch has two full-time officers, together with seven administrative staff and a further four employed in the casual pay office.

NGA

354. The London Region newspaper members of the NGA are organised into a News Department, membership of its Trade Committee being restricted to representatives drawn from each trade in the national newspaper industry. In 1974, 20% of the Region's members worked in the national newspaper industry. The Region itself has undergone substantial organisational changes in recent years, brought about by the series of union amalgamations that, in the process of creating the NGA, particularly affected London (there are, at present, about 65 different subscription rates within the Region). The Region covers all districts lying within a 15-mile radius of Charing Cross. The 21-member Regional Council has representation from each trade category.

355. The London Region structure (see Appendix 9, Table 9) was developed to ensure that contact between chapel members, officers, regional council members and the various committees was well maintained. All journeymen employed on daily and Sunday newspapers are members of the News Department, which holds two delegate meetings annually to receive reports from the News Trade Committee. The News Trade Committee has similar functions to the other trade committees, in that it is comprised of Regional Council members from the appropriate department, together with additional elected members. The committee deals with all matters appropriate to it under the instructions of the Regional Council. The News Trade Committee has been the forum in the Region in which NGA policy on new technology has been discussed and developed.

356. The Region has two unattached members' chapels which were established in 1973, namely the Electrotypers' and Stereotypers' Casuals Chapel, and the Machine Managers' Casuals Chapel; unemployed members are entitled to send delegates to delegate meetings of the Region. The decline of the printing industry in the London area and the loss of employment opportunities for NGA members has been a matter of considerable concern to the union since the mid-sixties. The NGA has adopted a policy of not accepting individual applicants for membership in an effort to contain and reduce membership levels, and of placing limitations on apprenticeship entry and transfer of members from other regions, while at the same time organising new firms, or those previously not unionised, in order to create employment opportunities for its members.

357. The NGA also has an Executives, Technicians and Overseers Section (ET & O) based at its head office in Bedford, with a full-time officer responsible for servicing it. The Section, which had 2,257 members in 1975, was set up in 1970, and covers a wide range of employee categories including directors, works managers, electronics engineers, overseers, superintendents and estimators. Much of the day-to-day work of the ET & O Section is undertaken

at regional level by the regional secretaries. In 1975, the Section had 260 members working in London national newspapers and 76 in Manchester.

358. Manchester NGA members are organised by the Manchester Graphical Society (MGS), which is the largest NGA branch in the country. About half of the working members are employed on national newspapers, and the 15-member Branch Committee, elected on a sectional basis, reflects both the newspaper and jobbing membership of the Branch. The MGS has a News Compositors' Consultative Committee established primarily to discuss current problems of members in national newspapers, and responsible to the Branch Committee. The Branch has a number of replacement agreements with NATSOPA. These apply principally in the machine rooms where NATSOPA and the NGA share the filling of vacancies in the event of there not being an experienced NGA rotary letterpress member being available. A similar agreement, recently re-activated, applies to reading rooms, where, in the event of there not being a suitably qualified and unemployed NGA member, any vacancy is made available to NATSOPA revisers in the office concerned.

SOGAT

359. There are four branches of SOGAT organising members in the national newspaper industry in London; the London Central Branch (LCB), the Monotype Casters', Filmsetters' and Typefounders' Branch, the Printing Machine Branch, and the Circulation Representatives' Branch. The latter Branch, having a national coverage, also has members working for national newspapers in Manchester.

360. The LCB is the largest of SOGAT's branches and 30% of its employed members work on national newspapers. Since 1965 the Branch membership has fallen as a consequence of mechanisation, closures and redundancies in the London area. The Branch has a Newspaper Section to which all regular national newspaper members belong, and entry into which is controlled by membership card number. The majority of the Branch's membership works outside national newspapers in book publishing, bookbinding, newspaper and periodical wholesaling, in general printing and for HMSO.

361. A sub-committee elected from the 12-member Branch Committee is responsible for the national newspaper interests of the Branch, and all are FOCs on one or more of the titles. While wage negotiations with the NPA are conducted by national officers of SOGAT, the Branch deals with all other NPA and local matters, usually through the Branch Secretary, the sub-committee and the Branch Chairman (a lay member).

362. The Printing Machine Branch (PMB) had 3,420 members at the end of 1975, of whom 170 worked as pressmen (or proofpullers) and 30 as process provers (producing "virgin proofs" of the original copy) in the process departments of national newspapers. Process provers work in close conjunction with SLADE members, and relationships between the PMB and SLADE at both house and branch levels have been close over a period of many years. The PMB also has an associate card agreement with the NGA, whereby members wishing to progress from platen machines to larger printing machines

are given associate membership of the NGA. There is also provision for members wishing to work on litho equipment to transfer after an application has been accepted and a three-year training period completed, but this requires a full transfer of membership to the NGA. The PMB is organised according to the trade agreements under which members work; there is a Branch sub-committee to deal with Fleet Street affairs. The PMB is involved in two of SOGAT's trade sections (the General Print, Process and Typesetting Section, and the Newspaper Section) and their annual conferences.

363. A problem of major importance faced by the PMB has been the increase in redundancies amongst its members, particularly in the process and typesetting sections. These have been caused not only by closures, but also through the introduction of new techniques and technical changes, particularly the introduction of photosetting. The PMB shares this problem with the Monocasters' Branch (which has only eight members in national newspaper composing rooms)*.

364. The Circulation Representatives' Branch (CRB) organises members in both the national and provincial press, and in the periodical and book publishing industries. Whilst the Branch has a chapel organisation at house level this tends in practice not to be the principal organisational unit. The CRB is organised into 21 divisions which elect their own officers. The secretary of each division is a member of the CRB committee. The headquarters division also has in membership managerial circulation staff from national newspapers.

365. The four London SOGAT Branches mentioned above, together with the London Women's Branch and the Ruling, Manufacturing and Stationery Branch, meet three times annually in a London District Committee, which is a purely advisory body. It is analogous to the District Council unit of organisation in SOGAT's structure (see Appendix 9, Table 5) which has the objective of "securing more uniform conditions of labour and greater harmony between the Branches of the Society".

366. About 9% of the members of the Manchester SOGAT Branch work in national newspapers. They consist principally of drivers and distribution staff. While no separate organisational arrangements exist in the Branch for national newspaper members, meetings are occasionally convened between representatives of the seven SOGAT chapels covering these members at the Branch offices. The Branch, partly because its jurisdictional area in national newspapers is narrower than its London counterparts, has relatively few casual members.

SLADE

367. The London Branch of SLADE is the largest of the union's Branches and contains about a third of the union's total membership. Its members in national newspapers work principally in process departments, although there

---

* In April 1976 the NGA and SOGAT agreed a statement of intent to ease the friction between them in the London area over the manning of new photocomposition and lithographic machinery. It is possible as a result that a common union card will cover SOGAT's PMB and Monocaster membership and the NGA London Region.

are also 52 publicity artists, working, for example, in advertisement design. All national newspaper members come within the Branch News Panel which in addition to having an annual delegate meeting, has monthly meetings of its News Committee, which comprises the Branch's national newspaper FOCs. The newspaper process workers also have representation on the Branch's governing body, the District Committee.

368. Unemployment is probably the Branch's largest single problem, particularly in the process area, where, in 1975, there were 167 unemployed members, 15% of total commercial process membership. Subscriptions were increased in 1975 by imposing a membership levy specifically to assist the financing of benefits to the union's unemployed members. The Branch has a growing membership in a number of areas, particularly in litho houses. However, the London Branch suffered a 60% drop in its photo-engraving membership between 1963 and 1973 with many leaving the trade completely*. The litho membership, while having increased, did not make up for this loss, and the Branch's overall membership fell in the period by 18%.

369. About 12% of the Manchester Branch members work on national newspapers. The Branch has a similar organisational structure to its London counterpart, with a News Section and Committee composed of the five national newspaper FOCs reporting to the Branch committee. The Branch does not have such a serious unemployment problem as the London Branch, although the change from letter-press to litho reproduction equipment, and the introduction of photo-reproduction equipment in the national and provincial press has considerably reduced employment opportunities in the commercial process area, particularly in blockmaking.

EETPU

370. The EETPU has a separate Fleet Street Branch, which is part of the union's London 27 Area which covers all printing and newspaper production members in the region. The Branch has a total strength of nearly 1,000 members, of whom over 80% are employed in the national press. The national press membership includes not only electricians and electrical assistants, but also electrical engineers, overseers and managers. As well as the Branch's involvement in the joint administration (with the NPA) of an apprenticeship scheme, provision is also made for the upgrading of electrical assistants to electrician status, subject to joint agreement between the Branch and the appropriate house management. According to the Branch officers, there is not a great demand on the part of union members for jobs in the national newspaper industry partly because comparable or higher earnings are available elsewhere (for example in the electrical contracting industry). The Fleet Street Branch Secretary and Branch Chairman, although employed by newspaper houses, are virtually full-time officers. Negotiations with the NPA are undertaken by them, together with the area official and two lay members of the Branch. The Manchester area membership is represented by its Executive Councillor and the secretary of the EETPU's Manchester Press Branch.

---

* With the advent of new technology SLADE, and the Graphic Reproduction Federation, an employers' organisation, agreed in 1976 jointly to explore a retraining scheme for photo-engraving members in photo-litho work, where a demand for skilled labour was likely to arise.

AUEW

371. The AUEW Fleet Street Branch has a special position recognised by the union in that it is a trade branch within the North London District. The Branch has 1,018 members, (as compared with 720 in 1967) 640 of whom work in the national press, 189 in "flat-bed" houses, and 25 in other engineering trades (the rest are retired members). Some 24 AUEW members working for national newspapers are members of other London AUEW Branches.

372. The Fleet Street Branch, because of its special position, is able to act with some independence within the District. The secretary, the chairman and three (of the 14) committee members comprise the negotiating committee. Regular meetings of the 21 AUEW FOCs are held to approve house agreements, which are then forwarded to the District Committee for ratification.

373. There is also an AUEW Manchester Press Branch. Regular monthly meetings take place between the Branch's officers and the Manchester Divisional Organiser and their opposite numbers in London.

NUJ

374. The NUJs London national newspaper membership is organised by three Branches, the largest of which is the Central London Branch. The Branch organises all full-time journalists in the London national newspaper industry; news agency journalists (previously members of the Branch) are now organised by the London News Agency Branch. The Branch Committee is comprised of all Fleet Street FOCs together with elected members from chapels.

375. Most of the members of the NUJ's London Evening Papers Branch work for either of the two major London Evening Newspapers (but 8% work for provincial evening newspapers). The other London NUJ Branch with members working on national newspapers is the Freelance Branch which has about four times the membership of the London Evening Papers Branch. Members are for the large part self-employed, although some may be employed by freelance agencies.

376. The NUJ Branches, compared with those of the other unions, are weaker in relation to their chapels. This may be partly because they play a less vital role in labour supply than the Branches of the printing unions and because the latter indirectly provide casual and permanent employment and certain fringe benefits (for example, unemployment pay) to their members, and apply more stringent requirements on attendance at both branch (and chapel) meetings by delegates and members. The progressive abandonment of national level bargaining in favour of that at house level since 1974 (see Chapter 16) has also increased considerably the functions of NUJ chapels at the expense of their Branches.

377. A principal function of the NUJ Branches is to act as a channel for communication and as a forum for developing policy and to monitor journalists' entry into Fleet Street according to the provisions of the NPA/NUJ 1965 Memorandum (see paragraph 581). A major problem for the Branches concerns finance. Subscription collection has become more difficult with the devolution of responsibility to chapels although the extension of check-off

arrangements is regarded as a counterweight to this problem. The London branches are supervised by the Inner London Area Council, whose officers are elected from among the branches' delegates.

378. Some 73% of the members of the NUJ Manchester Branch work on national newspapers. The remainder are employed in weekly newspapers in the Greater Manchester area, and in broadcasting, public relations and local government.

379. Under the new structure of the NUJ approved at its 1975 Annual Delegate Meeting, (see Appendix 9, Table 8) there is an Industrial Council for National Papers and Agencies, composed of 12 members (seven for NPA, non-federated and evening papers in London, two for news agencies, one for NPA and metropolitan papers in Scotland, and two for national and metropolitan papers outside London, in England, Wales, and Northern Ireland). The industrial councils promote and supervise negotiations and agreements for members in their sectors, with the autonomy to determine policy within the confines of the union's general policy.

IOJ

380. The IOJ rules allow for organisation by divisions or branches. The London Region of the IOJ has the largest membership, and is composed of three districts one of which covers Fleet Street. The pattern of local organisation of the IOJ is not well developed, but in 1975 membership had increased by 50% from the 1971 total to almost 2,400, with the General Secretary reporting that there were "nearly 100 chapters (the equivalent of chapels) in existence for the first time ever". In 1975 about 150 IOJ members were employed by national newspapers in London.

Inter-Union Relationships

381. Inter-union relationships within the printing industry can be discussed at a number of levels, ranging from those occurring in-house (see Chapter 8), those between union branches, those at national level to those at an international level.

IGF

382. The International Graphical Federation, established in 1949, resulted from the fusion of three established printing trade union international organisations; the Typographers, the Lithographers and, the Bookbinders. The IGF, which has three trade-groups (typography; bookbinding; and lithography, offset, photogravure and process engraving) exists to protect and further the "occupational, economic and idealistic interests of print workers". SLADE, the NGA and SOGAT are affiliated to it. The NUJ is a member of the International Federation of Journalists.

P & KTF

383. The printing trade unions established the P & KTF in 1901, with the object of co-ordinating matters of common interest to all printing unions (who were later to include the NUJ). The P & KTF had seventeen unions affiliated to it in 1945, and, as a result of amalgamation, nine affiliates in 1971 (although this included an additional union in membership, the Wallpaper Workers' Union).

384. The P & KTF was not solely a national body, but required affiliated unions "in places where two or more branches of affiliated unions are established" to instruct their branches to co-operate and form local federations. Between the individual local and national federations, regional federation of groups were constituted, each of which held an annual conference of delegates appointed by their constituent organisations.

385. Until its dissolution in April 1974 when it had six affiliates the P & KTF provided arrangements for the settlement of disputes between unions, conducted the main negotiations on wages and conditions with the NPA on behalf of the separate unions, and acted in its own right in making agreements on matters such as basic hours, holiday arrangements and apprentices' wages.* Any agreement reached as a result of joint negotiations which were conducted by the P & KTF Executive (composed of the affiliated unions' general secretaries) had to be submitted by each union to its members for approval, and the agreements themselves were held by the individual unions with the employers' associations. The unions retained their right to negotiate independently, and on occasions submitted their own special claims in addition to the general P & KTF claim.

386. While the P & KTF by rule could not interfere in the internal arrangements, rules or customs of any union, it did maintain inter-union disputes machinery. Any matter in dispute was first referred to a conference of the contending unions, and then, failing settlement, to the executive of the P & KTF. Should there still not be settlement an arbitration board was convened, to which each of the parties appointed two members selected from a panel composed of the delegates to the P & KTF Administrative Council for that year, together with a chairman appointed by the Executive. Such an arbitration board had to be convened within 14 days of the parties failing to agree and the decision of the board was binding on all parties.

387. The P & KTF began to weaken in the late 1960's following a major period of union amalgamation during which the NGA and SOGAT had been formed. In both 1968 and 1972 motions proposing the winding up of the P & KTF were only narrowly defeated at its annual conference, and following the 1972 conference, SOGAT severed its connection with the Federation. Efforts were made to restructure the organisation, and proposals drawn up to make it solely a co-ordinating body or bureau, but these proposals fell in the absence of both SOGAT and NATSOPA's agreement to participate.

TUC PIC

388. In 1974 the TUC Printing Industries Committee (PIC) was established and is in many ways the successor to the P & KTF. It is a forum for information exchange between unions on claims and settlements and its activities encompass health and safety, the work of industry training boards, and monitoring developments affecting printing, publishing, paper and paper products manufacture. The PIC includes the general secretaries of NATSOPA, SOGAT, NGA, NUJ and SLADE, together with representatives from the EETPU, AUEW and Wallpaper Workers' Union. (Whilst the AUEW and EETPU were not members of the P & KTF, representatives did attend P & KTF conferences and received its minutes and working papers).

* The NUJ was not party to these agreements.

389. Whilst the PIC, which is serviced by TUC staff, is still relatively young, it has not developed local committees as was the case with the P & KTF. The six regional groups and 100 local branches of the P & KTF were themselves instrumental in the settlement of disputes both between unions and employers and between unions themselves. Both NATSOPA's and SOGAT's disillusionment with the P & KTF was in part associated with the belief that it was a hindrance in the formation of one union for printing workers. A number of unions and their branches, while not wishing to re-establish the P & KTF, have expressed a desire to form a liaison body at local level to develop common policy. At the 1974 Annual Conference of the London Region of the NGA the Regional Council were urged "to re-establish the links, previously embodied by the (London) P & KTF ... and (to) contact the London Branches of the various printing unions with the intention of establishing a common policy towards a similar organisation".

Other Links

390. While at present no such formal links have been established, considerable informal contact takes place. When NPA agreements are subject to review and renegotiation it is generally the case that national or branch officers of the various unions meet together to consider a common policy. Each union reserves the right to withdraw from any joint submission and to negotiate with the NPA separately.

391. The amount of contact and the relationships between unions have improved considerably since 1975 in the London area. This has largely been stimulated by the introduction of new technology and other proposed changes in the national newspaper industry. It has been noted earlier (paragraph 363) that closer working and a possible new structure may evolve from discussions between the NGA's London Region and the two London-based craft branches of SOGAT.

392. The AUEW and EETPU have a joint-branches' sub-committee which meets bi-monthly to develop common policy on NPA matters. Arrangements for joint co-operation between unions tend generally, however to be *ad-hoc* and are activated by particular circumstances. These may be over matters of demarcation, transfers or upgrading of membership (eg between the NGA and NATSOPA), or organisational questions. Such arrangements do not occur exclusively between the production unions. The NUJ, for example, and the Art, Technical, Administrative, Executive and Sales (ATAES) Branch of SOGAT formed a committee in 1976 to organise a joint recruiting campaign in publishing houses among both journalists and office staff in the London area.

Part D: Industrial Relations Procedures and Practices

CHAPTER 10: THE NEGOTIATION OF PAY AND CONDITIONS

393. Pay and conditions of employment within the industry are governed by agreements of four broad kinds:
   (a) national agreements between the NPA and the unions, resulting in industry-wide basic rates and "extras"* which are applied in each office and form the basis for other components of earnings;
   (b) company/union agreements negotiated at house level and applying to all or most employees within the house;
   (c) agreements between houses and individual chapels;
   (d) agreements between houses and groups of chapels.

National Bargaining

Past Joint Institutions

394. None of the attempts that have been made in the past to establish formal comprehensive negotiating machinery at national level have survived the pressure of controversy. Two such attempts have been made since the 1962 Royal Commission on the Press but both failed essentially for the same reason: the disparities between the objectives of the parties to the machinery allied to their tradition of independent action made positive action impossible.

395. The first attempt resulted in the Joint Board for the National Newspaper Industry established in 1964 under the independent chairmanship of Lord Devlin. It sprang from a recommendation of the 1962 Royal Commission. In making its proposal the Royal Commission was particularly concerned about the failure of efforts to improve efficiency. In 1960 the NPA and unions made a joint declaration of co-operation in the introduction of improved working arrangements. Any savings were to be applied to the mutual benefit of employers and employees; the introduction of new techniques was to be facilitated whilst individuals were to be protected; disputes procedures were to be strictly followed. The Royal Commission two years later could not see any significant improvement as a result of the agreement and recommended that new consultative and negotiating machinery should be set up to revise and agree manning standards, reduce casual working, standardise "extras" and ratify house agreements. It also proposed that a joint standing body of employers and unions should oversee planning and development in the industry with the aim of promoting technical development, manpower planning and training requirements, and devising redundancy and pension schemes.

---

* Extras, while calculated from industry basic rates, are only paid when the particular task is performed or when the circumstances (eg bank holidays) arise.

396. The Joint Board began ambitiously in widely defining the scope of the questions with which it intended to concern itself. At an early stage the Board decided that it needed an agreed factual background upon which to base its negotiations, and commissioned a survey by the Economist Intelligence Unit (see Appendix 17(*a*)). It established three committees to handle the different aspects of the survey covering capital structure, production and managerial efficiency, and social benefits. Once the major investigating aspects of the Board's work were completed (in 1966), however, difficulties in taking key decisions, especially concerning the distribution of productivity savings, became apparent. Enthusiasm waned and the Board withered.

397. The second brief attempt came in 1970 when following a dispute with SOGAT and as part of the 1970 wages agreement, a National Newspaper Steering Group (without an independent Chairman) was established. Its main aims were to work towards a more equitable wages structure, make more effective use of human and technical resources, improve two-way communication, provide adequate training and re-training, and introduce "workable and written procedures for all employees embracing employment conditions, redundancy, claims and disputes". The objectives of the Steering Group were in many ways a revival of those of the Joint Board. Again, however, it proved impossible jointly to agree major changes, especially since the difficulties of the *Daily Sketch* and the growing unemployment in the industry prevented the unions from making agreements on manning reductions. Neither the Joint Board nor the Steering Group effected any major changes in the structure of the industry basic rates.

The Present Position

398. Currently, then, the major settlements in the national newspaper industry on basic wages and conditions are achieved in the absence of any formal joint negotiating machinery. Revisions of basic rates may be negotiated between the NPA and the unions acting either separately, jointly, or some independently and some together. In recent years the unions have acted collectively except in 1974 when the NGA and the EETPU each negotiated separately with the NPA, as did the AUEW in 1975 (see Appendix 10, Table 1)*. The reasons why the unions have not always adopted a joint approach have included differences in national union policy over pay restraint, differing views on the proportioning of increases between the lower-paid and the higher-paid, the non-TUC affiliation of one union†, different objectives between unions and branches, and disagreement over differentials between the unions.

399. Until its dissolution in 1974, the P & KTF (see Chapter 9) acted for those printing unions wishing to negotiate with the NPA collectively, co-ordinating each individual union's claims prior to presenting the collective claim on their behalf. Each union, as is the case today, retained its autonomy and the right of individual approach to the NPA. The valuable consultative function and the co-ordinating role of the P & KTF led the craft unions in particular to seek to

---

* In 1972 the NATSOPA clerical workers also negotiated separately from the NATSOPA production workers and other unions. A consultative body of clerical workers representatives was elected to advise and accompany the union's negotiators. This arrangement was not maintained in subsequent negotiations.

† ie the NGA which, contrary to TUC policy, registered as a trade union under the Industrial Relations Act 1971 and was required to disaffiliate from the TUC as a result. The NGA reaffiliated at the end of 1975.

establish a co-ordinating bureau to replace the P & KTF in 1973. Consultation and co-ordination between printing unions on national newspaper wage claims, while partly the province of the TUC PIC, is largely carried out at informal meetings convened by the chairman of the PIC between national and local area officers of the various unions.

400. Each union or branch formulates its individual claims on a wide range of matters, and the co-ordinating meetings act as a forum in which the possibilities of adopting a common negotiating stance are explored. Such a stance is usually agreed. Practice varies between unions with regard to the composition of their negotiating teams, which may comprise entirely full-time officers or a mixture of full-time officers and lay officials (see Chapter 9). National officers of the trade unions generally conduct the principal wage negotiations with the NPA, while branch representatives become involved at a later stage in determining subsidiary items and "domestic" issues (see paragraph 405).

401. Before 1955 maintenance employees (members of the AUEW and EETPU) had their rates of pay adjusted in accordance with the general settlement made by the print unions. Following a stoppage by them in 1955 over the differential between their rates and those for similar workers in other industries they were invited to join negotiations in the same way as federated unions who individually decided whether to take part in a collective approach to the NPA. The EETPU and AUEW were never affiliated to the P & KTF, which would only accept into membership unions whose predominant membership strength was in the printing industry.

402. Most basic wage agreements made at national level are held between the NPA and each individual union. Moreover, there is a separate agreement for many of the main occupational categories. There are some thirty national agreements of this type applying to stereotypers, readers, machine and process workers, publishing room employees etc, and about 70 different basic rates. Since 1974 agreements have been annual but before then they were of two or three years' duration.

403. The form of settlements has also changed. Before 1970 revisions in the NPA agreements tended to include a percentage increase in basic rates and the payment of weekly cost of living bonuses based on movements of the retail price index beyond an agreed point during the currency of the agreement. Such agreements usually incorporated previously accrued cost-of-living bonuses into basic rates.

404. These agreements did not apply to journalists, publicity artists, and circulation representatives. Each of these groups is covered by separate national agreements with the NPA*. The same was true for maintenance workers (AUEW and EETPU) until 1970, when they joined with the other printing unions in collective negotiations for the first time since 1960.

National "Domestic" Matters

405. While all the principal substantive items are dealt with during the collective national negotiations matters of interpretation, subsidiary points, and "domestic issues" are dealt with by branch representatives from each union

---

* Negotiations for these groups are conducted for the NPA by the Industrial Relations Executive, although there may also be representatives present, dependent on the work group, from the Editorial Committee or Circulation Executive.

separately following conclusion of the main negotiations. Domestic issues in this context refer to matters which primarily concern a single union, rather than to matters involving individual houses. The NPA's policy is not to make concessions on such domestic claims if they in any way repercuss on other groups. Domestic issues most commonly arise in relation to the RIRMA Branch of NATSOPA (for most of its occupational groups), the London Central Branch of SOGAT (eg for tobymen and evening newspaper outside commission staffs) and from SLADE (particularly in regard to the London/Manchester differential for process workers).

National Bargaining Strategy

406. Since 1970 the NPA has generally limited its negotiating role to revisions to wage rates, hours of work, premium payments for overtime, night work, sixth shift work, Saturday/Sunday working, bank holiday working, periods of notice and holidays. Pensions and sick pay arrangements have been regarded as matters for negotiation at house level, and NPA policy on basic rates has been largely one of not allowing disturbance in the relativities within the national wage structure, and not conceding to any union better terms than those offered to all costs and to secure from the trade unions commitments both to fund any pay improvements by savings from manning reductions and to limit or prevent a further stage of negotiation at house level.

407. The NPA's negotiating strategy is circumscribed by the financial circumstances and ability to pay of each house. The tendency is thus for the NPA to react to issues and claims, and to be governed in its decisions on them by the circumstances of its less financially successful members, or what has been termed "the lowest common denominator approach."

408. The trade unions have found it difficult on occasions to present a collective claim to the NPA. The desire of the NGA to negotiate percentage increases to maintain existing differential relationships* has sometimes contrasted with the non-craft unions' policy to seek flat-rate increases, both to improve the position of their own lower-paid members† and to prevent the widening of money differentials with craft workers. Similarly, the AUEW negotiated separately in 1973 because it wanted to pursue a claim for a reduction in the working week, whereas SOGAT and NATSOPA wished to concentrate attention on the lower-paid.‡

---

* The merger of some of the craft unions from 1964 onwards to form the NGA led to a growing concern within the new union that the incorporation of cost of living bonuses into industry basic rates between 1960 and 1970 had progressively reduced their craft differentials, particularly in what one NGA officer has referred to as "the sensitive areas—the machine areas and the readers' department". There was also a growing desire to deal with the widening differentials that were developing between NGA members employed in the different NPA offices. At the 1974 Annual Conference of the NGA London Region it was the view of one delegate for example that "there is a limited amount of money to be shared out by NPA offices and it should be shared out to the best possible advantage of the lower-paid".

† While "second tier" negotiations at house level for journalists have been proscribed from time to time by national agreements (eg in January 1971: see Chapter 16), the nature of such negotiations for production workers differs considerably, principally because the latter take the form of ongoing task or productivity bargaining.

‡ During the 1974 industry negotiations NATSOPA, in an information circular to its members on the progress of discussions with the NPA stated that "despite a lot of ill-informed talk about the high level of wages paid to print workers in the national newspapers, there are 65·55 per cent of our people who are earning less than £42 per week". (Average weekly earnings in manufacturing industries in April 1974 were £43·60.)

409. The limitations on the NPA's own manoeuvrability, together with the difficulties on the trade union side of developing a common approach to negotiations combine to ensure that any union wishing to engage in separate negotiations has their outcome largely predetermined by the settlement achieved by other negotiating groups. The process thus gives added momentum to the pursuance of the different and at times conflicting objectives of each union in house level bargaining.

General Company/Union Bargaining

410. Only two newspaper houses within our terms of reference are outside the NPA and are formally not covered by NPA/union agreements. The *Morning Star* has never been in membership but for many years has been sent copies of the settlement and has, where appropriate, applied them.

411. Since its departure from the NPA in 1974, the MGN has negotiated its own "MGN basic" rates. This is the only current example in Fleet Street of comprehensive house level bargaining for production workers and is worth closer examination if only for that reason. Several interesting features of the MGN experience should be noted. First, the MGN 1974 general agreement was negotiated with SOGAT, NATSOPA, SLADE, AUEW and EETPU national and other officers as a collective body, and, in all its main substantive features, separately with the NGA. Second, the agreement differed substantially from the NPA agreement on both length and content. It was to last for 18 months, and to provide (staggered) pay increases of $17\frac{1}{2}\%$. Third, the pay improvements were tied to a non-automatic replacement (NAR) clause. The latter was intended to establish "minimum maning levels in all departments in which (the signatory unions') members are involved." The agreements were drafted to ensure that there would be no additional chapel entitlement to a share of any savings and that the acceptance of the policy would not be tied to the life of the agreement.

412. The 1974 negotiations in theory enabled MGN to take a much tighter hold on chapel bargaining: the NAR clauses theoretically put the decision on whether or not to refill vacancies permanently back into the hands of management and no further payment was called for to lower manning requirements. MGN's immediate policy was to replace men who retired or otherwise left with casuals or not to replace them at all. However, the process of manpower reduction on this basis proved slow and between October 1974 and the beginning of 1976 negotiations have taken place with chapels so that the company could achieve a meaningful return from the policy in the shortest possible time and so that the chapels, for their part, could re-establish agreed manning levels departure from which would require further negotiation with them.

Bargaining between Managements and Chapels

413. At NPA level joint approaches from unions for agreement revisions are common: at house level joint approaches of any kind, whether from unions or chapels within individual unions, are comparatively rare. This is partly the result of the concentration of national bargaining on areas (the increase in the cost of living, the situation of the industry etc.) in which all the unions have a common experience, and the productivity-orientated bargaining of chapels, in which the situation of each chapel is argued to differ. But it is also due to the jealousy

with which each chapel maintains its own bargaining rights. The number of chapels with which management may be required to negotiate may range from 20 or more in single-title houses to 50 or more in dual and multi-title houses, and the scope of bargaining units varies widely (see Chapter 8).

414. The bargaining process is characterised by the absence of formal procedures and the wide range of matters which are negotiable. While agreements may contain a review clause which is activated at six-monthly or annual intervals, negotiations are initiated by management or chapels at any time as a result of changing circumstances at the work place. Before the introduction of comprehensive agreements (see Chapter 5) most production and ancillary staffs were paid at the appropriate industry (NPA) basic rates supplemented by a wide range of additional payments depending on the changing workloads and circumstances applying to the chapel at any point in time. These payments were negotiated at departmental level between chapel officials and overseers on an *ad hoc* and continuous basis.

415. The purpose of comprehensive agreements and their deficiencies in the eyes of managements have already been described. From a bargaining point of view the most difficult task of management is to reconcile the maintenance of differentials with productivity bargaining with individual chapels. In areas where chapels regard the maintenance of such formal or informal pay relationships as a priority, any savings accruing to managements as a result of a negotiation of staffing levels or changes in working practices with one chapel can be largely lost should the related chapel claim restoration of the previous differential relationship without commensurate concessions on its own part. Such balancing acts in the bargaining process are further complicated in that they may disadvantage those chapels which have high productivity levels and little or no "fat" to bargain away.

416. Day-to-day bargaining takes place at departmental level between overseers and chapel officers over claims for either extra payment in the form of overtime hours or extra manning (ie casual labour) as a result of abnormal working circumstances such as the cleaning of oil patches on the machine room floor, the production of special editions, special maintenance or modifications made to existing equipment and plant, emergency distribution arrangements, physical conditions of working, and any extra work outside the norm and not specified in the agreement.

Volume and Pattern of Chapel Bargaining

417. The pattern of bargaining varies both within and between houses. The implementation of industry-wide wage awards negotiated at NPA level are not the subject of negotiation at house level. Single title houses, with one exception, review every chapel agreement on an *ad hoc* basis, matters being raised by either the chapel or the management at any time. In one single title house all agreements are subject to regular joint annual review. In multi-title houses the pattern of review of agreements is more diverse. Most agreements are reviewed as necessary and about a third are regularly reviewed annually (see Appendix 10, Table 2).

418. The fact that chapel agreements may be subject to regular annual (or more frequent) review does not mean that changes necessarily are made if the circumstances do not warrant it. Nor does it seem to be the case that within each occupational group the volume of day-to-day bargaining is great. During our in-house interviews we sought from overseers, managers and chapel representatives information about local negotiations in which they had been involved in the last few years. The responses were varied. Apart from comprehensive agreement revisions some chapel representatives and management said that no day-to-day bargaining took place and that overtime was extremely rare. In other cases, it was said that some small issue, not necessarily requiring extra payment, arose every week and, occasionally, every day. Overall, both chapel and management representatives gave the impression that day-to-day negotiations are not especially frequent, affect relatively few employees, and do not result in any substantial budgetary on-cost. Indeed, any negotiation which did potentially involve such on-cost would rapidly be escalated up the management hierarchy.

419. We also asked houses to complete for 1973, 1974 and 1975 a Table showing the number and type of agreements reached with each chapel. The returns that houses have been able to make together with the comments of those concerned tend to confirm the comments in paragraph 418. There also seems to be no special significance in the timing of the reviews of comprehensive agreements as a whole. This does not mean that a review of one agreement will not stimulate a review of other agreements related formally or informally to it. Such knock-on agreements are fairly common (for example, in composing or machine rooms) but a complete cycle of agreements either does not occur or takes so long to work itself out that it is not obvious to participants. In some houses managements recognise that agreements are more difficult to reach with certain chapels* but in no case was there a strategy to settle with some chapels before others; indeed it would be difficult to develop such a strategy given the rather haphazard way in which comprehensive agreements were originally negotiated.

Bargaining between Houses and Groups of Chapels

420. There is relatively little joint bargaining between houses and groups of chapels. We have already touched upon the limited negotiating functions of the FHCs (see Chapter 8), the background to the Joint Pressroom Agreement at MGN, the special arrangements in the *Sun* machine room, and the close links between the PMB chapels of SOGAT and the SLADE process chapels. The existence of NGA imperial chapels, SOGAT liaison groups and combined chapels, NATSOPA federations, and the like enable some bargaining co-ordination, albeit loose and informal, to take place and managements do meet these collective groups of chapels from time to time to discuss matters of common interest. It has not been the practice, however, for chapels within most of these groups to present joint claims on pay.

Bargaining Strategies

421. Management bargaining strategies are only operable within the restraints of the bargaining situation. In most houses there is no written, defined policy on

---

* This was exemplified in a debate at the 1974 Annual Conference of the NGA London Region on wages when one machine managers' chapel FOC stated that "Everyone has sympathy with chapels which are being underpaid but when it comes to the crossroads we look after our own chapel. In the machine room we would defend the $12\frac{1}{2}$ per cent differential (over NATSOPA machine assistants) to the death—make no mistake about that".

pay and manpower policy in general. Industrial relations management regard a principal constraint in the negotiation of agreements to be the maintenance of acceptable differentials. All houses attempt to pursue a policy of giving new money to production workers only in exchange for definite economies. It is and has been for some years the view of managements that pay structure reform is necessary and that a pre-requisite for this is the reform of bargaining practices. Some managements, either formally or informally, have as their long-term objective the development and encouragement of plant bargaining, by minimising the amount of wage bargaining at chapel level and maximising that at house level. Although MGN has negotiated joint union house agreements (see paragraph 411), bargaining with individual chapels followed this, and the normal Fleet Street pattern of general, followed by chapel, agreements has been maintained.

422. The vast majority of chapels, as we have already noted, adhere firmly to their independent bargaining rights*. Any collective bargaining strategy between chapels within houses is very loose and worked out within the framework of the federations, liaison groups and imperial chapels described earlier. Individual chapels rarely have any strategy extending beyond the next negotiation. Only occasionally during our study did it appear that chapel representatives had considered the future of the bargaining system, and only a handful had seen or had knowledge of any of the previous inquiries whose reports and recommendations had touched upon this area (see Chapter 17 and Appendix 17(a)). We did nevertheless seek the views of FOCs on the question of extending house level bargaining. A majority favoured such an extension though only a minority thought it a practical possibility in current circumstances. We shall return to this point in Chapter 19.

423. The question of differentials has been touched on in Chapter 5. Though chapel representatives may have fairly firm ideas of the relationship their members' pay should bear to the pay of employees in other chapels, inter-chapel comparisons in support of claims are not made (except where a definite relationship has by agreement or custom and practice evolved) and management will not generally accept any such comparisons. It is difficult to judge how far such comparisons, whilst not figuring formally in claims, influence chapels in fixing the level of claims when genuine productivity changes are mooted, or influence them in attempting to devise other grounds for making a claim. Convincing evidence that chapels have a good knowledge of the level of pay and other terms and conditions of employment in other departments has not been forthcoming (see Chapter 13): there is certainly no formal mechanism through which information on pay levels may be transmitted within individual houses.

Influence of Union Branches and NPA on In-House Bargaining

424. While all negotiations other than those at industry level with the NPA, originate at chapel level (apart from within the *Morning Star* and, since 1974, MGN) the negotiation of agreements at this level is closely monitored by trade union branches and regions (see Chapter 8). There are two broad areas of chapel bargaining, one concerned with issues specific to the workplace, and the other involving the pursuance of union policies determined at either local or national levels.

---

* Expressed usually as a desire not to be swamped or outvoted by other groups, or as one FOC put it "where people can control their own destiny it is democracy at its best".

425. While comprehensive agreements had been present in one form or another in some houses for some years before 1968, the impetus for their now widespread application was the then Government's incomes policy, and its objective of securing improved productivity and efficiency in return for wage increases above the pay norm. Comprehensive agreements provided managements with the opportunity to improve efficiency and rationalise payments (see Chapter 5). They have also provided union branches with the opportunity to pursue and achieve their policy at house level more effectively than has been the case at industry level. The bargaining objectives of chapels in the negotiation or review of comprehensive agreements are strongly influenced by branches, and not least by the employment position within each individual branch. One NATSOPA machine chapel, for example, during negotiations on the introduction of new equipment and a management initiative to reduce overall manpower requirements, set out three alternatives open to its negotiators. These were, first, acceptance of management's proposals which "would have required redundancies, be regarded to be detrimental to the interests of the chapel as a whole, and further strain the already problematical employment situation in the London Machine Branch". A second alternative of voluntary redundancies was given, which while of advantage in some respects, would have "allowed (those affected) to seek work within the Branch". The third alternative, which was adopted, involved the pursuance of a policy for a shorter working week "with the belief that technology should bear fruit for all" and at the same time obviate the need for redundancies and maintain "to an acceptable degree, the overall manpower requirements".

426. The union branch is an important medium for the exchange of information between FOCs, and for the development of policy on a wide range of issues. Having established negotiating objectives the branches monitor and control developments, vetting, and in some instances rejecting, proposed chapel agreements. Examples of recent branch policy decisions which have been effected in some offices include the nine-day fortnight or a reduced working week, narrowing of inter-office differentials, equalisation of fringe benefits (such as sick pay arrangements between houses) and the regularisation of casual workings.

427. The NPA has initiated several attempts to influence the outcome of house level claims which were likely to have repercussive effects on the industry as a whole. In 1964 a House Claims procedure was introduced and lasted for about a year, each management submitting details of the claim and chapel concerned in order that joint consideration and advice might be given by the NPA in order to deal with it. In 1972 the procedure was reinstituted, but as a result of the operation of incomes legislation at the time fell into disuse after twelve months. The present position is described in paragraph 229.

Sanctions in Negotiations

428. One of the criticisms of some managers on the bargaining practices of chapels is that they resort too quickly to the use of sanctions and, in so doing, breach agreed procedures. We discuss this more fully in Chapter 11, and put the counter-argument of the chapels. However, two points should be noted here. First, the threat of sanctions is often related to an attempt to relocate

negotiations to a higher level in the management hierarchy. Chapels are aware of the tight budgetary constraints on overseers and junior managers and sometimes feel they need to threaten action to reach a stage of meaningful negotiation. Second, quite important negotiations in Fleet Street tend to take place at the last possible moment before a necessary change is imminent. This may be due to early chapel intransigence or to management obstinacy, but whatever the reason such brinkmanship can increase the chances of industrial action if only because there is limited time in which to disentangle unforeseen problems.

CHAPTER 11: DISPUTES AND DISPUTES PROCEDURES

The Incidence of Disputes

429. The incidence of industrial disputes and industrial action is one indication among several of the way industrial relations are conducted within a firm or industry and of the climate of industrial relations. But it does not follow that a high level of disputes can necessarily be equated with "bad" industrial relations or that the absence of open dispute indicates a completely satisfactory situation. The existence of strong employer and employee organisation and of comprehensive procedures for the resolution of disputes do not, and cannot, guarantee industrial peace. The system of pay determination within a firm or industry may be such that the opportunities for dispute are many, and this may have been accepted by the parties as the necessary price for the preferred system of pay determination. Conversely, the absence of disputes may simply disguise an absence of collective organisation, inadequate collective bargaining procedures, low productivity, weak management, and/or high labour turnover and absenteeism.

430. It is worth starting with this general point in view of the emphasis placed within the industry on the disputes record and on the characteristics of disputes and the sanctions applied in relation to them. Some managements consider the incidence of disputes and of industrial action associated with them to be among their greatest problems. They complain of irresponsible and specious claims by chapels which ignore the terms of current substantive agreements and the economic situation of the companies; of the unreasonable use by chapels of a variety of sanctions which take advantage of the vulnerability of the product; of action taken unconstitutionally outside agreed disputes procedures and with little or no warning; and of the inability, or unwillingness, of union full-time officials to control the behaviour of chapels.

431. The unions, too, have expressed concern about disputes, especially given the current economic situation of newspapers. In May 1976 the TUC PIC expressed its concern about "the industry's ability to survive recurring stoppages". To ensure that disputes are dealt with through the appropriate procedures the TUC PIC has set up a disputes liaison procedure through which unions must keep each other informed about problems which may lead to industrial disputes.

The Official Figures of Stoppages

432. Appendix 11, Table 1, shows selected Department of Employment (DE) statistics for stoppages of work, days lost, and incidence rates of days lost between 1970 and 1975. The figures are of comparative value only because the notification procedures of the DE in this respect mean that not all industrial action is recorded. Nevertheless, assuming the extent of under-recording to be similar in all industries, the Table shows that in each of the six years the incidence rate of days lost per 1,000 employees in the paper, printing, and publishing industries (ie including the national newspaper industry) was lower than the average for all manufacturing industries. The incidence rate for the national newspaper industry was very considerably lower than either the all manufacturing industries' average or the average for the rest of the paper,

printing and publishing industry until 1974. In the last two years the incidence rate per 1,000 employees and the number of days lost (both direct and indirect) from each work stoppage in the national newspaper industry has exceeded that in all manufacturing industries and in the rest of the printing industry by a substantial margin. The absolute number of disputes recorded by the DE in the national newspaper industry has also risen. Too much should not be made of this, however. Appendix 11, Table 1, also, for comparative purposes, gives corresponding figures for the motor vehicle industry where the incidence rates have consistently been well above those in the national newspaper industry (though rather less so in the last two years).

Industry Statistics: The Limitation of the Figures

433. The official figures are lacking in a number of respects. They are not a complete record of stoppages in the industry nor do they take account of the fact that the sanctions available to chapels can fall short of a stoppage of work and still cause disruption and financial damage. Even the threat of industrial action may be a potent weapon against a vulnerable management. "Non-co-operation" or "go-slow" by any group directly involved in the production process can have a crucial effect on a night's run which may culminate in the disruption of normal distribution schedules. Companies can then be faced with the choice of more expensive methods of distribution (such as a road run where a train has been missed) or with a certain area losing its copies and the consequent loss in revenue, reader goodwill and advertiser confidence. Similar consequences will occur when action by a chapel results in the loss of part of a night's run. Action taken by a chapel or chapels at one point in the production process may result in the necessity to pay for overtime later in the process to maintain distribution schedules. Some managements claim that sabotage has taken place during disputes. An example given is the deliberate tearing of newsprint reels in the machine room; paper breaks are a normal occurrence and can be easily induced and managements claim it is almost impossible to prove that any are deliberate. During the dispute between Beaverbrook Newspapers and its engineers in 1975, crucial parts were removed from machines to ensure that the industrial action was effective in preventing production of the newspaper.

434. Managements thus feel that chapel members stand to lose very little in the short term by actions which are financially damaging to the newspaper companies. A meeting during work time may result in the deduction of an hour's pay from those involved, but cause very substantial loss to the company. Non-co-operation may have the same consequences and cost chapel members nothing. The cost to chapel members of a particular action may bear little relationship to its eventual consequence. The financial and competitive situations of some houses mean that resistance to a claim appears to make little short-term financial sense. A claim may appear negligible when compared to the consequences of losing a night's revenue where liquidity problems make that revenue crucial or where competition between newspapers may mean that the loss of a night's run involves the permanent loss of readers. Managements feel they have few, if any, counter-sanctions at their disposal in disputes where chapels are disrupting production. No national newspaper has lay-off agreements with any of its chapels and thus houses must go on paying chapels not involved

in an action who report for work. Protective notice is felt to be a blunt weapon because of agreed or statutory notice requirements; it also worsens relationships with chapels not directly involved in a dispute, and would involve great difficulties if it became operative. Dismissal of those involved in disputes is also felt to be impracticable and undesirable. According to some managers, full-time union officials are often of little help during disputes, being unwilling or unable to prevent unconstitutional action by chapels even where they might privately agree a claim is unjustified. Some were also said to be difficult to contact when disputes arise.

Stoppages: The Industry Record

435. Our inquiries within the industry sought to piece together a picture of industrial action and industrial disputes falling short of industrial action for 1973–1975. We asked employers to provide details of every dispute and industrial action in this period, including the subject of each dispute, the chapel(s) involved, the dates of any industrial action taken in connection with any dispute, the duration of any action, the type of action, the warning given of action, the stage of the procedure when action was taken, and the sales lost as the result of any action. We also sought information in this area from the NPA and from chapel and management representatives during our in-house studies.

436. Due to the recording procedures of houses (and often their absence) it is not possible to present a comprehensive statement for the whole period. However, from information from a number of sources, it can be said with some certainty that from mid-1974 to the end of that year there were eleven disputes leading to industrial action which either resulted in substantial numbers of lost copies or a total print loss. The corresponding figure for 1975 was fifteen, and in 1976, to the end of May, six. Appendix 11, Table 2, gives a more detailed picture of industrial action in 1975 in nine newspaper houses. There were 38 recorded industrial actions of which over 40% were stoppages of work. Nearly all the remaining actions consisted of unauthorised meetings in working hours, a sanction especially favoured by NUJ chapels, and restrictions of output. In about a fifth of the actions copies were lost (but see paragraph 433) though in some of these cases the number of such losses were relatively small. The duration of recorded industrial action in 1975 varied between a half-hour stoppage to one lasting 48 hours and from one unauthorised meeting to a series over a period of weeks. Appendix 11, Table 3, shows that over half the action taken in relation to over half the disputes leading to any action lasted for less than 24 hours, and 60% of those lasted for less than one shift.

437. In 15 of the 23 disputes for which the relevant information exists no warning was given of industrial action, according to house records, before it was actually taken. Where warnings were given they ranged from $2\frac{1}{2}$ hours to 14 days. Of course, the fact that no warning was given prior to the action does not mean that the issue over which the action took place had not been under active discussion for some time. Appendix 11, Table 3, also shows the time elapsing between when the issue was first raised as a matter requiring discussion and resolution and when industrial action was taken. In 11 of the 25 disputes

(ie 44%) for which this information was provided, action was taken 24 hours or less after management was aware that the issue had been raised. Caution has, however, to be exercised in drawing conclusions from this. A number of FOCs told us that it was not unusual for matters to be raised with overseers to no effect until some pressure was exerted by the chapel. This could mean that overseers may not register that an issue has been raised until it is clear that industrial action or the threat of it is imminent.

438. Only two disputes involving industrial action reached the national procedure before the action began. In several cases the action began before the procedure had progressed beyond the overseer level (see paragraph 450) though usually even where the issue had been raised only 24 hours before the action began, the procedure had progressed to its final stages within the house.

Disputes not Involving Industrial Action

439. The figures of industrial action are, for reasons already stated, only the most visible sign of disputes within houses. Only a few houses, however, were able to provide any details of disputes other than those leading to stoppages and even some of these were incomplete in some respects. Nevertheless, the information is adequate to illustrate the general picture. In one house, for example, there were an average of two disputes per chapel during 1975 (with the number varying from none to 15 per chapel). 14% of all disputes led to some form of industrial action, and 4% to a loss of copies. The corresponding combined figures for those houses for which information is available are one, 14% and 5%.

440. Several obvious points should be made about the pattern of disputes that emerges from the figures. First, the bargaining system within houses provides frequent opportunities for disputes to arise. Independent bargaining on pay, manning and other terms and conditions of employment takes place with some 360 chapels in Fleet Street. Moreover, the system of task bargaining essentially persists. Chapels consider new work, different methods or schedules for dealing with the existing workload, or adverse physical working conditions to be legitimate reasons to open negotiations with management for payment related to the "new" task which they have been asked to undertake, and which they do not consider to be covered by the payments agreed in current comprehensive or other agreements. For example, chapels have claimed extra payment for the cleaning tasks within their department which they do not feel are covered in agreements. One house claimed that just such a demand, coupled with a refusal to start work until it was conceded, cost the company £20,000 in lost production. Task bargaining thus provides one area where disputes can arise, but there are others. The annual review of a comprehensive agreement may result in a failure to agree, or there may be in-house difficulties over the implementation of a national agreement. The overwhelming majority of disputes and of stoppages and other industrial action involve individual managements and individual chapels: rarely are chapels or unions jointly involved directly in disputes.

441. Second, many of the "disputes" that arise are not serious matters and are often settled quickly and amicably. This may be one reason for the dis-

crepancy we found between the information provided by chapels which suggested that a high proportion of chapels had been involved in no disputes in recent years and the figures given to us by some employers: chapels simply do not register as "disputes" issues which are raised in the normal course of negotiation and over which there may be some disagreement and friction, if a settlement is eventually reached without too much trouble. Senior industrial relations managers are at the apex of the in-house procedures and feel the brunt of all serious disputes that occur within the house.

National Disputes Procedures

442. The NPA has agreed disputes procedures with all the unions with which it has substantive agreements. National disputes procedures in the national newspaper industry are embodied, for the most part, in a series of agreements made with the printing trade unions during 1947, 1948 and 1949. These agreements combined substantive and procedural clauses. Few, if any, amendments seem to have been made to them. The mergers among print unions since 1947 have led, in many cases, to a situation where there are variations in the current disputes arrangements applying to different sections of the same union, though these variations seem to have little practical effect.

443. The fourteen procedures themselves are similar in form in many respects (see Appendix 11, Table 4). All allow either the employers or the unions to refer a matter in dispute to a joint committee consisting of three nominees of the NPA and three nominees of the union concerned (or, occasionally, five nominees from each side). The function of the committee is to arbitrate* on the dispute concerned. In one case, the procedure applying to London Stereotypers, there are no further stages. The most common second and final stage is for the committee to appoint a "referee" to arbitrate on points upon which it has failed to agree. In some cases, there is provision for the committee to ask an outside body (then the Ministry of Labour) to appoint an independent arbitrator if it cannot agree on one and in all cases the decision of such an arbitrator is final. One agreement, covering London compositors, has a second stage consisting of an appeal committee of three; a mutually-acceptable independent chairman and a representative each from the NPA and the union.

444. The agreements covering the London Branches of NATSOPA allow for a second stage of a conciliation committee made up of equal numbers from each side. This can be by-passed (by mutual agreement) and the issue may be referred to the NPA Council and the NATSOPA National Executive (the third stage). There is then a final arbitration stage.

445. Disputes procedures applying to Manchester normally allow for referral of a dispute to a committee consisting of the NPA Manchester Managers' Committee and six nominees of the union concerned. Failure to agree by such a committee is followed by a referral to the NPA Council or its nominees and the Executive Committee of the union concerned. Some Manchester agreements also allow for independent arbitration.

446. All the national agreements are drafted so that disputes arising in relation to house agreements can be dealt with through the national procedures

---

* The agreement between the NPA and the old LTS specifically calls its five-a-side committee a "Committee of Arbitration".

after having progressed through any domestic procedures. All the national procedures contain clauses which preclude hostile action by either side until the procedure is exhausted. Only one specifies time limits of any kind in relation to the procedure*.

447. Following its withdrawal from the NPA, MGN was technically no longer party to the agreements made between the NPA and the unions concerned. In common with other houses MGN's domestic disputes procedures fed into the NPA procedure. The company submitted a proposed new disputes procedure to the unions late in 1974. This outlined five internal stages at the apex of which was a meeting between the managing director and the manpower director for MGN and a national officer and the branch secretary of the union(s) concerned. The entire procedure was to take no longer than three weeks with not more than seven days between the stages. Once the in-house procedure had been exhausted the proposal was for the dispute to go to conciliation and, if necessary, arbitration by the (then) DE conciliation and arbitration services. The draft procedure also contained a "no hostile action" clause.

Domestic Disputes Procedures

448. Most of the national newspaper houses have written disputes clauses in their agreements with most or all chapels. The clauses vary from a simple "no hostile action for 72 hours in the event of disagreement" to more sophisticated staged procedures. In some cases, an individual grievance procedure exists in harness with the disputes procedure. If the company has no written agreement on the procedure for dealing with disputes with a chapel it has the "safety net" of the NPA disputes procedures. In practice all domestic disputes procedures can feed into the NPA procedures whether or not this if formally agreed in-house. Some domestic procedures provide for the issue to go to the NPA procedures if it remains unresolved after a specific period of time (eg seven days).

449. Even where there are no written procedures, custom and practice has tended to evolve a commonly accepted way of dealing with disputes; it became clear during our inquiries that the procedure was often the same whether written or unwritten, and that the important factor in deciding how a dispute was handled was the gravity with which the situation was viewed by chapel and management. This will be discussed in more detail in the next section.

450. The written disputes procedures normally require a dispute or grievance to be dealt with first by the appropriate overseer or head of department and then, if unresolved, to be progressed through the management hierarchy, which varies in complexity. Most procedures provide for the matter to be dealt with at board level if necessary, and allow for the involvement of full-time union officials from an early stage, if required. All written domestic disputes procedures contain clauses stating that there shall be no hostile action by either side until the procedure is exhausted.

---

* ie The procedure relating to the London Branches of NATSOPA states that "there shall be no hostile action by either side during the fourteen days following the breakdown . . ." of the NPA Council/NATSOPA national executive stage of the procedure.

The Working of the Procedures

451. The patchwork of written and unwritten disputes procedures is not really reflected in the practical working of them. In houses where written and unwritten procedures exist side-by-side there is little or no practical difference between the way disputes concerning chapels in either category are dealt with. Similarly, it is possible to detect common elements in the way disputes are dealt with in all houses.

452. The typical procedure outlined in paragraph 450 is followed in most houses where a dispute concerns a minor issue with little prospect of industrial action and where no imminent action is threatened by the chapel. Issues where industrial action is threatened, or in fact takes place with little warning, lead to a by-passing of the early stages of the procedures and the rapid involvement of management at board level and union full-time officials.

453. We found a common perception among managements and some FOCs that it is chapel use of industrial action, or the threat of it, which determine the rapidity and the level of management with which a dispute is dealt. Few of the FOCs we interviewed during our inquiries could remember taking industrial action in pursuit of a claim or grievance in the past two years. This is broadly consistent with the figures reproduced in Appendix 11 especially where action leading to a loss of production is concerned. Those FOCs who could remember taking or threatening action felt that such behaviour was necessary to elicit a response from managers especially when they were not present during the night production shift and when they "hid behind the procedure" in order to postpone giving an answer to a claim. Managements tend to maintain that there is nothing wrong with the procedures, only the extent to which chapels adhere to them. Chapels, on the other hand, cite cases where responses to claims have been delayed for months.

454. Some FOCs are also impatient with procedures which, they feel, do not reflect the realities of power within the house management structure. If an overseer, or even a labour relations executive, is not empowered to concede a money claim FOCs are reluctant to negotiate with him, at least for any length of time. FOCs who have in the past negotiated on quite minor issues direct with the managing director and who have gained concessions, are conditioned to want to push through the procedure to talk to the managing director again. Those houses operating an "open door" policy may manage to avert industrial action designed to involve top management in disputes, but in the long-run they fuel FOCs' impatience with the lower echelons of management, who are seen as only empowered to say "no", and increase the burden at senior management level.

455. Most disputes are resolved before going into the formal NPA machinery. This is not to say that there is not NPA involvement in many house disputes*. Where a dispute has reached an impasse at house level, managements will often ask NPA staff to arrange meetings involving union full-time officers if such officers have not already been involved. Managements do tend to attempt to involve union officials in house disputes which appear unresolvable, sometimes to the annoyance of the chapels concerned. Most FOCs we spoke to regarded

---

* In fact, where industrial action is taken which causes substantial numbers of copies to be lost the NPA is almost certain to be notified of the dispute.

the intervention of branch, regional or national officials into a house dispute as a last resort, and felt that chapels were capable of resolving the majority of issues in-house. Managements complained of the unavailability of full-time officers at crucial moments during disputes and of their inability to control chapels. While FOCs we spoke to appeared unwilling to involve full-time officers, none felt that they would ever attempt to persuade their chapel to disobey a direct branch or union directive.

456. There is, then, an informal bridging stage between domestic and NPA disputes involving NPA officials using their good offices in attempting to settle a dispute. While FOCs accepted this conciliation function there was a reluctance to allow disputes to go into the formal NPA procedure. This appeared to stem from the feeling that chapel affairs should be settled in-house and that the NPA procedures are too prolonged. Some management representatives also had reservations about the joint arbitration provisions in the procedures, believing that they had led in the past to unacceptable compromises on unjustified claims. Few disputes involving production chapels seem to go into the formal stages of the NPA procedure. The NUJ appears to be more willing to use the procedure, especially for disputes concerning individuals. Of the ten cases on which NPA/Union disputes committees made findings between September 1973 and June 1975, eight involved the NUJ and the other two involved the AUEW and NATSOPA. This is by no means a complete picture of the NPA disputes activities. NPA staff estimate that they are involved in informal "good offices" meetings twice a month on average, and feel they have a fair success rate.

CHAPTER 12: WORK ORGANISATION AND OTHER PROCEDURES

Work Allocation

457. Chapter 8 indicated that the role of the production chapels and their officials extends considerably beyond the negotiation of terms and conditions of employment. The extent to which the chapels in these areas organise working arrangements and are responsible for man-management is such that these functions are virtually sub-contracted by management to chapels. An important part of the function of chapels is to maintain holiday rotas in accordance with the appropriate manning agreements, shift rotas, and, where necessary, overtime rotas. Few managers said during our inquiries that they wanted chapel responsibilities curtailed in these areas. The introduction of comprehensive agreements gave considerable impetus to the present arrangements. Many comprehensive agreements contain clauses on the allocation of work. One publishing agreement, for example, states that "nightly duties shall be allocated by the chapel and approved by the Publisher". With the exception of some composing departments, the chapels in most production areas allocate work through their officials. Departmental heads are generally content to keep a watching brief unless the work allocation impairs the efficiency of the department. In composing rooms, some attempt is made to keep the responsibility for work allocation with the departmental head. One agreement, for example, maintains that "the placing of staff shall be at the discretion of the Head Reader and the chapel shall undertake to provide full flexibility of working". Practice varies between offices on the strict adherence to such agreements, but it is common for head printers* to allocate work during edition shifts, and to be more closely involved in rota preparation with FOCs than is the case in other production areas.

458. An integral part of chapel work allocation in some departments is the operation and organisation of the blow system (see Chapter 5, paragraphs 175, et seq). The organisation of the system is in practice a chapel responsibility, allowing continuous working to take place throughout the shift.

459. In editorial and clerical departments work allocation is primarily the responsibility of departmental heads. Rota working arrangements in some clerical areas may nevertheless be a chapel responsibility. Such areas tend to be those in which employees work shifts and in which the work content is not always of a strictly clerical nature, such as telephone reporting, cashiers, syndication and classified advertising.

Recruitment

460. The operation of recruitment procedures, particularly those in production areas, is one of the clearest examples of the subcontracting relationship between managements and chapels. Recruitment of casual staff takes place on a day-to-day basis in the production areas, particularly in the machine and publishing

---

* In some offices head printers were strongly of the opinion that the authority to allocate "the best man to the most suitable job" should be restored to them. They felt that the present system reduced job satisfaction and resulted in every man in the composing room being reduced to working at the speed of the slowest man.

rooms, and, to a lesser extent, in the foundry. The system, as Chapter 4 indicates, is organised and administered by chapel officials and union branches in accordance with the manning requirements of the chapel agreements and the particular circumstances (pagination, sickness, holidays etc) applying in the offices at any point in time.

461. The practice for filling vacancies for permanent or regular staff in production areas varies between unions. In NATSOPA's case, vacancies are notified to and filled by the appropriate branch calls office, with a regular casual generally being offered the position on the basis of seniority in the first instance. Similarly in the publishing rooms any vacancy is notified by the chapel to the LCB of SOGAT*. Such positions are filled on the basis of union card number (in effect, by seniority of Branch membership).

462. Both SLADE and SOGAT PMB vacancies are notified to the appropriate branches and are filled by unemployed members. Overseers have no choice over applicants for vacancies in SLADE, SOGAT and NATSOPA membership areas, branch nominees being deemed to be the only acceptable applicants. Occasionally overseers may object to a branch nominee, on the grounds, for example, of inappropriate experience and background or because of a poor disciplinary record as a casual. Such objections are considered and their validity determined by the appropriate branch.

463. In the case of NGA vacancies in the composing rooms, the decision on engagement still rests in most offices with the head of department, although the chapel would make representations on the applicant's behalf if, on being rejected, they felt he had been unfairly treated. "Holiday frame hands" (compositors engaged on a six-month contract between April and September to cover holidays) are used in most offices and these are the main source of recruitment of permanent employees. The head printer will invite back those whose work is satisfactory the following year, after which time the member has the right to continue working as a holiday hand until a permanent position becomes available and can be offered to him. In the machine rooms and foundries NGA vacancies are filled by nominees from the London Region office, initially on a month's trial, at the end of which the appropriate departmental head has the right to end the engagement or make it permanent.

464. Where clerical vacancies occur some recruitment selection by management does take place. In most houses a common procedure operates whereby vacancies (including managerial vacancies) are initially notified by management to the chapel call clerk, who in turn notifies the NATSOPA Clerical Branch calls office and posts details of the vacancies internally. If there are no internal applicants the Branch is then called upon to supply applicants, all applications

---

* The situation on the two London evening newspapers is a little different. Van drivers' assistants ("round boys") are recruited direct from school at age 16, remaining non-unionised until they are taken into membership of the LCB at 17. They are often the sons of existing publishing room staff and are interviewed and recruited by the overseers. Promotion in these cases, based on seniority of chapel membership, is to commission-earning rounds boy ("topping-up" of newsagents with extra copies), van (or "parcel") driver, and depot man. The latter employee is essentially a newspaper vendor with a clearly-defined sales area and working on a commission basis. Promotion to this grade is by chapel seniority; the FOC submits a short list of applicants and the Circulation Manager selects the successful applicant.

being directed in the first instance to the chapel call clerk. Should no suitable applicants be forthcoming from the Branch after having been notified for four weeks, management is free to recruit through advertisement and other outside sources.

465. Selection and appointment in all houses is regarded as a management responsibility, but in all cases internal applicants have to be dealt with before outside applicants are seen. The ability of the Clerical Branch to supply suitable labour is dependent on the employment circumstances applying to its membership (including those in general printing) at any point in time, although in most houses it is usual for outside sources to be used for tele-ad sales and secretarial staff. New recruits, including internal transferees, are normally appointed on three months' probation, at the end of which, and subject to successful completion, the appointment is confirmed in writing.

466. Most managers we saw were generally satisfied with the industry's recruitment procedures, although a number told us that they thought more management control was necessary, particularly over access to more information for personnel records purposes about staff recruitment. Some managements also felt that they should be able to interview internal, Branch and external applicants at the same stage in procedure, subject to their recommending the successful applicant, if not already a union member, to join the appropriate union.

Promotion

467. In production areas there are two distinct aspects to promotion, one internal to the chapel and the other applying outside the chapel to supervisory and other managerial positions. The movement of employees from one grade to another is controlled by the chapels, usually on the basis of seniority of chapel membership. This has developed through custom and practice and rarely appears in written agreements. Chapels maintain seniority lists and when vacancies occur inform the appropriate overseer the name of the employee who is to fill it.

468. While written agreements on the movement of employees between grades generally do not exist, in the NATSOPA machine and SOGAT publishing areas agreements on manning do normally set out a breakdown of the numbers of employees in each grade. The grades applying in these chapels/departments, which may vary in number between offices, are described in Chapter 5, paragraphs 158 and 159 which also set out the somewhat different provisions applying to both NGA and NATSOPA members in the machine room at NGN. Temporary promotions between grades on a nightly basis may also occur when permanent members of the chapel are sick, absent or on leave, and again dependent on chapel seniority.

469. Most companies have a policy of attempting wherever possible to promote from within. In production areas, by custom and practice, in all promotions to the level of departmental head houses normally use internal candidates as their only source*. It is common for promotion to departmental

* In Manchester there is evidence of a greater variety of sources (including other newspaper houses, the provincial press and the general trade) being used to fill such positions in production areas.

head to be on the basis of seniority among the deputies, although this is not necessarily automatic. The procedure used to fill junior overseers' or staff hands' jobs varies both between departments and between offices. When a staff job becomes vacant, management will normally call for applications for the position. All applications have to be made through the appropriate chapel officials. In the publishing rooms the chapels generally draw up lists of approved candidates, largely on the basis of seniority of chapel membership, and then submit these to management. In at least one office the successful candidates are selected jointly by the publisher and the FOC.

470. In other production departments it is usual for the departmental head to discuss suitable candidates for staff vacancies with his immediate deputies, to then confirm the suitability of the candidate with the production manager and approach the employee privately, after which the FOC is informed. Staff positions may also be advertised internally, and formal interviews held with applicants. In some offices the departmental FOC may sit in on these interviews. In the words of one FOC, "this is very necessary because it is the member's last link with the chapel".

471. In production departments other than the publishing room, in which a number of unions organise employees, overseers are mostly drawn from the predominant craft union, the NGA (and SLADE in process departments). In some offices NATSOPA overseers are employed but it is unusual in any office for their responsibilities to extend beyond the supervision of NATSOPA members.

472. The interchangeability of overseers and managers between departments is limited by the constraints outlined above to fairly rigid vertical career development to middle management levels. Some houses have, within these confines, attempted to move away from promotion on the basis, as one manager put it "of whether the person was a good workman rather than good management material". In the past overseers have often been drawn from the older employees in a department, whose ability to adapt to a managerial role has in some cases been limited. Part of new policies on promotion has involved attempts to establish salary structures and other improved terms and conditions of employment to attract a wider range of applications for such positions (the relationship of existing terms and conditions to those of production workers generally has created some bad feeling; see paragraph 185).

473. In clerical areas the promotion policy is similar to that outlined in paragraph 464. In very few houses does promotion involve a transfer of union membership. We were informed that occasionally NATSOPA clerical members working in editorial areas had over a period developed their job content to the point where it became recognised as journalistic work, and had been accepted into membership of the NUJ. Similarly NATSOPA clerical members working in circulation departments have on occasions been promoted to circulation representatives' positions, and been accepted into membership by the CRB of SOGAT. Such positions are also open to application from members of SOGAT publishing chapels, although the CRB now has a policy that any circulation representative vacancies must be filled from the Branch's unemployed membership.

Discipline and Dismissal

474. Disciplinary procedures in the industry (see also Chapter 8, paragraphs 276 to 278) operate at two levels. Chapels not only take action on any misconduct which weakens their collective strength, but also reinforce discipline at the workplace. While managements in all houses regard the maintenance and upholding of discipline as their right and responsibility, the operation of disciplinary procedures in practice is very much a joint responsibility. Some re-examination of present disciplinary arrangements has, however, been made by NATSOPA as a result of matters arising from the union's own appeals machinery. The Executive Council reiterated its policy on workshop discipline; namely, "that industrial misdemeanours are matters for management and the Society's (NATSOPA's) disciplinary rules should not play a part unless the misdemeanours affect the reputation and well-being of the Society and its members".*

475. Few companies have compiled, or issued their employees with, copies of works rules although some offices do run induction courses for newly-recruited clerical and administrative staff. In practice, there is greater managerial control over discipline in these areas. Disciplinary procedures are formalised in a number of clerical house agreements and follow a standard format of verbal warnings, followed by written warnings (which may be expunged from the record after an agreed period of time) with the ultimate sanction of dismissal by the appropriate departmental manager. At every stage of the procedure the employee is entitled to have the FOC or chapel representative present. One clerical chapel agreement states that "the parties . . . . . . accept that they have a shared responsibility for the conduct of those staff covered by the Agreement to reach and maintain effective work standards. The Chapel agrees to assist departmental heads in the maintenance of standards of work within their departments". Most disciplinary issues are decided by custom and practice within the industry; there are few formally agreed procedures outside the clerical and editorial areas.

476. Most managements have, nevertheless, issued guidance to managers on discipline and the appropriate procedure to be followed†. The authority to dismiss is rarely given to those below the level of departmental head, and in production areas dismissal has generally to be authorised by a senior executive. In these areas it is usual, except in instances of gross misconduct, for an overseer to approach the appropriate FOC on a disciplinary matter relating to a chapel member. If the FOC agrees that the complaint is justified, it is usual for the member to be warned initially, with further offences being considered by the chapel committee. Discipline is not a source of major concern in production areas. Disciplinary action is relatively uncommon and dismissal rare (in one house in 1975 there were 23 disciplinary actions including five dismissals; in other cases there were far fewer, and one establishment reported having had none since 1973). Both chapels and their union branches tend to back justifiable management action on matters such as drunkenness, theft and poor timekeeping.

---

* "Workshop Discipline"—*Journal and Graphic Review*, November 1975.
† One house, in a document giving guidelines to its heads of department on discipline, summarised its procedure, which is fairly standard, as follows:—
"(1) Informal verbal warning; (2) Formal written warning; (3) Final written warning; (4) Disciplinary measure. Always (*a*) Involve the FOC; (*b*) keep full written records; (*c*) keep everyone advised; (*d*) spot trouble coming."

Redundancy

477. Most houses do not have formal redundancy procedures. Negotiations on redundancy take place within the established house negotiating procedures described in Chapter 10. In virtually all houses redundancy and early retirement terms exist and are widely applicable, having been developed by management alone rather than in any jointly determined setting. Individual employees wishing to take advantage of such voluntary severance terms initially inform their appropriate FOC and then approach management for further details. One large company indicates in its guide to redundancy and early retirement arrangements that "before applications to volunteer to be declared redundant can be accepted the employees, the employees' union branch and the management must all give their consent. It may not be possible to accept an application for voluntary termination where suitable alternative employment is available to the employee in (the) company.......... or where the employee is still required in his present job".

478. A number of houses, prior to the agreement reached at national level in 1975 agreeing to the establishment of the JSC, had given assurances to their employees of no compulsory redundancy made in the context of negotiations over manning reductions. A review of redundancy procedures has been carried out by the JSC.

The Chapel/Overseer Relationship

479. Many of the traditional aspects of man-management are, then, undertaken by the chapels in the production areas of national newspapers. The direct control of many chapels over recruitment, work allocation, promotion, and discipline inevitably means that overseers are largely concerned with technical and quality control matters (see paragraph 196 et seq.).

480. It would, of course, be possible to extend the functions of chapels still further. We questioned FOCs about this during our inquiries. Very few considered any extension of their role was either desirable or practicable, partly because in some cases it was argued that they "do everything already". Some chapel representatives did feel that they could make a bigger contribution if they were drawn into management planning functions at an early stage, particularly to advise on the practical effects of decisions in the workplace. They often thought that overseers had a low status in the hierarchy of the organisation and some even felt that overseers were largely superfluous given the extent of the chapel role. Only a minority, however, thought that the sub-contracting relationship could be developed to the extent of dispensing entirely with supervision in the production areas. The reasons for the reluctance to tread this path varied but a common fear was that a formal assumption of all or most managerial functions would place unacceptable strains on relationships within the chapels concerned.

481. Indeed, from the chapels' point of view the existence of overseers provides career prospects for members and employment opportunities. While no manning agreements as such exist to govern the number of overseers in each department, in many offices there are informal understandings about such matters between chapels and managements. In some offices, in the absence of a junior overseer (through holiday or sickness for example), a temporary replacement is "made-up" from the appropriate chapel to cover the position.

CHAPTER 13: CONSULTATION, COMMUNICATION AND DISCLOSURE

482. It seems paradoxical in a mass communications industry that communications between representatives of newspaper managements and unions should resemble a disorganised, and loud, conversation between two (or more) groups of the hard-of-hearing. Such, at least, is the first impression. Subsequent examination reveals that the procedures for, and apparent effectiveness of, joint consultation and communication, and the extent of disclosure, vary greatly both between houses and at different levels in the industry. The need for confidentiality in a competitive environment has to be set by houses against the need for consultation with, and information disclosure to, those whose co-operation has to be won in the process of innovation. The tendency for these two needs to pull against each other has led to an informal and often personal communications network. An outstanding feature of consultation and communication in the industry has been the relative absence of any comprehensive, formal arrangements to facilitate it.

Consultation and Communication at National Level

483. At national and at house/branch level there are relatively few senior industrial relations management, union and NPA officials and they have often worked within the industry for many years; personal relationships have developed and a good deal of two-way communication takes place. Such communication is often related to a particular issue or dispute: there has been little organised communication and, as far as can be judged, little advance consultation on future plans. Until the creation of the JSC and the preliminary discussions, representatives of management and unions gathered together only during pay negotiations or when a house management convened a meeting to discuss a crisis.

Consultation and Communication at House Level

484. Some houses have fairly elaborate, formal consultative and disclosure arrangements and policies (either operational or proposed) whilst others have no agreed commitment to consultation or disclosure at all. Company attitudes to consultation and disclosure in the past have been clearly influenced by short-term considerations such as their economic circumstances at any given point in time and their need to induce specific technological and other changes. The extent to which the absence of formal arrangements inhibits the easy and accurate flow of information partly depends on house size. The *Morning Star* and the *Morning Advertiser*, for example, experience fewer problems in this area, although even in these cases whilst there are no complaints about the process of communication we heard some criticisms about the content.

Formal Consultative Arrangements

485. **Beaverbrook Newspapers Ltd** has one of the most developed formal arrangements for consultation and disclosure. The impetus for more disclosure of information and consultation on future plans seems to have been the general company policy of cost reduction since 1971 and, in particular, the closure of the *Scottish Daily Express*. In 1973/74, the company set up three consultative committees covering the *Daily* and *Sunday Express* in London, the *Daily* and

Sunday Express in Manchester, and the *Evening Standard*. The main functions of these committees are to receive regular information on the company's trading position and finances and on future plans and prospects; to discuss any matters affecting the operating efficiency of the company or the interests of the employees; to enable each side to have the opportunity to understand the other's views and objectives; and to discuss future plans and new ideas.

486. The committees consist of representatives of each chapel concerned (the FOC and deputy FOC in all but one case) and the deputy chairman/managing director and his deputy, the production director and his deputy with labour responsibilities, the personnel director and the overseers of the machine room, foundry and publishing departments. The committees meet every two to three months and provide an opportunity for management to disclose financial information and for FOCs to ask questions related to it. At one stage FOCs retained the printed information presented by management at each meeting, but this is no longer so; the material is considered confidential and potentially damaging if revealed.

487. The company believes strongly in the value of the consultative arrangements as a means of overcoming any mistrust between management and chapels which may have grown up over the years. The seriousness of the financial positions of newspapers within the group seems to have made the company explore means of convincing chapels that the situation really was difficult. The group's plans for reorganisation and for introducing new equipment also required detailed planning with the chapels. The company has attempted to involve the chapels in the selection of equipment and on modifications which will be necessary for it to be used within the house titles. This has involved taking parties of FOCs to see and assess new equipment in action in this country and abroad.

488. **Mirror Group Newspapers,** too, has made substantial efforts in the last few years to improve its consultative arrangements. It has tried to provide a neutral forum for the exchange of views between managers and FOCs; improved its means of imparting information directly to employees as well as to FOCs; and attempted to create formal consultative institutions. In 1970 the company set up, under the auspices of its training department, a series of courses held at Windsor designed to provide managers and chapel representatives with the opportunity for extensive informal discussions away from the day-to-day environment. Since their inception thirty-five of these five-day courses have been held, with a total attendance of about 600 managers and FOCs. Some are held on specific subjects (on worker participation, for example) but most are fairly general and have a very low lecture input. Most of the time is taken up with discussions in small groups between managers and FOCs. Every year a two-day meeting is held at which all those who have been at Windsor during the previous year discuss and critically evaluate the scheme.

489. MGN has used three other methods to improve the flow of information to employees generally and to FOCs. First, as the result of a suggestion made during the Windsor consultations in Spring 1974, MGN introduced three internal telephone information services; dial-a-fact, dial-a-figure and dial-a-question. These, respectively, give five minutes of information about events

within MGN and the activities of particular departments; report the operating revenues, costs and trends at the end of each accounting period; and record individuals' questions to which written answers are given later. Directors normally record the necessary tapes and five internal lines are connected to each service. Altogether more than half-a-million calls have been made since the service was introduced in September 1974, and on average weekly calls to dial-a-fact and dial-a-figure have been running at about 3,500 each. Dial-a-question is hardly ever used.

490. Second, MGN also produces a free weekly house newspaper, *Mirror Group News*, which the company uses for the dissemination of key items of news. For example, MGN's development plans have been communicated directly to employees solely by this means. Third, in 1974 the company began to distribute to FOCs a monthly "detailed disclosure document". This provides an analysis of costs and profits, manpower statistics, circulation, and certain revenues and expenditures.

491. MGN has a number of departmental consultative committees, and in March 1974 and again in the NAR agreement of that year the company made proposals to its chapels to set up an employee consultative council. The aims of the proposed council were "to achieve an environment of trust and confidence with the company, thereby eliminating destructive industrial conflict" and to involve all employees in the running of the business. It was envisaged that the council would meet regularly every two months and that the employee side would comprise one elected member from each of six London constituencies (editorial and editorial services, graphics, machine, despatch, administration, engineering and supply services) and one from Manchester. It was further proposed that after a year a separate "area committee" in each constituency would be established on the same lines as the MGN consultative council. No response to the proposals had been forthcoming at the time the JSC began its deliberations. MGN's proposals differ from the arrangements in operation at Beaverbrook Newspapers in that the latter involve all FOCs in the consultative process whereas MGN are attempting to get employees to directly elect representatives across chapel lines. It is not part of the proposals that the employee representatives should have to be FOCs.

492. **The Financial Times** in September 1975 made a novel proposal that a joint supervisory board (JSB) should be established to supervise the implementation of the newspaper's technological plans for the composing room. Briefly, the proposal was that on certain conditions* the JSB, composed of national officers from each of the main unions and two directors of the *Financial Times* and chaired at first by the chairman of the TUC PIC, should be responsible, through four sub-committees, for ensuring that the details of the company's plans were fully understood by all employees and that employees concerned had the appropriate skills, for establishing and monitoring a job-evaluated payments system, for managing appropriate selection and

---

* Among the conditions was acceptance by the unions that ". . . the new technology would be introduced and accepted on a time scale determined by the company's requirements in order to achieve actual cost reductions in line with the specified reductions in staff".

training programmes, and for handling the proposed net income support system for redundant employees. The JSB proposal was cautiously welcomed by some union representatives but has not yet met due to the attempts being made in the JSC to agree similar arrangements in all houses.

Other Consultative Arrangements

493. Consultative and disclosure arrangements in other houses tend to be more *ad hoc*. In some houses the traditional means of talking to all chapels has been, where necessary, through the FHCs (see Chapter 8). FHCs are normally concerned with discussing issues of joint concern to chapels such as canteens and pensions, and have been a convenient method of communicating with all FOCs in the past. In one house the use of the FHC for joint consultation has been considered particularly useful, but the institution normally has a number of limitations for this purpose. Not every chapel in every house is a member of the FHC and chapels are suspicious of FHCs (see Chapter 8). FOCs are sometimes reluctant to discuss matters freely within the confines of the FHC.

494. During the financial crisis at the *Observer* in 1975 the FHC met only once, and then not for the purpose of receiving information from management. The company disclosed the extent of the crisis to a specially convened meeting of national, branch and chapel officials at a London hotel. During the redundancy negotiations the company opened its books completely to union and chapel officials. At national level, the unions made independent studies of the accounts. In-house, FOCs were taken line by line through detailed financial documents issued by the company. The *Observer* (which had only taken over the bulk of its workforce from Times Newspapers in 1974) had no fixed consultative arrangements with its staff before the crisis and management decided that the redundancy negotiations would have to be conducted in an atmosphere of the fullest possible disclosure. The company now intends to hold regular meetings with representatives of individual chapels to discuss the state of the newspaper, although there are doubts as to the practicality or desirability of continuing the detailed financial disclosure of information which took place during the redundancy negotiations.

495. The *Observer* pattern of *ad hoc* consultation and communication to meet particular circumstances is repeated in most other houses, although, in addition to MGN, *The Times* does have a telephone information service and a house magazine. The arrangements usually take the form of meetings between management at board level and all FOCs where news of particular company developments is passed on verbally (sometimes accompanied by documentation) and FOCs have an opportunity to ask questions. Some houses have attempted to regularise such meetings,* in others they are convened only when vital decisions have been made requiring communication to chapels. Where new equipment is envisaged, some houses have attempted to involve FOCs in the detailed planning of its introduction, with mixed success. The activities of Beaverbrook Newspapers in this direction have already been mentioned. At least one other house has set up a number of joint working parties in connection with its plans to introduce new technology (and the same house also intends setting up a joint working party to consider the question of profit-sharing by

---

* At the *Guardian*, for example, they are held every six months.

employees). Some houses have also attempted to improve in-house communications by ensuring that management information chains which end with the overseers have a further link which involves the overseer holding regular meetings to pass on information to the FOCs in his department.

Safety and Other Committees

496. Most houses have now established, or have proposed, joint safety committees. Most of these were created following the Health and Safety at Work Act in 1975, although some had been in existence well before then. The committees vary in their composition, but usually comprise the senior executive responsible for safety matters within the company as well as chapel representatives. They meet regularly, and consider such matters as safety statistics, new machinery, accidents and means of improving safety in the workplace. One constitution states that the committee's activities "shall not encroach upon existing management/chapel negotiating procedures" and this understanding appears to apply to all such committees.

497. A number of other joint committees exist within houses. Some pension, sick pay and welfare schemes have employee representation in their administration, such as an employee trustee. Some houses also have joint catering or canteen committees.

Areas of Disclosure

498. In most houses, policies for consultation, disclosure of information, and communications are unwritten and undifferentiated: it is difficult to distinguish separate policies in each area. Where detailed financial information has been disclosed, however, it has concentrated on areas such as circulation trends, predictions of profitability or loss and performance of individual titles. No house issues details of earnings levels within the house either on a general or a departmental level to FOCs. During our inquiries we found that FOCs often had surprisingly little knowledge of the working arrangements in departments other than their own, and in particular of precise earnings levels outside their own immediate area. Estimates made by FOCs of earnings levels outside their own departments were usually too high.

Working of the Arrangements at House Level

499. The bulk of communication and information disclosure within houses takes place within the framework of chapel bargaining. Although some houses are trying to develop their consultative arrangements most expressed reasonable satisfaction with the present state of affairs in this respect. Two main reservations were expressed about communications. The first concerned the difficulty which sometimes arises of communicating with the appropriate full-time union officers when disputes arise. This is felt to be partly a deliberate tactic on the part of the union officers concerned and partly the result of the work-load which union officers bear. In one house we even heard it suggested by senior managers that if unions were prepared to allocate officers to particular houses, the companies concerned might be prepared to meet some of the additional costs involved. The second reservation was over whether information given to FOCs reached all chapel members in a complete or accurate form. Relatively few houses have any means of direct, systematic communication with individual employees. Only

two houses have a house publication (in one other case the house publication was discontinued in 1972 for cost reasons) and telephone communications systems give even less assurance that information is universally received.

500. In every house criticisms were made by chapel representatives during our inquiries about consultative and disclosure arrangements. While chapel representatives in those houses which have made concrete attempts to improve such arrangements acknowledged them, their criticisms were often similar to those voiced in houses where the consultative arrangements are more rudimentary. Despite the variety among houses in policies and institutions for consultation, chapel representatives were fairly united during our inquiries in their views on consultation, disclosure of information and communication.

501. A common criticism was that arrangements were often designed simply to allow the one-way flow of information considered by houses to be "consultative". Meetings were held to pass on, explain and defend management decisions taken well beforehand. Recent meetings to divulge plans to introduce new technology were quoted as particular examples. The mechanics of the arrangements were also criticised. The practice in some houses of issuing detailed financial documents at meetings between management and FOCs was felt to deny FOCs the opportunity to ask meaningful questions as they had had so little time to consider the information. Question-and-answer sessions were said to lose value because of the size of meetings and of selective answering by management representatives.

502. Many FOCs feel that the communication process is inadequate and that rumour constantly misinforms employees, particularly in the current situation. Some FOCs alleged that a lack of information from managements had caused disputes and stoppages. For example, it was said that in one house, where no plans had been announced for the introduction of photosetting equipment, some equipment had been "secretly" brought in. Rumours about the equipment had spread rapidly and FOCs had been put under pressure to call a halt to work until further information was available. In the event, the equipment was for another part of the group not involved in the production of national newspapers.

503. In houses which have announced plans to introduce new technology, a common complaint from FOCs was that after the original announcement, promises to consult regularly on the progress of the plans had not been kept. Many FOCs appeared to be confused over the current situation in regard to the reorganisation and/or introduction of new technology being carried out within houses. Some FOCs felt that the newspaper houses lost financially through not consulting them enough over future plans; the experience of long-serving individuals was a wasted asset and it was alleged that expensive mistakes had been made by managements over reorganisation plans or new equipment hastily introduced without proper consultation.

504. Management attempts during consultative meetings to convince FOCs of the weak financial situation of many newspapers were often viewed with scepticism by FOCs. The reasons for this are linked to the criticisms made of the consultative process itself. With such deficiencies in the consultative process as those outlined in paragraph 499, some FOCs felt that they were not able to

form independent assessments on the financial situation of the houses for which they worked and thus had to rely on what they were told. This has led to a call from some FOCs for chapels to be able to make independent assessments (via their own accountants) of the financial situation of their companies. On the other hand, some chapel representatives are wary of seeking too much information because they believe it might inhibit chapel bargaining activities.

505. The credibility of management representatives had suffered, it was felt, by too many financial crises in the past which had been overcome without too much trouble. Some FOCs have developed a cynicism about recurring crises, and the task of present managements in persuading them that current problems are worse than those of the past is not an enviable one. Chapel representatives have told us that managements are more enthusiastic about consultation and disclosure when they feel the economic pinch or when they wish to secure some change to their advantage. In one case at least it is clear that the consultative arrangements were activated during a period of change and thereafter atrophied.

506. Managements are not unaware of some of these criticisms and realise that consultative meetings which seem invariably to involve the communication of bad news from management to FOCs inevitably jaundice the FOCs' views of the consultative procedure. In some houses managements have been inhibited from introducing new consultative procedures by what they feel to be union lack of enthusiasm, and in others there have been no plans for developments in this area.

CHAPTER 14: INDUSTRIAL RELATIONS TRAINING

507. Until comparatively recently, formal management training of any kind has had a relatively low priority in many newspaper houses. In 1966 it was possible to say of Fleet Street generally that there was little company policy on management training*, that there was little evidence of planned management training at supervisory level; and that in individual houses there was "comparatively little interest in training" with virtually no training of existing or future management, "a certain amount of lip service" to management training, no formal management training programme, and "no training of management staff".*

508. Such criticisms of management training in the industry are no longer sustainable. Much more interest in training has been developed, especially in the last few years, and translated into training organisation and training programmes. This is not to say that adequate management and other training is conducted and that the calibre and performance of managers is regarded as satisfactory. On the contrary, a common feeling within the industry is that much more could be and needs to be done in this area and our inquiries indicate that industrial relations training for both management and trade union representatives tends to be patchy.

509. There are several reasons why there has been relatively little emphasis on management training of middle managers and overseers. First, the responsibilities of such managers, particularly at the lowest level, have been limited. They have not been responsible for employee selection and recruitment or for functions other than of a fairly narrow technical and organisational nature. This has lessened the apparent need for general management training. Second, the industry has not been one associated with rapid technical and organisational change and training has not, until fairly recently, been stimulated by any such developments.

510. Third, most promotions in the production area are made from among existing employees: many overseers and managers have had long experience within their respective companies and have developed their skills within the confines of their day-to-day work. This, together with the fact that there is very little interchangeability of middle and junior management between departments has disguised the need for broader-based programmed training. As far as industrial relations is concerned, many managers have had long experience of chapel membership, and often chapel office, and have learned during their careers to handle routine industrial relations matters as they have arisen. This has led to a feeling in some quarters that further training is largely superfluous. FOCs, too, have tended to have held chapel responsibilities in other capacities for a number of years (see paragraphs 265 and 266) and to have had little, if any, formal training.

The Providers of Training
The PPITB

511. The Printing and Publishing Industry Training Board (PPITB) was established in May 1968 to increase the effectiveness of companies in the

---
* EIU Report, pages 56, 100, 25, 21, 37, respectively.

industry through progressive training and development. As with other training boards, one of its main principles is to ensure that there is an equitable sharing of training costs among firms. The Board is also concerned with the promotion of training "aimed at improving industrial relations practice, but (the Board) will not become involved in issues which are within the province of the industry's industrial relations system". The Board is composed of employer members, employee members, educational members and government assessors. All three major publishing sectors—book publishing, periodical publishing and newspaper publishing—are served by a main Training Committee. The 1973 Employment and Training Act led to the establishment of the Manpower Services Commission, which, through the Training Services Agency, now pays for the operating expenses of training boards and co-ordinates their work.

512. The 1973 Act also introduced a levy exemption system under which firms that meet the criteria and standards laid down by the Board can qualify for exemption from the training levy. Among the thirteen main criteria examined by the Board in making decisions on the granting of exemption are previous training performance, the existence of a clearly defined training policy which is communicated to all those with management responsibilities, the production of a training plan for at least one year ahead, the ability of each firm to draw upon expertise to prepare training programmes in accordance with the training plan, the provision of induction training to all employees, the maintenance of training records, and the existence of a method of assessing the effectiveness of the training. In 1975, the first year of operation of the exemption scheme, 12 out of the 20 national newspaper establishments in levy were covered by either clear or conditional exemption certificates, representing 83% of all leviable employees in the sector.

513. The PPITB gives practical help and advice on the formulation of training plans and their implementation. A PPITB Training Adviser maintains liaison on training matters with those primarily concerned with training within houses and in the NPA and assists those responsible to identify training needs and devise suitable programmes to meet the needs. Specialist help on particular areas of training is available if required.

514. The Board has a Management/Trade Union Sub-Committee to monitor its industrial relations training activities. Much of its work has concerned the development of a "Relations at Work" training package, which includes a guide to the assessment of needs for and objectives of any training and to the selection of appropriate training material from the package. The Board also runs day release courses for FOCs and supervisors, although most of the industrial relations training has been directed at areas of the industry other than that of national newspapers.

The NPA

515. Paragraph 225 describes the training activities of the NPA. Most houses take advantage of the NPA organised courses, especially those concerned with supervisory training. The NPA introductory courses on the principles of supervision last five days and have a substantial industrial relations content, emphasising the industrial relations implications of managerial activities.

516. The NPA has progressively developed its supervisory training courses the basic objectives of which are to encourage broader-based knowledge and skills among supervisors. The introductory course resulted from consultations held by the NPA's training department with the National Examination Board in Supervisory Studies. An average of five of these courses are run annually with about 15 participants on each (either from a number of houses or solely from one house). The NPA has also developed a number of module courses in conjunction with South West London College, and these include finance and costing, problem solving, safety, communications and workplace industrial relations.

517. The NPA and the Institute of Supervisory Management (ISM) have also arranged for overseers who have undertaken the basic introductory course in supervision and the modules to pursue a programme of ISM studies, the successful completion of which entitles the student to ISM membership and a joint NPA/ISM qualification.

518. The NPA has in the past organised joint courses in conjunction with each of the main printing unions on such subjects as work study appreciation, and has promoted courses on important current issues. In 1974 for example, a short course on controlling the use of newsprint was organised by the NPA, and training courses have been developed for advertising representatives.

519. These training activities are monitored by the NPA's training committee, which meets monthly. The future organisation of training is likely to change, however, as a result of the establishment by the Joint Standing Committee of a Training Education and Counselling Sub-Committee. This sub-committee will have a general responsibility for the monitoring of the technical development plans of individual newspaper houses, and to determine training arrangements, including standards of training, training facilities and programmes. The possibility of levying each house to provide training facilities for the new technology is under active consideration.

Newspaper Houses

520. The bulk of the training within the industry is handled by individual houses. The growing emphasis placed on training in recent years in most houses has several causes. The introduction of the PPITB exemption scheme is undoubtedly one. It has tended to encourage houses to think more systematically about training needs and programmes. Though the full potential benefits of the scheme have yet to be felt, the pre-existing levy/grant system is sometimes thought to have stimulated training on an unco-ordinated basis and not strictly related to need, in order that houses could maximise grants from the PPITB. One house told us during our inquiries that the new system operated by the PPITB has not been fully assimilated by all managers some of whom still think of training primarily with a view to collecting grant aid.

521. A second reason for increased attention to training, especially of middle and junior management, has been the explicit policy of some houses to devolve as much responsibility as possible to the lower levels of the management hierarchy. Though the success of such policies have been limited, there have

been some attempts to involve middle and lower managers more in the wider decision-making process, attempts which have sometimes highlighted the need for training.

522. Though training programmes have gained impetus in the last year or two, some houses have had fairly detailed training programmes for a substantially longer period. MGN, for example, between 1970 and 1974 spent some £600,000 on training and expenditure in this area is now running at about £200,000 a year. Beaverbrook Newspapers began to re-assess its activities in this area in the latter half of the 1960s, when a Group Training Manager was appointed. Other houses undertake, and have undertaken for some time, appreciable amounts of training, though not on the same scale and not invariably systematically. One smaller house in 1974–75 spent some £8,000 in providing over 200 units of management/supervisory training. Another house provided 355 units of such training between 1970 and 1976.

523. All houses now have a senior executive specifically responsible for training (the exemption criteria require this) and most houses have a manager or managers who work full-time in this area. In 1975 national newspapers and news agencies employed 17 full-time training officers and 11 part-time staff spending at least 40% of their time on training duties. There were also 11 full-time and 18 part-time instructors.

The Unions

524. Of the printing unions, the NGA is the only one to have a formal training, education and research department, which is staffed by two officers and two secretarial assistants. In 1972 the union reorganised its training and research activities, embarking on a series of experimental courses for FOCs and Branch secretaries at its head offices in Bedford.

525. The NGA's present training arrangements now include a six-part correspondence package, the running of 15 one-week FOC courses annually, together with two annual one-week Branch secretaries' courses and an FOCs' summer school also of one week. The FOCs' courses are generally intended for FOCs with less than two years' experience, each course having 20 participants. The courses are allocated to the union's regions according to membership size, the London Region having three. Each course is held in the region of the participants providing facilities are available. The courses cover a wide range of matters, including union finance and administration, communication with the chapel, interviewing management, grievance settlement, collective bargaining in printing, and employment legislation.

526. The Branch secretaries' courses, which each have 20 participants, are more orientated to NGA administration and accountancy matters, together with employment legislation. The FOCs' summer school is intended for FOCs who have completed the basic FOC course, and takes the form of a working conference. The NGA's training activities are the responsibility, through the National Council, of its Training, Educational and Research Committee. The union, in common with other printing unions, also makes grants available to members undertaking other approved courses, such as those run by the WEA and Ruskin College Scholarships.

527. Prior to its dissolution the P & KTF organised FOC summer schools, in which all affiliated unions participated. Extensive use is made by the printing unions of TUC educational courses. SLADE, SOGAT, and NATSOPA do not as yet have a regular and systematic approach to industrial relations training, although part of SOGAT'S intention in creating a research function in the future (see paragraph 328), is to develop training.

528. Similarly, it is NATSOPA's intention to develop its present training arrangements by use of the union's recreation centre at Rottingdean. Seminars have been held for FOCs on new technology and its effects on the newspaper membership of the union, together with courses for part-time branch secretaries on employment legislation.

House Training Policies

529. The general statements of company policy on training are influenced by the exemption criteria and are therefore similar. One house, for example, provides training resources to "improve its performance and create opportunities for employees to develop to their full potential". Another house aims to provide opportunities to employees to acquire the knowledge and skills necessary for their jobs, current and potential. A third tries to give employees the necessary technical and practical experience to undertake the relevant work and the opportunity to develop higher skills. Further elaborations of these general statements refer to induction training, and training on safety and health. These, too, are requirements of the exemption scheme. There is no specific requirement in the scheme for houses to make provision for industrial relations training.

530. Although the PPITB has secured some uniformity in the presentation of training needs and programmes, houses do give different emphasis to the various elements in their training, and varying amounts of industrial relations training have been carried out. The way in which training is administered by houses also varies to some extent. Generally, individual managers are formally given the responsibility for the training of their subordinates and in carrying out these responsibilities they may seek the advice of training specialists in their respective houses. In practice, training departments take rather more of the initiative in seeking to ensure that adequate training is done.

531. In several houses we were told that it is general policy to ensure that all managers receive some managerial training on appointment and further training as necessary on particular subjects, though our interviews with overseers and other managers indicated that this objective has still to be fully attained. Induction training is centrally promoted and monitored within houses though, as one management argued, since it was impossible to design a course for new managers to attend on their first day because they are appointed one at a time, it had to be left to the manager/supervisor of the new arrival to give the necessary induction using a pre-designed checklist. Even in this latter case it was hoped to introduce a short course for recently engaged staff to "foster corporate identity and break down the barriers between departments". Special management training programmes—for example, on new technology or on changes in production organisation—are also instigated, operated and evaluated by the relevant training executives within each house.

532. It is also part of the central policy of some houses to encourage joint management/FOC training programmes. The MGN Windsor "human relations consultations" in which both managers and FOCs participate have already been mentioned (paragraph 488). From them a number of other joint courses (on communication skills and interpreting accounts) have been developed. The joint courses are central to MGN's training policy and an integral part of its industrial relations policy. Other houses have also had joint management/FOC training programmes though not as extensive. For example, Beaverbrook Newspapers has run a number of joint seminars on industrial relations legislation (including the Trade Union and Labour Relations Act, the Employment Protection Act and the Equal Opportunities Act).

533. Much of the specifically industrial relations-orientated training within houses has been concerned with legislative developments. Many more general training programmes have an identifiable labour relations content and it can be argued that any training which improves the general competence and performance of managers is likely to have a beneficial effect on industrial relations in the long run. On the narrower definition of industrial relations training, the amount of such training for managers done by houses varies greatly. In some cases virtually none is sponsored by houses. At the other extreme, a substantial proportion of managerial staff have received some such training, though the depth of the training may leave something to be desired. In one house, for example, we were provided with figures showing that four-fifths of supervisory staff and all managerial and specialist staff had received some industrial relations training since 1970. On closer examination 82% of those said to have received such training had attended one half-day, in-house seminar on the Industrial Relations Act 1971, and otherwise had had no other such training.

Part E: Special Cases

CHAPTER 15: INDUSTRIAL RELATIONS IN THE MANCHESTER ESTABLISHMENTS

Organisation of Production

534. About a fifth of all national newspaper employees (ie some 6,400) work in Manchester at the three main production centres, namely:

Thomson Withy Grove (TWG). This company produces the *Daily Mirror*, *Sunday Mirror*, the *Daily Telegraph* and the *News of the World* on a contract basis. It also produces the *Sporting Chronicle* and *Weekly Handicap* for its parent company, and does a small amount of commercial printing. About two-thirds of all those employed at TWG are directly employed by the company. The remainder are employees of its customers.

Northprint. This company, formed in 1970 is jointly owned by Associated Newspapers and the *Guardian* and MEN*. Northprint supplies plant, building and maintenance services and employs directly some 300 workers, about a tenth of the number directly employed by the user companies, the *Guardian* and MEN, Associated Newspapers (*Daily Mail*) and MGN (*Sunday People*).

Beaverbrook Newspapers Ltd. This establishment is about two-thirds the size of the other two and publishes the northern editions of the *Daily/Sunday Express* and the *Scottish Daily/Sunday Express*. When the Glasgow plant closed in 1974 the labour force rose by about 100, with some influx from Scotland. In late 1975/76 the increase was partly counterbalanced by labour force reductions caused by pagination and circulation decline.

535. Each of these establishments will be (and, in one case, has been) affected by new technology. As far as Northprint is concerned, the *Guardian* and MEN has introduced and is in the process of introducing substantial technological changes. In 1961 the TTS link for transmissions between London and Manchester was established; in 1967, a computer for computerised typesetting for the *Guardian* and MEN was installed; in 1971 a more sophisticated computer was brought in, and in January 1975 all display advertising in the *Guardian* in Manchester and in the MEN began to be photocomposed. Magnesium platemaking was also introduced into the process department. It is planned that by mid-1977 classified advertising and some editorial feature material will be photocomposed. No technological changes in respect of the *Daily Mail* at Northprint have yet been announced.

---

* Before 1970 the Northprint complex was originally the home of the *Daily Mail* and *Sunday Dispatch*. The *Sunday Express* was also printed there for a while. Many agreements currently applying to employees within the establishment pre-date 1970.

536. Beaverbrook Newspapers is planning to introduce similar photo-composing equipment to that which will be used in London. Negotiations on its introduction will take place on a Group basis.

537. Plans for technological change at TWG were announced by MGN and the *Daily Telegraph* towards the end of 1975. The timing of MGN's plans has subsequently (18 February 1976) been amended following discussions with the unions. The Daily Telegraph Ltd is planning to use facsimile transmission from London for its complete newspaper from about the autumn of 1977. The end product will be magnesium plates ready for stereo moulding. It is also MGN's intention ultimately to facsimile all its northern editions to Manchester, though hot-metal composition will now be phased out over three years from the date of the commencement of facsimile transmission. The plans for Withy Grove have caused industrial relations difficulties, especially in relation to journalists and compositors (see paragraph 565).

Labour Force

538. The structure of the production labour force in Manchester differs markedly from that of Fleet Street. In Manchester only 4% of regular employees work less than a full week for any one establishment (the corresponding Fleet Street figure is 27%). The distribution of production staff between departments differs; the proportion of publishing room staff in Manchester is half that in Fleet Street and the proportion of composing room staff is 50% higher (Labour Survey).

539. The Manchester establishments depend marginally less than Fleet Street on casual employment (but see paragraph 543). In October 1975 436 men were called on to work on a casual basis on Saturday for the Manchester establishments (ie about 10% of the total production labour force compared with 11% in London). The number appears to have fallen somewhat since then. Most casual employees work on the *Sunday People, Sunday Express, News of the World*, and *Sunday Mirror* and most (see paragraph 543) are sixth shift workers who work permanently for the other national newspapers on the other five shifts often in the same office, another contrast with Fleet Street. Since the publishing rooms in Manchester are organised by NATSOPA the bulk of casual workers are NATSOPA members. SOGAT organises drivers and there are relatively few SOGAT casuals*.

540. The great difference between casual working in London and Manchester is that in Manchester a "pool" system operates for most casuals. The procedure is that the local NATSOPA FOCs establish the casual working requirements a day in advance and notify the Branch calls office. Members seeking casual work contact the calls office between 11 am–2 pm each day and are directed to the appropriate office. For Saturday night casual workings permanent employees at the establishment concerned may approach FOCs for work who in turn must submit such names to the Branch office. No permanent employee may be allocated Saturday night casual work until a quota of the casual members of the Branch have been taken on. The quota is fixed by the Central Branch Committee and is related to the numbers of Branch casual members. In addition to the

---

* One informed estimate we heard was that 40–50 might be employed on a Saturday night.

Branch calls office there is also an office at the NPA in Manchester staffed by NATSOPA employees (see Chapter 7). This office receives every Monday notice of the calls that have been made by each newspaper office made and filled during the previous week and calculates the payment each man should receive and the total liability of each office. Managements are informed and are required to forward the appropriate sums of money. The cash is then delivered to the NATSOPA calls office from where it is collected by the relevant members.

541. NATSOPA thus has comprehensive information about the pattern of working and numbers of its members who work on a casual basis. There is relatively little casual working in NGA areas, though substantial numbers of members (about 300) are currently available for Saturday night work. In the past, each of those available would have obtained a casual Saturday-night shift about once every 10 weeks. In the current situation unemployed members have priority over the few casual jobs available. In SOGAT's case, it is the FOC's responsibility to call in the casuals required by the house for which he works, though the Branch is to review this procedure to give itself control over the casual lists.

542. NATSOPA, the NPA and house managements are satisfied that the pool system has worked well for many years. We were told that the system, together with NATSOPA's policy of restricting entry into the industry, had made for smooth, relatively efficient production and had encouraged a "constructive atmosphere". NATSOPA restricts entry into the Branch (which covers members outside as well as inside national newspapers) and into the national newspaper industry. The number of members in the industry has remained fairly static over the last decade. Entry is by seniority of union membership and, currently, about 12 years membership is necessary before entry into national newspapers is possible. In February 1976 the Branch had 179 casual members divided into four categories: unemployed members (77), retired members who retain their rights to list for casual work (57), members who have accepted voluntary redundancy but who go on to seek casual work (24) (these members have the lowest priority for casual work) and temporary members (21).

543. The relatively small number of casual members depending entirely on casual work for employment indicates the extent to which permanent employees also undertake casual work. Between May and September 1975 an average of 449 casual Saturday night shifts were required in NATSOPA areas. Given the number of casual members on NATSOPA lists, about 60% of these shifts must have been worked by permanent employees. This highlights the contrast with the Fleet Street situation mentioned in paragraph 538. Although the extent of dependence on casual casual working in Manchester is comparable with that in London, the number of union members listed purely as casual casual staff is proportionately smaller. It can be estimated that the number of such staff is about 5–6% of the number of regular production staff in Manchester compared with the corresponding Fleet Street figure of about 12–13%.

544. Another interesting feature of casual working illustrates the relatively close relationship between the printing unions in Manchester. When casual work has been abundant NGA, SLADE and SOGAT unemployed members have been allocated work in NATSOPA areas. Indeed, at the height of the summer holiday season, Saturday night casual work in areas within NATSOPA's jurisdiction is often undertaken by members of other unions, with NATSOPA's full agreement.

Terms and Conditions of Employment

545. Many of the broad features of the terms and conditions of employment of national newspaper employees described in Chapter 5 are apparent in the Manchester establishments. The vast majority of Manchester production staff, except those working for the *Sunday People*, are covered by comprehensive agreements, and in many areas there are similar grading structure to those that exist in London. Most managers to whom we talked said that comprehensive agreements had been negotiated on a genuine productivity basis, sometime with agreed work measurement, and that they had brought substantial benefits. Average earnings in October 1975 were significantly lower in Manchester than in London for most broad occupational groups (Labour Survey) except in the machine room, and there are substantial differences in average earnings levels between similar groups working for different employers and newspapers, sometimes within the same establishment.

546. Different bonus systems have been negotiated, and bonuses are paid sometimes weekly, sometimes monthly and sometimes quarterly. Many chapels have pagination bonus schemes which have yielded relatively little since the decline in advertising. In one case, a chapel has increased its earnings by only one per cent in two years because of the loss of pagination payments. There is very little overtime and the overtime that is worked is carefully monitored. Problems over differentials arise as in London but seem to be less acute. NATSOPA's policy is to seek the $87\frac{1}{2}:100$ comprehensive rate ratio between its own and NGA members as a minimum position but, again as in London, this has by no means been fully achieved. Similarly, whilst there is some recognition that engineers' and electricians' rates should be parallel, such recognition is not universal.

547. The biggest differences in pay and payments systems between London and Manchester are probably to be found in the composing rooms. Average earnings of composing room staff in London in October 1975 were about 50% higher than the earnings of those in Manchester, a bigger earnings difference than for any other major group of printing employees. A major reason for this is that there is no division in Manchester between piece and time workers within composing rooms: all employees are paid on a time basis, though time-work payments may be supplemented by bonus payments. In one house, for example, composing room employees are paid a bonus based on the amount of setting done in excess of a target figure fixed after agreed work measurement. The bonus, paid quarterly to all NGA composing room employees, can be adjusted to take account of unduly low manning levels caused by sickness and, in the view of some of those associated with it, encourages the maintenance of low staffing levels. Comprehensive agreements have in Manchester generally led to increased flexibility in the composing area and it is not uncommon for men to transfer between sections. A single agreement and a single basic rate normally apply to all NGA composing room employees within each house.

The Managements: Inter-Relationships

548. The management of industrial relations in Manchester is complicated by the presence in two of the establishments of three or four employers each paying its employees different rates and each with its own plans for the future, and by

the contractual relationship at two of the establishments (but especially at Withy Grove). A further potential complication is the relationship of each Manchester management to its London parent. Whatever the precise formal relationship it seems fairly generally true that Manchester managements attempt to "keep as independent of London as possible".

549. **The Beaverbrook Newspapers'** establishment, being a "single house" establishment, has the most straightforward industrial relations management task. The production director in Manchester is responsible for industrial relations with production employees and there are three managers whose prime responsibility is in the labour relations field. The general manager in conjunction with the northern editor deals with industrial relations matters affecting editorial staff. Industrial relations in the Manchester establishment are, at least on a day-to-day basis, managed separately from industrial relations in Beaverbrook Newspapers as a whole. This managerial separation is perhaps facilitated by the low incidence of open industrial relations conflict in Manchester (see paragraph 565) and seems to have grown in the last few years.

550. **The Thomson Withy Grove** situation is, by contrast, much more involved. The *Daily/Sunday Mirror* have been printed under contract there for over 20 years and the present contract extends to 1981. The northern *Daily/Sunday Mirror* are entirely produced at TWG except for one or two matted advertisements from London. The *Daily Telegraph* has been produced at TWG since 1940. Much of its display material is prepared in London and can be put directly onto TWG presses. The *News of the World* is largely composed in Manchester, though some moulds are sent from London.

551. Four managements thus have an interest in industrial relations at TWG. One of these, MGN, is not in the NPA. The "customer" managements directly govern the pay and conditions of employment of those concerned with all functions before copy is passed to the composing room (journalists, clerical and advertisement staff, wireroom employees, copytakers and library staff), and indirectly influence industrial relations relating to production staff employed by TWG. Many such staff work on both the *Daily Mirror* and the *Daily Telegraph*. The composing room is, for example, fully integrated and composing room costs are divided notionally between the customers. There is normally no direct contact between the customer managements and the TWG chapels* though TWG obviously has to bear in mind the interests of its customer houses in dealing with industrial relations matters. The normal procedure would be for any substantial claim from a TWG chapel to be costed by TWG management which would consult the customer managements before responding. TWG's individual and cumulative decisions in these areas are important for its customers especially where their contracts are on a cost-plus basis. Clearly, TWG has to balance the interests of its customers, which may not invariably coincide, and also take into account its own long-term credibility with its employees in dealing with industrial relations. The reconciliation of these factors has sometimes been difficult, especially during disputes.

552. The TWG management has recently been in a still more difficult situation in relation to the plans of the user houses on new technology. First, the MGN

---

* Though representatives of customer managements have participated in meetings about technological change.

and *Daily Telegraph* plans were announced at different times but within a few weeks of each other in October/November 1975, and this created some confusion and contributed to worsening industrial relationships. Second, the announcements sparked off a strong reaction from the TWG composing room staff. TWG thus had to deal with an industrial relations problem not created by its own direct action, and try to handle it in a way which its customers felt was not against their interests.

553. The broad managerial remit of MGN, *Daily Telegraph* and TWG managements is similar to that of the Beaverbrook Newspaper Manchester management. Day-to-day management at TWG, for example, is entirely in the hands of local directors and managers. The managing director of TWG reports to the managing director of Thomson Regional Newspapers Ltd. and consults closely with him on major investment plans affecting Withy Grove and on any other important policy matters. As far as the customer managements are concerned, general industrial relations policy is developed in liaison with their respective parent organisations and the execution of policy is largely in the hands of Manchester management. The Northern General Manager of MGN reports directly to the chief executive of MGN and the functional managers in Manchester (for example, the production controller at Northprint) report both to the Northern General Manager and to the appropriate director in London. This is to ensure a proper balance between local decision-taking and general company policy.

554. **The Northprint** board consists of three representatives of Associated Newspapers, three of the GMEN and two others. The plant is fully utilised: the *Manchester Evening News* is produced during the day, the *Guardian* and *Daily Mail* at night, and the *Sunday People* on a Saturday night. Some thought was originally given to the suggestion that there should be integrated employment in *Daily Mail*/GMEN production departments on the grounds that these newspapers were in competition editorially but not in production areas* and that such an arrangement would be the most efficient. In the event, only the stereo department was integrated; the remainder are staffed according to title. In this situation, the main difficulty of management is to prevent comparative bargaining between chapels within the various houses. The *Guardian* and *Manchester Evening News*' production is not integrated: about three-quarters of the chapels come under the auspices of one or other of these newspapers, though they negotiate with the same managers†.

555. The various managements are careful to avoid approaches from chapels representing employees not formally coming within their individual areas of control but concessions by one management do sometimes lead to claims being presented to the others. The only stoppage of work specifically by a Northprint chapel since the company was formed occurred when the engineers who worked on the *Sunday People* felt their earnings were falling behind those of MGN

---

* This was the only example we found during our inquiries of two managements explicitly considering the place of wage costs in the competitive process and where there was some feeling that such costs should be formally removed from inter-house competition.
† About a third of GMEN employees work solely on the *Guardian*.

employees following MGNs withdrawal from the NPA*. There are no formal inter-management committees covering all the managements at Northprint, but informally liaison is close and continuous.

556. If anything, the managements at Northprint have greater freedom to regulate routine industrial relations within the establishment with minimal intervention from London. The production of both the *Guardian* in Manchester and the *Manchester Evening News* is the responsibility of the MEN board. The *Daily Mail* management in Manchester similarly has considerable latitude on matters other than major policy questions.

Management Organisation

557. It is important to remember in the Manchester context that management teams are relatively small. One house has a middle and senior management team of eleven and other teams are still smaller. Not surprisingly they do not invariably contain a manager solely responsible for labour relations matters though they do usually contain managers with long experience of industrial relations in the newspaper industry. As in Fleet Street, there have been some attempts to devolve more responsibility to overseers for at least some aspects of industrial relations. Nevertheless any negotiation of more than marginal significance is done by senior managers though overseers may be present and contribute to the discussion. In some cases overseers work at their trade in addition to performing their managerial functions.

Trade Union Organisation

558. The principal differences in union membership patterns between Fleet Street and the Manchester establishments are described in paragraph 318, and the union branch structures are also outlined in Chapter 9. There are no formal joint arrangements designed to encourage policy co-ordination between the unions. Contacts do, however, take place on an *ad hoc* basis and relations between the unions are said to be good. Demarcation problems do crop up from time to time but appear usually to be settled amicably (see for example paragraph 358).

559. Within the Manchester establishments chapel organisation differs in some respects from that in London. As far as the MGS is concerned, there are no local chapels in the composing area. There are seven SOGAT chapels in the establishments. Despite NATSOPA's pre-eminence in the publishing, machine, clerical and other areas only one NATSOPA combine chapel exists (this links the machine and publishing chapels within one of the houses). In 1953 the NATSOPA Branch abandoned its policy of encouraging combine chapels. SLADE has one chapel in each house, as does the NUJ.

560. In total, there are about 140 chapels in the Manchester establishments with a smaller average size than their London counterparts (29:47). The links between chapels of different unions within individual houses appear even more

---

* In a recent case involving TWG and the NGA, members of the NGA working at TWG claimed in April 1976 that rates of pay agreed between MGN and the NGA (which appeared to the NGA chapels to be higher than the increases agreed between the NPA and NGA) should be reflected in payments to their members. The claim was eventually submitted to a board of arbitration constituted by ACAS which found against it.

fragile than in London. There are Federated House Chapels covering the *Guardian*/MEN and Beaverbrook Newspapers Ltd, and there is a liaison committee at TWG which performs the same functions as an FHC though it does not enjoy the support of all the chapels. Elsewhere there are either no joint chapel working arrangements or arrangements that have operated intermittently and imperfectly.

561. The functions of and facilities available to chapel officers are similar to those described in Chapter 8. A rather higher proportion of chapels (about a quarter in those houses providing relevant information) are party to "check-off" arrangements (see paragraph 296), and many chapels have office and telephone facilities. A very small proportion of FOCs spend significant proportions of normal working hours on chapel duties.

Pay Determination and Collective Bargaining Machinery

562. The terms and conditions of employment of national newspaper employees in Manchester (apart from MGN employees) are governed by NPA agreements. The details of the implementation of NPA agreements in Manchester are normally handled by the accountants sub-committee of the Manchester NPA (see paragraph 234). There are no separate Manchester negotiations about the general size or form of pay increases. Though MGN has left the NPA it co-operates closely with other newspaper houses in Manchester. Indeed, the integration of the composing area at Withy Grove and the use by MGN of the casual "pool" arrangements necessitate its close involvement in any discussions affecting these areas. An MGN representative is occasionally invited to meetings of the Manchester Managers' Committee and the MGN receives all NPA circulars. Conversely, MGN is careful not to embarrass NPA members by setting precedents that breach NPA agreements.

563. Within establishments the framework within which negotiations are conducted is much the same as in Fleet Street. Some houses review their comprehensive agreements annually and others have agreements that are subject to review only when a change in working conditions warrants it. The frequency of joint chapel negotiation with management is probably greater in Manchester than Fleet Street. In one house joint negotiations have taken place involving NGA and NATSOPA machine room chapels, and also NGA and NATSOPA reading room employees. In another, the engineers and electricians negotiate jointly with management though they have separate, practically identical, agreements. In a third it is said to be "not uncommon" for management to negotiate with two or more chapels jointly and recent examples were given during our inquiries of joint negotiations involving NATSOPA and NGA machine room chapels and NATSOPA and NGA machine and publishing room chapels.

564. Nevertheless, most chapels negotiate independently. The pattern of house negotiations is similar to that in Fleet Street though the incidence of negotiation seems, if anything, rather less. In 1975, about a third of the chapels for which information is available (ie about half the total number) were involved in no formal negotiations which resulted in an agreement. A further 35% were involved in one or two negotiations during the year which resulted in agreements, and the bulk of the remainder were involved in three to five negotiations. Only

one or two chapels had an average of one or more negotiations a month. It should, of course, be emphasised that many of the negotiations are quite minor in character and involve little, if any, money. Certainly wage drift was said by managements to be very low. In one case in 1975 labour cost variance from labour cost forecasts was of the order of one per cent, or, as one manager in another house described his establishment's wage drift, "peanuts". Negotiations were predominantly concerned with regular reviews of comprehensive agreements, manning or other productivity changes, and payments for abnormal working conditions for small groups of employees within individual chapels. In one house in 1975 fringe benefits, holidays and hours were a particularly frequent subject of negotiation.

Disputes and Disputes Procedures

565. Paragraph 555 has already referred to the low level of industrial action initiated by Northprint chapels. In other houses, the number of industrial actions has also been comparatively low. For example, in one case there have been only three stoppages of work or other industrial action leading to lost copies over a period of many years. In another, no disputes, grievances or issues arose in 1975 over which any industrial action was taken or threatened; and in a third there have been eight disputes since 1973 leading to a loss of copies and several of these were related to questions outside the power of the establishments concerned to determine. Stoppages that occur in Manchester may be the result of decisions taken in London, and these may be partly affected by the Fleet Street industrial relations situation. The MGN departure from the NPA, for example, provoked some difficulties in Manchester the following year (1975). Similarly, the plans for photocomposition announced by MGN and the *Daily Telegraph* prompted meetings in working hours and stoppages by NGA and NUJ chapels. Between 28 October 1975 when the MGN made its announcement (the *Daily Telegraph* announcement was on 21 November 1975) and the middle of January 1976 some two dozen such meetings and stoppages are on record.

566. London disputes do not normally overspill into Manchester, though they may have some effect on newspaper production in Manchester. For example, in one composing area nearly 30% of the work dislocations were the result of poor copy flow from London because of industrial relations difficulties there. Conversely, however, production problems in London from whatever cause may be partly compensated by increased output in Manchester.

567. The Manchester NPA disputes procedure has been outlined in Chapter 11. Within houses in Manchester the usual procedure, not always in writing, is that issues arising are first raised with overseers/heads of departments; then, if unresolved, they are handled by a senior manager and the union Branch may become involved; finally, the NPA procedure may be invoked. Whilst the warning given of industrial action may be short or non-existent some management records suggest that action takes place at a more advanced stage of the procedure than in London. The kind of comments made by Manchester managers and union representatives about the working of the procedures contrasts sharply with the comments commonly made in Fleet Street about the handling of disputes there. One manager told us that chapels adhere "scrupulously to agreements". In another house the feeling was that chapels generally followed the procedure

(which, in this case, was fairly protracted) though they sometimes threatened not to do so. As in London most disputes are settled within the house machinery. Branch officers and the appropriate managers are said to be easy to contact and there is less reluctance to use the NPA machinery on the part of unions. Though relatively few issues are referred to the NPA machinery most that do reach that level are settled there. There seems to be a mutual reluctance on the part of managements and unions to allow matters to be referred to the IRE and national officers in London.

Joint Negotiating and Consultative Machinery

568. We have referred in paragraph 563 to the joint negotiations that sometimes take place between two or more chapels on the one hand and house management on the other. Such joint negotiations are not normally standing arrangements and there is no formal joint negotiating machinery that involves two or more chapels in regularly reaching joint agreements with management. Joint consultative arrangements are almost as rare. Health and safety committees exist or are in the process of formation in all houses and canteen committees and similar institutions sometimes exist. Only in Beaverbrook Newspapers is there a broad-based consultative committee on which all chapels are represented. The committe had its first meeting in November 1973 and meets every two months.

Views of the Parties

569. A fairly common view in Manchester is that there are two main reasons why industrial relations are easier in Manchester than in London. First, it is thought that Manchester managements are not as competitive. Day-to-day competition between newspapers is principally manifested in Fleet Street. Manchester managements may be affected by inter-house competition in the longer term but not in their daily relations with each other. It is argued that this encourages an easier flow of information between NPA and non-NPA managements (though there are still some inhibitions in this connection), and facilitates a common managerial approach to industrial relations problems. On the union side, strict control into the industry, fewer casual employees, and different membership and Branch structures to those in Fleet Street are thought to contribute to a more stable situation.

CHAPTER 16: EDITORIAL STAFF

570. It would be wrong to draw too sharp a distinction between editorial staff* and other employees within national newspapers. We deal separately with editorial staff here partly for convenience, and are conscious that with the introduction of photocomposition as planned by the *Financial Times*, *Daily Telegraph* and *The Times* (see Chapter 3), the traditional lines between editorial and composing functions will be blurred. The NUJ and the printing union consult closely within the TUCPIC on matters of joint concern (as, for eaxmple, over the NUJ dispute with the *Daily Telegraph* in May 1976); the NUJ was party to the joint submission of the unions and publishers to the Royal Commission in February 1976 and is a member of the JSC; and, within houses, NUJ chapels are normally represented on FHCs.

571. Nevertheless, editorial staff do possess a number of distinct characteristics most of which derive from the fact that they are at the "sharp end" of the business: the output of editorial staff determines the nature of the product and is a major factor in a newspaper's success or failure. The journalist's job is to find, select, present, interpret and even make, news. The process demands flair as well as practical skills; experience, which is partly related to age, and imagination, which is not. The nature of the work done, the qualifications required to do it, and the environment in which it is carried out are very different for journalists than for most other employees. In addition, journalists, concerned essentially with news rather than newspapers, have wider job opportunities than most other employees in the industry. A career in Fleet Street might be a stepping stone to a job in broadcasting or public relations, areas in which opportunities have grown immensely in the last twenty years. Journalists also have more opportunity for in-house career progression than production workers and movements from one Fleet Street newspaper to another, though not common in a tight employment situation, are more frequent for journalists than production staff.

572. It was often argued during our inquiries that journalists have a stronger identification with the product than other employees, and that they expect to derive job satisfaction rewards from their creative work beyond their material ones (one house agreement for journalists contains a clause in which this is formally recognised†); a statement that is less true of production and clerical staff. It is certainly the case that in industrial relations terms there are fewer problems among editorial staff than among other employees, and this is probably a reflection of the job differences referred to in these paragraphs. Notwithstanding a more aggressive approach by NUJ chapels in negotiations in recent years and recent disputes related to the introduction of new technology, there is a lower incidence of management/chapel conflict in the editorial than in the production area. There are fewer difficulties in relation to the payments systems (though these are rudimentary), and the union organisation of journalists is simpler.

---

* "Editorial Staff" are defined here as all NUJ and IOJ members and potential members. It should be remembered, however, that other staff (such as NATSOPA copy takers, messengers and clerical staff) are employed in editorial departments.

† The clause states ". . . the company shall seek to make work rewarding for its staff. With this in view the editor will, where practicable, endeavour to let individuals extend their experience and responsibility". In exchange for this the journalists have agreed to work flexibly.

Distribution of Editorial Staff

573. The use of the term "journalists" to cover all those employees who are actually or potentially members of the NUJ or IOJ can disguise the fact that there are widely differing types of journalist with different job contents, work patterns and career and promotion expectations. The popular image of the journalist is of the reporter on an outside assignment but only 38% of full-time editorial staff fall into the category of reporters and correspondents. The working lives of the sub-editorial staff (about a fifth of all editorial staff) are based on routine attendance at the newspaper office. These two categories comprise 61% of the total editorial staff. The remainder consists of editors, deputy editors, photographers, researchers, statisticians in city offices, and cartoonists. About a fifth of full-time editorial staff work in Manchester.

Casual and Freelance Working

574. In addition to the 3,600 full-time editorial staff working for national newspapers there are large numbers of casual and freelance journalists. Although an individual may undertake both casual and freelance work, it is important to distinguish between them. "Casual" journalists have an affinity with casual production workers in that they work as direct employees of a newspaper usually for fewer shifts during a week than permanent staff journalists, though where a casual journalist is called in to cover holidays, long-term sickness, special projects or a staff vacancy, he may work the same number of shifts as permanent staff for a limited period. Editors usually maintain an on-call list from which such "casual" journalists are employed.

575. Sunday newspapers rely heavily on regular casual news sub-editors. Many of these have staff jobs with other newspapers (sometimes part of the same group), others are freelances supplementing their income. Some freelances also work as casual casual journalists. There has been discussion within the NUJ on the desirability of fifth-day working by individuals who are regularly employed elsewhere, when the union has unemployed members qualified to do such work.

576. Freelances are for the most part self-employed, although some are employed by freelance agencies. The owners of such agencies, invariably freelances themselves, are allowed full membership of the NUJ. Freelances often specialise in a particular subject area, and their work may be commissioned by a newspaper or may be put forward on a speculative basis.

577. There is one main Freelance Branch within the NUJ which has about 1,700 members. Casual journalists are not members of the NUJ chapel in the house in which they work, but are usually invited to chapel meetings. The position of casuals in relation to NUJ chapels has been under discussion, however.

578. The national negotiations between the NUJ and the NPA settle minimum casual "Daily", "Sunday Paper" and "Weekly" rates for London and Manchester*. The latter rate has the same sub-division according to length of NPA experience as the agreement relating to regular staff journalists (see paragraph 584). Minimum freelance rates are also settled nationally, although during separate negotiations at which there is Freelance Branch representation. These

---

* Technically the IOJ also negotiate with the NPA; in practice it follows the NUJ agreements.

negotiations may take place in advance of the main national negotiations or after them, and there is no automatic link between the increases made to national minimum rates and the increase in minimum freelance rates. The 1975 round of house agreements included, at the NUJ's request, domestic rates for casuals*. Although most of the agreed rates are higher than the national minima, it is generally thought that the growth in importance of house agreements (the provisions of which have, until now, only applied to regular journalists) has caused unfair differences in earnings between journalists doing very similar work. This has caused some regular casual journalists to question whether their interests are adequately served by the existing chapel structure and to seek to set up "casual chapels". In some houses regular casual journalists enjoy the same conditions of employment as regular staff in relation to holidays, pensions, sick pay and the like.

579. Apart from the general misgivings within the NUJ about casual employment there is concern within some Fleet Street NUJ chapels over the extent of casual working within their houses. Some chapels have agreed limits on the amount of casual working with managements. Some agreements specify that a casual casual will be invited to join the regular casual staff after he has completed an agreed number of consecutive regular casual engagements. Similarly, some agreements state that a regular casual will be invited to join the regular staff if he completes an agreed number of consecutive full working weeks as a casual. Other NUJ chapels express concern over the amount of news agency material used by their newspapers, and feel this poses a threat to the employment of journalists.

Training and Entry

580. The major part of the burden of journalists' training falls upon provincial newspapers. Although the 1965 NPA/NUJ Memorandum on the subject of journalists' entry into Fleet Street (see paragraph 581) to some extent formalised this arrangement, it has long been the case that the provincial press provides a training ground for the editorial staff of national newspapers. The training of journalists is supervised by a joint industrial federal body, the National Council for the Training of Journalists (NCTJ) and is based on collective agreements between the unions and the employers' associations. The NCTJ is supported, through its grant system and through advisory services, by the PPITB, which has NUJ representation. Basic training is provided through two routes: direct entry into "apprenticeship", and pre-entry courses of one year followed by a reduced apprenticeship. The apprenticeship consists of supervised on-the-job vocational training in offices and of associated further courses. At the end of the training period the trainee takes the NCTJ proficiency test to obtain the Council's Certificate of Proficiency. At least one company with provincial newspaper interests, MGN, uses a provincial group of newspapers as a basis for a training scheme which it feels provides a good supply of journalistic talent to its national titles.

581. In 1965 a joint NPA/NUJ sub-committee drew up a memorandum on the appointment of unqualified journalists. Unqualified journalists are defined as those who have not undergone the necessary provincial training. The joint committee accepted "the traditional notion" that Fleet Street is not normally a

---

* A few houses have now also agreed domestic minimum freelance rates with their NUJ chapels.

suitable training ground for unqualified juornalists. It also recognised, however, that editors must be able to recruit journalists "from other than conventional sources". This clause was designed to cover specialists such as financial experts, and mention was made of direct graduate entry into newspapers. Even with these exceptions, the joint committee felt it was unreasonable that a significant number of NUJ members employed in Fleet Street were not covered by NPA/NUJ agreements as they had not entered from the provinces. It was recommended that:

(a) qualified entrants over the age of 24 should receive at least the minimum NUJ rate not later than six months after their engagement;

(b) unqualified entrants aged between 23 and 24 should receive the minimum rate after 12 months' service;

(c) unqualified entrants under the age of 21 would not normally be engaged,

582. The NUJ remained concerned, however, about the scope to recruit unqualified journalists which they felt editors still had. An exchange of drafts and correspondence between the NUJ and the NPA attempted unsuccessfully to tighten up the agreement. Some editors maintained their objections to the original memorandum on the grounds that it tended to deter the best talent from newspapers.

583. Our inquiries revealed few current industrial relations problems associated with the Memorandum. The vast majority of journalists working on national newspapers are qualified within the terms of the agreement. Although there were complaints from managements about "restrictive" interpretations of the Memorandum by editorial chapels (and a good deal of dissatisfaction was also voiced in oral evidence to the Royal Commission by managements and editors), there were also those who were firmly in favour of it. Some chapels are attempting to negotiate domestic agreements which strengthen the terms of the Memorandum, in particular to require editors to reach agreement with chapels about "doubtful" appointments, rather than merely to consult about them as the Memorandum requires; indeed, some such agreements already exist.

Terms and Conditions of Employment
Salaries and Grading

584. Following the report in 1969 of the National Board for Prices and Incomes on journalists' pay,* there were attempts within houses to rationalise salary and grading structures. At least one house and NUJ chapel did consider the introduction of job evaluation, but found the exercise so difficult that they abandoned it. Rather than adopt the NBPI's suggestion of job analysis, NUJ chapels have worked towards salary structures containing minimum salary provisions related to length of service and level of responsibility. In consequence, nearly every house has some system of incremental service payments and many have a grading system with minimum salaries for each grade of journalist. The complexity of these systems varies and some chapels have been more successful than others in codifying the payments made by the house over and above the NPA minimum. In one house there are four grades which qualify for extra payments above the basic house scale: assistant editors and similar staff, heads

---

* Report No 115, "Journalists' Pay", Cmnd 4077. HMSO.

of department and similar staff, deputy heads of department; and special writers, specialist sub-editors and similar staff. Other agreements also make special payments for responsibility. In one case where the grading structure covers all (except very senior) staff within five scales, a specific set of "grading principles" has been agreed. These require editors to "assess the comparative value of the job to the company ... (then to) ... consider the special qualifications required and possessed by staff to fill the posts". The latter are given as experience in journalism generally, special experience, ability to work long hours and to work with others, initiative, acceptance of responsibility etc. This five-grade system is agreed by management and chapel to have worked satisfactorily for the most part.

585. Whether these developments have led to a more rational or equitable distribution of salaries is debateable; merit payments still complicate the picture. These have survived in every house and are given at the editor's discretion, although in some houses there is agreement that the editor will take heed of chapel representations on the distribution of merit payments. A few houses have agreed with their chapels on what the total sum given in merit payments will be during the life of a house agreement although the allocation is left in the hands of the editor. In one major house, for example, attempts are made to ensure that the sum available to editors for merit payments is around 2% of the salary bill. Moreover, not only is the chapel informed about the total number of staff who receive merit increases but also about the broad occupational areas in which they are paid. The editor must also take into account the chapel's written views before completing the merit review. At the other extreme the question of merit payments remains a controversial area between chapel and managements.

586. As well as merit payments, the salary structure can be affected by journalists who join the newspaper at well above the minimum salary (perhaps where there is competition for his or her services) and by journalists who may negotiate increases individually where they feel that their market value is being underestimated. In addition a special category of exceptionally talented writers exists and it is accepted that these "star" journalists or writers, some of whom have fixed-term contracts, will negotiate their own salaries with the newspapers. There are no house agreements which cover editors.

587. What emerges is that managements and chapels have been negotiating over both the size of the salary bill and on how it should be distributed. Although some NUJ FOCs feel that merit payments are divisive and open to abuse many think them to be an inevitable part of the creative editorial environment, together with meteoric promotions and equally dramatic falls from grace. There also seems to be an acceptance that there will always be "star" journalists. Some managements complained during our inquiries that chapel pressure over service and merit payments have compressed differentials, and that there is now insufficient scope for editors to properly reward talent and effort. The existing system in most houses seems to be a compromise between the chapels' desire to regulate the distribution of the salary bill and the management's wish to retain the right to reward individuals whom they feel deserve it.

Other Terms and Conditions of Employment

588. An examination of agreements affecting journalists in Fleet Street reveals two interesting areas of comparison. The first is with those agreements applying

to production and clerical workers, and the second is between the individual agreements applying to each house. In the former case, the most obvious difference is in the type of bargain struck. Whereas agreements covering production chapels tend to concentrate on the detail of the work which it is agreed chapel members will undertake and on pay, hours and holidays, those covering journalists make only limited reference to the work performed, and have provisions about wider "staff" conditions of employment such as sabbatical and maternity leave. It is difficult to compare the basic conditions of employment of production and editorial staff because of the wide variations of conditions for staff in the former category.

589. A comparison of NUJ house agreements shows that there are marked similarities between them. Most house agreements embody the nationally-agreed hours of work for journalists (40 hours per week for day workers and 35 per week for night workers: night workers are usually defined as those regularly finishing after 19.00 hours, or starting before 0.630 hours), although at least one house improves on these. Most houses now allow journalists to work a four-day week and occasionally other flexible arrangements (eg a nine-day fortnight or 18-day month) operate. On holidays, some houses give the NPA minimum of four weeks but most give five weeks plus a number of days off in lieu of statutory public holidays.

590. All houses also grant sabbatical or training leave to their journalists. A typical provision is for four weeks' leave after every four years' service, although some agreements differ slightly from this. Sabbatical leave is said to be for a journalist to "widen his experience". Most agreements state that such leave should not be taken during peak holiday times and that a journalist is not permitted to work for another UK newspaper while on sabbatical leave. Another common feature of house agreements is maternity leave, although there is a variety of provisions. All agreements make reference to journalists' expenses and allowances. Among the most common allowances are those for telephone rental, the purchase of newspapers and periodicals and the costs of running a motor vehicle. Expenses and allowances form the area over which there are most day-to-day management/chapel discussions.

The Management of Editorial Staff

591. The organisation of editorial management reflects the view of most companies that editorial staff should, for industrial relations purposes, be set apart from those employed in the clerical and production areas. One justification for this is that where companies produce more than one title the demands of editorial autonomy lead to editorial management being based in individual newspapers: this is not always the case with other staff and is becoming even less so. Journalists working for the same house but on different titles are sometimes employed under significantly different terms and conditions of employment. In the majority of houses industrial relations management of editorial staff is distinct from that of production and clerical staff, even where there is a specialist industrial relations department within the company.

592. In most houses the managing editor generally has responsibility for administrative matters in the editorial departments, including day-to-day

dealings with the chapels. This frees the newspaper's editor from such tasks so that he can devote more time to the contents of the newspaper. Day-to-day problems may also be dealt with by the appropriate departmental editor or his deputy. Negotiations on journalists' house agreements usually involve the editor, the managing editor and one or more members of the board. Editorial house negotiations in Fleet Street seem to be the only ones consistently to have board involvement. In only one house are production, clerical and editorial staff covered by an integrated management structure below board level for negotiating purposes.

Union and Chapel Organisation

593. Whereas the production areas are fully unionised as a consequence of pre-entry closed shops, as in these areas are the managerial staffs who are mostly promoted from within the existing workforce (see Chapter 6), the level of unionisation in editorial and administrative departments whilst high, is generally less than 100%. No comprehensive figures on the extent of non-membership of trade unions in national newspapers are available but in one large multi-title house 1% of the editorial and editorial services employees are not in membership of any union, and 9% of the administrative, circulation and advertising staffs are not union members. In two other multi-title houses, the editorial staff are 98% and 96% unionised. Most house agreements for journalists include a clause encouraging membership of the NUJ, although these vary in their firmness from the more common forms which state that "it is the established and normal practice for journalists employed by the company to be members of the NUJ", to one which states that "if legislation allows the company will require journalists . . . to belong to the Union [NUJ] on taking up their employment, and to remain in membership". Only in the *Daily Telegraph* is there an IOJ chapter which has negotiating rights for its 74 members, although six smaller chapters do exist in Fleet Street and similar rights have been requested elsewhere without success.

594. Where houses produce more than one title the pattern of NUJ chapel organisation varies as Appendix, 16 Table 3 shows. Sometimes the chapel covers the editorial staff of more than one newspaper (as with Beaverbrook Newspapers and the Daily Telegraph Ltd); other companies have separate chapels for different titles. Journalists employed in the Manchester establishments are organised into separate chapels.

595. NUJ members employed on national newspapers are currently covered by three branches. The Central London Branch (CLB) includes in its membership all NUJ members employed on national newspapers in London except those employed on the London evening newspapers, who are members of the London Evening Papers Branch. The NUJ Manchester Branch covers journalists employed on national newspapers in Manchester. In addition, members of the Freelance Branch provide material for national newspapers.

Determination of Terms and Conditions of Employment
Developments in Wage Bargaining

596. The NPA and the NUJ have had agreed minimum rates for Fleet Street and Manchester editorial staff for over fifty years. Agreements have also covered

conditions of employment such as hours and holidays. In the 1950s and early 1960s these rates were fixed at meetings held every two to three years. Although the nationally agreed minimum rates and general increases provided the basic rates of pay, most journalists received other payments which included "merit" increases granted periodically, usually annually, by editors. These payments were becoming a major source of grievance in the mid-1960s. Quite apart from what some journalists considered to be the paternalistic connotations of merit payments, they militated against the older "average" journalists whose job mobility was less than that of his younger colleagues. The subjectivity of editors' judgements brought complaints of favouritism and inconsistency. Some journalists felt that trade union activity in Fleet Street was inhibited by the fact that the determination of individual salary levels was firmly a management prerogative.

597. There was also widespread and growing resentment among journalists at what they felt were anomalous relationships between their own earnings and those of skilled production workers employed on their newspapers. It was felt that the journalists had been left behind in the struggle for higher earnings. A document presented by the General Secretary of the NUJ during the wage discussions of 1966 argued that the rates of pay for Fleet Street journalists had manifestly failed to keep up with the cost of living.

598. General increases in basic rates were agreed between the NPA and the NUJ in 1964 and in 1967. However, the pressures described above led to a clause in the 1967 agreement committing both sides to examine the suitability of the existing minimum rates. Later in that year the NPA and the NUJ set up a joint working party to look at the possibility of a nationally negotiated salary structure for journalists and of distinguishing between the rates for "creative" and "non-creative" journalists, the latter being those editorial staff employed mainly on statistical/clerical work.

599. The report of this working party was the basis for the December 1968 agreement which laid down staged increases to the minimum rates of pay and established differentials between three categories of journalists based on length of service with a national newspaper or national newsagency. The three categories were for journalists with under two years', with two to five years' and with over five years' such experience. At this stage the NBPI was asked to examine the settlement and its "repercussions on the pay of all journalists employed by the newspapers covered by the settlement and its relationship to pay negotiations for other groups of journalists". The Board felt that these terms of reference demanded that it examine "the appropriateness of the negotiating procedure as well as the pay increases to which they give rise".

600. A number of the Board's findings are of interest here. For example, it was found that actual increases and actual earnings "differed considerably" from those laid down in the national agreement. Earnings had "moved steadily upwards" while the rate had been increased "only intermittently". The two major contributors to this drift were merit payments and the growing trends towards house agreements. The Board felt that clear steps, including the introduction of job analysis to ensure that jobs of equal content received equal

pay, should be taken towards a radical restructuring of journalists' pay at house level. There should also be "a more objective system of staff appraisal and a grading of salaries which would enable good performance by a journalist to be rewarded by his being placed above the mid-point of the range of pay for his particular grade". The Board further recommended that the "exceptional" journalist continue to be rewarded by merit payments but that the gross amount paid in such merit payments be kept within bounds; that the relationship between the national and house negotiations should be made explicit, and that the former should be put onto a more formal footing. A new standing joint NPA/NUJ Committee should have three main functions: to establish minimum salaries, to establish guidelines for the new salary structures the Board felt should be constructed at house level and to vet house agreements before implementation.

601. While the Board was deliberating, however, IPC, following a withdrawal of labour by journalists in Manchester, had negotiated a house agreement with its journalists which seems to have set the pattern for Fleet Street. It established five categories of editorial staff with separate rates for each, and payments were given for NPA and house service. The principle of a four-day week was agreed. Formal recognition was also given to the need for regular consultation between management and staff, and a domestic disputes procedure was introduced.

602. Other houses followed IPC's example, and the general increases in salaries agreed nationally in 1969 and 1970 were accompanied by general increases in some houses. The 1971 NPA/NUJ agreement, which increased the minimum Fleet Street rate by 47% and gave a guaranteed minimum increase of £400, included an embargo on further house increases during its tenure. This agreement caused fierce argument within the NUJ which culminated in a debate at the 1971 Annual Delegate Meeting. The ADM carried by a large majority a motion which instructed the NEC "not to recommend or enter into any future agreements with employers that inhibit the bargaining power of individual chapels on wages, holidays or conditions". Although the draft agreement had been balloted and accepted by the Fleet Street members of the NUJ, there had been many unofficial withdrawals of labour by chapels in attempts to persuade managements to negotiate.

603. The national agreement of June 1972 removed the embargo, increased minimum rates and gave staged guaranteed minimum increases in salary of £250 and £150. The agreement was for eighteen months and was thus due to terminate in December 1973. During its currency IPC had lost several million copies by refusing to settle with its NUJ chapel above the limit agreed by all the NPA members. It emerged, however, that one house had already settled at a higher figure. When the agreement elapsed the incomes policy in operation at the time prohibited further increases until June 1974, one year after the second staged increase had become payable. The NUJ wished to open early negotiations with the NPA for a new national agreement to run from June. The opening of negotiations was delayed, however, and IPC, in February 1974, again came under pressure from NUJ chapels to settle in-house before the NPA had opened negotiations on a new national agreement.

604. IPC's journalists claimed that the company had given an undertaking that house negotiations would commence before the NPA negotiations and industrial action by journalists on the *Daily Mirror* and the *Scottish Daily Record* resulted in more lost copies. IPC, believing that, as in the previous year, another company had already settled with its journalists, withdrew from the NPA, opened negotiations with its chapels and settled on a new house agreement two months later.

605. When the national negotiations did commence, the NPA and the NUJ were unable to agree. The NPA claimed that the financial position of newspapers prevented them from meeting the NUJ claim, and it was agreed that negotiations would have to be carried out on a house basis. House agreements between individual managements and their NUJ chapels were rapidly concluded, however, and there seems to have been little variation in the size of increases agreed in the various house negotiations. Many, if not all, were in excess of the maximum offer which the houses had collectively felt able to offer during the NPA negotiations.

606. The NPA and NUJ set up a working party to reach agreement on the national minimum rates for regular and casual journalists to be operative from July 1974. The working party finally agreed on the new rates (obtained from the lowest money elements of the 1974 house agreements) in May 1975.

607. The 1975 negotiations began with the NPA insisting that it could only agree to "one tier" negotiations; that is, either a series of house level agreements with no national agreement, or a nationally-agreed increase with an embargo on further house increases as in the 1971 agreement. The NUJ negotiators were precluded from an agreement of the latter sort by the decision of the 1971 ADM. In addition, the *Guardian* and *Observer* felt unable for differing reasons to commit themselves to a national agreement. In these circumstances house agreements were again negotiated. As in the previous year, there do not seem to have been wide variations between the increases agreed within different houses. Contact between NUJ FOCs in Fleet Street on the level of their increases and a determination that no house would be allowed to become too poor a relation in terms of the salaries paid to its journalists seem to have contributed to this outcome. At national level a similar exercise to that of the previous year was carried out to arrive at new national minimum rates for regular and casual journalists.

608. Although incomes policy has made the question of house or national negotiations somewhat academic, the events of the past seven years seem to have firmly entrenched the importance of house agreements for Fleet Street editorial staff. There seems little possibility of Fleet Street's NUJ chapels relinquishing their right to negotiate house agreements which improve on the NPA agreement. Among the FOCs and the Branch and national officers to whom we spoke, however, there is some feeling that agreements at national level should be continued. One of the main reasons given is the problems which the present situation causes for casuals and freelances (see paragraph 578). In addition, it is felt that national agreements act as a "safety net" for journalists employed on the financially weaker national newspapers. There is

a belief, among NUJ members and elsewhere, that the pay of editorial staff is an area where certain of the newspaper houses feel they might be able to embarrass their competitors and consequently there is little chance that the national negotiations will ever again supersede house negotiations in importance. Despite this belief, which is not well supported by the evidence, all current house agreements refer to the national agreement. The clauses vary in strength; one, for example, states that nothing within the house agreement shall derogate from superior terms in national agreements, and another that should agreements be made at national level which improve on house terms then discussions will take place between chapel and management.

The Conduct of House Negotiations

609. Whereas the Manchester journalists' chapels usually work closely with the Fleet Street chapels of their respective newspapers and are generally covered by the same agreement, the extent of inter-title co-operation between NUJ chapels in the same multi-title house varies considerably. Wherever there is more than one NUJ chapel within a house there is invariably informal co-operation and exchange of information, but a comparison between the coverage of chapels and the coverage of agreements within such houses (see Appendix 16, Table 3) shows that joint negotiation by such chapels is by no means universal. Those NUJ chapels which have members working on two newspapers (the *Daily Express/Sunday Express* and the *Daily Telegraph/Sunday Telegraph* chapels) have single agreements with managements which cover both newspapers. In some cases there is dual-working between newspapers owned by the same company.

610. The situation has not always been as shown in Appendix 16, Table 3. For example, between 1969–70 and 1974 MGN's NUJ chapels negotiated as a group and were covered by a single agreement. The *Daily Mirror* chapel broke away from the group and there were separate negotiations and separate house claims in 1975. However, in making separate claims each chapel emphasised that it would not settle for less than the others received and the company has attempted to keep the separate settlements in line. News Group Newspapers' *Sun* and *News of the World* chapels also negotiated together until 1973.

611. The extent of differences between agreements by the NUJ chapels of multi-title houses also varies. In some cases such differences are considerable, whereas in others the agreements reached are practically identical. Both situations seem to have been the result of deliberate management policy, in the latter to maintain consistency and (in at least one case) to demonstrate the house view of the futility of fragmented bargaining, and in the former to ensure that journalists' terms and conditions of employment reflect the differing profitability of the newspapers concerned.

612. Although chapels negotiate independently in-house, claims and proposed settlements must be approved by the union's National Executive Council. This procedure is intended to ensure the expertise of national negotiators is brought to bear, that clauses are inserted that are considered necessary from a national point of view (such as those establishing the relationship between house agreements and NPA agreements), and that chapels do not insert clauses in agreements which run counter to union policy.

Disputes and Disputes Procedures

613. The growth in militancy of the NUJ in the 1960s and 1970s, which has been acknowledged within the union itself*, has been marked by a growth in disputes involving editorial staff. Paragraphs 596 to 608 outline the events of 1967 to 1975: during this period strikes and other forms of industrial action became more acceptable to editorial staff, many of whom felt that their past unwillingness to consider such action had resulted in journalists slipping down the earnings ladder. The industrial action that has been taken has mainly been concerned with the negotiation of annual house agreements, however, and there is little day-to-day bargaining over the actual work performed by editorial staff and thus few disputes arise which are not connected with the negotiation or interpretation of house agreements. Major issues such as redundancy have, of course, caused serious disputes involving editorial staff.

614. Most day-to-day grievances involving editorial staff are of an individual nature. The payment of expenses and allowances is an area where such grievances commonly arise. Individual complaints about grading or status and the allocation of merit payments also occur from time to time, and where these are not quickly settled chapel officers often become involved.

615. All houses have agreed† domestic disputes procedures with their NUJ chapels. Commonly these have stages involving meetings between the FOC and the editor and/or the appropriate editorial executive. Subsequent stages involve the appropriate NUJ official and/or the chapel officials and, in most cases, an executive board member (usually the managing director). All the procedures (except of course MGN's) then feed into the NPA/NUJ procedure.

616. Despite not being able to agree a new national wage agreement in 1974, the NUJ and NPA did agree in October of that year that the procedural agreement for the settlement of disputes should be revived. The current agreement requires the officials of the NUJ and/or the NPA to attempt to settle the dispute using their "best endeavours". In common with disputes agreements with other unions in the industry, the agreement allows for the setting-up of a "three plus three" joint panel if the conciliation stage is unsucessful. The "five plus five" stage, however, differs from those in the disputes procedures with other unions in that it requires the membership of the panel to be drawn from the NUJ's National Executive Council and from the NPA Council. The third stage of the procedure is left to the "five plus five" panel to decide upon should the dispute remain unresolved. Both sides agree that there shall be no hostile action while the procedure is in operation. The IOJ is also party to similar procedural arrangements.

617. An examination of the utilisation of the NPA disputes machinery since 1974 shows that editorial chapels are much more willing than other chapels to allow domestic disputes to go to the NPA disputes procedure. Many of these disputes concern individuals. A chapel may claim, for example, that an individual appointed by management is not qualified within the terms of the 1965 Memorandum or that a casual journalist is being unfairly refused his holiday entitlement. Although collective issues have gone to the NPA/NUJ procedure, few have been concerned with annual house agreements.

---

* The union's president in his address to the 1971 ADM called 1970 "the most militant year in the union's history".
† One house was in the process of agreeing a domestic disputes procedure during our inquiries.

Consultative Arrangements

618. Most agreements with editorial staff include a commitment that the house will consult regularly with the chapel on matters of mutual concern. Again, these agreements differ from the mass of agreements applying to other staff. Some specify that meetings be held monthly, others bi-monthly or quarterly. One agreement requires the editor to convene meetings of all the editorial staff of his newspaper in London and Manchester at least every six months to discuss matters of mutual concern. Some of the agreements specifically exclude editorial policy from the matters of mutual concern that may be discussed. In no case is editorial policy the subject of joint consultation between chapel and management, though one chapel has claimed the right to elect the editor of the newspaper and nominate a director to the house board. The claim has been rejected.

619. In one case editorial house agreements have a very wide disclosure clause in which the house undertakes to "provide the chapels with the maximum possible information" about the company. The clause goes on to specify that the management will agree at the chapels' request to a mutually acceptable accountant investigating the company's finances. This provision has been used and the accountant's report to the chapel enabled it, during its pay claim, to argue specifically on the basis of how many journalists were employed by the various titles within the house, and to cost each management proposal. The accountant's report was, in the view of the chapel, instrumental in more than doubling the company's first offer.

Part F: Conclusions

CHAPTER 17: DEVELOPMENTS SINCE THE 1962 ROYAL COMMISSION ON THE PRESS

620. Appendix 17(a) outlines the conclusions of the 1962 Royal Commission on the Press on industrial relations in the national newspaper industry, and the findings of the EIU (1966), the NBPI (1967, 1969, 1970) and the 1967 Court of Inquiry into the problems at Southwark Offset Ltd. The 1962 Royal Commission made four key industial relations recommendations. It suggested that management should give more attention to fostering good industrial relations; that the NPA and P & KTF should be invested with more authority; that within national newspaper offices more authoritative machinery for negotiation and consultation should be established; and that the new machinery should include a joint standing body to oversee "planning and development over the whole field of national newspaper production". The aim of the recommendations was to improve production efficiency and to reduce costs so that in the short term at least there would be no further reduction in the number of national newspapers. In the longer term cost reductions uniformly made across houses would not, it was recognised, alter the balance of the competitive pressures. It is useful briefly to summarise at this point how far the recommendations of the Royal Commission have been achieved or what other developments in industrial relations have taken place.

The Industry

621. The external circumstances in the context of which industrial relations have developed have not been easy. Circulation has fallen by some 16% on average since the 1962 Royal Commission reported with the popular Sundays (an 18% fall) and the London evenings (52%) taking the brunt of the decline. The price of newspapers has risen considerably faster than the index of retail prices (in the case of national daily papers, more than twice as fast), and the proportion of revenue from advertising has steadily declined since 1960 (see Table E9 in the current Royal Commission's Interim Report), and especially sharply since 1973. Two national newspapers have been wound up since 1962: the *Sunday Citizen/Reynolds News* in 1967, and the *Daily Sketch* in 1971.

622. In some ways, the difficult external circumstances faced by national newspapers have promoted internal change in management organisation and techniques, and consequently in the kind of agreements sought and made by managements with chapels. They have also resulted in extensive reappraisal of procedures and practices within the industry.

Disputes and Disputes Procedures

623. Few developments have taken place in national joint disputes procedures since 1962. Their form has not altered and there appears to have been no significant change in the extent to which the procedures are formally used. Within houses there has been more codification of procedures but this does not seem to have affected in practice the very flexible way in which procedures operate in most cases. We have the impression, however, that in recent years there has been a conscious attempt, not always successful, to involve overseers and other line managers to a greater extent in negotiations on disputes occurring in their departments.

624. No comprehensive figures are available to establish trends in the incidence of disputes over the whole period. The trends in house bargaining might imply that, if anything, the incidence of internal house disputes has risen. Such figures as are available from official sources suggest that the number of stoppages in the newspaper and printing industries generally began to rise in the mid-1960s as did the incidence of days lost per 1,000 employees. There has certainly been no diminution in the concern of employers and unions (see Chapter 11) about the damaging effect of major disputes. Indeed, the employers have had one more worry in this direction in recent years. They have felt themselves to be particularly badly affected by "political" stoppages. Between 1970 and 1975, there were seven such stoppages of work lasting a total of 11 days which affected the whole of Fleet Street. The stoppages were not only estimated by employers to cost £150–200,000 each but caused problems related to hours, and for what payment, any backlog of work should be cleared. Most of these stoppages were, however, concerned with the Industrial Relations Act 1971 and there have been none since May 1974.

Employers' Organisation

625. Employers have given more consideration to industrial relations since 1962. In most houses one or more reorganisations have taken place which have tended to give greater weight to industrial relations management. The number of staff specialising in this area has risen, rather more attention is paid to training, and a few houses have tried to work out a new approach to industrial relations generally. In a number of cases management consultants have been employed by houses to advise them on aspects of their management systems. As a result initially of employers' initiatives comprehensive agreements have been widely introduced and payments structures have been simplified (see Chapter 5). Overtime, by joint agreement, has been reduced.

626. The current criticisms of inter-house employer organisation have been set out in Chapter 8. The Royal Commission's plea in 1962 that the NPA should be given more authority finds an echo in submissions to the present Royal Commission. However, the Association has changed structurally in a number of important ways (see, for example, paragraph 252, and footnote) and especially in the development of its advisory facilities. This has not prevented the MGN departure from the NPA nor a serious reappraisal by other houses of their position in relation to the Association. The Royal Commission in 1962 pointed to an earlier agreement that if the publication of one NPA member's publication were stopped the other members would not publish. The agreement

had lapsed but in the Royal Commission's view "unity in defence" (where, for example, unconstitutional action was taken) was sometimes essential. In this area, too, the NPA has attempted to make progress.

Union Organisation

627. A great deal has happened in the field of union organisation since 1962. In 1962 there were 13 organisations (including the IOJ and NUJ) with members wholly or mainly in the printing industry. The present figure is six, and would have been five had the NATSOPA/SOGAT merger attempts been successful. This important development has counter-balanced the demise of the P & KTF, and indeed was partly responsible for it. The TUC PIC has already begun to supplant the P & KTF.

628. Union organisation has also improved at a more basic level. The boundaries of clerical membership have widened and the services available to members have grown. Overseers and other managers have in some houses begun to associate across traditional union lines.

629. However, organisational developments at chapel level are more limited. Union amalgamations have in some cases resulted in closer working between chapels within the same union but the inter-union chapel joint working arrangements have not improved and in some houses have deteriorated (see paragraph 306). There have been some chapel mergers where agreed changes in production arrangements have eradicated the working boundaries between two chapels within the same union, but these have been relatively infrequent.

Joint Working Arrangements

630. There have been few developments in bargaining or consultative machinery within houses since 1962 (but see Chapters 10 and 13), although there have been several important attempts to create joint national machinery. Chapter 10 outlines the birth in 1964 and death of the Joint Board for the National Newspaper Industry and, in 1970, of the National Newspaper Steering Group, and we have referred in passing to the recent establishment of the Joint Standing Committee (JSC). The JSC has emerged from the joint talks between the publishers and unions which began at the end of 1975. The JSC constitution has been agreed (see Appendix 17(*b*)) and during a meeting on 26 May the publishers and unions agreed that the JSC "should operate forthwith". A bank account was authorised and auditors were appointed.

631. The JSC and the previous *ad hoc* talks between employers and unions have been directly supported by all the national newspaper houses (except the *Morning Advertiser* and *Morning Star*) and by all the major print unions other than SLADE. Before the formal creation of the JSC, the joint talks between publishers and unions resulted in the establishment of three joint working parties. The problems faced by the working party dealing with the system of casual employment have already been noted (see paragraph 124). Reports from the other two working parties, dealing with pensions and voluntary redundancy, were available at the time of the May meeting. The working party handling pensions has been exploring the possibilities of establishing minimum pension standards within the industry in relation to levels of future pension and post service pension, and to ancillary pension provisions (eg widows benefit and

transferability). The voluntary redundancy working party has been concerned with the monetary aspects of voluntary redundancy. A number of alternative schemes designed to harmonise voluntary severance terms applicable in each house have been considered.

632. The JSC is potentially an important vehicle for change in the industry. The scope of its activities are more widely drawn than its predecessors, and its objectives are more ambitious. Among its plans, it intends to monitor and co-ordinate the plans of houses on new technology and manpower; encourage the regularization of all employment; deal with demarcation problems in relation to new technology; devise redundancy policies and procedures; and devise and monitor comprehensive procedures for the settlement of disputes. The committee is to be serviced by a joint secretariat of NPA and TUC officials. In all its objectives it has made some progress.

New Technology and Closer Joint Working Arrangements

633. Chapter 3 has outlined the plans of houses so far in introducing new techniques into composing rooms. The prospect of major changes of this kind has promoted closer joint working between the unions. Unions again are considering in general terms the prospects for amalgamation. On 15 June 1976, for example, the General Secretary of SOGAT referred publicly to the possibility that SOGAT, NATSOPA and the NGA, and any other relevant union, might come together to discuss the creation of a single print union*.

634. The amount of detailed thought that has been given to the industrial relations problem thrown up by new technology differs between houses (see Chapter 3) and is obviously related to the stage the plans of each house have reached. Similarly, the unions vary in the extent to which they have considered the detailed implications of new technology. The union most directly affected, the NGA, has given considerable thought to its approach. Its general position is that the introduction of photocomposition on the right conditions should not be opposed, though its first consideration is the employment of its members within the new systems. The view of the London News Committee (see Chapter 8) is that the LSP should be ended as new systems are introduced, that once the transitional period during which the new systems and process are completely installed is over, progress could be made towards job flexibility; that there should be a number of basic photocomposition grades (perhaps two) separated by a fixed percentage differential; that the objective should be the establishment of a common base rate across all offices; and that the general objective should be to establish wage rates that are related to new skills and responsibilities. These and other broad views of the committee have been worked out in some detail and discussed by Fleet Street chapel representatives. Both the way in which the proposals have been developed and the content of the proposals themselves represent in the eyes of some of those to whom we talked a significant advance in practice in this area.

---

* Speaking at the 1976 NGA Delegate Conference in Bournemouth. At the conference a resolution was passed instructing the NGA National Council "to make a determined approach to the other print unions to bring about one union for the industry". Similar resolutions had previously been passed by NATSOPA and SOGAT. Preliminary discussions between the NGA and NATSOPA have taken place.

CHAPTER 18: THE CASE FOR CHANGE

635. The report so far has outlined in some detail the state of industrial relations within national newspapers. It is for the Royal Commission, of course, in the context of its general remit, to draw its own conclusions on what reforms, if any, should take place in this field. In this and the two subsequent chapters we attempt to crystalize our own thinking on the industrial relations problems of the industry and how best they might be tackled, in the hope that our assessment may assist the Royal Commission in its future work.

Some Preliminary Considerations

636. In examining the industry's industrial relations problems it should be acknowledged from the outset that there are those within the industry who argue against any substantial industrial relations change and point, often with some justice, to features of the current situation which, at least from the employees' point of view, are worthy of preservation. Earnings within the industry are relatively high and the industrial relations system has contributed to this situation; the execution of managerial functions by chapels has taken place, to a unique degree in British industry, with either the active or tacit agreement of houses and can be seen as an example of worker participation; and there has been a gradual rationalisation of union structure within the whole newspaper sector. Moreover, as Chapter 17 has related, important changes have taken place within the industry since the 1962 Royal Commission on the Press in an industrial relations setting that has remained fairly constant.

637. These are many countervailing arguments put forward by the publishers, and sometimes by the unions themselves and other critics. Many of the criticisms of industrial relations are, in our view, valid as this Chapter and Chapter 19 will try to show, but they are not all straightforward and capable of simple proof. For example, it has been said during our inquiries that the power of veto effectively in the hands of chapels has stifled initiatives to improve efficiency and worsened the economic position of the industry; that the complexity of the system has absorbed too high a proportion of management and union resources; and that essential elements of joint control at the workplace have been lost.

638. Each of these points can be debated. A study in 1970* on the relationship between union policies and technical change in the printing industry (including national newspapers) concluded that "only the installation of mechanised publishing in national newspapers appears to have been generally delayed by union policies." Elsewhere other factors had been of more direct importance than union policies in determining the timing of the introduction of new equipment, though agreements had been made which affected the efficiency of the new equipment and therefore the return on investment. It seems possible, in view of statements by those involved during our inquiries, that a similar judgement may be able to be made about the introduction of photocomposition. None the less it is true that the negotiation of any major change can be considerably complicated by the existence of several independent negotiating groups whose interests may not have been reconciled up to the point of negotiation.

* "Labour Problems of Technological Change": L C Hunter, G L Reid and D Boddy. George Allen and Unwin. Page 109.

639. The argument that industrial relations takes up too much of the time of management, particularly production management, can also be seen in two ways. On the one hand production managers do spend a high proportion of their time on industrial relations questions (see Chapter 6) and many feel that this time is largely wasted or that their efforts are unnecessarily duplicated. On the other hand, there is insufficient awareness of the degree to which industrial relations, particularly in the newspaper industry, is an integral part of production management. Some of the managers/overseers to whom we have spoken have felt that all or the overwhelming part of their work should be concerned with the technical and organisational aspects of production and that industrial relations could and should largely be divorced in some way from these functions. The process of management by negotiation and agreement that has become a central feature of the national newspaper industry has by no means been fully accepted by all managers.

640. On the issue of joint workplace control several points can be made. First, management "loss of control" is sometimes overstated. It is normally the case, for example, that holiday and other rotas are shown to, and agreed with, the appropriate manager and/or that if the manager concerned is dissatisfied with the way the rotas are working he makes representations to the FOC and changes may result. The chapel "rota" functions are not generally exercised arbitrarily. Nor, of course, does the chapel—particularly in the clerical, editorial and maintenance areas—invariably exercise rota or job allocation functions. Second, as Chapter 6 outlines, the functions performed by chapels have been those which, by and large, managements, for valid management reasons, have wanted them to undertake. Though the way in which chapels exercise these functions (for example, the use of the seniority principle) can create managerial problems the alternatives to this situation apparently pose far greater problems; few of the managers we interviewed wished to disturb existing arrangements and we found only one case where managers had attempted specifically to reassert management initiative on job allocation*.

641. The third point is that whilst managements may have delegated certain day-to-day functions to chapels they have retained control over the absolute rate of output of the product to a greater extent than in many other industries. Managements decide, within the context of the market, how many newspapers to produce, how many pages are necessary, the number of editions, and the number of changes within an edition. The printing of the newspaper has remained very subordinate to editorial objectives†. Continual complaints are made by printers and compositors about the "unreasonably late" demands made upon them by journalists (and by journalists about the difficulties raised by compositors when late editorial changes are thought necessary), but on the whole managers and chapels responsible for printing the newspaper see it as their function to produce whatever is editorially determined. Complaints from those concerned with production usually concern alleged lack of foresight or reasonable consultation by editorial staff.

---

* This was done in the despatch room of one house in the early 1960s. Managers, rather than FOCs, allocated men to jobs for two or three nights but because of the difficulties then gave up the task.
† This is most ostensibly so where the newspaper is printed under contract by a separate organisation, as with, for example, the *Daily Telegraph*, *Daily Mirror*, *Sunday Mirror*, and *News of the World* in Manchester (printed by Thomson Withy Grove).

642. The arguments about the need for industrial relations change then are not all one-sided and there are undoubtedly some areas where the present arrangements appear to have worked reasonably well. During our inquiries we asked managers/overseers and FOCs how they would describe the state of relations between management and chapel(s) within their own department. A large majority commented favourably on relationships in this respect, though they were critical of some wider aspects of industrial relations in their houses. This did not mean that inter-departmental arguments and disputes did not arise between managers and chapels, indeed many often did, but that such disputes were usually amicably settled without escalating into active industrial conflict (see Chapter 11). At shop floor level day-to-day management/chapel relations are reasonably good, aided perhaps by the fact that overseers have often held chapel office before stepping into the ranks of management and that the role of the chapel is fully recognised and accepted at shop floor level.

Basic Problems

643. Nevertheless, whilst there are features of industrial relations in the national newspaper industry that are well worth preserving and developing, there are undoubtedly areas where substantial improvements need to take place. Chapter 2 has referred to some of the areas in which the parties have sought reforms or over which they have expressed concern. The problems of the casual system of employment have been outlined in Chapter 4. It has been established, in our view, that the system can be unfair to casual staff themselves and can have adverse effects on in-house industrial relations. Other employment questions have sometimes caused difficulty to house managements—the operation of the blow system in certain respects (paragraph 176), the effect of chapel control of recruitment and promotion on the optimum allocation of the human resources of the industry, and the limitations imposed by demarcation lines on the placement of managers and the general efficiency of production. There have often been deep divisions amongst unions, and amongst managements, on policies or the means of pursuing them, and both sides, as our inquiries have shown, have been open to criticism on organisational grounds (eg see paragraphs 205, 246, 333, 455). Payments systems (see Chapter 5) do not, by fairly general consent, create generally accepted and stable differentials; comprehensive agreements have solved some difficulties but have created others; and the piecework systems in the composing rooms have led to strains between different employee groups in that area and must shortly give way to new systems where photocomposition techniques are to be introduced. The incidence, unpredictability, and handling of disputes has been a constant source of concern to union and management representatives, who accuse each other of making inadequate responses to the problem. Consultative mechanisms and communication procedures in Fleet Street (or their absence) have been widely criticised during our inquiries, and union criticisms on this score were illustrated by references to the way in which the introduction of new technology is being handled (see Chapter 13). Above all, bargaining arrangements at house level are highly fragmented, and this increases the opportunity for friction and dispute.

Union Sectionalism

644. At the root of many of these problems lies the sharply sectional approach by unions and employers to industrial relations questions. On the union side this

has occurred at both national and chapel level. One of the deepest divides has been between NGA and AUEW craftsmen on the one hand and their assistants in NATSOPA on the other. In some areas in the past, as the report has noted, the divide has been bridged and NATSOPA assistants have been able to progress from assistants jobs to "NGA" jobs, not, in the view of the NATSOPA assistants, a move which has required a great deal more skill than they already possessed. This is now possible in only rare cases because of the difficult employment situation.

645. Although the use of the terms craft and non-craft to describe a union in the industry is less relevant now than formerly (see Chapter 9) and it is agreed that jobs held by time-served craftsmen, for example in the machine room, do not require such high skill levels, craft consciousness is still an important factor in the sectionalism of unions and chapels. During our inquiries we asked chapel representatives about their attitudes to the amalgamation of unions within the industry. Whilst our questions evoked a broadly favourable response on the principle of amalgamation, many doubts were voiced on the practical effects it would have on demarcation and the craft/non-craft interface. One particularly striking aspect of the responses was the tendency of NGA and SLADE FOCs to favour amalgamation only if craftsmen were separately organised within the larger body. Many felt that no amalgamation would eradicate the craftsmen/assistants boundaries in the foreseeable future*. The NGA's members, being the highest paid production employees, have been regarded as the craft elite within the industry and the tenacity with which they have maintained their position has created some resentment within houses.

646. At national level whilst the unions have strongly defended their respective interests against each other, they have from time to time made serious attempts to act jointly. Apart from the merging of unions outlined earlier, national negotiations have been conducted with the unions acting largely in concert; the new Joint Standing Committee may be an augury for future close joint working; and the TUC PIC, with its disputes committee, has helped, and should increasingly help, the unions to adopt common policies, or at least to understand each others' problems more intimately.

647. Below this level, however, there is much less joint working between unions. With the demise of the P & KTF there is no natural forum within which London Branch officers can meet to consult and co-ordinate policy. The NATSOPA London Branches do have machinery for liaison (see Chapter 10) as do, to a less elaborate extent, the SOGAT London Branches. But inter-union contacts at this level are spasmodic and Branches and their officers act independently within their own union machinery. Even within that machinery some branches, as Chapter 9 has shown, have scope for independent action.

---

* That union amalgamations do not easily remove demarcation lines was illustrated in 1970 when the *Sunday People* was transferred from Long Acre to the Associated Newspapers' plant. At the Long Acre plant reel porterage was handled by SOGAT (then the NUBP & PW) members but elsewhere in Fleet Street it was a NATSOPA job. Though the arrangement had been that the Long Acre practice would be preserved within the Associated Newspapers' plant, when the transfer took place the press room staff of the *Evening News* objected to SOGAT "A" members being involved in the press room. A demarcation dispute was sparked off. The problem was eventually resolved by drawing a notional line in the press room up to which reels were taken by SOGAT "A" members and beyond which they were handled by SOGAT "1" (NATSOPA) members.

648. At chapel level the habit of sectional action is deeply ingrained. The fragmentation of house bargaining procedures has been fully described in Chapter 10. Several points need to be re-emphasised here. First, practically all of the 360 chapels in Fleet Street negotiate their own house agreement, covering from a handful to nearly a thousand employees. The great majority of these agreements are negotiated independently by chapel representatives with no formal liaison with other chapels. The major exception is in the composing rooms where the IFOCs take a leading part in negotiating agreements for each of the local chapels which comprise the Imperial chapel, but even here IFOCs have said to us that they do not allow an agreement they may have participated in reaching for one local chapel to influence them in negotiations they may lead on behalf of another. Even where agreements are felt to bear a strict relationship to each other (ie as between the AUEW and EETPU) they are negotiated separately by the chapels to which they apply.

649. This does, of course, lead to many difficulties. Where chapel agreements are supposed to be reviewed only when warranted by changes in working conditions or practices, there is an inherent contradiction between maintaining stable differentials and improving productivity on a chapel-by-chapel basis. The contradiction can be resolved only by making parallel improvements in productivity in chapels the pay of whose members is related, in exchange for parallel improvements in pay. This, indeed, is an exercise that has to be attempted by many managements and, although a chapel's right to receive pay increases resultant from changes in the working practices of its members is accepted by most chapels, there are unwritten boundaries within which this right can be freely exercised without causing repercussions. Managements may be responsible for reviewing anything up to 50 agreements with chapels each year. This is usually done at a fairly senior level and it is at this level that the difficulties of maintaining sensible and generally acceptable pay relationships between groups with different working practices (and, therefore, different potentials for productivity improvements) is most clearly apparent. In view of their experience of such difficulties it is not surprising, perhaps, that the views of senior managers contrast with those of their juniors (see paragraph 642) on the state of industrial relations.

650. A second point to make about fragmented house bargaining is that in few cases has there been any attempt by either side to re-organise the bargaining arrangements. An important reason for this is that managements have become conditioned to the existing situation. Managers normally have spent all or a large proportion of their working lives in the industry, have had little experience, direct or indirect, of industries other than the national newspaper industry and have received little training. They have mostly worked in a fairly static technological environment which has permitted the present bargaining arrangements to develop and have watched the role of the chapels grow to its current extent. In short, they have become accustomed to the system of in-house bargaining to the point where many of them cease to question its efficacy.

651. Furthermore, though the bargaining arrangements have their longer-term drawbacks, in the short-term they can prove expedient. Given the intense pressures managements feel themselves to be under in dispute situations because of the potential losses houses can incur from quite small disputes, the ability to negotiate a settlement with a relatively small group within the house can provide managements with a vital degree of short-term flexibility. It is possible, of course,

that a settlement made with one chapel because of short-term considerations may provoke a response from another, related, group. But this normally takes some time and meanwhile the prime object of the management is achieved: the newspaper appears. It may also be that repercussions can be avoided or at least slowed. If each agreement embodying a pay increase can be linked to a change in working practices peculiar to the chapel concerned, the increase, however unjustified management may think it is in reality, can be represented as having no implications for employees outside that chapel. An important factor in preventing or delaying ripples from any settlement is secrecy. Agreements by long tradition are the property of management and individual chapels and their branches; they are not made available generally to chapels within the house. The awareness of chapels about the contents of each other's agreements is generally sketchy (see Chapter 10), and whilst managements often contest this and maintain that the contents of agreements are not incompatible they do not generally favour a wider disclosure of agreements because they believe that it would stimulate each chapel to seek the most favourable clauses from among all the agreements without being prepared to make (or being able to make, in some cases) comparable changes in work practices. We shall return to this point in Chapter 19.

652. In day-to-day practical terms it is often in management's interests tacitly to endorse the fragmented bargaining structure and the independent bargaining philosophy of most chapels. This approach encourages or creates many of the other problems referred to in this report: the conflicts over differentials and the absence of coherent payments structures, the lack of comprehensive consultative arrangements, and the incidence of disputes. But aside from the fact that in the short-run the current bargaining arrangements may give a useful flexibility to management, they are extremely difficult to modify in the face of chapel attitudes.

Employer Sectionalism

653. The previous paragraphs already indicate that a sectional approach to problems is not simply a union characteristic. Managements, too, have behaved independently and sectionally. One of the reasons for MGN's departure from the NPA was its belief that the Association's members were incapable of united action in difficult situations, and similar criticisms are not uncommon throughout Fleet Street.

654. Within individual houses managers normally spend much, if not all, of their working lives as managers within a single department. Whilst the reasons for this are clear, it does mean that the full managerial potentialities of a house are not necessarily fully exploited. In industrial relations terms, managers at and below departmental head level tend to have relatively little appreciation of the situation of the whole house; they operate simply within a departmental framework. Indeed, they often do not have a complete set of house/chapel agreements either because they are said not to need them or because distribution of the agreements on this scale could cause "leaks". In one house a review in 1974 of management practice at the more senior levels concluded that they should know and understand current policies; that their levels of authority should be restated, agreed and generally known; and that they should take risks individually and identifiably. These proposals were to meet deficiencies in the house management that had parallels throughout the industry.

The Need for Change

655. The effects of sectional behaviour are damaging. It is understandable that a management representative or a chapel or union officer should take as his first point of reference the particular organisation, department, or group of members for which he works, but that he should take such narrow allegiance as his only point of reference can be counter-productive. It can obscure the basic fact that unless newspapers are sold in large quantities, and compete successfully with other media for advertisements and the interest of the public, well-paid employment in the industry is jeopardised. We have heard it argued that management rivalry has influenced the location of production in Fleet Street and that sectionalism on the part of unions has affected the geographical distribution of publishing arrangements within the country (see Chapter 3).

656. Sectional behaviour and its effects would themselves argue for reforms in industrial relations procedures and practices within the industry. They have contributed to inefficient working and loose manning in some areas, ineffective management in some cases, and an uneasy industrial relations atmosphere in many houses at the best of times. The industrial relations climate has not, to say the least, been conducive to innovative management, and it is only with great effort and under the pressure of external circumstances that innovation in the technical and the industrial relations fields is coming about. The fact that the industry is undergoing a period of technical and economic change is a strong argument in itself for industrial relations reform. The choice facing the industry is between planning necessary changes in manpower deployment, payments systems and other terms and conditions of employment through comprehensive bargaining and consultative machinery designed to seek to harmonise the interests of those involved as far as possible, or to introduce change without such machinery and reach a less satisfactory result only after bitter conflict. The rational choice must surely be the former.

Prospects for Change

657. In Chapter 2 we indicated our view of the importance of two factors in producing over a long period the main features of industrial relations described in this report. The influence of the product market has been profound in determining the management approach to industrial relations, the response of unions and chapels within the bargaining situation, and the extent of joint working arrangements. The long history and stability of the chapel and its scope in practice for independent action have influenced attitudes towards co-operative bargaining; the idea that chapels can best defend their interests by acting independently is deeply ingrained and has been continually reinforced by the management reactions in the context of the product market. The past success of the industry has in some ways added to its current problems. Economically it has been able to support relatively high wage levels and has therefore proved attractive to printing union members in general printing. This has facilitated the casual system, encouraged the progressive development of generous manning levels in some areas, and caused the national newspaper industry to be seen as a provider of employment especially when there is unemployment in the general trade. The level of unemployment in the general trade is currently fairly high. We asked each union branch about the numbers of members registered as unemployed in the last few years and they each indicated that unemployment had risen

and sometimes substantially*. This obviously is a difficulty when change is needed.

658. Given the factors militating against industrial relations reform, it might be argued that the prospects for change are discouraging. In our view this is not so, for at least three reasons. First, the economic climate is now so altered that product market pressures on houses in dispute situations have been counterbalanced to a degree by the economic necessity to restrain costs in order to survive. The economic situation has imposed a discipline on managements (and, indeed, on unions) that in the past they have been unable to impose upon themselves. This has caused some managements not only to resist claims from chapels that they may have reluctantly conceded in more favourable economic circumstances but also to take substantial initiatives in reorganising production.

659. Second, six of the nine principal houses have announced plans for the introduction of photocomposition and another house is seriously considering the alternatives. There remain, as Chapters 3 and 17 point out, many problems to be resolved before the plans materialise but matters have progressed far enough to be sure that the new techniques will be introduced. They will not only provide improved editorial facilities but also an opportunity to reappraise the payments systems and joint working arrangements in the composing and related areas and will also have an impact on pay comparisons made within the house generally.

660. The third and most important reason for optimism that industrial relations changes will be forthcoming is that the parties have shown that they want them. The emergence of the JSC and the wide range of questions being tackled by the Committee is a symbol of the wish of at least the leaders of the industry to seek a way out of many of its difficulties.

---

* For example, within the London Region of the NGA there was no unemployment in the years 1966–70 and since then the figure has grown to 320 (1976), having risen particularly steeply since 1974 when the figure was 42.

CHAPTER 19: CONCLUSIONS

661. There are two reservations that should be registered at this point about the assessment we have made about the state of industrial relations in the national newspaper industry and the conclusions and proposals that we shall go on to make in this Chapter. The first is that unavoidably it has been necessary to generalise. Chapter 2 referred to the differences between houses of different sizes, producing newspapers for different markets. Whilst they may be facing industrial relations problems of the same kind such problems may vary markedly in degree. The text has tried to highlight the most striking differences but it will be for individual houses to measure their own situation against the broad prescriptions for improvement outlined herein to see to what extent they are already moving in the direction proposed or how far their particular situation warrants a different line of approach. In most houses there is considerable room for reform and in no house are no improvements necessary.

662. The second reservation concerns the time span of industrial relations change. It is necessary for problems to be tackled with a sense of urgency and in a number of areas this is already happening. Our proposals, if agreed, could not be implemented or bring the hoped-for results overnight. The process of change requires consistent commitment over long periods and such commitment will not be easy to engender or to sustain. Historically in the newspaper industry this has been shown to be so. The path trodden by the industry is littered with discarded ideas and institutions which both at the time of their creation and of their rejection, had considerable value. The pattern has been for ideas initially adopted with enthusiasm ultimately to come to nothing because either insufficient resources were devoted to ensuring they had a reasonable chance of survival, or because a change in economic or other circumstances dissipated the early commitment to change. A main aim of our proposals is to break this pattern.

663. One more comment should be made about our proposals. They are framed within the current industrial structure. The Royal Commission has been asked to consider structural change of a quite radical kind. The Labour Party, for example, has proposed the creation of a National Printing Corporation which would take into ownership all publishing plant for national newspapers*, and the TUC similarly has recommended the creation of a National Press Finance Corporation which would first promote the growth of new publications and over time perhaps come to own all the printing plants in the country. Even aside from these suggestions, it is not unlikely that, left to itself, the industry would develop structurally. Any structural changes thought desirable by the Royal Commission and implemented, or any such changes spontaneously emerging, would undoubtedly present their own industrial relations difficulties. Our proposals have sought to avoid pre-judging the Royal Commission's recommendations in this respect. Whatever structural changes come about the major industrial relations problems outlined in this report will remain to be solved, and the same principles will need to be employed in their solution.

The Area of Change

664. Implicit in some of the representations that have been made to us in the course of our work has been the idea that we should apportion blame for past

---
* "The People and the Media." Evidence of the Labour Party to the Royal Commission on the Press.

failures and current weaknesses in industrial relations within national newspapers. This would have been a fruitless, if not impossible, task and we have avoided this approach. It is important, in our view, for all those concerned to concentrate on the constructive possibilities for the future and to accept that the current structure of industrial relations, imperfect for whatever reasons, must be the starting point for change. There has been a tendency in the past for attempts at reform to give insufficient weight to the practical difficulties of securing change at plant level. Current attempts should, and we believe will, seek to remedy this failing.

665. During our inquiries we were also urged by some chapel and management representatives to recommend appropriate manning levels, settle demarcation questions and suggest appropriate pay differentials between different groups of employees. We accept the verdict of many of the union and employer representatives in the industry that manning levels in many areas are generous, and that restrictive, or protective, practices are employed by chapels to defend what they see as their best interests. Both chapels and branches have been strongly influenced in their attitudes to such practices by the twin objectives of maintaining employment in the national newspaper industry and of maximising job opportunities in the London printing industry generally (see paragraph 37). Nevertheless, these practices in some cases can hinder effective management and blight the individual career prospects of employees.

666. But we have not seen it as the purpose of our inquiry to make substantive recommendations on manning, pay and similar issues. The current position in relation to these matters has been reached after many years of collective bargaining and only the parties themselves can settle upon new manning, demarcation and pay levels and relationships. There are no absolute rules that can be applied on manning, "job ownership", or pay except, perhaps, that they should be determined by agreement between strong representative organisations of managements and employees. Yet there is fairly broad agreement in the industry that the existing bargaining arrangements have produced problems in these areas and that other difficulties are likely to arise. Unions and employers have agreed at national level that a more effective use of manpower could be made, and it is clear that some major hurdles have to be overcome before photocomposition can be successfully introduced. It is for the parties immediately concerned to argue and agree on what, for any job, is the appropriate work content and what is the appropriate pay, or which members of which union can and should perform the new work created by photocomposition techniques. In this report we are rather more concerned with exploring whether the appropriate machinery exists for determining these issues (and there is no doubt that they do require careful discussion), whether the parties to the machinery are strong and representative, and whether current industrial relations practices and procedures require modification.

667. Our answers to these questions are that appropriate machinery is lacking, that the parties are organisationally weak in important respects and that practices and procedures within the industry do require modification. There are, however, several qualifications that should be made. First, some new machinery has been created (see paragraph 646) and this may give rise to yet further institutional reform. Second, the parties have made attempts in recent

years to improve their organisations; and, third, further definite changes to industrial relations procedures are already planned in outline form (see paragraph 695). Our proposals are an attempt to build on and support the progress that has already been made.

668. Chapter 18 discusses the nature and effects of sectionalism within the industry and the prospects for change. In many ways the effects stimulate the causes. The pressures of newspaper competition and the pattern of production have strengthened the chapel as an independent negotiating unit, have resulted in agreements that often bear no strict relationship to each other between adjacent chapels in individual houses, and in narrowly-based productivity bargains. In turn, the number of agreements augments the possibility of disputes and increases the pressure on managements, leaving them less time and opportunity to work out and implement comprehensive industrial relations strategies. The need of the employers to restrain comparative bargaining and the growth of the wage bill, and of the chapels to protect their independent bargaining position, encourage attempts on both sides to prevent the free flow of information on the terms and conditions of employment. The understanding that any significant changes within the house need to be negotiated with individual chapels has discouraged some employers from seeking to consult chapels jointly on a systematic basis, as it has some chapels from involving themselves in such consultative arrangements.

669. The situation within houses has inter-acted with the situation outside. The greater development of in-house bargaining has reduced the significance of national bargaining. The relative position of the chapel has been enhanced and the difficulty of translating plans developed nationally on a joint NPA/union basis into concrete action locally is made more complex.

670. Until the economic down-turn and the resultant losses incurred by newspapers and their cash flow crises, little was happening within the industry before 1976 to encourage the belief that any comprehensive long-term reappraisal of industrial relations was taking place. This is not necessarily the fault of those concerned, who were and are heavily beset by day-to-day problems. The shock of crisis and the ramifications of new technology have provided an opportunity for such reappraisal. The question is what precisely should be the objectives of any new policy, and how should it seek to break into the self-reinforcing process described in paragraph 668.

671. Several complementary objectives need to be pursued within the industry:

  (a) First, much more attention needs to be given to the development of more comprehensive bargaining and consultative arrangements within individual houses.

  (b) Second, current developments in joint procedures at national level need to be supported as strongly as possible, and national procedures should be designed to inter-link with those at house level.

  (c) Third, managements both individually and collectively, and unions both individually and collectively, should ensure that their organisation and policies are designed to promote broader based, authoritative collective bargaining.

672. To assist the development of more comprehensive arrangements within houses and to counteract the divisive effects of newspaper competition and extreme sectionalism within houses, managements will need to impose upon themselves a disclosure of information policy that in the short run they might find difficult, and unions will need radically to reconsider their joint working arrangements. We will return to these points later in this Chapter. It is important to stress here that the encouragement of broader-based arrangements for consultation and bargaining does not mean that chapels would lose their identity or independence. The aim would be within such broader arrangements to give chapels more opportunities of working together and involve them to a greater extent in the wider planning process. What they would surrender in pooling some of their authority with other chapels in wider joint arrangements they would more than gain in securing better terms and conditions of employment for their members in the longer run, and in helping to maintain future employment prospects.

Joint Procedures at House Level
Bargaining Arrangements

673. The NBPI recommended in 1970 that bargaining on a chapel-by-chapel basis needed to be replaced by plant-wide bargaining*. Its recommendation evoked little, if any, response. One reason for this may have been the inability by those who saw the sense of the NBPI's recommendation to envisage how to achieve that end. During our inquiries we sought the views of chapel representatives on the concept of plant or house bargaining. A majority favoured wide joint bargaining at this level but a majority also thought that the idea was impractical given the number of chapels, the differences in their current agreements and working arrangements, and the attitudes of certain of the chapels within each house. It was also noticeable that some chapel representatives made immediate assumptions, not on a par with those of the NBPI, about what house level bargaining would concern itself with and who would participate in the process. Some thought that house level bargaining would replace national, rather than chapel bargaining. Indeed, that is what has happened at MGN since 1974. Others thought that it referred to an FHC performing the normal FHC functions in relation to pensions and sick pay and felt (where there was no FHC within the house) that even this might not work; and relatively few instantly understood and approved of the NBPI's proposal. The idea of plant bargaining over the whole range of terms and conditions of employment was foreign to most chapel representatives: their main concerns were about the relationship between their own terms and conditions of employment and those of members of other chapels adjacent to them in the production process. They had been conditioned in their views by the tradition of chapel bargaining; few had given possible alternatives any careful thought.

674. We think that it would be advantageous for managements and chapels to pursue the ultimate aim of house bargaining over the widest possible area with full involvement of chapel representatives as well as full-time union officers. Only in this way can the disadvantages of sectional bargaining referred to in Chapter 18 and the difficulties of reconciling the maintenance of differentials with chapel-by-chapel negotiations be minimised. The JSC in its constitution

* "Costs and Revenue of National Newspapers". *Ibid*, page 26.

has indicated its intention to draw up a model constitution for joint committees at house level (see Appendix 17(*b*)). This is in our view one of the most important results of the joint talks between publishers and unions and we feel that the model constitution should be drafted and implemented as a matter of priority. The joint house committees (JHCs) should, we believe, deal with consultation on future planning and current issues and should take over any existing negotiating functions of FHCs. They should also have the special job of monitoring the introduction of new techniques and dealing with associated questions in much the same way as has been proposed at the *Financial Times* (see Chapter 13). Clearly, whatever the functions and membership of the new committees they need to be more effective than, for the most part, the FHCs have been. The FHCs generally meet infrequently, depend on the efforts of relatively few people, have minimal functions, are prone to internal squabbles and to fragmentation. The new joint committees would start with the full authority and weight of the unions and publishers behind them, but to be effective in the long-run they would need the consistent support of the unions and managements and would need to develop effective working routines. This means, in our view, that at least one seat on the committee should be available to a full-time officer from each major union; that a senior management team, including if possible the chief executive, should attend meetings; that the committee will require a proper joint secretariat which will be able to collect information, draft papers, and write minutes; and that meetings of full committees will need to take place more often than once a year. Once a quarter would be more appropriate* though sub-committees of the JHCs might meet more frequently than this.

675. Whilst the objective might be gradually to expand the negotiating role of the JHCs we do not think it makes practical sense to give them the immediate job of negotiating over the whole range of terms and conditions of employment. The first stage in the development of joint bargaining arrangements between chapels might be to encourage wherever possible links between chapels within particular departments. The precedents of the MGN Joint Pressroom Agreement and the machine room arrangements within NGN have already been noted, as have the arrangements that seem likely to develop in composing areas. Such arrangements should be encouraged wherever possible. It seems sensible that assistants and those whom they assist should negotiate jointly. Similarly, joint arrangements should be developed covering engineers and electricians. Managements will need to take the initiative in this but in doing so they will require the agreement of union branches fully to accept and promote joint negotiations and closer working relationships.

676. At present most chapel agreements are reviewed annually. Negotiations on departmental agreements such as those proposed above would similarly not take place with greater frequency. But we believe that joint contacts between chapel representatives within each department and the departmental managers on a more regular basis are necessary. Informal person to person contacts do, of course, take place currently but they are no substitute for joint discussion between representatives of all the chapels within a department and appropriate managers on current problems and future plans. What we propose is that departmental committees with these functions be set up. The precise delineation

---

* This refers to regular meetings. In particular circumstances much more frequent meetings may be necessary.

of the departmental coverage of each committee would be for the JHC to decide in each house. As with the JHC, the departmental committees would need to be properly serviced and to keep minutes. They would operate under the auspices of the JHCs and the minutes of the two institutions would be exchanged. The most senior departmental managers would need to be present at departmental committee meetings, and such managers would naturally require to be kept fully briefed, a matter we return to later in this Chapter.

677. The institution of departmental committees might help to bring out into the open and encourage joint discussion on matters which one or other of the parties determines independently and which cause dissatisfaction among others affected. For example, some managers feel that the work organisation procedures —the allocation of jobs and the operation of the blow system—do not always function smoothly. Agreements make the operation of the blow system, sometimes felt to be grossly abused, a matter for joint determination but the fact is that in some cases we have heard complaints from managers about its working and about the occasional inappropriateness of job allocation that have never, it seems, been calmly discussed with the chapel officers concerned. Where this occurs it may be a sign of inadequate management, or of unapproachable chapel officers. This kind of problem, if recurring, should be vigorously taken up by managements and could be explored within the proposed committees. It should certainly be the case that where the appropriate division of responsibilities between chapels and departmental managements is unclear or is causing difficulties it should be the subject of joint departmental scrutiny and, where possible, agreement.

Disclosure of Information

678. In making these proposals for closer joint working between chapels and between chapels and managements, we lay particular emphasis on the need for a review of policy on disclosure of information. The Employment Protection Act requires (Section 17) an employer to disclose, with certain qualifications (Section 18) information without which trade union representatives would be to a material extent impeded in conducting collective bargaining, and which it would be in accordance with good industrial relations practice to disclose for collective bargaining purposes. ACAS is required to produce a Code of Practice on disclosure of information and a draft consultative Code was issued on 7 July 1976. In the context of the national newspaper industry we believe that in some areas disclosure of information can have potentially important beneficial longer-term effects. Chapter 13 has referred to current policy on disclosure. In some houses practice on disclosure has already seen encouraging changes, with some houses even "throwing open the books" to some chapels, but in others the policy on disclosure is restrictive. In no case, however, are agreements between managements and chapels revealed to chapels not directly involved in negotiating them. The reasons why are given in paragraph 651 but in our view when reviewing disclosure policy generally managements and chapels should reconsider their attitudes on this question.

679. We say this for several reasons. First, it is clear that in negotiating agreements chapel negotiators do attempt to ensure that the pay of their members bears a reasonable relationship to pay in other parts of the house. Moreover, it is not unreasonable that this should be one of the factors in determining the point

at which a settlement is reached. Indeed, if the intention is that a jointly-agreed payments structure should operate on a house-wide or even on a departmental basis, the intention cannot be realised and maintained without full knowledge on the part of the chapels covered by such a structure of all the rates (and conditions attached thereto) of employees within it. Second, a full disclosure of agreements would help to counteract market pressures. Managements would find it harder to give way to one group of employees without provoking a swift reaction from the rest. To return to the point made by the *Observer* to the Royal Commission and quoted in paragraph 16, the costs of conceding a minor claim would no longer be " . . . initially at least comparatively small". The true costs of individual chapel agreements would be more apparent and this could be expected to have its effect both on those senior managers whose interests are not especially in the industrial relations field, and on the chapel approach to collective bargaining over a broader area.

680. We do accept, of course, that the sudden disclosure of agreements might create short-term problems for managements and, conceivably, for chapels, and that any revised disclosure policy in this area might have to be phased in. At the very least we would suggest that any new or revised agreement negotiated from a current date be submitted for information to members of the new JHCs and be available on request to any chapel officer within the house. Whilst on the subject of new agreements, managements and unions should aim, in our view, to follow the practice adopted in some houses of drafting agreements according to a standard format. This should help to harmonise agreements and avoid unnecessary anomalies.

681. On disclosure policy generally the emphasis should be on the fullest possible disclosure. We refer in Chapter 15 to the feeling of some managements that too much disclosure, or too precise a disclosure procedure, on such subjects as the house financial situation could prove embarrassing to houses. Each house must make its own judgement on this, bearing in mind the Employment Protection Act and our Code of Practice. However, especially in such a close-knit community as Fleet Street, once it is decided to make information available, less-than-full disclosure stimulates rumour which can be just as damaging, and probably more so, than a straightforward presentation of all the facts. An effective consultative policy cannot be built on anything less than possession by all the parties concerned of all relevant information.

Disputes Procedures

682. No disputes procedure, however well designed, can prevent disputes arising where irreconcilable conflicts of interest arise. We have been told by managers that chapels often do not adhere to the procedures, and that they are prone to take action in breach of the procedures leaving insufficient time for the question at issue to be resolved. Chapel representatives have said that industrial action is often the only language managers understand and that without recourse to it problems raised by chapels are never resolved.

683. Three points arise from these statements. First, the arguments about adherence to the procedures and the speed of management reaction to problems raised are long-standing. It is certainly true that procedures are breached, and that managements are sometimes dilatory in dealing with (often non-money) points

raised by chapels but the size of the problem is hard to gauge. There are no comprehensive records which are systematically analysed showing what issues are raised, the chapels raising them, the period taken between successive stages of the procedure, how the problem was resolved, and any industrial action taken. Second, there were few complaints about the procedures themselves, even where they differed somewhat within the same house. The only substantial problem that occasionally appeared to arise in this connection was in relation to Saturday-night-only workers some of whose representatives said that their pattern of work meant that a question raised on one Saturday night often took weeks to sort out.

684. Our first suggestion on domestic disputes procedures is that, where it is not already so, they should be standardised throughout the house and embodied in the procedural agreement setting up the JHCs, as well as in local agreements. Given the similarity of management structures within the industry there seems no reason why the house procedure cannot closely follow the JSC model (see paragraph 695). Second, managements should ensure that adequate records are maintained of the progress of issues in procedure. Some industrial relations managers have said to us that given the pressure of work of production managers it would be difficult to persuade them that this was really necessary. This is a short-sighted approach. Anything which can help to identify the problem areas and indicate where management or unions need to give support or to consider procedural modifications will in the longer-term ease the pressures on managers. Moreover, the recording process can be quite simple and need not take longer than a few minutes each time a dispute occurs. Our third suggestion is that the records should be monitored centrally and analysed periodically for presentation to managers, chapel representatives, and members of the new JHCs. The procedures should be regularly reviewed by the JHCs in the light of this evidence of their functioning.

Clerical and Managerial Staff

685. There remains the question of how, if at all, managerial and clerical staff would fit into the arrangements proposed so far. As far as overseers and other managers are concerned, many would sit on the JHCs and departmental committees as part of the management teams. It would be possible for representatives of overseers and other managers, where appropriate organisations of managers exist (see paragraph 287), to sit on JHCs if only as observers, and JHCs might give consideration to this. However, separate arrangements are needed, in our view, to discuss the special problems of overseers to which we have referred to in this report.

686. Clerical staff often already have their own consultative arrangements, although these do not always work smoothly and should be jointly reviewed. They also have a tradition of working within the FHCs. The clerical consultative/ negotiating committees are, or could become, the equivalent of the departmental committees we recommend above, and we see no reason why clerical representatives should not participate fully in the JHC arrangements.

Joint Procedures at Industry Level
The JSC

687. The creation of the JSC is an essential step in the direction of improving relations at all levels in the industry. Had it not spontaneously emerged, we would

have recommended that such an institution be set up. Already, the publishers and unions have made important progress in attacking major problems confronting them. No doubt as the JSC progresses it will develop its own methods of working to meet the needs of the situation and to avoid the fate of the Joint Board and the National Newspaper Steering Group (see Chapter 10). There are, however, several suggestions that we should like to offer in this area.

688. The first concerns the coverage of the JSC. It was vital for the future of the JSC that MGN agreed to participate on the employers' side, thus ensuring a full representation of major employers. It is equally important in our view that there should be full representation on the union side and, whilst understanding the reasons for SLADE's non-participation on the JSC, we would hope that the present position will shortly be reassessed by those concerned.

689. Second, one of the risks inherent in the current situation is that national discussions will get out-of-touch with local problems; that the pressure of events on national decision-takers will tend to inhibit a realistic assessment of the local possibilities. This is one of the rocks on which earlier national machinery has foundered. Conversely, there is also the danger that managers and FOCs generally will not be aware of the thinking behind JSC decisions. Such a breakdown in co-ordination between the various levels of decision-taking in the industry can lead at best to tension and frustration and at worst to a collapse of the machinery. The union and management organisations do, of course, provide an essential means of communication with their respective members but this, in our view, is not enough. We found, for example, despite the efforts of the unions and managements a good deal of scepticism, confusion, or simply ignorance, among FOCs and managers about what was being agreed in the joint discussions between unions and publishers at the end of 1975 and the beginning of 1976. What are now required are, we believe, measures to ensure that there are formal links between the machinery at house and industry level. In part this can be done fairly simply by circulating the minutes of the JSC members of the JHCs and making JHC minutes available to JSC members. In this way members of the JHCs would be able to see and comment on the ideas and discussions of the JSC and vice-versa and, most importantly, comments would be able to be taken into account by the initiating body.

690. In addition, however, the JSC might give consideration to the creation of a JSC/JHC liaison sub-committee. This might consist of the union side chairmen and secretaries of the JHCs and appropriate management and union representatives from the JSC, and might meet regularly to consider current issues arising. The need for regular meetings is in our view apparent also at JSC level and a number of standing dates might be set aside for this purpose. Given the scope of function and frequency of meetings of the JSC and its sub-committees and the burden of work involved in drafting papers, writing minutes and executing JSC decisions, adequate resources must be made available to the committee to maximise its effectiveness. We return to this question in paragraph 708.

National Wage Bargaining

691. Given the low, and falling, level of national rates in relation to earnings (see Chapter 5), the prospective changes in internal pay structures, and the proposals we have made in seeking to foster joint bargaining at departmental

level leading eventually to the widest possible area of joint bargaining at house level, it might be thought that there is a strong case for ending national wage bargaining. Indeed with MGN outside the national machinery, the process can no longer be called "national" with complete accuracy. An alternative proposition that has been made is that the national rates should be retained and revised to bring them more into line with current earnings (this would at least have the effect of solving the problem on overtime referred to in Chapter 5). A third idea is that there should be separate negotiations and rates in respect of employees working for the different categories of newspaper: evening, popular daily, popular Sunday, quality daily, and quality Sunday newspapers.

692. The parties might consider a "one-off" jump in the rates though care would have to be taken that this did not lead to consequential increases within houses. Apart from this, however, we do not on balance favour either of the other two suggestions as immediate possibilities. As far as the former is concerned, our inquiries have shown that the increase in the national rates is significant for employees, and there is little current desire to dispense with national bargaining. Even with MGN there is some feeling on the part of FOCs that national is preferable to company bargaining because, it is argued, the company is less able within a national framework to drive a hard bargain relating to its own circumstances. The argument seems to be that the more general the bargain nationally, the more room for individual chapels to negotiate locally (in saying this, the FOCs concerned evidently had the NAR agreements (see Chapter 10) in mind). If true the argument might imply that the less national bargaining, the more opportunity to foster joint relationships at house level.

693. In bald terms we believe this statement to be true, but we do not consider that winding up the national wage bargaining machinery before having created the JHCs and having given them a chance to establish themselves is the best way of stimulating better relationships at house level. It would be preferable, in our view, to create the new house level machinery and to permit individual houses to secede from the national wage bargaining process and bargain separately as confidence grew that the JHCs, with support from full-time union officers, were able to handle such negotiations. In this way, the importance of house-level bargaining would grow over a period and industry-level bargaining would gradually atrophy, though it would be possible for a set of minimum rates to be maintained in much the same way as happens now for journalists (see Chapter 16). It may happen, of course, that having created the JHCs and having paused to enable them to settle down, no further secession from the national bargaining machinery takes place. When and if this point is reached, there would be a case for the parties to consider whether to cease altogether to bargain nationally on minimum rates.

694. Because our proposals envisage a diminishing emphasis on national wage bargaining, the suggestion that such bargaining at national level might be conducted on some different basis than it is at present is not attractive. Moreover, our inquiries have shown that earnings levels of similar employees working for newspapers in the same market categories are no longer very close. Apart from these factors national bargaining by newspaper category could lead to a number of practical difficulties.

National Disputes Procedures

695. The constitution of the JSC indicates the intention of the NPA and unions to review the national disputes procedures. We outline in Chapter 11 how the procedures have operated in recent years. When industrial action is taken before the exhaustion of the appropriate procedure, the procedure in theory cannot continue. In practice, when industrial action is imminent, the procedure works swiftly, or informal meetings are quickly convened to deal with the problem, despite the general absence in the national procedures of time limit clauses. The formal national procedures are invoked relatively infrequently by representatives of production workers, partly because of the time it can take in normal circumstances to convene a "three-plus-three" or "five-plus-five" meeting, partly because there are the informal methods of disputes settlement, and partly because once the national disputes machinery is brought into action the union full-time officer(s) are involved and the chapel concerned relinquishes part of its control on the dispute's outcome.

696. In conducting its review of the industry's national procedures we would urge the JSC to consider the following matters. First, there are 14 national procedures varying, often slightly but in one or two cases quite significantly, between unions and between different parts of the same union. We would doubt whether there is justification for this proliferation of procedures; joint agreement on a single national disputes procedure would add to its authority and to understanding within houses about its provisions. It would be a rather odd situation to have uniform joint disputes procedures within houses and occasional disparities thereafter. Second, each of the current disputes procedures makes provision for "three-plus-three" joint arbitration and it can prove difficult to assemble such committees at short notice. It might help to speed the consideration of disputes if the number of nominees from each side were reduced to two. The inclusion of time limits in the procedure might also encourage chapels to believe that disputes that go into the machinery will be dealt with expeditiously. Third, the current procedures have a variety of final stages but usually there is the possibility of the recourse to independent arbitration. Where a dispute, in the view of the employers and unions involved, directly concerns more than one house or has important implications for other houses and unions, there is a case that there should be provision for it to be considered by the JSC. Such a provision would seem to complement the TUC PIC disputes procedure (see Chapter 11). As to final arbitration or independent conciliation, we would remind the parties of the full range of ACAS services available.

697. Paragraph 682 refers to the dispute procedures within houses that might be drawn up by the JHCs. It seems sensible that the national procedures should complement the local ones. It would be appropriate, in our view, for the JSC to draft a model procedure for use in houses which could be adopted by JHCs or modified by them to suit the local situation.

Other National Issues: Decasualisation

698. Of the working parties set up by the unions and publishers (see Chapter 17) to consider major issues confronting the industry only one, the Casuals Joint Working Party, had not reported back by the beginning of June 1976. The nature of the differences inhibiting progress have already been described and can only be resolved by continued and detailed discussion between those concerned. Whilst

the solutions to the difficulties that have been encountered will be difficult to find and to carry through the broad conclusion we reach from our inquiries is that the objective of eliminating casual working should be pursued with all possible vigour. If there is any practical help we can give the parties in this area we will naturally do all in our power to do so. Some measures can be, and have been, taken to minimise the extent of casual working (for example, spreading holidays evenly throughout the year to equalise calls). When agreement on the principles to be employed in eliminating, or at least progressively reducing, casual working is reached it will be important, in our view, for a properly co-ordinated approach to be made to all chapels involved by union and management members of the JSC.

Management Policy and Organisation

Policy Formulation

699. In paragraph 667 we state our conclusion that in important respects the organisation of management and unions is weak. On the management side one of the most important deficiencies lies in the absence of authoritative policy formulation and its communication to all levels of management. In few cases does the house have a written industrial relations policy. In fewer still is there any real understanding on the part of overseers (and even managers at a more senior level) on what the company objectives are in this field other than generally to avoid disputes and rigorously maintain budgets. The unwritten policy of some houses seems to be to accept the organic development of industrial relations but to be unwilling to accept the consequences.

700. In our view, even where it may seem to houses that they do not want procedural changes within the house, it would be a valuable exercise for each house to set out in writing the main aims of its industrial relations policy. Indeed, if the work of the JSC is successful procedural changes will be required in every house and a reappraisal of policy will have to take place. Any statement of policy might cover many of the matters touched on in this report, for example, negotiating and consultative procedures and practices, dispute settlement, wage structures and payment systems, overtime, work organisation procedures and practices, training and promotion, safety, health and welfare and the specific role of each level of management in industrial relations, etc. Under each heading each statement would outline the company's objectives, the difficulties in the way of meeting the objectives and ways of overcoming the difficulties. It is important that the policy statement be discussed and approved at board level within the house to give it the necessary authority.

Communication and Implementation of Policy

701. No policy can be successful if not fully communicated and explained to managers at all levels and to employees and their representatives. The commitment of all managers to the policy will improve its chances of success and this means bringing as many managers as possible into the process of policy formulation. Our inquiries indicated that this is inadequately done at the moment. Several measures might be considered. First, not only should a summary of the board's policy statement be made widely available but communications policy generally should be reviewed to ensure that regular written and oral information reaches managers at all levels, FOCs and employees. Regular briefing group meetings and executive circulars are useful means of achieving this. House

journals can also be effective communication vehicles and can be still more valuable if employees and their representatives have easy access to their columns to make their own contributions. Houses might also consider a regular written statement to all employees of the progress of the house in the previous period and its current position and aims.

702. Second, the effect of the house industrial relations policy should be monitored and regularly reviewed, and managers and FOCs can with advantage be involved in this. We have already referred to the need for improved recording systems but junior managers might also be involved in discussion within the regular management meetings on wider industrial relations questions concerning the appropriateness of the house policy and the identification of areas where it might be modified or extended. The views of managers should be relayed to those responsible for managing industrial relations who should take account of them in preparing an annual industrial relations report for the board which would form the basis of its annual policy review. It would encourage informed joint consideration of the industrial relations problems facing the house if the industrial relations report, or at least the bulk of the report, were submitted to the JHC and the departmental committees for discussion. Indeed, the board should seek JHC agreement to its policy and the subsequent policy reviews.

703. Our proposals so far would create, at least in the short-term, substantially more work for senior managers concerned with industrial relations. In only three houses is there a board member whose responsibilities are exclusively in the manpower or industrial relations field. We believe that, especially in view of the major changes imminent in the national newspaper industry, it would yield practical dividends for boards to contain a director concentrating on manpower and industrial relations questions and we urge houses, resources permitting, to give serious consideration to this.

704. At director and senior executive level it is especially important for good industrial relations management that continuity of policy and management is maintained. We have been given examples during our inquiries of industrial relations being adversely affected by management changes in conjunction with inadequate management development and succession planning. Houses should re-examine their practices in this area to ensure that as far as possible, when key personnel leave or retire, well-trained, experienced replacements are available. This does not mean that we think that recruitment within the industrial relations sector should invariably be from within the industry. Whilst we have heard cases where the use of outside expertise has caused problems because the newcomers were not always fully attuned to the idiosyncrasies of the industry or house, this is largely due, in our view, to inadequate induction and training. The judicious employment in industrial relations of managers with experience outside the industry can provide a useful stimulus for improvement. At the moment (see Chapter 6) a large majority of industrial relations/personnel managers within the industry do not have the benefit of experience outside it.

Training

705. Chapter 14 outlines, as far as records show and our interviews with managers indicated, the extent of management training. Three points stand out. First, the past few years have seen significant improvements in the performance of some houses in this area, with the help of the NPA and PPITB. Second,

despite this improvement many overseers have received no training in industrial relations, or very general training, or training which took place near the beginning of their careers as overseers and which has never subsequently been followed up. Third, hardly any of the industrial relations training has been related to the specific policy of individual houses if for no other reason than that there have been few such policies.

706. We have recommended that board industrial relations policies should cover training. We think that following the formulation of the board's policy and its discussion within the JHC, efforts should be made to ensure that within a reasonable period every overseer and more senior managers receive training in this area. Previous training has tended to concentrate on legislation in industrial relations. Whilst this is important, future industrial relations training should be orientated towards the situation within the house and the problems it faces. A normal part of the induction of new overseers should include training of this kind. Any training scheme on this model would require an input by the senior industrial relations managers/directors and, through encouraging inter-management discussion, would itself stimulate the formulation and improvement of policy.

707. The Employment Protection Act places an obligation on an employer to permit employees who are trade union officials to take reasonable paid time off to carry out certain industrial relations duties and undergo relevant training. Suitable systematic training should be devised by unions for FOCs where this has not already been done, and the arrangements for releasing FOCs to have training should be discussed and agreed within the JHCs following parallel discussion within departmental committees.* In some cases joint management/FOC courses† have been held and, provided that the contents and administration of such courses are jointly agreed and they are not seen as a substitute for separate management and FOC training, this kind of exercise might usefully be extended.

The NPA

708. We have recounted in some detail the criticisms made of the NPA or, more precisely, of the degree of commitment to united action by NPA members. It is said that the NPA is wrongly structured and that its labour relations functions should be hived off from its other activities; that even in the commercial field the performance of the NPA has been inadequate; that the council of the NPA (or, in a re-jigged NPA, of the new commercial body) should have the power to make binding decisions; that the NPA should merge with the Newspaper Society (NS); that the NPA is under-staffed; that it absorbs too great a proportion of the management resources of individual houses; and that, partly because of the last factor, it inhibits the proper development of chapel/management relationships within individual houses.

709. The first point we would make is that there is quite clearly a need for a continuing and continuous association of employers within the industry. Had the current members of the NPA decided to disband the association when MGN

---

* ACAS, in accordance with its duty under the Employment Protection Act, and has issued a Draft Code of Practice on Time Off for Union Officials and Members.
† These are more an extension of the consultation/communication process than rigidly structured training courses.

withdrew in 1974 they would in 1975 have needed to create a new, and probably very similar, organisation to deal with the joint talks then beginning with the unions. The range and scale of matters which require to be handled, or at least co-ordinated, on an industry-wide basis is impressive in both the industrial relations and commercial fields. At the moment, there is the rather odd situation that despite MGN's non-membership of the NPA, the company and NPA members work together and jointly contribute towards activities of mutual benefit in relation to the work of the JSC and in the commercial field, and co-ordinate their joint activities through NPA officials. Only in relation to wage bargaining and the resolution of disputes does MGN operate separately (and even on the latter, as we have mentioned, the JSC intends to review procedures). If our proposals are accepted and acted upon it would be possible for NPA members to do within the organisation what MGN is doing outside it.

710. We do not think that NPA membership and commitment to its work need detract from the urgent need to develop better chapel/management joint procedures and practices within individual houses. The NPA, in our view, will never be in a position to impose rigid conformity on houses, and recognition of this partly by encouraging individual houses to negotiate their own house agreements will encourage more comprehensive arrangements at house level. It is true that in the past it has been necessary for some houses to devote substantial amounts of senior management time and energy to carrying out their responsibilities in connection with the NPA. This may have been a reflection of the tight management manning situation in the houses concerned or of the uneven distribution of "NPA" work between members.

711. We would suggest that the whole structure and functions of the NPA be reviewed by publishers. Such a review would need to take into account possible future developments in industrial relations, and in particular the future of national wage bargaining which we discussed in paragraphs 691–694. The assessment made would condition any changes in the composition and functions of the IRE and LLC which were felt necessary in order more effectively to utilise the management resources each company devotes to these committees. Similarly, the future role of the JSC within the industry will affect the part played by the NPA. There are two other main areas which we would hope would be considered. The first would concern relationships with the NS. We do not feel that, however superficially attractive, a merger between the two organisations would yield dividends that would not be forthcoming from other forms of co-operation. Indeed, such a merger could add to the difficulties of both organisations. But we are clear that closer links would be useful particularly in the training and technical areas. Second, the NPA's advisory and research functions should be further developed. This would not only involve more resources but the willingness of houses to provide information. The NPA might revive its annual earnings survey, monitor manning and productivity within the industry, maintain a library of house substantive and procedural arrangements that can be consulted by members, and provide other similar services. The experience of some European newspaper publishers' associations might be examined in this context.

Union Policy and Organisation

Closer Working Arrangements

712. A precondition for many of the industrial relations improvements outlined in this Chapter is that the unions within the industry continue to develop

closer working relations. It is encouraging that despite all the tensions the principal union officers have been able to work together within the TUC PIC. Less formal discussions have also been proceeding in recent months. It has long been an ideal of trade unionists to have one printing union covering all those working in the industry. In Chapter 18 we describe the reservations of some chapel representatives about this and warn against any simple belief that a merger of all print unions would solve at a stroke all the problems of sectionalism we have described. Nevertheless, we are convinced that such problems will not be solved without a single union organisation for the industry as a whole. Union boundaries can entrench occupational differences which are becoming less and less relevant, and which, in any case, are also partly reflected within separate branch structures.

713. The problems to be surmounted in achieving a single union are large. To begin with two of the largest unions, NATSOPA and SOGAT, have made one attempt to amalgamate and the result, whilst in formal terms successful for a time, ultimately failed and left behind a good deal of scepticism, especially at chapel level, about future prospects for amalgamation. Second, the memberships of unions in the industry, and particularly of the NGA, are in the process of contraction and a situation in which unions are each trying to defend the employment prospects of their members is not the easiest in which to talk constructively about amalgamation. There are also organisational questions to be resolved. Should an industry-wide union take the form of a federation? In other words should another layer of organisation be laid on top of the existing structures or should the top of the existing structures be replaced? What relationship should the London branches bear to the new central organ? Should further amalgamation begin on a bi-lateral basis? Should a new union embrace only members of those unions with no interests outside the printing and associated industries? What about AUEW and EETPU members and what about journalists?

714. The answers to these and other questions depend largely on the attitudes of the union organisations concerned. We would hope that any new organisation will be as broadly-based as possible and that steps will now be taken by the unions concerned to begin formally to explore the detailed possibilities and difficulties. The signs are encouraging that this will happen (see Chapter 17). The help and advice of TUC officials or of an independent chairman of the discussions might ease the path to amalgamation. In any new joint body the availability of research facilities should be reviewed. Indeed, such a review might be begun immediately by individual unions. It is important that the unions and the TUC PIC bring to bear adequate resources on the detailed problems facing the industry, and this may require additional research and other personnel.

Joint Union Organisation

715. There is no reason why all unions should not progressively develop joint organisation. The *Financial Times* has, for example, suggested that employees working in areas affected by new technology should become members of a "joint technology section" of all the unions concerned. Every union would receive subscriptions from all those within the joint technology section and the differences between subscriptions actually paid by employees and paid to unions would be met by the houses concerned. The details of the proposals are contained

in Appendix 18(*a*). The idea has its difficulties, as the *Financial Times* acknowledges, not the least of which, in our view, would be that the unions concerned would be dependent for a significant and growing portion of their income on company contributions*, and that lines of responsibility of the section to the unions concerned might be difficult to establish. However, whilst questions of replacement and expansion within the new technology area might resurrect the demarcation problem, the *Financial Times* proposal would minimise the immediate impact of new technology on union jurisdiction, would encourage joint union collaboration in composing and related areas, and is worthy of consideration by those concerned.

716. Unions might also immediately consider joint organisation in the management area. The formation of management associations in some houses and the comments to us of overseers and other managers in the houses indicate that management personnel feel under-represented and in need of common representation. The principal unions each have their own arrangements for managers that do not, and individually cannot, meet the requirements of those covered by them. We suggest that the unions now form a joint overseers'/managers' section responsible to the unions jointly and paying common contributions into a separate fund under the combined control of the unions. In the event of amalgamation of the unions a unified means of representing overseers and managers will, in any case, be required. Our proposal might simply be the precursor of more thorough reorganisation.

717. Any discussions on amalgamation or progressive joint organisation, however urgently begun, will inevitably take some time to bring to fruition. In the meantime the unions will continue to conduct their relationships within the existing framework. On demarcation matters it is proposed that the JSC should play a prominent role. We welcome this proposal but feel that, in addition to joint management/union discussion, the unions themselves require separate machinery to deal with demarcation issues. The P&KTF had special rules for dealing with inter-union disputes (see Chapter 9) and similar machinery could usefully be developed under the auspices of the TUC PIC.

Liaison between London Branches

718. There is currently no formal machinery for liaison between London branch and regional officers and little informal contact. In the light of the aim of our proposals so far to encourage closer working between chapels and between the unions nationally, it is clearly necessary to improve communication between the intermediate elements of the union machinery. We suggest that a London Joint Union Committee (LJUC) be set up, perhaps under the auspices of the TUC PIC. The LJUC would be solely to facilitate the discussion of common problems, would meet regularly, and would comprise the London branch officers and the General Secretaries (or national officers as deputies where appropriate) of all the unions recognised by the NPA. We do not envisage that such a body should preclude a reorganisation of London branches in the event of union amalgamation. Indeed, in some respects such reorganisation might be as important as amalgamation itself.

---

* This could be avoided, of course, by raising the pay of the employees concerned so that they, and not the company were responsible for paying the multiple contribution.

Chapel Organisation

719. The institutional arrangements we have proposed within houses would require and stimulate closer links between chapels within houses. At the moment, even where chapels work in close proximity to each other in the production process there is sometimes a wary, if not hostile, atmosphere. This is partly because of the competition in marginal areas for jobs, partly because the union boundaries institutionalise this competition, partly because of suspicion on the part of groups attempting to bargain comparatively with inadequate information, and partly because of the policy of branches and the personalities of chapel representatives.

720. During our inquiries we found examples of chapels whose plans to merge had been halted by their union in an attempt to maximise the number of jobs available. Sometimes the position is reversed and it is the chapels that resist merger, or dual-working proposals for the same reason. Occasionally, as with the London Region of the NGA, the official union policy is to oppose any extension of dual working, except under exceptional circumstances. This has tended to mean that separate chapels continue to exist for similar employees on different newspapers within the same house, though there is no reason why this should necessarily have to be so. Some FOCs told us that their impression was that their union branches were not in favour of the growth of formal links between chapels within the same union within a house, which might lead to joint bargaining. Branches have, indeed, varied in the strength of their efforts to achieve joint working between chapels but we are assured that in no case is any branch hostile to such developments.

721. In our view, new initiatives should be taken by union branches and chapels to reduce the number of chapels, where appropriate; to promote closer links between chapels within the same union in each house; and to develop inter-union joint chapel arrangements within particular departments. Each union branch should reiterate individually and collectively through the LJUC its support for such arrangements and review, house by house, the current position. The LJUC might also facilitate joint bargaining within departments by harmonising as far as possible union branch policies applying to negotiation, disputes, consultation and other procedures. At house level, chapels should enter into discussion on a departmental and a union basis, and the progress of discussions should be carefully monitored by branches and the LJUC.

722. The new JHCs and joint departmental committees, and the joint working arrangements between chapels, will require the availability of proper facilities to chapels. Chapter 8 has indicated that the present basic facilities for most, but not all, chapels are adequate. There is a need, in our view, to reach agreement within each JHC on the standard facilities each chapel should be afforded.

Joint Assessment of Terms and Conditions of Employment

723. We have already outlined in some detail the problems that have arisen in the past concerning payments systems and structures. It has been said that the LSP causes difficulty; that pay differentials do not reflect skill differences; that work study and similar techniques are inadequately used; that comprehensive agreements are too "loose"; and that grading structures require revision.

724. Changing technology will affect some of these problems, and we believe that the disclosure proposals we have made, in conjunction with the new institutional arrangements, will provoke more joint discussion and agreement on acceptable differentials. In some houses the rationalisation of the rates structure within individual departments already means that most production employees are covered by about a dozen basic rates; a plant-wide rates structure appears to be evolving naturally though there is not yet any joint regulation of the whole structure. To assist progress towards such joint regulation we make four proposals. First, figures of earnings with the house should be made regularly available to JHCs. Second, now that comprehensive agreements cover the vast majority of production employees in Fleet Street, a review of the progress of comprehensive arrangements should be conducted by the JSC and, within each house, by the JHCs. Where necessary the comprehensive principle should be consolidated in agreement revisions and, we hope, a new series of joint agreements between managements and all chapels within individual departments. The use of jointly-agreed job evaluation techniques in arriving at new structures would be helpful. Third, attempts should be made within the JHCs to standardise fringe benefits for all production employees within each house.

725. Finally, renewed efforts to introduce integrated house clerical payments structures using job evaluation techniques should be made by both sides, where such structures do not already exist (see Chapter 5).

Industrial Relations in the Manchester Establishments

726. The industrial relations problems of the Manchester establishments of the national newspapers are altogether different in kind and somewhat different in degree to those of Fleet Street. Managements and unions in Manchester are largely united in believing that their biggest problems are not of their own making and that they are on the receiving end of the difficulties resulting from the inability of managements and unions in London sensibly to organise their affairs. It is felt that the casual system of employment is better regulated in Manchester; that management/union relationships are superior; that production is more efficient; and that inter-union links are closer and less turbulent. Despite the amendments to the development plans for Manchester (see Chapter 3) there is undoubtedly some bitterness that Manchester is to be adversely affected; in the view of some of those to whom we talked it would be preferable considerably to expand the Manchester operations. There is also some on-going feeling that the views of Manchester managers and union representatives are not given the attention they deserve in London.

727. Several of these points are made with some justice. Union organisation is simpler in Manchester, inter-union links are, informally, closer than in London, payments systems in the composing rooms are less complex, and, leaving aside the recent troubled period caused by fears about the effects of new technology, disputes seem to have been less frequent (see Chapter 15). But institutionally procedures are as in need of development in Manchester as in London. Our general recommendation is that the proposals we have made for institutional change in Fleet Street should also be applied in Manchester. One complication is that the TWG and Northprint establishments contain employees of more than one employer. Each group of chapels will require its own separate arrangements since the terms and conditions of employment of employees within it are determined on an employer, rather than a plant, basis. However, in each plant

for broad consultative purposes a committee composed of representatives of all the managements and chapels within the plant should be set up. This would, of course, require closer consultation between different employers within each plant concerned and between representatives of employees of different houses in each plant.

728. We do not think that separate wage negotiations between the NPA and the unions in Manchester would do other than complicate the situation and cause greater difficulties. Moreover, with the emphasis being placed progressively more heavily in future on house bargaining, the concept of separate "national" bargaining in Manchester is less relevant. The employers and unions when considering matters of national concern in NPA or JSC discussions and negotiations should, however, take steps to ensure that the separate interest of the Manchester establishments is adequately recognised.

Industrial Relations in Journalism

729. This report has drawn attention to the significant differences between journalists and other newspaper workers in occupational content, working routines and employee aspirations and characteristics. There are also differences in union and chapel organisation and practices. NUJ members have not been, except marginally, in competition with members of other unions for work in Fleet Street, have identified themselves more closely with the product than other workers, and have had career prospects based more on individual performance than collective strength. These factors have affected their approach to industrial relations. Whilst substantive questions were raised with us by journalists' representatives during our inquiries, only three main procedural or organisational matters call for consideration here.

730. The first concerns the relationship between the NUJ and IOJ. This is related to the closed shop issue which, under the terms of our inquiry, we did not examine in detail (see paragraph 9). We confine ourselves to expressing regret that it has proved impossible since the collapse of the amalgamation scheme in 1972 for the two organisations to devise any other form of joint working arrangement. The present state of relationships between the two bodies does not augur well for the future. The two organisations presently face in practical terms a choice between collaboration leading to amalgamation, or of attrition. If conflict ensues it will benefit members of neither organisation. While not underestimating the problems or the differences that exist between the two organisations, discussions between IOJ and NUJ representatives should, in our view, be reactivated, perhaps under an independent chairman, with a view to exploring the possibilities of formal joint working arrangements, leading to amalgamation.

731. Second, we have called for links between chapels of the same union to be developed within houses. In our view, the case for such links is, if anything, stronger for NUJ chapels, between whose members there are no distinctions of job content, than for other union chapels, whose members may be doing substantially different work. We would urge managements, chapels and the NUJ to seek, where there is more than one NUJ chapel within the house, joint chapel bargaining and consultative arrangements.

732. Third, there is the question of relations between the NUJ and the other unions and their respective members. Relationships nationally are quite close. At

branch level contact is more distant, and at house level the main contact seems to be through the FHCs, where they exist. Yet the work and pay of journalists and production staff are likely to become more inter-related. Journalists have sought to compare their terms and conditions of employment with those of compositors and, if current plans materialise, photocomposition will in some houses give journalists even greater influence over the final product. Where journalists and other staff are employed to key material into the computers the work of the two groups will overlap to an unprecedented degree. In our view this will call for the closest possible relationships between journalists and other staff. The LJUC should include NUJ representatives and the NUJ chapels within houses should give their full support to the union side of the JHCs. NUJ chapel representatives should also, in our view, participate on the full JHC but would not involve themselves in negotiations on terms and conditions of employment relating solely to production workers. The closer the integration of journalists and production workers for industrial relations purposes, the more the separation of the management of industrial relations for the two groups (see Chapter 16) must be called into question. This matter should be kept under constant review by managements.

733. There is one final point that has been made to us in relation to journalists. It concerns their payments structures in each house and the influence on them of merit payments. Most of those to whom we talked had no special complaint in principle about the existence of merit payments but there was some feeling that such payments if not carefully monitored could distort even the fairly rule-of-thumb structures that currently operate. Some chapels are given general information about the distribution of merit payments each year but, though useful, this is not an adequate control. There is often no means available to chapels to satisfy themselves that the cumulative effect of merit payments and individual negotiation is not distorting the salary structure to an unacceptable degree. We propose, first, that after the annual merit awards have been paid statistics be made available to chapels showing the broad distribution of journalists' salaries within the house. Second, we suggest that managements and chapels review their payments structures along the lines suggested by the NBPI in 1969.

Conclusions

734. The proposals we have made together with the changes already being discussed and agreed within the industry would take some time to implement and firmly establish. Our inquiries have convinced us that change is necessary, that there is fairly widespread recognition that this is so, and that with a jointly-agreed strategy supported by all the parties beneficial reforms can be brought about. This does not mean that with reform there would be no further conflict within the industry but that the creation of joint institutions at all levels, the growth of broader-based bargaining and other procedures, and organisational changes by the parties, would diminish conflict detrimental to the long-term future of the industry and the employees who derive their livelihoods from it. Nor does it mean that change will be easy or achievable without consistent effort and the commitment of resources. We have already indicated our willingness to help the parties in relation to their examination of the casual system of employment (see paragraph 696) and, on a wider front, we remain ready, within the limits of our own resources, to provide such further appropriate assistance the parties jointly may request.

CHAPTER 20: SUMMARY OF CONCLUSIONS

735. In this Chapter we summarise the main conclusions outlined in Chapter 19. The order of the conclusions is, however, rearranged as far as possible in the form of a plan for action.

General Conclusions and Areas of Change

736. The industrial relations problems of houses may differ markedly in degree but in most houses there is considerable room for reform (paragraph 661).

737. Problems should be tackled urgently, but consistent commitment to improvement over long periods is also necessary (paragraph 662).

738. Our proposals are relevant whatever structural changes may come about within the industry (paragraph 663).

739. Manning, demarcation, differentials, and similar matters should be, and in some cases are being discussed between the parties. There is some agreement that the present situation is unsatisfactory and that changes in these areas are necessary. Our report deals with the machinery through which these questions should be settled (paragraph 665).

740. Appropriate machinery has been lacking; the parties are organisationally weak in important respects, and industrial relations practices and procedures require modification (paragraph 667).

741. Sectionalism has produced agreements that bear no strict relationship to each other, narrowly based productivity bargains, a high disputes potential, and short-term industrial relations policies by management (paragraph 668).

742. In-house bargaining has increased in importance, the relative position of the chapel has been enhanced, and the relationship between national decisions and local action is more complex (paragraph 669).

743. The objectives of a new policy should be to pay more attention to the development of more comprehensive procedures within houses; support current developments in joint national procedures; and strengthen the organisation and policies of unions and managements to promote broader-based authoritative collective bargaining (paragraph 671).

Matters for Management Action

House Management Policy and Organisation

744. It would be a valuable exercise for each house to set out in writing the main aims of its industrial relations policy, which should be discussed and approved at board level to give it the necessary authority (paragraph 700).

745. Any industrial relations policy statement should be comprehensive, covering many of the matters touched on in this report, and should include objectives, the difficulties in meeting them and ways in which the difficulties might be overcome (paragraph 700).

746. A summary of the industrial relations policy should be widely available, and communications policy generally should be reviewed in each house to ensure that regular written and oral information is received by managers at all levels, FOCs and employees (paragraph 701).

747. The effect of the house industrial relations policy should be regularly monitored and reviewed, and an annual report should be prepared by those responsible for managing industrial relations to form the basis of the board's annual policy review (paragraph 702).

748. Informed joint consideration of each house's industrial relations problems would be encouraged if the industrial relations report was submitted to the JHC for discussion; the board should seek JHC agreement to its policy and policy reviews (paragraph 702).

749. Where resources permit, houses should give serious consideration to the inclusion of a director concentrating on manpower and industrial relations questions on their boards (paragraph 703).

750. Houses should re-examine their practices in regard to management development and succession planning and attempt to ensure that when the appointment of key personnel is required continuity of industrial relations policies and management is maintained by well-trained, experienced replacements; the judicious employment of managers with industrial relations experience outside the industry can also provide a useful stimulus for improvement (paragraph 704).

751. While there have been significant improvements in the performance of some houses in management training in the past few years, many overseers have received little or no planned training in industrial relations, and the training that has been carried out has not been related to the specific policy of individual houses (paragraph 705).

752. Following formulation of the board's industrial relations policy and its discussion with the JHC, efforts should be made to train every overseer and manager in this area; such training should be a normal part of the induction of new overseers (paragraph 706).

Provision of Information

753. The policy of houses on disclosure of information is sometimes restrictive. Houses should review their disclosure policies, taking into account Section 17 of the Employment Protection Act, and in doing so should reconsider their attitudes to the general disclosure of agreements (paragraph 678).

754. At the very least, any new or revised agreement negotiated from a current date should be submitted for information to members of the new JHCs and be available to chapel officers. Chapel agreements should be drafted according to a standard format (paragraph 680).

755. On disclosure policy generally, the emphasis should be on the fullest possible disclosure. This is a prerequisite of an effective consultative policy (paragraph 681).

The NPA

756. There is quite clearly a need for a continuing and continuous association of employers within the industry (paragraph 709).

757. The NPA will never be in a position to impose rigid conformity on houses, and recognition of this partly by encouraging individual houses to negotiate their own house agreements will encourage more comprehensive arrangements at house level (paragraph 710).

758. The present manpower resources of the NPA are stretched, and likely to become more so as the JSC develops its work, and it would seem necessary for both the effectiveness of the NPA and the JSC for the staffing requirements of the NPA to be reassessed (paragraph 710).

759. A review of the whole structure and functions of the NPA should be undertaken by the publishers. Working relationships with the NS need to be reconsidered and advisory and research functions should be developed. The information gathering and disseminating activities of some European newspaper publishers' associations might be examined in this context (paragraph 711).

Matters for Union and Chapel Action
National Level Initiatives

760. It is encouraging that despite all the tensions the principal union officers have been able to work together within the TUC PIC. A merger of all print unions would not solve at a stroke all the problems of sectionalism within the industry, but these problems will not be solved without a single union organisation for the industry as a whole (paragraph 712).

761. There are a number of practical problems to be surmounted in achieving a single union, but any new organisation should be as broadly-based as possible. Steps should now be taken by the unions concerned to begin formally to explore the detailed possibilities and difficulties. Third-party assistance might ease the path to amalgamation (paragraphs 713 and 714).

762. There is no reason why all unions should not progressively develop joint organisation. The *Financial Times*' proposals in this area would minimise the immediate impact of new technology on union jurisdiction, would encourage inter-union collaboration and are worthy of consideration by those concerned (paragraph 715).

763. The unions should form a joint overseers'/managers' section responsible to the unions jointly and paying contributions into a separate fund under the combined control of the unions; this might be a precursor of more thorough reorganisation (paragraph 716).

764. It is intended that demarcation problems will be discussed within the JSC, and this is welcome. However the unions themselves require separate machinery to deal with demarcation issues; machinery similar to that of the old P & KTF might be developed under the auspices of the TUC PIC (paragraph 717).

Initiatives for Branch and Chapel Reorganisation

765. A London Joint Union Committee (LJUC) should be set up, perhaps under the auspices of the TUC. The LJUC would be solely consultative, would meet regularly, and comprise the London branch officers and general secretaries of all the unions recognised by the NPA. Such a body would not preclude a reorganisation of London branches in the event of union amalgamation (paragraph 718).

766. The institutional arrangements proposed within houses will require and stimulate closer links between chapels within houses. Branches have varied in the strength of their efforts to achieve joint working between chapels, but have expressed no hostility to such developments (paragraph 720).

767. New initiatives should be taken by union branches and chapels to reduce the number of chapels; to promote closer links between chapels within the same union in each house; and to develop inter-union joint chapel arrangements within particular departments. The LJUC could facilitate such joint arrangements (paragraph 721).

Matters for Joint Management/Union Action

Industry Level Consultative and Negotiating Procedures

768. The creation of the JSC is an essential step in the direction of improving relations at all levels in the industry (paragraph 687).

769. The coverage of the JSC should be as wide as possible. The present position should shortly be reassessed by those concerned (paragraph 688).

770. The future of national wage bargaining is called into question by a variety of factors; there are a number of alternatives to the current situation. National wage bargaining might be done away with; national rates brought into line with current earnings; or separate negotiations might take place for different categories of newspaper (paragraph 691).

771. There is little current desire to dispense with national bargaining. New house machinery should be created and individual houses should be allowed to secede from the national wage bargaining as the ability of the house machinery to cope with house level bargaining grows. In this way, national-level bargaining would gradually atrophy, although it might be possible to maintain a set of minimum rates (paragraph 693).

772. The suggestion that bargaining at national level might be conducted on a different basis is not attractive (paragraph 694).

773. Formal links need to be created between the machinery at industry and house level. Minutes should be exchanged and a JSC/JHC liaison sub-committee of the JSC should be set up (paragraph 690).

House Level Consultative and Negotiating Procedures

774. It would be advantageous for managements and chapels to seek house bargaining over the widest possible area with full involvement of chapel representatives as well as full-time union officers (paragraph 674).

775. The JSC should draft the model constitution for house level JHCs as a matter of priority (paragraph 674).

776. The JHCs should deal with consultation and take over the existing negotiating functions of FHCs. They should monitor the introduction of new techniques within their respective houses. They should comprise, on the union side, full-time as well as chapel representatives, and, on the management side, a senior management team. Meetings should be regular and each committee should have a joint secretariat (paragraph 674).

777. A number of our proposals will require the availability of proper facilities to chapels; agreement should be reached within each JHC on the standard facilities each chapel should be afforded (paragraph 722).

778. Training policy generally and the facilities to be made available to FOCs to receive training should be discussed and agreed by the JHCs following discussion within departmental committees (paragraph 707).

779. JHCs should consider the possibility of representatives of overseers and other managers sitting on JHCs, if only as observers. However special arrangements are needed to discuss the problems of overseers (paragraph 685).

780. Clerical consultative arrangements should be reviewed but there is no reason why clerical representatives should not fully participate in the JHC arrangements (paragraph 686).

Departmental Level Negotiating and Consultative Procedures

781. The first stage in the development of comprehensive wage bargaining arrangements at JHC level within each house might be to encourage wherever possible joint bargaining links between all the chapels in particular departments and managements. Managements and unions need to take positive steps in this direction (paragraph 675).

782. Departmental committees should be created as vehicles for departmental consultation and, where appropriate, negotiation. They should be constituted under the JHCs (paragraph 676).

783. The departmental committees, among their own functions, might discuss matters which one or other parties decides independently and which cause dissatisfaction among others affected (paragraph 677).

National and Local Disputes Procedures

784. The working of national disputes procedures is related to whether or not industrial action is associated with a dispute. FOCs representing production workers are reluctant to invoke the formal national procedures (paragraph 695).

785. In conducting its review of the industry's national procedures the JSC should consider producing a single national disputes procedure; reducing the "three-plus-three" committees to two representatives from each side to ease the arranging of meetings; and enabling a dispute which directly concerns more than one house or has important implications for other houses and unions to be considered by the JSC (paragraph 696).

786. The JSC should draft a model procedure for use in houses to be adopted by JHCs or modified to suit local circumstances (paragraph 697).

787. At house level disputes procedures are breached, and managements are sometimes slow in dealing with points raised by chapels. No comprehensive disputes records are kept. Domestic disputes procedures should be standardised and should be embodied in the procedural agreement setting up the JHCs. Records of the progress of issues in procedure should be maintained by management and records should be monitored, analysed and presented to members of JHCs. Disputes procedures should be regularly reviewed by JHCs (paragraph 682).

Joint Management/Union Action on Substantive Issues

Decasualisation

788. The objective of eliminating casual working should be pursued with all possible vigour. When agreement on the principles to be employed in eliminating

or reducing casual working is reached a properly co-ordinated approach should be made to all chapels involved by union and management members of the JSC (paragraph 698). If there is any practical help ACAS can give in achieving this objective we will do all in our power to do so.

Other Matters

789. To assist progress in individual houses towards a joint regulation of a plant-wide rates structure it is suggested that figures of earnings within the house should be made regularly available to JHCs; that a review of the progress of comprehensive arrangements should be conducted by the JSC, and within each house, by the JHCs; and that JHCs should attempt to standardise fringe benefits for all production employees within each house (paragraph 724).

790. Efforts should be made to introduce integrated house clerical payments structures using job evaluation techniques (paragraph 725).

Industrial Relations in the Manchester Establishments

791. The industrial relations problems of the Manchester establishments of the national newspapers are altogether different in kind and somewhat different in degree to those of Fleet Street (paragraph 726).

792. Union organisation is simpler in Manchester, inter-union links are, informally, closer, payments systems in composing rooms are less complex and disputes appear to have been less frequent (paragraph 727).

793. Institutional procedures are as in need of development in Manchester as in London, and the general proposals for institutional change in Fleet Street should also be applied in Manchester; in each plant for broad consultative purposes a committee composed of representatives of all the managements and chapels within the plant should be set up (paragraph 727).

794. Separate negotiations between the NPA and unions in Manchester would complicate the situation and cause greater difficulties, but employers and unions, when considering matters of national concern in NPA or JSC discussions should ensure that the separate interest of the Manchester establishments is adequately recognised (paragraph 728).

Industrial Relations in Journalism

795. A number of factors differentiate journalists from other newspaper workers, and these factors have affected their approach to industrial relations. Three main areas call for consideration: the relationship between the NUJ and IOJ; the links between NUJ chapels within the same house; and the relations between the NUJ and the other unions (paragraph 729 et seq.).

796. The practical choices facing the NUJ and IOJ are straightforward; either attrition or a further attempt to obtain closer formal joint working/amalgamation. The two parties should re-open discussions towards this latter end, perhaps with the aid of an independent chairman (paragraph 730).

797. The case for closer links between chapels of the same union within houses applies equally, if not to a greater extent, to NUJ chapels. Managements, chapels and the NUJ should seek joint chapel bargaining and consultative arrangements where there is more than one NUJ chapel within the house (paragraph 731).

798. Developments within the industry will call for the closest possible relationships between journalists and other staff. The NUJ should participate in the LJUC and NUJ chapels should participate on the full JHCs. Closer integration of journalists and other staff will call into question the separate management of the former for industrial relations purposes, and this should be kept under constant review by managements (paragraph 732).

799. Merit payments are a cause for concern among journalists where they distort payments structures. After merit payments have been paid statistics should be made available to chapels showing the broad distribution of journalists' salaries within the house. Managements and chapels should review their payments structures along the lines suggested by the NBPI in 1969 (paragraph 733).

National Newspaper Industry

APPENDICES

Appendix and chapter numbers correspond. Since some chapters do not refer to appendices, the appendix numbers are not consecutive (ie after Appendix 11).

LIST OF APPENDICES

			Page
APPENDIX 1.		— Royal Commission's Terms of Reference … …	215
APPENDIX 2.		— Comparative European Newspaper Study … …	216
APPENDIX 3.	Table 1	— The newspaper companies … … … …	230
	Table 2	— National newspapers: numbers employed (1970–75)	232
	Table 3	— Numbers employed in printing and publishing of newspapers and periodicals … … …	233
	Table 4	— Numbers wholly unemployed in newspaper printing and publishing … … … … …	233
	Table 5	— Closures and redundancies affecting NGA and NATSOPA members … … …	234
	Table 6	— NGA: unemployment figures 1971–1976 … …	234
APPENDIX 4.	Table 1	— Casual shifts worked in London, October 1975 …	235
	Table 2	— Regular part-time production employees in London, October 1975 … … … … …	235
	Table 3	— Weekly totals NATSOPA calls required 1975–1976	236
	Graph to Table 3 … … … … … … …	237
	Graph A	— Demand for casual staff from calls office. April–June 1975 … … … … …	238
	Graph B	— Demand for casual staff from calls office. September–November 1975 … … … …	239
	Table 4	— Daily average number of calls, 1975 … …	240
	Table 5	— Distribution of non-production staff, October 1975…	240
APPENDIX 4a.		— Union rules relating to casual employment …	241
APPENDIX 5.	Table 1	— Average weekly earnings of production workers 1961–1975 … … … … … …	248
	Table 2	— Average weekly earnings of full-time production workers 1975 … … … … …	249
	Table 3	— Earnings comparisons between newspaper categories 1975 … … … … … …	250
	Table 4	— Examples of comprehensive wage make-up …	251
	Table 5	— Movement of NPA rates, 1960–1976 … …	252
	Table 6	— NPA basic rates since 1970 … … … …	253
	Table 7	— Earnings/rate relationship, 1961–1976 … …	256
	Table 8	— Relationship between NPA rates, and all industries rates, 1961–1975 … … … … …	257
	Graph to Table 8 Rate of increase of SOGAT LCB average weekly rates … … … … … …	258
	Graph to Table 8 Comparative indices of average weekly earnings	259
	Table 9	— Average earnings and NPA rate differentials 1970	260
	Table 10	— Average earnings and NPA rate differentials 1975	261
	Table 11	— Comparative ranking of selected production workers 1960–1975 … … … … … …	262

APPENDIX 6.	Table 1	— Typical house board level organisation	263
	Table 2	— Distribution of principal industrial relations responsibilities	264
	Table 3	— Typical management structure in production areas	265
	Table 4	— Analysis of wage and salaries, 1970-1975	266
	Table 5	— Wages and salaries as a proportion of total costs, 1970–1975	266
	Table 6	— Analysis of operating costs, 1970 and 1975	266
	Table 7	— Experience of personnel/industrial relations staff	267
APPENDIX 7.	Table 1	— Organisation and structure of the NPA	268
	Table 2	— Departments and staff of the NPA, 1970–1975	269
APPENDIX 8a.		— Code of principals for NATSOPA chapel rules	270
	Table 1	— FOCs' length of office	272
	Table 2	— FOC elections	273
	Table 3	— Chapel size and facilities (multi-title houses)	274
	Table 4	— Chapel size and facilities (single-title houses)	275
	Table 5	— Chapel discipline	276
	Table 6	— Distribution of chapels by size	277
	Table 7	— Annual salaries paid to chapel officials	278
	Table 8	— Weekly chapel subscriptions	278
APPENDIX 9a.		— Trade union development: abbreviated account	279
	Table 1	— Trade union amalgamations, 1945–1976	282
	Table 2	— National membership of printing trade unions	283
	Table 3	— Printing trade unions: branches with members in national newspapers	284
	Table 4	— NGA organisation	285
	Table 5	— SOGAT organisation	286
	Table 6	— SLADE organisation	287
	Table 7	— NATSOPA organisation	288
	Table 8	— NUJ organisation	289
	Table 9	— National newspaper trade union organisation	290
	Table 10	— NGA London Region organisation	291
APPENDIX 10.	Table 1	— NPA/trade union negotiations, 1951–1976	292
	Table 2	— Review of agreements in four houses	294
APPENDIX 11.	Table 1	— DE record of stoppages, 1970–1975	295
	Table 2	— Recorded industrial action in nine newspaper houses, 1975	296
	Table 3	— Industrial action—duration and warning 1975	297
	Table 4	— Variations in basic disputes procedures	298
APPENDIX 16.	Table 1	— Typical editorial organisation chart	302
	Table 2	— Full-time editorial staff	303
	Table 3	— Multi-title house agreements—London	304
APPENDIX 17a.		— Summary of previous Fleet Street inquiries	305
b.		— Constitution of JSC	310
APPENDIX 18a.		— *Financial Times* proposals on joint union organisation	314

APPENDIX 1: ROYAL COMMISSION ON THE PRESS: TERMS OF REFERENCE

To inquire into the factors affecting the maintenance of the independence, diversity and editorial standards of newspapers and periodicals, and the public's freedom of choice of newspapers and periodicals, nationally, regionally and locally, with particular reference to:—

(a) the economics of newspaper and periodical publishing and distribution;

(b) the interaction of the newspaper and periodical interests held by the companies concerned with their other interests and holdings, within and outside the communications industry;

(c) management and labour practices and relations in the newspaper and periodical industry;

(d) conditions and security of employment in the newspaper and periodical industry;

(e) the distribution and concentration of ownership of the newspaper and periodical industry, and the adequacy of existing law in relation thereto;

(f) the responsibilities, constitution and functioning of the Press Council; and to make recommendations."

APPENDIX 2: COMPARATIVE EUROPEAN NEWSPAPER STUDY

1. Towards the end of our inquiries in the national newspaper industry in Britain a short study was set in hand to compare industrial relations procedures and practices in Britain with those in a number of European countries. A rather more extensive study than that contemplated by us (and one on rather different lines) had already been completed for the Royal Commission by Mr Rex Winsbury in relation to the United States. *The countries selected for the detailed ACAS study were the Federal Republic of Germany, Sweden and the Netherlands and the inquiries concentrated on the organisation of unions and management both within newspaper houses and outside them; bargaining procedures within houses and nationally; consultation, disputes and other procedures at all levels; joint institutions within houses and nationally; and new technology and the way in which associated industrial relations problems are being handled. ACAS representatives paid a short visit to each of the countries concerned and held meetings with appropriate trade union and employers' association representatives in addition to visiting and having talks at individual newspapers. We are indebted to all those who helped us in this work.

2. For the purposes of this report we have prepared a summary of our European study report. A fuller version is available from ACAS separately on request.

General comments

3. In any international comparisons in the industrial relations field caution must be exercised. The development of industrial relations procedures and practices in any country is related to its history, legal traditions, and economic situation. If the cultural setting of two countries differs there may be difficulties in transposing institutions and procedures from one to the other. Considerable differences between the newspaper industries of the UK and the countries we visited do exist. To begin with the structures of the industries vary. The West German daily press, for example, has only four "national newspapers" and the circulations of two of them are largely regional. In Sweden, whilst there is a small number of daily newspapers with relatively large circulations, outside Stockholm and the other main urban centres they meet strong competition from the provincial daily press. Also in Sweden the Swedish trade union confederation (LO) owns the second largest national newspaper in the country and owns or gives financial support to some two dozen other newspapers. The Netherlands, considering its population size, has a relatively large number of national newspapers (eight major newspapers three of which circulate mainly in their city of origin), but it has no Sunday newspapers.

4. Another structural factor which may have important consequences for industrial relations is that the organisation of production and distribution differs between the UK national newspaper industry and its European counterparts. In Germany, many newspapers are linked for editorial purposes and share national and international news with at least one other newspaper. The largest regional newspaper produces thirty-five local editions each of which share national and international news but are otherwise designed to meet the local market. There are over 400 newspapers in Germany producing about three times as many local editions. However, the 400 or so newspapers come under the auspices of some 120 editorial units. Whilst there has been some tendency for the editorial and production units to separate in Germany, there has also been a measure of production rationalisation, and the latter is also reflected in actual or prospective developments in Sweden and the Netherlands.

5. Most newspapers in the countries visited, notably in Germany and the Netherlands, are sold by subscription, and the distribution of newspapers to each subscriber is

---

* "New Technology and the Press—a study of experience in the United States." Rex Winsbury. HMSO, 1975.

handled by separate networks under the management of each newspaper house*. Joint distribution arrangements between publishers rarely operate and, particularly in Germany and the Netherlands, the vast bulk of distribution is by road. This contrasts with the British situation and has two immediate effects. First, it means that whilst each newspaper management has to maintain tight daily production schedules, the scheduling is not quite so inflexible as in the British national newspaper industry. Second, the extensive practice of sale by subscription coupled with the control by individual publishers of their own distribution networks from the point of production to each reader makes it difficult for a reader, in the event of the non-availability of the newspaper for which he has subscribed, to switch to another newspaper. In the short-run at least this affects the competitive relations between newspapers. The intensity of the day-to-day competition in Fleet Street described in the body of this report is not apparent in the countries we visited and this may be a further conditioning influence on the behaviour of managers, union representatives and employees in the industrial relations context.

6. In addition to the differences in the economic structures of the newspaper industries in the UK and in Europe there are wide differences in the general industrial relations traditions and the legal frameworks which apply in this area. Enough has been written about this elsewhere† to obviate the need for further detailed elaboration here. The most obvious distinction to be drawn between the UK industrial relations system and those of its European counterparts is that the latter are more strictly governed by law. There are closely defined rules on the institutional arrangements for consultation, for example, in each of the countries we visited, and each tends to have developed more centralised bargaining practices. There are fewer local disputes leading to industrial action than in the UK newspaper industry and fairly rigorous conditions applying to the situations in which industrial action may be sanctioned by unions.

7. Though these differences between the UK and the other European countries concerned have to be taken into account in any comparative assessment, there are also some similarities, particularly where their newspaper industries are concerned. The newspaper industry of each country has in recent years been going through a difficult time economically. Costs have risen and the level of advertising has declined. In Germany, less than half of the newspapers were profitable in 1974/75 and in the Netherlands the proportion of newspapers that were profitable was about half. Over a longer timescale there has also been a tendency in each country for the number of independent newspaper publishers and newspaper titles to decline. Between 1967 and 1975 the total number of "editorial newspaper units" in Germany fell by nearly a quarter, and the number of Dutch independent newspaper publishers dropped by 30%. Since 1950 the number of Swedish daily newspapers has dropped by 38%.

8. Each of the countries visited has also had to face the problems of introducing new techniques in its newspaper industry. The introduction of photocomposition has already gone considerably further than in the UK. In the Netherlands, for example, all daily newspapers have installed some form of photocomposition, and such techniques began to be introduced in the national newspapers in 1970. In Germany, about four-fifths of the circulation of German newspapers is produced by photocomposition systems, though the larger publishers appear not to have gone as far in this direction as the smaller ones. There are, however, important problems and questions still to be settled in relation to further technological developments in each of the countries we visited. The most common of the new systems currently in use do not extensively involve the input of material by journalists. In the Netherlands we were told that the printing unions' general position was that editorial matter could be input by journalists but that detailed plans would have to be examined house by house to determine work boundaries. In Sweden,

---

* In Sweden there is a joint distribution network distributing over 70 per cent of newspapers.
† See, for example, CIR Study No 4. "Worker Participation and Collective Bargaining in Europe". HMSO, 1974.

the typographical union achieved an early agreement specifying that its members should have sole input rights of non-administrative matter, an agreement which has subsequently been the subject of some criticism by employers. The respective roles of journalists and technical staff in "on-line" computer typesetting systems is also under discussion in Germany at national level, though so far the introduction of new methods has been largely a matter for local discussion and agreement. It is important to remember, especially when considering Germany and the Netherlands, that changes in production methods have so far taken place in a situation of labour shortage. This has minimised or obviated the need for redundancies.

9. Another similarity between the UK and other European newspaper industries is that within them both employers and employees are relatively strongly organised in associations and trade unions. Only in Britain and the Netherlands is there provision for the closed shop covering all print workers but in Sweden the print unions (ie including those representing clerical and administrative workers) cover almost 100% of those eligible to join and in Germany the IG Druck und Papier organises over half of all printing industry employees and a higher proportion of newspaper employees. This compares favourably with the proportions for the country as a whole. The employers' associations, too, have a fairly comprehensive coverage in each of the three countries visited. Only a small minority of publishers remain outside the appropriate associations.

10. There are some parallels and some differences between the UK and its European counterparts in wage bargaining practices. In the Netherlands there is a long history of national bargaining and the pay of print workers is largely determined by industry-wide negotiations which, in turn, are related closely to the national negotiations for all industries. A broadly similar pattern is followed in Sweden, though local bargaining seems more extensive. In Germany there is a certain amount of plant bargaining, but this is generally concerned with non-wage matters. It is certainly the case that in each country there is some bargaining at local level but it never matches the extent of local bargaining in Fleet Street. Even where technological changes are introduced locally, whilst there may be detailed discussions about how they are to be introduced and the implications for the print workers, there seems less of a tendency to modify pay levels following local bargaining.

11. Some of the key issues which we discuss in the main body of the report and which are also the subject of some debate within the UK national newspaper industry, are also live issues in one or other of the countries we visited. Information disclosure is one such subject. In Germany the requirement to disclose information to works councillors is limited by law in the case of the newspaper (and certain other) sectors, though employers may voluntarily disclose information. In the Netherlands regular financial and other information must be disclosed, covering a wide area including remuneration. Again local practice varies and some companies go far beyond the statutory requirement in this respect. In Sweden, employees' rights in this field are to be widened by new legislation shortly coming into force. Another example of an issue common to the UK national newspaper industry and to those in Europe is the question of payments structures. For some years the need has been felt in the UK to rationalise payments structures in the national newspaper industry and it seems possible that with the formation of the JSC a new attempt to accomplish this may be made. In the Netherlands, reform in this area has also been discussed and considerable progress has been made.

General Points

12. Several general points emerge from an examination of other European newspaper industries which may also be relevant in the British context:
- (*a*) new technology in European newspaper plants has often been introduced over a fairly long time-scale, thus minimising the social implications;

(b) changes in techniques in newspaper houses in the countries we visited have occurred after careful joint scrutiny by representatives of managers and employees in the houses involved. Works councils/unions often participate in the detail of planning through specialist joint project groups;

(c) there is closer central monitoring of the effects of the introduction of new techniques in the Netherlands (in particular) and this seems to have operated well;

(d) the central joint institutions in the countries we visited are well-supported by unions and employers, and have a record of stability and effective operation;

(e) at establishment level there are comprehensive consultative arrangements which encourage a unified approach from employees;

(f) there are generally fewer unions representing printing workers than in the UK and the tendency has been for unions to come closer together. The most obvious example is in Sweden, where the largest printing union has resulted from a 1973 merger of three formerly independent unions under the pressure of technological change. Interestingly, the merger has proceeded so successfully that local branch committees tend no longer to be elected on the basis that formerly independent union identities should be protected by rule;

(g) most of the employers' associations feel they are adequately staffed in relation to the size of the newspaper industries they serve. In the Netherlands the newspaper publishers' association publishes a comprehensive annual report, and runs a regular survey on earnings and employment in the industry.

SWEDEN

The industry

13. In 1974 the Social Democratic Press Holding Company (A-pressens), owned by the Social Democratic Party and the Swedish trade union federation LO, accounted for 20% of the daily newspaper circulation in the country. The LO also owns the second largest newspaper in the country, *Aftonbladet*, with a circulation of half a million copies. Apart from A-pressens, the industry is dominated by eight large groups with a family-based ownership. It is difficult to distinguish regional and local newspapers, and indeed, national and other newspapers. The dominating position of the major dailies is largely confined to Stockholm and the other major cities, the provinces having a strong daily press of their own. The Stockholm evening newspapers have nearly nation-wide distribution; the Stockholm mornings and the Goteberg and Malmo newspapers circulate outside their immediate region; there are ten other large regional newspapers and otherwise daily newspapers with small circulations. Since 1950 the number of daily newspapers has declined from 250 to 145 (in 1975).

14. Mean daily circulation of newspapers in 1974 was over 4·6 million copies. In 1975 the newspaper industry, with the exclusion of A-pressens, employed 31,260 people. A-pressens is the largest newspaper group using photosetting techniques and is the only group that as yet has introduced such techniques into the national daily press. Most provincial newspapers make some limited use of such techniques, and at least half use them to set all their material.

The unions

15. There are seven unions organising newspaper workers. The Grafiska Fackforbundet (GF) with 40,000 members organises about 95% of technical and production print workers. There is one journalists' union in Sweden, the Svenska Journalist-Forbundet (SJF), which includes freelances. The union organises about 98% (9,000) of all active journalists.

16. There are two unions organising clerical and administrative workers in the industry, HAF and HTF. Foremen and supervisory staff are organised by SALF, a national union which represents almost all of those eligible for membership. Distribution workers are organised by the transport union, STF. Together with a small number of clerical and technical employees in SIF, the unions with the smallest proportions of organised workers in the printing industry are SALF and STF.

17. Sweden's labour force is highly organised with over 80% of all wage and salary earners belonging to trade unions. The largest labour organisation is the LO, with 25 affiliated unions totalling almost 2 million members mostly organised on an industry rather than craft pattern. The GF, HAF and STF are affiliated to the LO, whereas the journalists, HTF, SALF and SIF are affiliated to the TCO, the central organisation of salaried employees which has 24 member organisations and 950,000 members.

18. The GF resulted from a merger in 1973 of the typographers, lithographers and bookbinders unions. The merger was largely spurred by the changing technology of the printing industry, and also by the need for closer working between the unions as a result of new employment laws on redundancy, dismissal, safety, information disclosure and involvement in management decision-making.

19. At plant level each union has at least one works or personnel "club" established by decision of the local branch. The functions of such clubs range from the recruitment of new members to the negotiation of local wage rates within the framework of the current collective agreements.

Employers' associations

20. There is one newspaper employers' organisation, Tidningarnas Arbets Givareforening (TA). It has 125 members, the only major group not affiliated to it being A-pressens. The TA has close links and shares premises with the newspaper publishers' organisation (TU), of which it was a part until 1939. The TU now deals with matters without industrial relations content, such as advertising, newsprint and newspaper prices, although it co-ordinates with the TA on some matters such as freelance agreements and picture agencies (the TU having a greater membership than the TA, although companies may be members of both organisations).

21. The TA is governed by a council that meets quarterly, negotiations being conducted by a specially elected executive committee of between eight and ten newspaper managers. Its member companies do not in the main have industrial relations managers and rely to a considerable extent on advice and guidance from the TA in the conduct of plant-level industrial relations.

22. The dominant national employers' organisation is the Svenska Arbetsgivare Foreningen (SAF) which comprises 25,000 organisations affiliated to 39 employer associations. In 1973 its members had 1·22 million employees, of whom 780,000 were manual workers. The organisation was established in 1902 and its primary task is the representation of employer interests in trade union negotiations. Every affiliate must submit a draft of each collective agreement to be approved by the SAF Board before it is signed. The Board may also issue binding instructions as to the application of an agreement, and no affiliate can order a lockout without its consent.

Collective bargaining

23. The foundation of industrial relations and the procedure for negotiating agreements were established between the LO and SAF in 1938 in the Saltsjobaden Agreement. Originally introduced to forestall legislative intervention against conflicts which threatened vital public interests, it also covers the procedure for termination, disputes, stoppages and layoffs. Other agreements have since been made covering industrial safety, vocational training, work study, works councils, occupational health services, women in industry and the status of shop stewards.

24. Prior to the central negotiations which generally take place early in the spring, the LO circulates its affiliates with proposals on which SAF agreement is sought. A congress is held in the autumn to determine a common claim which is then presented for negotiation. The SAF-LO agreement in 1974 was the first since the 1950s to run for only one year, largely due to the uncertain economic situation. These central negotiations co-ordinate the various negotiations at an industry-wide level and determine the amount of wage increase (normally a minimum cash increase on an hourly basis), the legislative framework (both of the agreements and in relation to pressure on national government), and the movement of fringe benefits such as holidays, pensions and hours of work.

25. At the conclusion of the SAF-LO negotiations, industry level negotiations commence. In the newspaper industry negotiations and agreements between the TA and the unions are carried out separately, and are made annually. There are six agreements covering journalists, production staff, HAF members, foremen, HTF and other union memberships, and kiosk salesmen (most of whom are employed by individual newspapers). Such negotiations are generally limited to deciding the actual distribution of the increments allowable under the SAF-LO limits, although it is possible to exceed these limits in the case of productivity bargains.

26. The basic agreement between the TA and graphic industry unions was made in 1937, both sides agreeing not to resort to industrial action but to resolve differences through mediation and arbitration. The agreement was renewed in 1969 to last until 1980, a similar agreement having been signed in the same year between the SJF and TA.

27. Strikes in the newspaper industry are thus forbidden by agreement, and are rare in the printing industry generally. Industrial action short of strike action is, however, apparently not uncommon, with, for example, go-slows having prevented the publication of newspapers during disputes. The introduction of new technology has also resulted in a number of disputes both with managements and between unions. These have not involved strike action, but have delayed publication of the titles involved or resulted in greatly reduced paginations.

House level bargaining

28. The principal industry agreement sets out a claims procedure which requires that requests for negotiations be made without unreasonable delay at house level. If the circumstances on which the claims are based have been known for four months by either the TA or the unions, or to their local organisations then the party forfeits the right to request negotiations on the claim. Requests for negotiations may not refer to conditions that terminated more than two years before the claim was made. In the event of negotiations reaching deadlock at house level, they must be referred to the central organisations (ie TA and GF) and taken up within a month of their referral by the two parties.

29. Bargaining at house level is undertaken by the personnel clubs, with assistance from full-time union officers when required. Wage bargaining at house level generally takes place at the conclusion of the industry level negotiations (late summer/autumn).

30. Payments systems for production workers in no case involve piecework but are made up from time, shift pay, and bonus payments. Differentials between semi-skilled and skilled production employees are very small as a result of the LO's wages policy, and similarly, differentials between production employees and senior managerial staff are relatively small because of the formers' shift and overtime enhancements. Earnings have traditionally been lower in the newspaper industry than in the printing industry generally, although printers are second only to the miners in national earnings levels. While journalists are the highest-paid group of employees in the industry differentials

are very narrow between senior editorial staff and journalists. This has allowed the development of a policy in some titles of allowing journalists to move to senior editorial work and to return to their original jobs with considerable ease.

Information disclosure

31. In 1976 the TA came to an agreement with the printing unions that joint personnel clubs would be established for consultative purposes in each house. The joint personnel club, or an economic sub-committee of it, is entitled to secure the services of an independent accountant to audit the accounts of the newspaper. Financial information has to be disclosed by employers in order that the performance of each title can be identified. A number of outstanding problems remain, including questions of confidentiality, extended education arrangements for union representatives and matters of detail, including for example, the extent to which an employer's budget for labour and pay increases is disclosed. No permanent consultative body exists at industry level, the GF and TA having regular meetings at which a wide range of matters are discussed.

32. Under the Democracy at Work Act, due to become effective in 1977, employers will have a duty to inform recognised union representatives on matters such as production, finance, economic prospects and personnel policy, and to give any further information requested by the unions for negotiating purposes. The act also provides, where a collective agreement exists, for the employee's side to call for the negotiation of an additional agreement concerning a right of joint regulation "in questions which concern the making and termination of contracts of employment; management and distribution of work, and the operation of the business in other respects."

Changing technology and consequent problems

33. The 1969 principal collective agreement established a trust fund for supplementary payments in connection with unemployment, which in its preamble stated that "rationalisation measures or other operational changes which may affect the job security of employees be preceded by information and consultation . . . It is urgent that information and consultation concerning the measures in question take place already at the planning stage". The GF initiated negotiations with the TA on this basis which resulted in an agreement that typographical workers would have sole rights to input all material or data of a non-administrative nature associated with the introduction of new composing equipment, together with a guarantee of no redundancy.

34. The TA considered that they were not fully prepared to negotiate such an agreement at the time and that they conceded rather more to the GF than they would have wished. Problems arose in 1975 between the GF and HTF over the application of the agreement in regard to which union's members were entitled to operate computer systems as they applied to advertisements. The problem has also resulted in union membership disputes detween the GF and HTF in regard to data and computer programmers.

35. A compromise was reached in 1976 in the form of an open-ended agreement allowing a continuation of central negotiations at the same time as allowing plant level negotiations to take place. This policy has had a mixed success. In one national newspaper, attempts to settle in-house have led to disputes between the GF and HTF, with the title being published but with a reduced pagination. On the other hand one morning newspaper has concluded an agreement allowing flexibility on the new equipment of all employees, irrespective of union membership.

THE NETHERLANDS

The industry

36. There are at present in the Netherlands 28 independent newspaper companies publishing 49 newspaper titles, whereas in 1967 there were 40 independent companies

publishing 56 titles. Of the titles presently published, national morning newspapers account for a circulation of almost 1·25 millions, national evening newspapers of over 0·5 million, and regional daily newspapers of nearly 2·4 millions. The Netherlands has eight national newspapers. There are no Sunday newspapers, as working on Sunday is forbidden by law.

37. Over 95% of daily newspapers are sold by subscription and distribution and delivery is the responsibility of each newspaper publisher. Less than 1% of newspapers are distributed by rail. In 1975 about half of the country's daily newspapers were profitable, and the large regional daily press which has a monopolistic position apart from competition with the national newspapers, is on the whole highly profitable. The three largest newspaper publishers in the country are the NDU, the Perscombinatie and the family-owned *De Telegraaf*. Most national newspapers are owned by publicly quoted, but family-based, companies. Between 1955 and 1974 the market share of circulation of the four largest companies increased from 26·3% to 62·7%. In recent years rising costs have prompted an integration of production centres, the NDU and Perscombinatie each having joint newspaper production centres for their titles.

Printing unions

38. Employees other than journalists are orgainsed by three unions, the Algemene Nederlandse Graphische Bond (ANGB), the Graphische Bond NKV (GBNKV), and the Nederlandse Christelijke Graphische Bedrijfsbond (NCGB). The ANGB is a general/socialist trade union with about 33,000 members, whereas the other two are of a religious nature, the Catholic GBNKV having some 17,000 members and the Protestant NCGB having about 7,000. There were until the end of 1975 three separate trade union federations* to which the majority of Dutch unions are affiliated according to their denominational or secular status, with a combined membership total of 1·65 millions†. In 1976 the NVV and NKV merged to form a new federation, the Federatie Nederlandse Vakbeweging (FNV).

39. The three printing unions have similar organisational structures, with sectional representation for different trade groups, including a newspaper and letterpress section, each section having its own advisory council. Branches do not have the importance in organisational terms that they occupy in the structures of British printing trade unions. The emphasis on centralisation both in union structure and bargaining is further enhanced by the limited development of union organisation at plant level. The printing unions have one or more representatives at floor level in every plant but their role is more one of liaison with the union branch rather than that of plant level negotiators. The printing industry has since 1914 had a closed shop agreement applying to production workers and overseers. Almost every newspaper company has check-off arrangements for the collection of union subscriptions.

Employers' associations

40. The Dutch newspaper publishers' association, the Nederlandse Dagbladpers (NDP), has 45 of the 48 newspaper concerns in the country in membership. While the NDP has no official links there is close contact between it and the Koninklijk Nederlands Verbond van Drukkerijen (KNVD), the federation of master printers.

41. The NDP has an executive board of nine members representative of the various newspapers in membership including those with small and large circulations and those with political and religious tendencies employing some 13,200 people‡. It employs 12 full-time staff to service its various activities. It has three principal committee groupings covering economic, social and technical matters.

---

* The Nederlans Verbond van Vakvereinigen (NVV-socialist with 696,000 members) the Christelijk National Vakverbond (CNV-protestant with 235,000 members) and the Nederlans Katholick Vakverbond (NKV-catholic with 356,000 members).

† At the end of March 1973, 39 per cent of the working population belonged to a trade union.

‡ 4,500 production workers, 4,000 administrative staff, 2,500 journalists, 1,500 external services staff (advertising representatives etc) and 700 managerial and executive staff.

Journalists

42. There is one principal trade union for journalists in the Netherlands, the Nederlandse Vereniging van Journalisten (NVJ) which organises 3,500 (between 80 and 85% of the country's journalists. The density of union membership varies in the industry as a whole, but is at its strongest in national newspapers and weaker, although increasingly less so, in journals and magazines. The union has seven sections, each with its own council and annual meeting. They cover editors-in-chief, freelances, sports journalists, magazine journalists, free-distribution newspaper journalists, daily newspaper journalists, and those working in radio and television. In addition to the NVJ's 14 local and regional branches, there is in each house an NVJ editorial "commission" whose responsibility it is to ensure that the appropriate national collective agreement is properly applied.

43. At industry level the NVJ are parties to five agreements one of which covers all daily newspapers. The daily newspaper agreement is negotiated with the NDP, and separate from the production workers. No attempt is made to relate the terms and conditions of the journalists to other groups, although the NVJ normally try to negotiate after production unions.

44. At house level editors-in-chief are generally responsible for setting journalists' salaries, which are dealt with on an individual basis. The NVJ at house level do not bargain on wage matters, but engage in consultative and decision-making arrangements. The NDP and NVJ have agreed that from January 1977 each house shall agree jointly a version of an editorial statute giving journalists the right to consultation on the appointment of editors, including the right to submit their own lists of candidates and the right to consultation on any matters which influence the working patterns of editorial staff. In many newspapers editorial councils have been established for such consultative purposes, on which editors-in-chief and proprietors are present.

Joint industry institutions and procedures

45. The Dutch printing industry is characterised by the extent and centralisation of joint machinery for consultation and decision making, which is much more wide-ranging than in other industries in the country. There are, indeed, few if any matters which are outside the coverage of the industry's collective agreements or not the subject of joint regulation, wage matters being but one element in the bargaining process. There is a joint central bureau at industry level, the Central Bureau voor de Graphische Bedrijven, on which the three print unions (the ANGB, GBNKV, and NCGB) and the employers' associations (including the bookbinders and blockmakers and engravers) are represented. There are three national joint committees of the bureau for collective bargaining, social policy and disputes, all of which meet regularly. Collective agreements are made in the main in the name of the union federations.

46. The industry has had a low level of industrial disputes for many years. The joint disputes committee meets monthly at national level to determine disputes and interpretations of the collective agreement, their decisions being binding on the whole industry. All disputes follow an agreed procedure which, at plant level require negotiation in the first instance with line management and then with plant management together with a union full time official. If still unresolved, the dispute is referred to one of 33 regional joint disputes committees, and then to one of the six industry branch joint disputes committees. The national committee is the final stage of procedure, between 10 and 15 cases reaching this level each month.

Collective bargaining

47. The industry's principal collective agreement is negotiated between the CBGB and the three unions. It limits the extent of house level bargaining by its very nature,

its broad application having been progressively developed since 1914, ranging from wages, training, manning, redundancy compensation and the procedure for company mergers. Such house level bargaining that does take place is conducted by works councils, which are representative of all work groups in the plant concerned.

48. Incentive payments systems are not favoured by the print unions and none operate in the newspaper industry. The industry's collective agreement sets out minimum pay levels based on work content, age and experience and the differential relationships between each grade. Overseers receive a fixed amount over and above the earnings of those they supervise. Earnings of newspaper workers are higher than in the general printing industry. Wages at plant level are, on average, 10% above the national minimum rates, but in the west of the country where labour is in short supply the figure rises to between 20% and 25%.

49. A rationalisation of the industry's wages structure is currently being discussed at national level with the intention of reducing the present 28 wage grades to 6. The joint committee has identified 150 jobs and negotiations are being held to determine the pay levels and relationships between each of the grades.

Information disclosure

50. Regular financial information has to be disclosed to the works council, but, unless otherwise instructed, it is given on a confidential basis. Councils must have a half-yearly opportunity to discuss the general situation of their companies in the presence of members of their supervisory boards. The data disclosed includes that of general recruitment policy, training, promotion, dismissal, investment plans and remuneration.

51. The practice on disclosure varies between companies, although the industry's collective agreements have extended the areas of disclosure beyond those set out in legislation. In some companies the works council receives the same information as the board of directors. Works council representatives are entitled to paid leave for training purposes, particularly in financial and accounting matters. Works councils are also entitled to call on the services of independent financial accountants (paid for by the company) to examine and report on financial performance.

52. Whereas at works council level information disclosure is part of the consultative process, it is at national level that information disclosure is used for collective bargaining purposes. Companies are obliged to supply the unions with similar information which is examined by specialist staff; in cases of redundancy, merger, or new investment no information requested by the unions can be withheld by the employer.

Changing technology and consequent problems

53. All daily newspapers have installed photocomposing technology (such as photosetting and letterflex printing plates) together with computerisation in some limited degree. The "production-type" system is most commonly in use, with journalists not directly inputting material into the system. Informed observers feel that by 1980 all newspapers will be using computer typesetting with direct input or "on-line" systems.

54. New composing room technology in national newspapers began to be introduced in 1970, and since then the production workforce has declined by about 15%, while the numbers of journalists and administrative staff have increased by about 20%. The major problem presently faced by the industry is posed by the material input demarcation issues arising from the proposed introduction of "on-line" systems, and the by-passing of the keyboard operation stage. Detailed discussions between the printing unions and the NVJ have been held and it would appear that the former are prepared to allow the input of creative work by journalists, but that all advertising and non-editorial matter will be regarded as part of the graphic process. (A view strongly resisted by the NDP, who wish to have administrative staff operating keyboards.)

55. The CBGB has a social policy committee which includes among its responsibilities the joint monitoring of the effects of the introduction of new technology. Under the terms of the collective agreement an employer wishing to introduce new equipment, engage in major investment or reorganisation, including proposals for merger, must refer such intentions to the CBGB. The joint social policy (or technical) committee then has a three-month period in which to evaluate the plans and question the employer in all aspects of the business in order to determine whether redundancy is justified, or whether redeployment and retraining may be necessary. The unions have a right to independent audit of all relevant information they require from an employer in such a situation on a confidential basis, the actual introduction of new equipment being left to house level agreement between the employers and works councils.

56. Redundancies are generally avoided and it is unusual for an employer not to give guarantees of security of employment when introducing change; special compensation arrangements apply to any person made redundant. In the case of those aged 60 or over who are not suitable for retraining the provisions allow for them to be phased out on full pay (inflation protected) until retirement. Employees nevertheless have the right of refusal to redundancy, and anyone accepting must first obtain the approval of his union branch. In the case of employees under 60 years of age accepting redundancy earnings guarantees apply if earnings in the new employment are over 10% less than those previously earned.

WEST GERMANY

The industry

57. The West German daily press consists almost entirely of local and regional publications. There is only one publication with a truly national coverage with a circulation of over four million copies. Three other newspapers are read nationally but the circulations of two have a significant regional bias. Total sales of all daily newspapers amounted to over 19 million copies in 1975. There are currently 120 separate editorial units covering the whole spectrum of news, with just over 400 separate newspapers. Many newspapers thus share national and international news with at least one other paper but provide their own regional and local news services. The regional newspapers in fact form the largest group of daily newspapers, the five principal regional newspapers having a combined daily circulation of over 5·3 millions.

58. The distribution of West German newspapers and periodicals relies heavily on subscription, about 90% of newspapers being sold in this way. Newspapers run their own delivery systems for the bulk of their subscription sales using the postal system for deliveries outside the main circulation areas. Half of all daily papers are sold by the three largest publishers and two-thirds by the four largest. Very few of the major publishers have significant interests outside newspaper and periodical publishing. In 1974–75 over half of all West German newspapers made losses, but there were indications at the beginning of 1976 that the industry had begun to return to general profitability.

59. There has been an increasing tendency in recent years not only for the industry to become more concentrated, but for editorial units to separate from printing and production centres. The separation of editorial units from production facilities applies not only within newspaper groups but also to the use by a number of separately-owned titles of common printing facilities.

The unions

60. There are three unions organising employees in the newspaper and printing industry. The largest is the Industriegewerkschaft Druck und Papier with about 164,500 members, including about 5,000 journalists in its DJU section. The largest union for journalists is the Deutsche Journalisten-verband (DJV) with about 12,000 members.

The third union is the Deutsche Angestellten-Gewerkschaft (DAG) which organises white collar workers, although the IG Druck represents more clerical employees in the printing and paper industries than does the DAG, with whom it competes for members.

61. The IG Druck has eight regional (Land) divisions, each with their own full-time officials, below which each has a district and branch organisation. It is one of 16 industrial unions affiliated to the German trade union federation, the DGB.

62. At plant level the Works Constitution Act (1972) established a network of works councils throughout German industry and commerce representing exclusively employees in any enterprise with more than five workers. Though works councillors do not have to be union members and are elected by all employees of the firm, more than 80% of the country's works councillors are members of DGB industrial unions. The union members in a plant also elect union trustmen or confidants, usually on a departmental basis. Their function is to represent the interests of union members to the works council (works councillors are meant to reflect the social structure of the labour force of the enterprise in its entirety, not particular interest groups).

The employers' associations

63. Three organisations represent employers in the German newspaper and periodical industry. The Bundesverband Druck (BD) represents companies employing technical printing staff. Such staff may be employed on newspaper or periodical printing or on general printing. The Bundesverband Deutscher Zeitungsverleger (BDZV) is the organisation of newspaper publishers, 98% of whom are in membership. The Verband Deutscher Zeitschriftenverleger (VDZV) represents the publishers of periodicals.

64. An individual newspaper company may belong to all three organisations if it prints its own newspaper(s) and publishes a periodical. The BDZV and the VDZV are largely unconcerned with production workers whose wage negotiations are conducted between the IG Druck and the BD. However, they each negotiate with the journalists and with the white-collar unions agreements covering the editorial staff employed on newspapers and periodicals. The BDZV has twenty full-time employees and has a research department. The VDZV has eleven full-time employees. Both organisations are run by councils which are composed of senior officers of the Land (regional) employers' associations. Thus member companies are not directly represented on the central bodies. The size of the BDZV's Land associations varies; the biggest have two or three full-time employees while the smallest have none.

Journalists

65. There are three unions party to collective agreements for editorial staff. The DJU and DJV collectively represent about 80% of all journalists in the German press, there being a small number of journalists in membership of the salaried employees' union, DAG.

66. The DJV sees itself as a professional association for journalists with interests that are separate and distinct from those of the production workers, whereas the DJU is orientated more towards being an effective and strong collective bargaining body through its association with the production workers. Each union attempts to ensure that it has at least one elected representative in each house to carry out the role of organiser, and both encourage their membership participate in works council activities.

67. The journalists' unions, together with the DAG, negotiate jointly with the employers at national and Land levels. Separate agreements are negotiated and applied to editors and journalists. At national level while negotiations theoretically take place with the BDZV at the same time as those of the print union, in practice they are held after the conclusion of the production employees' negotiations and follow the broad outline of the agreement. These national rates are minimal and must be paid without exception at house level.

Collective bargaining

68. Two different types of agreement exist in the industry—those that result from trade union bargaining and those that result from bargaining by works councils. Works councils can only negotiate on matters not the subject of local, regional or national collective agreement, such agreements always superseding plant agreements. Works agreements can, however, supplement collective agreements with more favourable conditions than those already established.

69. Production workers' wages and conditions are negotiated between the collective bargaining committee of the IG Druck and the BD. The IG Druck's objective is to strengthen and develop the importance of national level negotiations as far as possible in order to co-ordinate and exercise its full bargaining power in one set of negotiations. The nationally-negotiated increases must be applied in all plants, and in recent years employers have attempted to absorb such increases by subtracting from them the value of extra payments negotiated at house level. This resulted in employees in a number of locations having had little or no increase in earnings, and contributed to the militancy of print workers during the 1976 negotiations. Regional negotiations between the local employers' organisations of the BDZV and regional sections of the union follow the national agreement, but these concern the pay of clerical and production supervisory staff.

70. The works councils have an equal say with management in deciding such matters as job evaluation, wages structures, working hours, overtime and shift arrangements, manpower policies, social plans in the case of redundancy, training and discipline. Subject to the limitations of the Works Constitution Act as it applies to the newspaper industry, hiring, firing and promotion, allocation of work and transfers all require the consent of the works council before implementation.

71. Works councils can have their plant bargaining rights overriden by the union should the latter wish to negotiate at a higher level. By law, no works council can call a strike in support of plant bargaining, although it may make use of lesser actions such as overtime bans. Works councils can veto management decisions where the Works Constitution Act allows them to do so, and may also refer matters in dispute to arbitration. Decisions on strike action can only be made by the national council of the print union.

72. The press comes under the Tendenzbetrieb (tendentious industry) provisions of the Works Constitution Act and the Co-Determination Act. This limits the rights of works councils in regard to the disclosure of financial information and related matters, and also excludes employees from the right to elect representatives in an enterprise to a supervisory board to oversee company policy. Workers in the press have no authority to challenge the proprietor's right to establish the editorial policy of the newspaper and to appoint editors-in-chief.

73. Under the industry agreement there are five grades of unskilled and semi-skilled employees. The agreement sets out both minimum weekly and hourly rates, together with their percentage differential relationships with the basic skilled rate. There are no piecework systems used in the printing industry, earnings being composed of basic rates, house extras, shift and overtime premia, cost-of-living payments, and special payments. Extra payments are made for particular or specialist work (for example, compositors may receive extra payments for setting stock exchange prices or foreign language copy). Cost of living payments, where made, result from negotiations at works council level.

Disputes procedures

74. The procedure for settling house disputes relating to conditions of work involves reference to an *ad hoc* arbitration board. Either party can refer a dispute to such a board, and the Labour Court can, in some cases, put the arbitration procedure into

operation against the wishes of one party. The board consists of an equal number of works council and management representatives, together with an impartial chairman.

75. When there is failure to agree during national wage negotiations, the normal procedure is for three negotiators on each side to agree on a conciliator, a neutral man who must have the confidence of both sides. In attempting to obtain agreements the conciliator may recommend a figure which he feels would be a basis for settlement. Failure to agree at this stage is followed by a five-a-side commission of both sides (plus one non-voting member each to present the case) which is chaired by the same independent individual who now has a casting vote. Each side has one week to decide whether the resultant figure is acceptable to them, and if either side rejects it there is a further 48 hour "duty for peace" period before a strike can be called. In the negotiations for manual print workers it is apparently quite common for the negotiations to go to the first stage above, and sometimes to the second.

Changing technology and consequent problems

76. It has been estimated that more than 80% of the total circulation of West German newspapers is produced by photocomposition methods using computers for hyphenation and justification. Of a total of 121 publishers producing 450 newspapers about 100 have photocomposition with the use of computers. Those companies which have not yet introduced photocomposition or computers tend to be the larger ones.

77. Under the provisions of the Works Constitution Act, closures, staff reductions, and reductions and alterations is the scale of production that requires the consent of the works council. In the case of major change the employer has to establish and jointly agree with the works council a social plan providing employment elsewhere in the firm, retraining, or should this not be possible, severance pay for the affected workers. In the event of disagreements arising from the development of a social plan either party can bring the case before a joint arbitration committee under an independent chairman for compulsory arbitration, the decision being binding on all parties. While on economic policy matters the arbitration committee cannot ultimately override the employer, it can in respect of social plans.

78. The IG Druck's approach to new technology has been to insist that retraining costs are part of investment costs and must therefore be included in all capital expenditure plans. The time-scale of introduction, the union argues, should be of at least five years duration, thus allowing for a 10% reduction in the labour force (between 5 and 6% by natural attrition, the remainder being made up of those employees over 60 years of age accepting the early retirement provisions of social plans).

79. Considerable attention has also been paid in the introduction of new equipment to working hours. It is argued, and generally accepted by the employers, that the new equipment, particularly VDUs, considerably increases stress. The print union argues that nobody can work for more than four hours at the screen terminals, thus placing a requirement for two groups of operators to work in shifts at the keying apparatus and video receivers connected to computer installations to replace a single eight-hour shift. The union's view is that the remaining four hours would be taken up by other duties, thus allowing the work available to be shared among as many people as possible. While at industry level both the employers' organisations and the unions have had some part to play in an advisory capacity, introduction of new techniques has been predominantly a matter for discussion and settlement between works councils and local managements.

APPENDIX 3

TABLE 1
THE NEWSPAPER COMPANIES

Publisher	Ownership	Title	Average Circulation Oct 74/Mar 75	Average Circulation Oct 75/Mar 76	Location of printing	Other interests
Associated Newspapers Group Ltd	A subsidiary of the Daily Mail & General Trust Ltd, controlled by the Harmsworth family and Viscount Rothermere	Daily Mail (1896) Evening News (1881)	1,721,747 710,986	1,728,466 588,891	Northcliffe House, London Northprint, Manchester Northcliffe House, London	Group also has interests in provincial newspapers, restaurants, North Sea oil, commercial radio, market research and transportation. Also publishes Weekend, (1904) printed by Bemrose's in Liverpool (Average circulation July-Dec 1975: 807,423).
Beaverbrook Newspapers Ltd	Majority of the voting shares held by Sir Max Aitken and the Beaverbrook family	Daily Express (1900) Sunday Express (1918) Evening Standard (1827)	2,982,100 3,876,863 527,930	2,667,508 3,496,128 444,091	Fleet Street, London Ancoates Street, Manchester Printed and published in Fleet Street, but composed in Shoe Lane	Editions of the Scottish Daily & Sunday Express have been printed and published in Manchester since 1974 following the closure of the Group's Glasgow printing plant. Considerable investment has been undertaken by the Group in new equipment in recent years. Other interests include local newspapers, oil, jobbing printing and printing matrices.
The Daily Telegraph Ltd	Shares in the company are owned through trusts by the Berry family	Daily Telegraph (1855) Sunday Telegraph (1961)	1,367,034 766,523	1,315,061 738,990	Fleet Street, London Thomson Withy Grove, Manchester Fleet Street, London	The Daily Telegraph Magazine is printed by Bemrose's in Liverpool. Other interests include television, The Morning Post and M Winston and Co Ltd.
The Financial Times Ltd	A subsidiary of Pearson Longman Ltd, which is owned by S Pearson and Son Ltd. The latter company is owned by Lord Cowdray and family trusts	Financial Times (1888)	188,487	175,415	Bracken House, London	Pearson Longman have interests in provincial newspapers, book publishing and printing.
The Guardian & Manchester Evening News Ltd	Owned by a trust fund set up by the Scott family	The Guardian (1821) Manchester Evening News (1868)	346,114 376,5571	307,787 361,6122	Farringdon Road, London Northprint, Manchester Northprint, Manchester	Other interests of the company include printing, television, Northprint Manchester (50% owned), property and newsagents.

230

Mirror Group Newspapers Ltd	Owned by Reed International Ltd, with no dominant shareholders.	Daily Mirror Sunday Mirror Sunday People Sporting Life Reveille	(1903) (1963) (1881) (1822) (1940)	4,105,446 4,431,379 4,407,272 84,323 595,227	3,864,923 4,090,938 4,089,126 81,375 551,994	Holborn & Stamford St, London Thomson Withy Grove, Manchester New Carmelite House and Commercial Wharf, London Northprint, Manchester Holborn, London Stamford Street, London	Other interests of the parent company include paper, paper products, building and decorative products.
Morning Star Co-operative Society Ltd	People's Press Printing Society Ltd	Morning Star (previously the Daily Worker [1930])	(1966)	49,842[3]	43,419[4]	Farringdon Road, London	(The title is printed on web-offset machinery.)
News Group Newspapers Ltd	A subsidiary of News International Ltd, owned by K R Murdoch, with a large shareholding by the Carr family	Sun News of the World	(1969) (1843)	3,386,384 5,741,627	3,520,723 5,231,452	Bouverie Street, London Bouverie Street and Thomson Withy Grove, Manchester	Other interests include local newspapers (owned through the Berrow's Organisation Ltd), magazines, Eric Bemrose Ltd (printers), paper manufacture, warehousing, transport, and television.
The Observer Ltd and The Observer Magazine Ltd	Subsidiaries of the Observer Holding Co Ltd, which is owned by Cushion Trust Ltd	The Observer	(1791)	794,161	685,915	Queen Victoria Street, London	The Observer Magazine is also partly owned by Purnell & Sons Ltd. Other interests include property and television.
Society of Licensed Victuallers	The owners are a non-profit making body governed by Royal Charter	The Morning Advertiser	(1794)	c. 65,000[5]		Effra Road, Brixton	(The title is printed on web-offset machinery.)
Times Newspapers Ltd	A subsidiary of the Thomson Organisation Ltd, itself a subsidiary of Thomson Scottish Associates Ltd, a company owned by Lord Thomson and family interests	The Times The Sunday Times The Times Literary Supplement The Times Higher Educational Supplement The Times Educational Supplement	(1785) (1822) (1902) (1971) (1910)	334,936 1,450,077 38,349[6] 20,185[6] 112,548[6]	312,475 1,387,864	Gray's Inn Road, London	(The Sporting Chronicle is published by Sporting Chronicle Publications Ltd, and is one of Thomson Newspapers Ltd.) Other interests of the parent company include provincial newspapers, book publishing, travel, television, property and oil. The Sunday Times Magazine is printed by Sun Printers Ltd in Watford.
		Sporting Chronicle		67,166	63,974	Thomson Withy Grove, Manchester	

[1] Jan–June 1975
[2] July–Dec 1975
[3] 1974 (year) } Source: COI Handbooks
[4] 1975 (year)
[5] Source: ACAS inquiries
[6] July–Dec 1975

Source: Audit Bureau of Circulations (circulation figures), and ACAS inquiries.

TABLE 2

NATIONAL NEWSPAPERS: NUMBERS EMPLOYED* 1970–1975

Category	September 1970	March 1971	September 1971	March 1972	September 1972	March 1973	September 1973	March 1974	September 1974	March 1975
Popular newspaper establishments	30,491	30,092	30,208	29,849	27,628	28,066	26,606	26,597	26,887	26,518
Quality newspaper establishments	11,089	11,151	10,982	11,054	10,778	10,793	10,767	10,881	10,723	10,849
Total	41,590	41,243	41,190	40,903	38,406	38,859	37,373	37,478	37,610	37,367

Source: PPITB.

*For the purposes of the PPITB, an employee is defined as anyone working for at least two-thirds of the normal working week.

Notes:

1. The Table shows the number of employees at each establishment in London and Manchester and includes those in Scotland, the Midlands and the West of England for Mirror Group Newspapers (including *Scottish Daily Record* and *Sunday Mail*) and News Group Newspapers.
2. The Manchester employees at the Thomson Withy Grove establishment have been included in the popular newspaper category.
3. The Table does not include employment figures for the *Morning Advertiser* or *Morning Star*, but includes all nine of the major publishers defined for the purposes of the ACAS study.

TABLE 3 APPENDIX 3

NUMBERS EMPLOYED IN PRINTING AND PUBLISHING OF NEWSPAPERS AND PERIODICALS ('000) GREAT BRITAIN

Year	Males	Females	Total
1969 (June)	112·9	38·4	151·3
1970 (April)	116·1	39·7	155·8
1971 (April)	114·9	39·6	154·5
1972 (April)	112·3	38·8	151·1
1973 (April)	105·8	34·3	140·1
1974 (June)	110·1	36·8	146·9
1975 (May)	107·3	36·6	143·9
1976 (Jan)	105·2	35·6	140·8
1976 (Feb)	104·6	35·5	140·1
1976 (Mar)	104·2	35·3	139·5

Source: DE Gazettes.

TABLE 4

NUMBERS WHOLLY UNEMPLOYED IN NEWSPAPER PRINTING AND PUBLISHING, GREAT BRITAIN

May 1969	May 1970	May 1971	May 1972	May 1973	May 1974	May 1975	May 1976
1,597	842	1,129	1,748	1,089	1,484	1,688	2,568

Source: DE Gazettes.

TABLE 5

APPENDIX 3

LONDON: CLOSURES AND REDUNDANCIES, 1965–1974, AFFECTING
NGA LONDON REGION AND NATSOPA MACHINE BRANCH MEMBERS

	NATSOPA Machine Branch		NGA London Region	
Year	No. of closures or redundancy exercises	Members affected	No. of closures or redundancy exercises	Members affected
1965	50	695	11	—
1966	14	174	40	—
1967	19	199	35	—
1968	3	8	26	—
1969	1	—	61*	344
1970	29	196	72	403
1971	34	330	82	1,073
1972	33	82	74	696
1973	18	156	(April 1973) 9	30
1974	5	10	N/A	N/A
Total	206	1,850	410	2,546

*Of the closures shown in the column between 1969 and 1973, 16 resulted from companies transferring out of London.

Source: ACAS inquiries.

TABLE 6
NGA: UNEMPLOYMENT FIGURES, 1971–1976

Branch/Region Year	1971	1972	1973	1974	1975	1976
*NGA London Region	150	90	20	42	201	320
Manchester Graphical Society	16	12	8	4	70	N/A
Total	166	102	28	46	271	320

*In the years 1966–1970 inclusive, there was no unemployment within the London Region.
Source: ACAS inquiries.

TABLE 1 APPENDIX 4

CASUAL SHIFTS WORKED IN FLEET STREET, OCTOBER 1975

	Quality				Popular				Total	
	Daily	%	Sunday	%	Daily	%	Sunday	%		%
Composing/Reading/Process	13	0·2	43	0·6	37	0·5	34	0·5	128	1·8
Foundry...	118	1·6	38	0·5	320	4·4	136	1·9	612	8·4
Machine...	368	5·0	108	1·5	934	12·8	417	5·7	1,826	25·0
Publishing	939	12·9	315	4·3	2,542	34·8	936	12·8	4,732	64·8
Total	1,438	19·7	504	6·9	3,833	52·5	1,523	20·9	7,298	100·0

Source: Labour Survey.

TABLE 2

REGULAR PART-TIME PRODUCTION EMPLOYEES IN LONDON, OCTOBER 1975

	Number of shifts normally worked								Total	
	1		2		3		4			
	A	B	A	B	A	B	A	B	A	B
% of overall total of such employees	54	9	2	1	1	13	3	16	61	39
% of total employees in relevant categories	89	22	4	3	2	33	5	42	100	100
% of A and B staff in each shift category	86	14	68	32	9	91	17	83	61	39

Source: ACAS inquiries.

A—Where one shift worked is a Saturday night shift.
B—Where none of the shifts include a Saturday night.

Note:
The absolute totals of regular part-time employees given by houses and used for the basis of this Table substantially exceed the probable real totals because of the double-counting arising from the dual pattern of working between different houses of many part-time regular casuals.

TABLE 3

APPENDIX 4

WEEKLY TOTALS OF NATSOPA CALLS REQUIRED FROM THE CALLS OFFICE 1975 AND 1976

Week Ending		Dailies	Sundays	Total	Week Ending		Dailies	Sundays	Totals
Jan	5	638	181	819	July	6	1,017	237	1,254
	12	453	184	637		13	1,158	360	1,518
	19	393	135	528		20	1,135	291	1,426
	26	339	185	524		27	1,204	292	1,496
Feb	2	384	251	635	Aug	3	1,236	315	1,551
	9	436	180	616		10	1,298	271	1,569
	16	425	225	650		17	1,402	329	1,731
	23	469	191	660		24	1,429	329	1,758
						31	1,249	304	1,553
March	2	585	212	797	Sept	7	1,152	262	1,414
	9	572	228	800		14	1,177	249	1,426
	16	476	263	739		21	979	332	1,311
	23	469	191	660		28	797	230	1,027
	30	846	227	1,073					
April	6	680	178	858	Oct	5	707	188	895
	13	526	229	755		12	628	178	806
	20	606	212	818		19	675	202	877
	27	791	194	985		26	724	251	975
May	4	756	195	951	Nov	2	461	194	655
	11	621	186	807		9	421	182	603
	18	592	165	757		16	409	194	603
	25	931	237	1,168		23	623	174	797
						30	585	159	744
June	1	993	196	1,189	Dec	7	652	170	822
	8	1,091	257	1,348		14	1,192	335	1,527
	15	960	261	1,221		21	1,328	343	1,671
	22	1,064	276	1,340		28	1,002	480	1,482
	29	1,025	291	1,316					

1976

		Dailies	Sundays	Total
Jan	4	968	418	1,386
	11	817	415	1,232
	18	980	456	1,436
	25	1,018	396	1,414
Feb	1	1,045	395	1,440
	8	1,016	475	1,491

Source: ACAS inquiries.

APPENDIX 4
GRAPH TO TABLE 3
WEEKLY TOTALS OF NATSOPA CALLS REQUIRED 1975–76

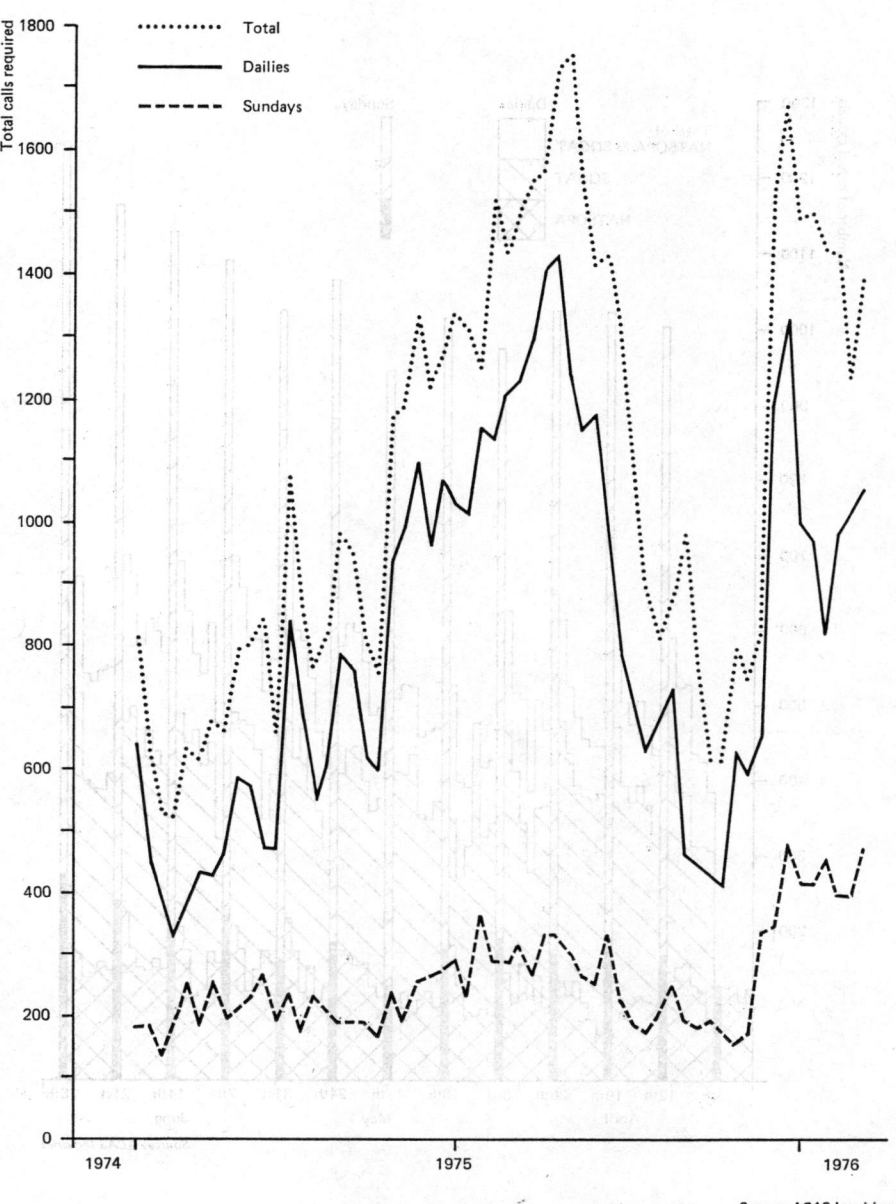

Source: ACAS Inquiries

APPENDIX 4: GRAPH A
CASUAL CASUAL WORKING BY NATSOPA AND SOGAT MEMBERS APRIL–JUNE 1975

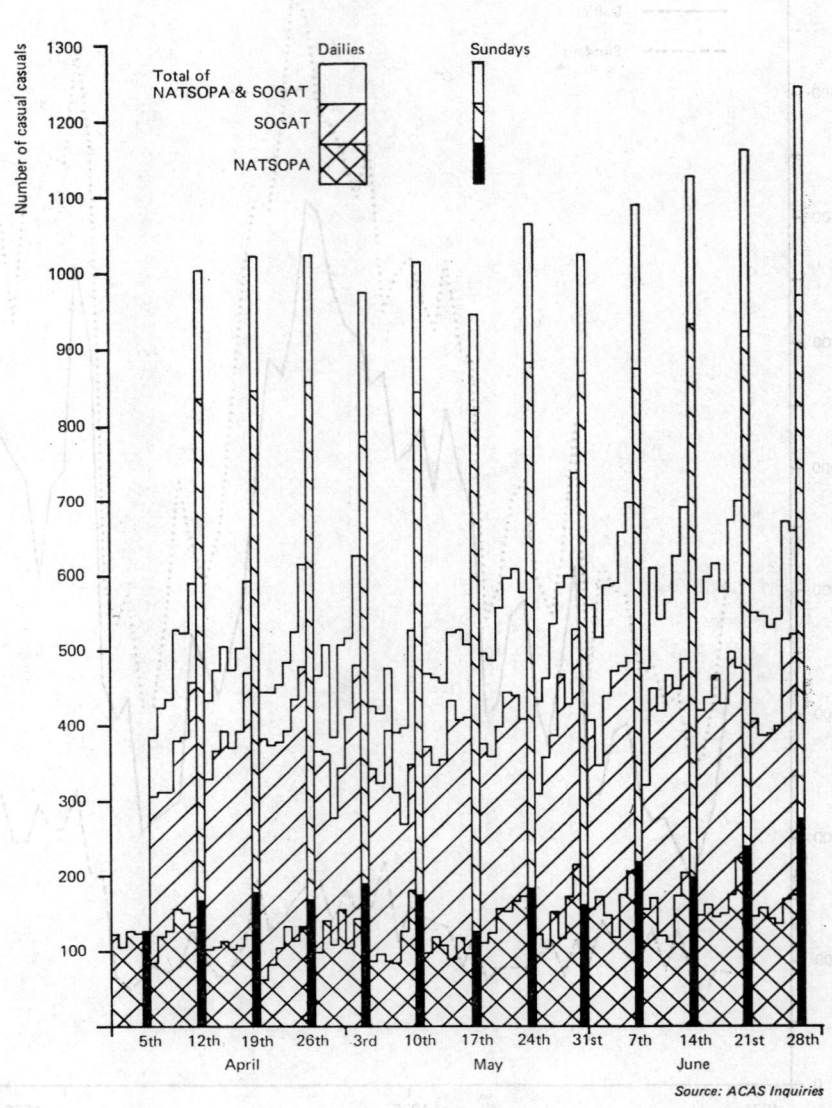

Source: ACAS Inquiries

APPENDIX 4: GRAPH B
CASUAL CASUAL WORKING BY NATSOPA AND SOGAT MEMBERS
SEPTEMBER-NOVEMBER 1975

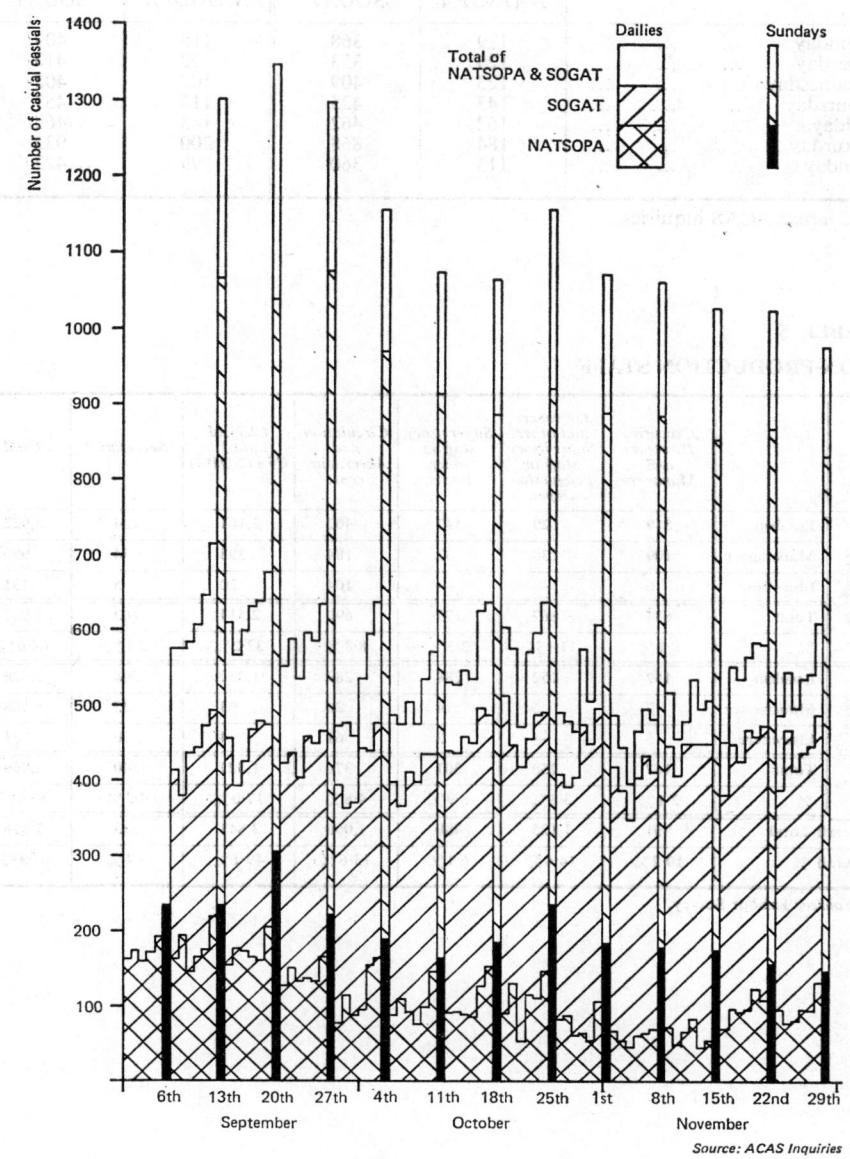

TABLE 4 APPENDIX 4

AVERAGE DAILY NUMBER OF CASUAL CALLS MADE ON NATSOPA AND SOGAT CALLS OFFICES, LONDON 1975

	April–June		Sept–Nov	
	NATSOPA	SOGAT	NATSOPA	SOGAT
Monday	129	368	115	409
Tuesday	125	353	99	410
Wednesday	123	409	107	408
Thursday	143	425	116	457
Friday	162	462	143	468
Saturday	184	868	200	932
Sunday	113	360	99	422

Source: ACAS inquiries.

TABLE 5

NON-PRODUCTION STAFF

		Executive Directors and Managers	Overseers and other Supervisory staff in Production Depts.	Supervisory staff in other Depts.	Circulation and Advertising reps.	Clerical staff (NATSOPA)	Secretarial	Total
Popular Newspapers	London	519	629	147	402	2,101	124	3,922
	Manchester	109	238	32	184	393	34	990
	Elsewhere	6	—	—	104	20	5	135
	Total	634	867	179	690	2,514	163	5,047
	%	8·1%	11·1%	2·3%	8·8%	32·2%	2·1%	64·6%
Quality Newspapers	London	157	252	284	289	1,230	308	2,520
	Manchester	7	6	14	26	93	22	168
	Elsewhere	3	—	3	61	4	10	81
	Total	167	258	301	376	1,327	340	2,769
	%	2·1%	3·3%	3·9%	4·8%	17·0%	4·3%	35·4%
Overall Total		801	1,125	480	1,066	3,841	503	7,816
Overall %		10·2%	14·4%	6·1%	13·6%	49·1%	6·4%	100%

Source: Labour Survey.

APPENDIX 4(a)

UNION RULES RELATING TO CASUAL EMPLOYMENT

A.   NATIONAL GRAPHICAL ASSOCIATION (LONDON REGION)

Rule 47: Regular and Casual Engagements

Regular Engagements

1. The allocation of notified regular engagements shall be through the medium of the Call Books, which shall be available for unemployed members, in accordance with the requirements set out below.

1(*a*). Every vacancy for a regular engagement within the E & S Trade Group shall be notified to the London Region. No member of the E & S Trade Group shall be allowed to fill any vacancy unless it has been offered in accordance with the employment policy of the E & S Trade Committee as ratified by the Regional Council.

2. Unemployed members holding clear cards of membership and not more than four weeks in arrear, as well as those holding temporary working cards, may insert their names, in order of arrival, in the Call Books, which shall remain open from 9.00 am to 3.30 pm from Monday until Friday subject to clauses 2(*a*) and 2(*b*) below. The Call Books shall be available to members at the London Region Office.

    (*a*) Any member writing another member's name in the Book shall forfeit his own position as well as that of the member for whom he signs.

    (*b*) No member shall be allowed to sign the Book whilst in work, or while not in a position to accept work.

3. The following shall be the regulations governing members who have signed the Call Book:—

    (*a*) All calls received at the Region Office shall state for what class of work members are required, and shall be given to the members first on the list who are able to accept such calls.

    (*b*) Any member whose name appears on the Call Book must accept whatever appropriate call may come to his name (except in cases involving excess travelling or special qualification subject to adjudication by the Regional Council), or have his name erased from the Call Book for a period to be determined by the Regional Council.

    (*c*) All calls shall be taken from the Call Book, excepting where an officer is satisfied that specialist requirements are necessary.

    (*d*) Any member, after having obtained a call, who forfeits such call by neglect or irregularity, shall be dealt with by the Regional Council in accordance with Association rules.

    (*e*) Any member sent from the Region shall bear a document signed by the Secretary, certifying the bearer to be the member officially sent for the call. No call shall be transferred to another member, except with the approval of the Secretary.

    (*f*) Should any Officer be proved to have abused the provisions of this rule, he shall be immediately suspended by the Regional Council, and be dealt with having regard to Rules 2 and 18, and in accordance with Association rules.

    (*g*) No member of the Region in receipt of strike pay shall take precedence of calls at the Region offices.

(*h*) Any member intercepting in the street or elsewhere, a messenger with a call that is intended for the Region, shall be dealt with by the Regional Council in accordance with Association rules.

(*i*) All calls to be notified to the Region.

(*j*) All calls shall be recorded with the name of the member, or members sent, the time and the nature of the call responded to. Such record shall be kept for at least six months, and shall be accessible to any member or members, upon application to the Secretary.

4. Whenever a member is aware of a vacancy he must communicate such knowledge to the London Region Office.

5. A member working in a firm as the sole NGA member shall, when giving or receiving notice to leave, inform the Region before the expiration of the first week of such notice, or be subject to such penalty as may be decided in accordance with Association rules on the recommendation of the Regional Council.

Casual Engagements

6. The Regional Council, or its appointed sub-committee, shall deal with all matters concerning casual engagements, of any kind, affecting any member of the NGA, subject to NGA rules and, where applicable, National Council rulings. Members signing solely for casual employment shall be deemed to be in full employment, and shall pay the highest rate of subscriptions in accordance with Regional Rule 36, irrespective of earnings.

7. All regular casual engagements must be approved by, or registered with, the Regional Council.

8. All casual engagements, other than those dealt with in Clause 7, shall be allocated by the Regional Council under the provisions of Clause 6. All calls for casual engagements must be referred to, and dealt with by the London Region Office. Such calls shall be allocated between members available for casual calls, ie members not in regular employment, or unemployed, or when such members are not available, between members in regular employment prepared to undertake work of this character, to the satisfaction of the Regional Council.

9. Any regulations necessary for the execution of the responsibilities set out in the preceding paragraphs, shall be formulated by the Regional Council and such regulations shall be binding on all members. The regulations must be laid before the Annual Conference of the London Region, or Special Conference for endorsement by such meeting, and any alterations must also be endorsed by the same procedure. Decisions of the Regional Council in this regard shall be binding on members until a Regional Conference has declared upon them.

10. Nothing in this rule shall be deemed to preclude any member or chapel from appealing against any decision of the Regional Council as laid down in Rule 18.

REGULATIONS OF THE REGIONAL COUNCIL IN ACCORDANCE WITH THE PROVISIONS OF CLAUSE 9, RULE 47

1. The Regional Council shall issue a document authorising members to undertake casual work. The form and contents of such document shall be determined by the Regional Council and may be altered from time to time as may be deemed necessary by the Regional Council, in such cases the provisions of Rule 47 would apply.

2. Every member must have the document issued by the Regional Council in respect of casual work when reporting for, or undertaking, casual work. This must be shown to the Father of the Chapel or authorised Chapel Official before commencing work. If a member cannot present this document he shall not be allowed to commence or continue work. The Chapel Officers shall be required to insist on production of the document. Failure to carry out this requirement shall be dealt with by the Regional Council in accordance with Association rules.

3. Casual engagements shall be made available to:—
   (a) Members not in regular employment.
   (b) Unemployed members.
   (c) Members on regular casual engagements.

In the event of there being insufficient members in sub-sections (a), (b) and (c) to cover the calls available, then the following provisions of sub-section (d) will apply.
   (d) Members in regular work who are prepared to take extra work on a casual basis as allocated by the Regional Office, providing that this is not to the detriment of the member's regular engagement or the normal obligations attached thereto, or any member who has left a position of regular employment of his own volition.

When a member wishes to transfer from the unemployed list to the casual list, or *vice versa*, he shall make his application in writing to the Regional Council.

The Regional Council shall determine the allocation of work to members in the categories referred to in this clause, according to the circumstances prevailing. The principle of maintaining the manning officially recognised shall be the prior consideration at all times.

4. Earnings for each casual working shall be recorded and shown. The Father of the Chapel shall be required to furnish accurate information of the earnings of each casual working to the Regional Office as requested.

5. All members engaged on jobbing or temporary employment shall be paid the same week in which they have worked, or at the expiration of their engagement, however brief.

6. All regular casual engagements must be registered by the member with the Region and shown by the Father of Chapel on the monthly Chapel return. Regular "dual working" in the same office will not be classed as casual work. No member may accept a regular casual working until approval has been obtained from the Regional Secretary.

7. All members temporarily or casually employed (including regular casuals) in either general printing or newspapers, shall be regarded as having completed a week's work where they have been engaged for a maximum of five days or four nights, or four workings where both days and nights are worked in the same office, or a combination of offices, from Monday, 8.00 am to the following Monday, 8.00 am.

Such members must not accept engagements in excess of the above, unless permission has been granted through the medium of the London Region Office. Permission will be granted only if all other members temporarily or casually employed have completed, or will be completing, a week's work as specified above, or if such members, as specified in these regulations, are not available. Overtime immediately prior to, or following on, a temporary or casual engagement, is excluded from the calculation of a week's work.

This clause in no way invalidates the existing operation and control of Lino grass cards. These cards, issued to members for employment on solo Sunday newspapers are at all times subject to withdrawal, without notice, at the direction of the Regional Council in accord with a previous decision of the members.

The existing directives in operation in respect of stereotypers (casual or regular) regarding limitation of shifts, will also continue, until the Regional Council recommend such alteration as may be required.

8. Every member shall be given a copy of these regulations. Any member contravening any of these regulations shall be dealt with by the Regional Council in accordance with Association rules.

9. Any unemployed stereotyper, machine manager or reader member prepared to undertake such casual work as may be available, will signify his preparedness to do so by signing the "Members available for casual working book", kept at the office of the London Region for this purpose. Members referred to in categories (b) and (c) of Clause 3 of these regulations will also sign to signify their availability, subject to the provisions of these regulations. Members so signing shall be required to undertake any casual work allocated to them from the London Region Office. Failure to undertake such work will disqualify the member from casual working until such time as the Regional Council shall restore his eligibility.

10. Calls will be allocated by the London Region Office on the basis of sharing available work amongst those members available.

11. Signatures will be used solely for establishing availability for casual work. Such signatures shall confer no entitlement to benefit or to reduce subscriptions.

12. Should any member, after having obtained a call, forfeit such call by neglect or irregularity, he shall be suspended for such time as the Regional Council may determine.

No member shall transfer a call allocated to him by the London Region. Should an emergency arise at a time when it is not possible to make contact with the Regional Office, the FOC to be informed immediately, who will make arrangements to obtain a replacement. Such alteration shall be advised to the Regional Office within 48 hours. The FOCs, when notified of an absence, either regular or casual, shall telephone the Regional Office to obtain a suitable replacement.

B. NATIONAL SOCIETY OF OPERATIVE PRINTERS GRAPHICAL AND MEDIA PERSONNEL

Rule 34: Calls and Vacancies

1. Call books shall be supplied for every Branch, and they shall be signed each day by all members out of employment whether in benefit or not. Members not signing the call book shall be considered employed.

2. A list of members who are signing the call book shall be drawn up by the Branch Secretary every week and placed in the waiting-room every Saturday morning. Members' names are to be placed in rotation on the list in the order in which they are entitled to answer calls, according to the number of times they have signed the book the previous week.

3. Any member doing a night's work shall not be entitled to sign the book the following day, and any member obtaining day work must miss signing the book once for each day's work done. Members doing a Saturday night's work shall miss signing the book the following Monday. Any member breaking this clause shall be fined a sum not exceeding £10, expelled, or otherwise dealt with as the Branch Committee shall determine and shall be suspended from all benefits until such fine be paid.

4. Upon a call being received at the offices of the Society, the call shall be answered by the member whose name is first on the list (provided he is qualified to do the work) and in the event of his being absent, by the next highest on the list who is able to do

the job. The member answering the call shall have his name removed from the list. Any member not answering his name at a call off for six consecutive times, his name shall be removed from the list.

5. In the event of any member being sent for men, or having knowledge of men being wanted, it shall be his duty immediately to give information of the same to the Secretary, and on no account engage anyone without the Secretary's sanction. Any member breaking this rule shall be fined a sum not exceeding £10, expelled, or otherwise dealt with as the Branch Committee shall determine. In cases of special calls the Secretary shall use his discretion.

6. Members not signing the book through illness will still retain their position on the list, provided they give notice thereof to the Secretary within 48 hours.

7. Whenever a member knows of a vacancy or leaves one situation to go to another, or gives or receives notice to leave his employment, he shall give information thereof to the Secretary within three days, failing which he may be fined a sum not exceeding £10, expelled, or otherwise dealt with as the Branch Committee may determine.

8. Any member knowingly making an application for a member's job before such member has actually left, without the sanction of the Secretary, shall be fined a sum not exceeding £10, expelled, or otherwise dealt with as the Branch Committee shall determine.

9. Any member commencing regular work must inform the Secretary where he is at work within 48 hours, and also give his rate of pay within two days of receiving same, or failing which he may be fined a sum not exceeding £10, expelled, or otherwise dealt with as the Branch Committee may determine.

London Machine Branch Bye-law

There shall be restriction of transfer to work on national newspapers within the London Machine Branch.

Applications for transfer will not be accepted from members with less than four years' membership in the general printing trade.

There shall be no restriction of movement within the London Machine Branch of those with more than 20 years' membership of the Branch.

Vacancies on national newspapers for those with less than 20 years' membership shall be filled on the basis of seniority of application through the Branch Committee. Where a number of applications are received on the same date, seniority of membership of the Society shall be the deciding factor.

As from 1 January 1976 members aged 65 and over retiring from their employment with a company pension shall seek their work at the branch office on the same basis as unattached members.

C. SOCIETY OF GRAPHICAL AND ALLIED TRADES
(LONDON CENTRAL BRANCH)

Rule 31: Members' Working Hours

Members working for Newspapers and Wholesale Newsagents. No member who is in regular employment (ie 5 days, 5 nights or three and one) shall do any work whatever for another employer or employers, or more than eight hours' overtime in one week for his own employer or employers without the sanction of the Branch Secretary, such sanction only to be given in cases of emergency or for special work which could not be done by an unemployed or jobbing worker.

Where permission has been given, all such cases to be reported to the Committee at the following meeting, and no member who is jobbing shall be allowed to do more than 56 hours in any week.

In dispute emergency the Branch Committee shall have power to reduce the 56-hour limit for the period of the dispute.

For the purpose of this Rule, jobbing or casual hands' time shall count as follows:—

Night	10 hours
Saturday night	11 ,,
Saturday half-night	6 ,,
Day	10 ,,
Half-day	5 ,,
Sunday early morning (member's own pedal cycle or motor vehicle)	3 ,,
Sunday early morning (driving firm's vehicle)	5 ,,
Wholesaler's early morning	4 ,,
Wholesaler's Sunday early morning	5 ,,
Wholesaler's full night or day	10 ,,
Wholesaler's half-day	5 ,,

With regard to work not specified in above schedule, the Branch Committee shall have power to decide how many hours such work shall count.

Any member working a full week of half-days or early mornings shall not be allowed to work more than 56 hours in any one week. But in dispute emergency the Branch Committee shall have power to reduce the 56-hour limit for the period of the dispute. If through any unforeseen circumstances, he is compelled to work beyond the limit, he shall at once acquaint the Secretary of same, who shall notify the Branch Committee at their next meeting.

Rule 34

Regular Hands and Jobbing Hands. The working week to count from 8 am Saturday to 8 am the following Saturday. That prior to going on holiday members be permitted to work overtime if required as a continuation of the working day or night provided that same terminates before 8 am on Saturday. The reference to "regular hands" in this Rule is for overtime purposes only.

Rule 37: Signing Unemployed Book

(a) Members working any night from Sunday to Friday must miss signing the Call Book the following day.

(b) Members working a day or earning 21s. or over are not eligible to sign Call Book on day worked. In the case of members working after having signed the Book, they must miss the following day.

(c) Members working Saturday (night or half-night) must miss signing the Book on the following Monday. Members employed on Sunday (day or early morning) must miss signing on the following Monday.

(d) Members working as in paragraph (c) above, on Saturday, Sunday or Sunday night consecutively, must miss signing the Book once for each job done, on the next Monday and following days.

(e) In the case of members working two half-days or two early mornings in any working week, they must miss signing once after the second half-day or early morning. But, if a sum of 20s. or more is earned in one half-day, a signature must be missed, in accordance with Clause (b) above.

Rule 38

The Branch Committee shall have power to decide the times the Call Room shall be open; the times at which calls are made, also the procedure and regulations governing calls, in every respect, subject only to such procedure and regulations being approved by the National Executive Council and subsequently posted at the Branch Office.

Rule 39

It shall be the duty of the Father of the Chapel to report any member breaking these Rules. Any member proved guilty of breaking any of these Rules shall be dealt with by the Committee, who shall have power to fine up to 40*s*.

TABLE 1
AVERAGE WEEKLY EARNINGS OF PRODUCTION WORKERS

APPENDIX 5

	1961			1964			1967			1970			1972			1975 (APRIL)		
	£	Rank	£	% Increase since 1961	Rank	£	% Increase since 1964	Rank	£	% Increase since 1967	Rank	£	% Increase since 1970	Rank	£	% Increase since 1972	Rank
Lino Ops.	36·60	3	44·17	20·68%	3	51·24	16·01%	2	69·86	36·34%	1	90·41	29·42%	1	153·96	70·29%	1
Time Hands	26·69	10	32·92	23·34%	10	38·63	17·35%	9	56·64	46·62%	8	67·14	18·54%	7	103·68	54·42%	4
Piece Case	40·64	1	47·23	16·22%	1	53·00	12·22%	1	71·65	35·19%	2	89·36	24·72%	2	137·54	53·92%	2
Readers	25·34	12	34·52	36·23%	9	37·38	8·29%	13	53·69	43·90%	9	63·96	19·13%	8	96·61	51·05%	8
Revisers/Copyreaders	18·88	20	25·52	35·17%	19	29·36	15·05%	20	41·73	42·13%	20	51·23	22·77%	19	77·57	51·42%	14
Proof-Pullers	19·85	19	26·10	31·49%	17	30·52	16·93%	18	41·45	35·81%	19	51·82	25·02%	18	75·88	46·43%	15
Lino Assistants	20·89	18	28·80	37·87%	15	32·04	11·25%	17	43·25	34·99%	17	52·22	20·74%	17	75·32	44·24%	20
Process Workers	31·55	5	38·20	21·08%	6	39·42	3·19%	8	52·58	33·38%	10	62·11	18·12%	9	96·48	55·34%	9
Stereotypers	38·39	2	46·53	21·46%	2	49·14	5·61%	4	62·85	27·90%	5	74·01	17·76%	6	102·94	39·09%	6
Machine Managers	35·00	4	43·04	22·97%	4	46·93	4·39%	5	63·21	40·69%	4	78·59	24·33%	4	97·96	24·65%	7
Machine Assistants	28·84	8	35·20	22·05%	8	38·42	9·15%	10	51·63	34·38%	12	61·78	19·66%	11	77·73	25·82%	13
Publishing (I)	24·34	14	30·96	27·20%	14	35·61	15·02%	14	46·36	30·19%	15	58·45	26·08%	13	75·87	29·80%	16
Publishing (O)	25·27	13	32·09	26·99%	12	37·45	16·70%	12	45·37	21·15%	16	56·84	25·28%	14	75·54	32·90%	19
Engineers	30·45	6	39·19	28·70%	5	50·55	28·99%	3	65·33	29·24%	3	79·25	21·31%	3	103·05	30·03%	5
Electricians	26·19	11	31·78	21·34%	13	42·94	35·12%	6	61·64	43·55%	6	76·09	23·44%	5	108·51	42·61%	3
Eng. Assistants	21·12	17	25·17	19·18%	20	32·91	30·75%	16	48·02	45·91%	13	55·87	16·35%	16	79·43	42·17%	12
Elec. Assistants	22·43	15	25·84	15·20%	18	34·60	33·90%	15	46·90	35·55%	14	56·82	21·15%	15	74·59	31·27%	18
Phototech	21·59	16	26·29	21·77%	16	30·32	15·33%	19	42·40	39·84%	18	47·69	12·48%	20	75·63	58·59%	17
Telegraphists	29·05	7	32·69	12·53%	11	38·03	16·34%	11	—	—	(11)	61·98	—	10	83·84	—	10
Wire Room	28·05	9	38·10	35·83%	7	24·79	5·70%	7	—	—	(7)	60·00	—	12			
RIRMA	16·56	21	22·11	35·51%	21	40·27	12·12%	21	—	—	(21)	—	—	(21)	56·86	—	21

Source: ACAS inquiries.

TABLE 2 APPENDIX 5

AVERAGE WEEKLY EARNINGS OF FULL TIME REGULAR PRODUCTION EMPLOYEES IN LONDON BY DEPARTMENTS

		April 1975			October 1975		
		All Houses	Lowest paid House/title	Highest paid House/title	All Houses	Lowest paid House/title	Highest paid House/title
Composing	NGA	130·70	76	221	131	99·50	170
	NATSOPA	75·50	59	97	76·50	66·50	85·50
Reading	NGA	96·60	71	125	99	80	125
	NATSOPA	77·60	59	97	80	69	98
Process	SLADE	96·50	79	128	100	78	127
	SOGAT	95	63	121	91	63	120
Machine	NGA	98	87	119	98	87	119
	NATSOPA	78	70	95	81	79	94
Foundry	NGA	103	53	168	104·50	88	150
Maintenance	AUEW	103	86	125	102	88	108·50
	EETPU	100·00	63	112	95·50	86	101
	NATSOPA	79·50	73	92	80	68	88
News and	NGA	83·80	52	107	87·50	54	110
Pictures	NATSOPA	75·50	65	102	75·50	67	86
Publishing Indoor	SOGAT	75·80	56	90	85	62	110
Publishing Outdoor		75·70	70	99	79	64	102
Ancillary	NATSOPA	56·80	47	75	56	49	75

Source: Labour Survey.

TABLE 3　　　　　　　　　　　　　　　　　　　　　　　　　　　　APPENDIX 5

EARNINGS COMPARISON BETWEEN NEWSPAPER CATEGORIES APRIL 1975

	All Houses		Quality Newspapers		Popular Newspapers	
	Average Weekly Earnings	*Range*	*Average Weekly Earnings*	*Range*	*Average Weekly Earnings*	*Range*
Lino Ops.	167·65	107–221	154·63	108–209	178·26	107–221
Time Hands	103·68	76–125	99·72	76–125	106·90	78–120
Piececase	137·54	104–174	139·71	104–174	133·22	111–139
Readers	96·61	71–125	93·30	71–125	96·50	76–108
Revisers/Copyreaders	77·57	59–97	78·91	62–97	77·55	59–92
Proof Pullers	75·88	67–95	77·76	67–95	74·92	69–86
Lino Assistants	75·32	63–97	73·70	63–97	70·51	67–81
Monocasters	74·22	59–84	74·75	59–84	70·00	70
Process Workers	96·48	79–128	96·35	79–105	101·86	84–128
Process Provers	95·08	63–121	80·10	63–103	100·43	73–121
Stereotypers	102·94	53–168	120·92	53–168	99·19	64–123
Machine Managers	97·96	87–119	107·35	105–119	93·55	87–113
Machine Assistants	77·73	70–95	90·33	76–95	75·74	70–76
Publishing (Indoor)	75·87	56–90	87·19	56–90	75	72–76
Publishing (Outdoor)	75·74	70–99	90·83	84–96	74·99	70–99
Engineers	103·05	86–125	99·84	95–125	104·47	86–113
Electricians	108·51	86–112	98·73	86–111	108·73	98–112
Engineers Assts.	79·43	73–92	77·99	73–81	79·94	73–92
Electricians Assts.	74·59	63–95	75·13	70–95	74·39	63–85
Phototechnicians	75·63	65–102	69·43	65–72	79·57	70–102
Telegraphists	} 83·84	} 54–107	} 77·83	} 54–98	} 84·97	} 80–107
Wire Room						
RIRMA	56·86	47–75	58·05	58–59	54·42	47–75

Source: Labour Survey.

TABLE 4 APPENDIX 5

EXAMPLES OF COMPREHENSIVE WAGE MAKE-UP AND COMPREHENSIVE WAGE AS A PERCENTAGE OF TOTAL EARNINGS IN ONE WEEK

NGA Machine Managers		*NATSOPA Copyreaders*	
Components of comprehensive wage	% of total comprehensive wage	Components of comprehensive wage	% of total comprehensive wage
NPA basic	34·8	NPA basic	29·6
Additional duties	12·0	Production bonus	5·9
Comprehensive extra	14·9	Pagination bonus	4·6
Consolidated production bonus	14·4	Productivity/flexibility bonus (1)	13·7
Agreed overtime	21·7	New techniques bonus	2·3
House bonus	3·0	Productivity/flexibility bonus (2)	17·3
		Shift overtime	6·6
		Weekly overtime	5·2
		Weekly deferred meals	1·5
		House bonus	3·0
	65·2		70·4
	100		100
Comprehensive wage/total earnings: 91·3%		Comprehensive wage/total earnings: 97·8%	
NPA basic /total earnings: 30·7%		NPA basic /total earnings: 27·1%	

SOGAT Publishing (Inside)		*NGA Readers*	
Components of comprehensive wage	% of total comprehensive wage	Components of comprehensive wage	% of total comprehensive wage
NPA basic	40·3	NPA basic	32·9
Agreed overtime	17·3	Production bonus	5·4
Bonus	10·4	Pagination bonus	15·1
Consolidated production bonus	27·7	Productivity/flexibility bonus	26·6
House bonus	4·5	Cover bonus	3·0
		Shift overtime	13·0
		Deferred meals	1·2
	59·7		67·1
	100		100
Comprehensive wage/total earnings: 77·1%		Comprehensive wage/total earnings: 100%	
NPA basic /total earnings: 31·2%		NPA basic /total earnings: 31·9%	

Source: ACAS inquiries.

TABLE 5

APPENDIX 5

NPA RATE MOVEMENTS

Date	Amount of Increase		NPA Basic Example (LCB)
1. 4.60	BASE	Basic (+ COLB*) 3rd week	12. 7.0
1. 3.62		Consolidation of 1961 COLB	12.13.0
1. 6.63		Consolidation of 1961 COLB	12.19.0
1. 4.64		10% of basic (+ COLB)	14. 5.0
1. 3.65		Consolidation of COLB—6/-	14.11.0
1. 3.66		Consolidation of COLB—6/-	14.17.0
1. 9.67		Consolidation of COLB—6/-	15. 3.0
1. 9.68		3% of basic (paid 33/- COLB frozen) Consolidation of 11/- COLB	16. 3.6
1. 9.69		2% of basic (paid 22/- COLB frozen) Consolidation of 11/- COLB	17. 1.6
1. 7.70		5% of basic 4th week (paid 22/- COLB frozen) (Fall back to 10% of basic)	17.95
1. 7.71		5% of basic or £1.12½ (paid 22/- COLB frozen) (Fall back to 10% of basic)	19.0750
1. 1.72		Consolidation of 55p COLB (paid 55p—COLB frozen)	19.6250
1. 4.72		Consolidation of 55p (no COLB)	20.1750
1.10.72		8% of earnings (including threshold)	21.7890
1.10.73		8% of earnings (including threshold)	23.5321
1. 6.74		Threshold £1·20	
1. 7.74		Threshold + 80p = £2·00	
1. 8.74		Threshold + 40p = £2·40	
1. 9.74		Threshold + 40p = £2·80	
1.10.74		5% on earnings (threshold ceases and £2·80)	24.7087
1. 4.75		Min. guarantee (becomes house bonus) Up to £45—£4, £45—£50—£3·50, £50+—£2·75 2% on earnings	25.2029
1.10.75		Earnings supplement £6·00 (max.) No change in schedules.	

Source: NPA.

*Cost of living bonus.

TABLE 6

NPA RATES 1970-1976

APPENDIX 5

	July '70 £	July '71 5% (%) or £1·12½ (+) £	Jan '72 55p CoLB £	Apr '72 55p CoLB £	Oct '72 8% £	Oct '73 8% £	Oct '74 5% £	Apr '75 2% £
Compositors (Perm. Time)								
Morning papers	24·2250	(%) 25·4363	25·9863	26·5363	28·6592	30·9519	32·4995	33·1495
Evening papers	23·7500	(%) 24·9375	25·4875	26·0375	28·1225	30·3701	31·8886	32·5264
Sunday papers	21·8250	(%) 22·9163	23·4663	24·0163	25·9376	28·1026	29·4132	30·0014
Machine Managers								
Morning papers								
Night work								
Up to 3 rolls	22·4250	(%) 23·5463	24·0963	24·6463	26·6180	28·7474	30·1848	30·7885
Up to 4 rolls	23·3000	(%) 24·465	25·1050	25·5650	27·6102	29·8190	31·3100	31·9361
Up to 5 rolls	24·1500	(%) 25·3775	25·9075	26·4575	28·5741	30·8600	32·4030	33·0511
Up to 6 rolls	25·0000	(%) 26·2500	26·8000	27·3500	29·5380	31·9010	33·4961	34·1660
Day work								
Up to 3 rolls	18·7000	(%) 19·6350	20·1850	20·7350	22·3938	24·1853	25·3946	25·9025
Up to 4 rolls	19·1750	(%) 20·1338	20·6380	21·3380	22·9325	24·7670	26·0055	26·5255
Up to 5 rolls	19·625	(%) 20·6062	21·1563	21·7063	23·4428	25·3182	26·5841	27·1158
Up to 6 rolls	20·1000	(%) 21·1050	21·6550	22·2050	23·9814	25·8999	27·1949	27·7388
Evening papers								
Up to 3 rolls	20·4000	(%) 21·4200	21·9700	22·5200	24·3216	26·2673	27·5807	28·1323
Up to 4 rolls	20·8750	(%) 21·9188	22·4688	23·0188	24·8603	26·8491	28·1916	28·7554
Up to 5 rolls	21·3000	(%) 22·3650	22·9150	23·4650	25·3422	27·3696	28·7381	29·3128
Up to 6 rolls	21·7500	(%) 22·8375	23·3575	23·9375	25·8525	27·9207	29·3167	29·9031
Men on overlay or interlays	18·0000	(%) 18·9000	19·4500	20·0000	21·0600	23·3280	24·4944	24·9843
Readers								
Morning papers	24·2250	(%) 25·4363	25·9863	26·5363	28·6592	30·9519	32·4995	33·1495
Evening papers	23·7500	(%) 24·9375	25·4875	26·0375	28·1225	30·3701	31·8886	32·5264
Sunday papers	21·8250	(%) 22·9163	23·4663	24·0163	25·9376	28·0126	29·4132	30·0015
Stereotypers								
Daily (including evening) papers	21·2250	(%) 22·2863	22·8363	23·3863	25·2572	27·2777	28·6417	29·2144
Press Telegraphists								
1.	23·2750	(%) 24·4388	24·9888	25·5388	27·5819	29·7884	31·2779	31·9034
2.	19·9500	(%) 20·9475	21·4975	20·0475	23·8113	25·7162	27·0020	27·5421
3.	18·8250	(%) 19·7663	20·3163	20·8663	22·5356	24·3384	25·5553	26·0664

*An earnings supplement (£6·00 maximum) became payable from 1.10.75 but no change in the schedule took place.

Source: ACAS Inquiries.

TABLE 6—continued
NPA RATES 1970–1976

	July '70 £	July '71 5% (%) or £1-12½ (+) £	Jan '72 55p CoLB £	Apr '72 55p CoLB £	Oct '72 8% £	Oct '73 8% £	Oct '74 5% £	Apr '75 2% £
Process Workers	24·1000	(%) 25·3050	25·8850	26·4050	28·5174	30·7987	32·3387	32·9855
Workers in Machine Depts.								
Morning papers								
Brake Hands (octuple)	19·6000	(+) 20·7250	21·2750	21·8250	23·5710	25·4567	26·7295	27·2641
Brake Hands (sextuple)	18·9750	(+) 20·1000	20·6500	21·2000	22·8960	24·7277	25·9641	26·4833
Brake Hands (single)	18·7000	(+) 19·8250	20·3750	20·9250	22·5990	24·4069	25·6272	26·1398
Magazine Hands	17·9500	(+) 19·0750	19·6250	20·1750	21·7890	23·5321	24·7087	25·2029
Oilers	17·9000	(+) 19·0250	19·5750	20·1250	21·7350	23·4738	24·6475	25·1404
General Assistants	17·6500	(+) 18·7750	19·3250	19·8750	21·4650	23·1822	24·3421	24·8281
Evening papers								
Brake Hands (octuple)	18·8000	(+) 19·925	20·475	21·025	22·707	24·5236	25·7498	26·2647
Brake Hands (sextuple)	18·4250	(+) 19·55	20·1000	20·65	22·302	24·0862	25·2905	25·7963
Brake Hands (single)	18·3000	(+) 19·425	19·975	20·525	22·167	23·9404	25·1374	25·6401
Magazine Hands	17·575	(+) 18·7000	19·2500	19·8000	21·384	23·0947	24·2494	24·7344
Oilers	17·5250	(+) 18·6500	19·2000	19·7500	21·33	23·0364	24·1882	24·672
General Assistants	17·2250	(+) 18·3500	18·9000	19·4500	21·006	22·6865	23·8208	24·2972
Sunday papers								
All grades	18·2750	(+) 19·4000	19·95	20·5000	22·14	23·9112	25·1068	25·6089
Revisers/Monocasters								
Night work	18·2	(+) 19·325	19·875	20·425	22·059	23·8237	25·0149	25·5152
Day work	17·575	(+) 18·7	19·25	19·80	21·384	23·0947	24·2494	24·7344
Copyholders/Proof Pullers								
Night work	17·55	(+) 18·675	19·225	19·775	21·357	23·0656	24·2189	24·7032
Day work	17·0	(+) 18·125	18·675	19·225	20·763	22·4240	23·5452	24·0161
Linotype Assistants								
Night work	18·2	(+) 19·325	19·875	20·425	22·059	23·8237	25·0149	25·5152
Day work	17·575	(+) 18·7	19·25	19·80	21·384	23·0947	24·2494	24·7344
Other Assistants								
Night work	17·1250	(+) 18·2500	18·8000	19·3500	20·8980	22·5698	23·6983	24·1723
Day work	16·7750	(+) 17·9000	18·4500	19·0000	20·52	22·1616	23·2697	23·7351

*An earnings supplement (£6·00 maximum) became payable from 1.10.75 but no change in the schedule took place.
Source: ACAS Inquiries.

TABLE 6—continued
NPA RATES 1970–1976

	July '70 £	July '71 5% (%) or £1·12½(+) £	Jan '72 55p CoLB £	Apr '72 55p CoLB £	Oct '72 8% £	Oct '73 8% £	Oct '74 5% £	Apr '75 2% £
General Assistants	17·0250							
Cleaners, Porters, etc.								
Night work	16·7							
Day work	16·875							
Shift work	13·55							
Women cleaners, Packers, etc.								
Morning papers								
Night work	18·53							
Day work	17·95							
Evening papers								
Bench Elevators, etc.	18·65							
Others	17·95							
Weekly	17·95							
Motor drivers								
Morning papers	18·5	(+) 19·625	20·175	20·725	22·383	24·1736	25·3823	25·8900
Evening papers	17·95	(+) 19·075	19·625	20·175	21·789	23·5321	24·7087	25·2029
Electricians and Engineers								
Daily and Daily/Sunday								
Day work	22·25						28·6125	29·1848
Night work	25·3						23·5447	23·1854
3 rotating/shifts	24·2						31·1201	31·7425
4 rotating/shifts								
Sunday offices	23·775						30·5737	31·1852
Electricians' Assistants								
Daily and daily/Sunday offices								
Day work	20·025						25·7514	26·2664
Night work	22·025						28·3232	28·8899
3 rotating shifts	21·525						27·6805	28·2339
4 rotating shifts	21·000						27·0051	27·5452

*An earnings supplement (£6·00 maximum) became payable from 1.10.75 but no change in the schedule took place.
Source: ACAS inquiries.

TABLE 7   APPENDIX 5

RELATIONSHIP OF AVERAGE EARNINGS TO NATIONAL MINIMUM RATES 1961–1976

	Average Earnings as a Percentage of National Minimum Rates of following Categories of Employees:—								
	Time Hands	Readers	Copyholders	Process Workers	Machine Managers	Brake Hands	Publishing Outdoor	Stereotypers	Engineers	Electrical
1961 ...	152·51%	144·8%	154·67%	181·06%	208·96%	230·36%	204·62%	255%	183·43%	157·77%
1964 ...	165·22%	173·25%	180·4%	192·44%	225·34%	243·43%	225·19%	269%	198·93%	161·32%
1967 ...	185·5%	187·60%	195·19%	189·98%	234·65%	250·26%	247·19%	271·12%	219·07%	186·09%
1970 ...	233·81%	221·63%	231·34%	218·17%	271·29%	282·37%	252·76%	296·11%	258·22%	243·64%
1971 ...	243·39%	236·36%	254·83%	239·56%	238·14%	277·61%	278·58%	316·20%	NA	NA
1972 ...	234·27%	223·17%	236·6%	217·8%	284·64%	287·95%	260·87%	293·03%	NA	NA
1975 (April)	312·76%	291·44%	309·72%	292·49%	306·74%	313·22%	299·73%	352·36%	310·53%	326·98%

Source: ACAS inquiries.

TABLE 8 APPENDIX 5

INDICES OF THE INCREASE IN WEEKLY BASIC RATES AND AVERAGE WEEKLY EARNINGS FOR MANUFACTURING INDUSTRY AND THE LCB SOGAT

Date		LCB Basic Rate Index	Manufacturing Industries Basic Rate Index	LCB Average Weekly Earnings £	LCB Average Earnings Index	Manufacturing Industries Average Weekly Earnings £	Manufacturing Industries Weekly Earnings Index
1960	April	100	100*			14·82	
1961	April		105·54	25·27	100†	15·7625	100†
1962	March	102·43	109·53				
	April					16·19	102·71
1963	April		111·57			16·62	105·44
	June	104·86					
1964	April	115·38	117·63	32·09	126·99	18·2125	115·54
1965	March	117·81	121·17				
	April					19·44	123·33
1966	March	120·24	127·13				
	April					20·97	133·04
1967	April		132·43	37·45	148·2	21·13	134·05
	Sept.	122·67					
1968	April		141·11			22·825	144·81
	Sept.	130·97					
1969	April		148·94			23·2	147·18
	Sept.	138·26					
1970	April		164	45·37	179·54	27·4	173·83
	July	145·34					
1971	April			53·14	210·29	30·2	191·59
	July	154·45	182·64				
1972	January	158·91					
	April	163·36	203·23	56·84	224·93	33·6	213·16
	October	176·43					
1973	April		229·04			38·6	244·89
	October	190·54					
1974	April		267·86			43·6	279·61
	October	200·07					
1975	April	204·07	335·94	75·74	299·72	54·5	345·76

Source: ACAS inquiries.
*Basic rate Index for Manufacturing Industries—Base January 1960—for the following years from July.
†Average Weekly Earnings Index—Base April 1961.

APPENDIX 5
GRAPH TO TABLE 8
WEEKLY WAGE RATES FOR LCB SOGAT AND ALL MANUFACTURING INDUSTRIES

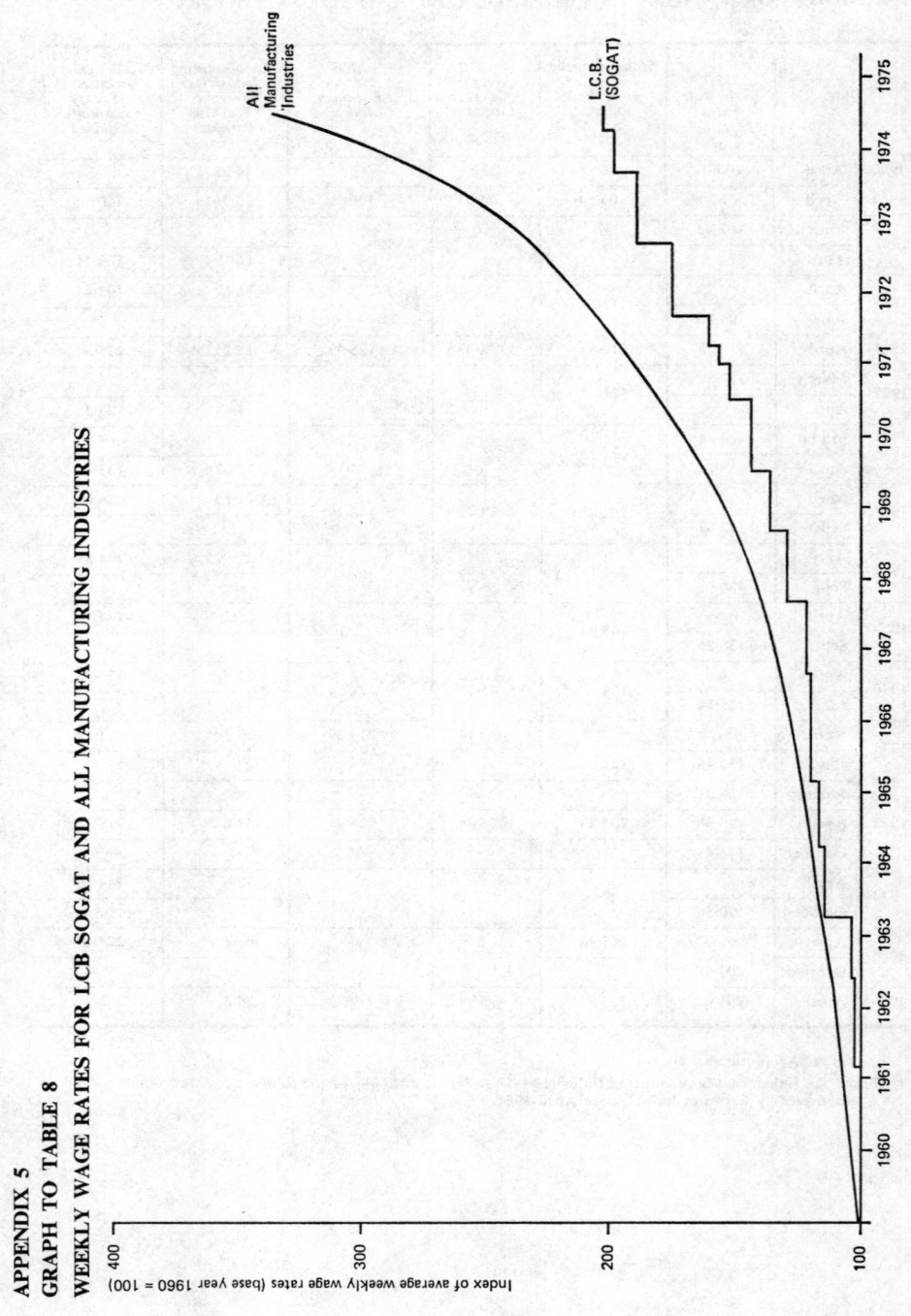

APPENDIX 5
GRAPH TO TABLE 8
COMPARATIVE INDICES OF AVERAGE WEEKLY EARNINGS FOR MANUFACTURING INDUSTRIES AND LCB SOGAT
BASE YEAR 1961

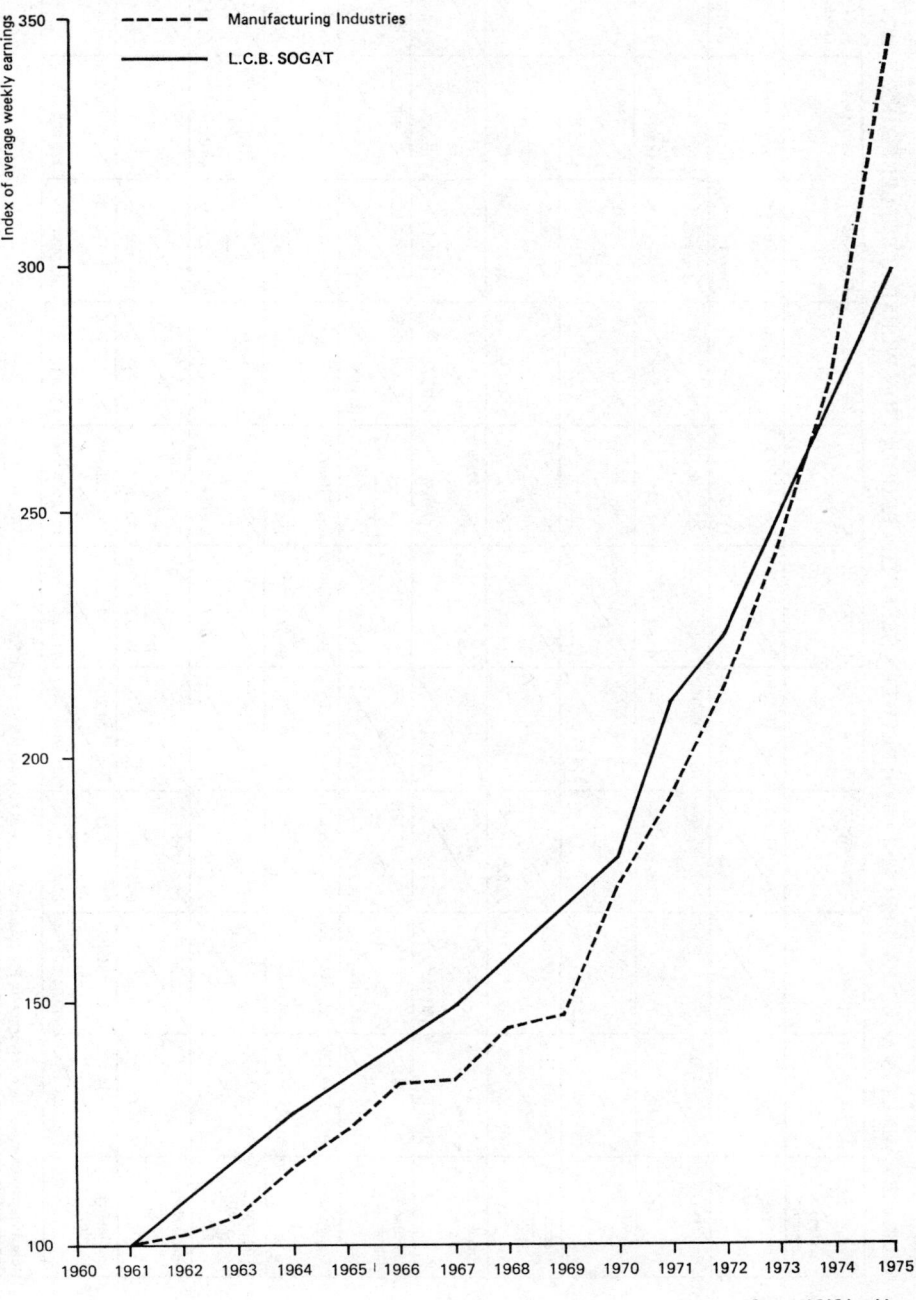

Source: ACAS Inquiries

APPENDIX 5
TABLE 9
AVERAGE EARNINGS AND NPA (PERCENTAGES) BETWEEN SELECTED PRODUCTION WORKERS IN FLEET STREET 1970

Basic Rate → / Average Earnings ↓	Timehands	Readers	Copyholders	Process Workers	Brakehands	Machine Minders	Stereotypers	Engineers	Electricians	Publishing Outdoor
Timehands	—	100% / 94.79%	71.45% / 71.68%	99.48% / 92.83%	78.33% / 94.60%	96.18% / 111.6%	87.62% / 110.08%	104.44% / 115.34%	104.44% / 108.83%	74.1% / 80.1%
Readers	100% / 105.49%	—	72.45% / 75.62%	99.48% / 97.93%	78.33% / 99.8%	96.18% / 117.73%	87.62% / 117.81%	104.44% / 121.62%	104.44% / 114.81%	74.1% / 84.5%
Copyholders	138.03% / 139.51%	138.03% / 132.24%	—	137.32% / 129.51%	108.12% / 131.97%	132.76% / 155.69%	120.94% / 153.57%	144.16% / 160.91%	144.16% / 151.82%	102.28% / 111.75%
Process Workers	100.52% / 107.72%	100.52% / 102.11%	72.82% / 72.22%	—	78.23% / 101.9%	96.68% / 120.22%	88.07% / 118.58%	104.98% / 124.25%	104.98% / 117.23%	74.48% / 86.29%
Brakehands	127.67% / 105.71%	127.67% / 100.21%	92.49% / 75.77%	127.01% / 98.13%	—	122.79% / 117.97%	111.86% / 116.37%	133.33% / 121.95%	133.33% / 115.04%	94.6% / 84.68%
Machine Managers	105.97% / 89.61%	103.97% / 84.94%	75.32% / 64.23%	103.45% / 83.18%	81.44% / 84.77%	—	91.09% / 98.69%	108.58% / 103.35%	108.58% / 97.52%	77.04% / 71.78%
Stereotypers	114.13% / 90.84%	114.13% / 86.11%	82.69% / 65.12%	113.55% / 84.33%	89.40% / 85.93%	109.78% / 101.38%	—	119.2% / 104.78%	119.2% / 98.86%	84.57% / 72.77%
Engineers	95.75% / 86.70%	95.75% / 82.18%	69.37% / 62.15%	95.26% / 80.48%	75% / 82.01%	92.09% / 96.75%	83.89% / 95.44%	—	100% / 94.35%	70.95% / 69.45%
Electricians	95.75% / 91.89%	95.75% / 87.1%	69.37% / 65.87%	95.26% / 85.3%	75% / 86.92%	92.09% / 102.71%	83.89% / 101.15%	100% / 105.99%	—	70.95% / 73.6%
Publishing Outdoor	134.96% / 124.84%	134.96% / 118.34%	97.77% / 89.49%	134.26% / 115.89%	105.71% / 118.1%	129.81% / 139.32%	118.25% / 137.43%	140.95% / 143.99%	140.95% / 135.86%	—

Note Percentages should be read vertically. For example, the rate of copyholders was 71.45% of the rate for timehands and the earnings of process workers were 84.33% of the earnings of stereotypers etc.

Source: ACAS Inquiries

APPENDIX 5
TABLE 10
AVERAGE EARNING AND NPA DIFFERENTIALS (PERCENTAGES) BETWEEN SELECTED PRODUCTION WORKERS IN FLEET STREET 1975

Each cell contains two values separated diagonally: the upper-right value is one differential and the lower-left value is the reciprocal differential.

Average Earnings ↓ / Basic Rate →	Timehands	Readers	Copyholders	Process Workers	Brakehands	Machine Managers	Stereotypers	Engineers	Electricians	Publishing Outdoor
Timehands	— / —	100% / 93.18%	74.52% / 73.79%	99.51% / 93.06%	78.89% / 80.01%	96.34% / 94.48%	88.13% / 99.29%	100.11% / 99.39%	100.11% / 104.72%	73.01% / 72.86%
Readers	100% / 107.32%	— / —	74.52% / 79.19%	99.51% / 99.87%	79.89% / 85.86%	96.34% / 101.4%	88.13% / 106.55%	100.11% / 106.67%	100.11% / 112.38%	73.01% / 78.19%
Copyholders	134.19% / 135.51%	134.19% / 126.27%	— / —	133.53% / 126.1%	107.21% / 108.42%	129.28% / 128.04%	118.26% / 134.54%	134.33% / 134.69%	134.33% / 141.9%	102.02% / 98.73%
Process Workers	100.5% / 107.46%	100.5% / 100.13%	74.89% / 79.30%	— / —	80.29% / 85.98%	96.82% / 101.53%	88.57% / 106.7%	100.61% / 106.81%	100.61% / 112.53%	76.41% / 78.30%
Brakehands	125.17% / 124.99%	125.17% / 116.47%	93.28% / 92.24%	124.55% / 116.31%	— / —	120.59% / 118.1%	110.31% / 124.1%	125.31% / 124.23%	125.31% / 130.89%	95.17% / 91.07%
Machine Managers	103.8% / 105.84%	103.8% / 98.62%	77.35% / 78.1%	103.29% / 98.49%	82.93% / 84.68%	— / —	91.48% / 105.08%	103.91% / 105.2%	103.91% / 110.83%	78.92% / 77.11%
Stereotypers	113.47% / 100.72%	113.47% / 93.85%	84.56% / 74.32%	112.91% / 93.72%	90.65% / 80.58%	109.32% / 95.16%	— / —	113.59% / 100.11%	113.59% / 105.47%	86.27% / 73.38%
Engineers	99.89% / 100.61%	99.89% / 93.75%	74.4% / 74.25%	99.4% / 93.62%	79.8% / 80.49%	96.24% / 95.06%	88.03% / 99.89%	— / —	100% / 105.36%	75.95% / 73.3%
Electricians	99.89% / 95.5%	99.89% / 88.98%	74.44% / 70.47%	99.4% / 88.86%	79.8% / 76.4%	96.24% / 90.23%	88.03% / 94.81%	100% / 94.92%	— / —	75.95% / 69.58%
Publishing Outdoor	131.53% / 131.53%	131.53% / 127.89%	98.02% / 101.28%	130.88% / 127.72%	105.88% / 109.81%	126.72% / 129.68%	115.92% / 136.27%	131.67% / 136.42%	131.67% / 143.73%	— / —

Note Percentages should be read vertically. For example, the rate of copyholders was 77.35 per cent of the rate for machine managers and the earnings of process workers were 116.31 per cent of the earnings of brakehands.

Source: ACAS Inquiries

TABLE 11 APPENDIX 5

COMPARATIVE RANKING OF SELECTED PRODUCTION WORKERS BY NPA BASIC RATE 1960–1975

Type of Work	1960–1969	1970–1975
Time Hands	1	3
Readers	1	3
Process Workers	3	5
Machine Managers	4	6
Engineers	5	1
Electricians	5	1
Stereotypers	7	8
Press Telegraphists	8	9
Photoprinters	9	10
Electricians' Assts.	10	7
Brakehands	11	11
Revisers/Monocasters	12	12
Motor Drivers	13	14
Lino Assts.	14	12
Copyholders/Proofpullers	15	15
Other Assts.	16	16
RIRMA (ancillary)	17	17

Source: ACAS inquiries.

APPENDIX 6
TABLE 1
TYPICAL HOUSE BOARD LEVEL ORGANISATION

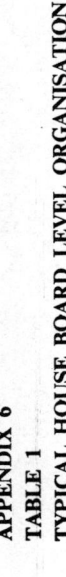

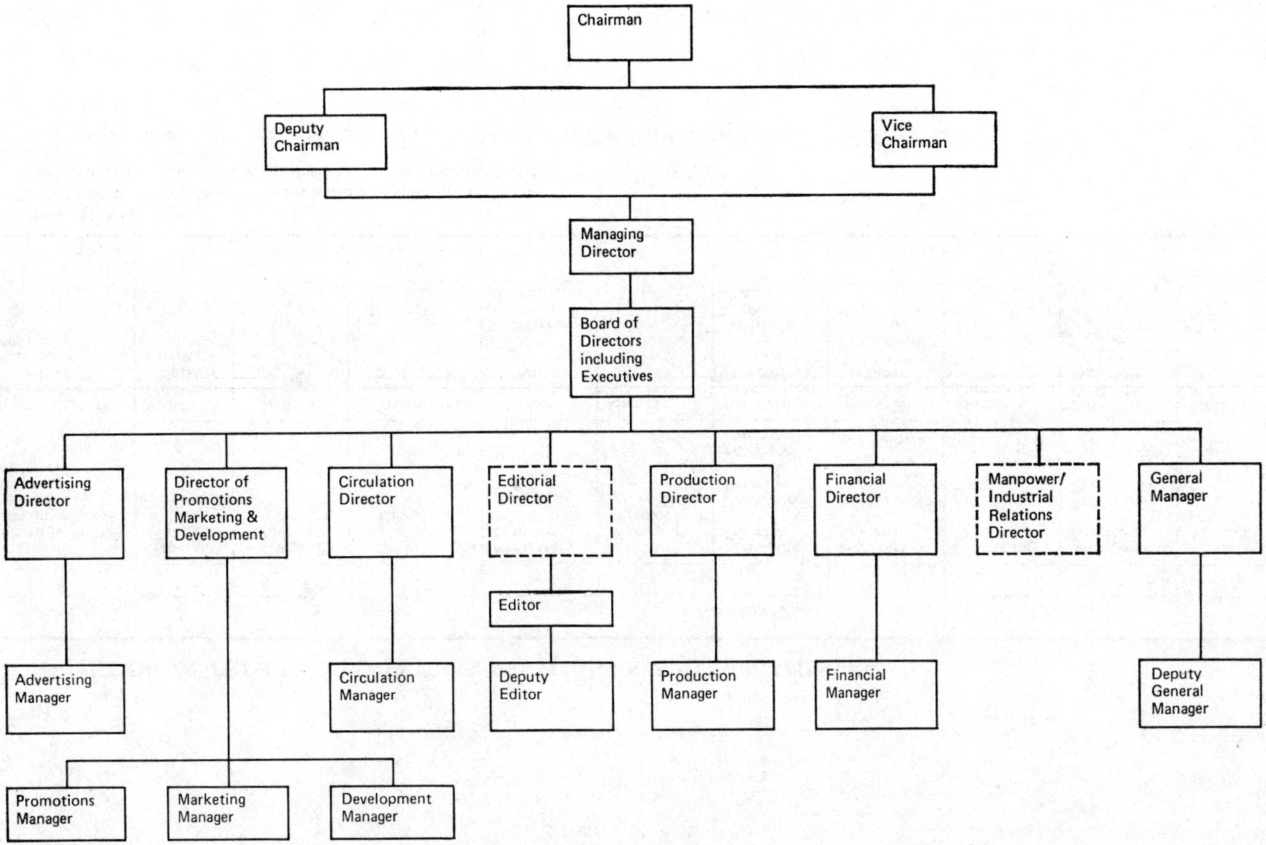

Note Dotted lines indicate that the individual concerned may or may not be an executive member of the board.

Source: ACAS Inquiries

APPENDIX 6

TABLE 2

DISTRIBUTION OF PRINCIPAL INDUSTRIAL RELATIONS RESPONSIBILITIES

Function	Newspaper Houses										
	1	2	3	4	5	6	7	8	9	10	11
Principal Board level responsibility for industrial relations matters.	General Manager	General* Manager	Deputy Managing Director	Manpower Director	Deputy Managing Director	Managing* Director — Production Director — Personnel* Director	General* Manager — Production Director	Managing* Director	Managing Director — Production Director	Production Manager	Industrial Relations Director
Senior Executive responsibility for industrial relations matters.	Senior Industrial Relations Adviser	General Manager	Production General Manager†	(Deputy Manpower Director) — Senior Industrial Relations Executive	General Manager	Assistant Production Director (Labour) — Assistant Personnel Director	Industrial Relations Manager — Production Director	Managing Director	Assistant Production Directors — †	Production Manager	General Manager — Assistant General Manager Senior Industrial Relations Manager

Source: ACAS inquiries.

*Includes a degree of responsibility for journalists' industrial relations.
†Clerical industrial relations the responsibility of the Company Secretary.

Note:
The houses include all those in membership of the NPA (nine) together with Mirror Group Newspapers and the *Morning Star*.

APPENDIX 6
TABLE 3
PRODUCTION AREAS: MANAGEMENT STRUCTURE

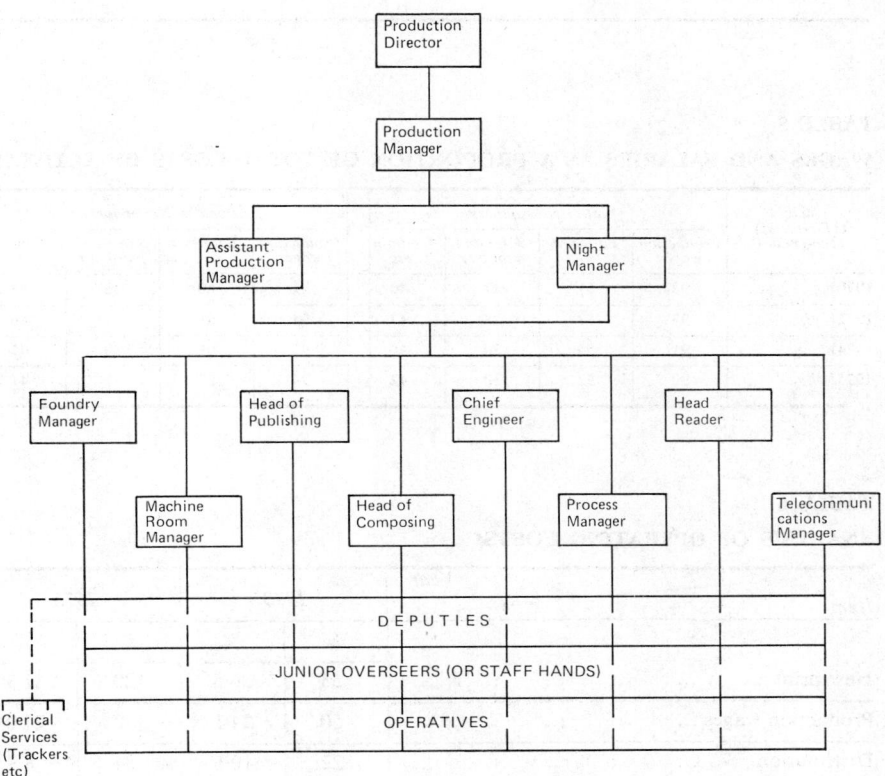

Source: ACAS Inquiries

TABLE 4
ANALYSIS OF WAGES AND SALARIES IN NATIONAL NEWSPAPERS*

APPENDIX 6

Percentage of total costs of	Financial years				Calendar	
	1970	1971	1972	1973	1974	1975
Newsprint...	26	26	26	28	32	31
Wages and salaries ...	43	43	43	43	39	40
Other	31	31	31	29	28	29
Total	100	100	100	100	100	100

TABLE 5
WAGES AND SALARIES AS A PROPORTION OF TOTAL COSTS BY ACTIVITY*

Year (†Financial) (‡calendar)	Quality Newspapers				Popular Newspapers			
	Production wages	Editorial	Sales and publicity	Admin etc.	Production wages	Editorial	Sales and publicity	Admin etc.
1970†	93	51	27	40	92	60	33	48
1972†	93	53	28	47	94	61	31	46
1974‡	91	55	30	46	95	61	30	45
1975‡	90	52	30	42	94	57	31	41

TABLE 6
ANALYSIS OF OPERATING COSTS*

Item \ Year	1970		1975	
	£	%	£	%
Newsprint	55	26·5	120	31·3
Production wages	50	24·1	92	24·0
Distribution	22	10·6	34	8·9
Editorial	32	15·5	41	10·7
Advertisement sales	5	2·4	9	2·3
Publicity	5	2·4	8	2·1
Administration	22	10·6	43	11·2
Other costs...	16	7·7	36	9·4
Total	207	100	383	100

Source: Royal Commission on the Press.
*Excluding the *Morning Star* and *Morning Advertiser*.

TABLE 7   APPENDIX 6

EXPERIENCE OF PERSONNEL/INDUSTRIAL RELATIONS STAFF

Length of service with the newspaper and general printing industry.	0 Years					0–2 Years					2–5 Years					6–10 Years					Over 10 Years					Total
Length of service outside the newspaper and general printing industry.	0	0–2	3–5	5–10	10+	0	0–2	3–5	6–10	10+	0	0–2	3–5	5–10	10+	0	0–2	3–5	5–10	10+	0	0–2	3–5	6–10	10+	
Length of service with house — less than 2	2	–	–	–	–	1	–	–	–	–	–	–	–	–	–	1	–	–	–	–	1	–	–	–	–	5
3–5	–	–	–	–	–	–	–	–	–	–	–	–	–	1	–	–	–	–	–	–	2	–	–	–	1	4
6–10	–	–	–	1	–	–	–	–	–	–	–	–	–	–	–	–	–	1	–	–	2	–	–	–	–	4
over 10	7	1	1	–	1	1	1	1	–	–	4	–	1	–	–	1	–	–	–	–	11	–	–	–	1	28
Total ...	9	1	1	1	1	2	1	1	–	–	4	–	1	1	–	1	–	1	–	–	16	–	–	–	2	41

Source: ACAS inquiries.
Note:
The Table is derived from information from eight houses, three of which do not employ distinct personnel/industrial relations staffs.

APPENDIX 7
TABLE 1
ORGANISATION AND STRUCTURE OF THE NPA

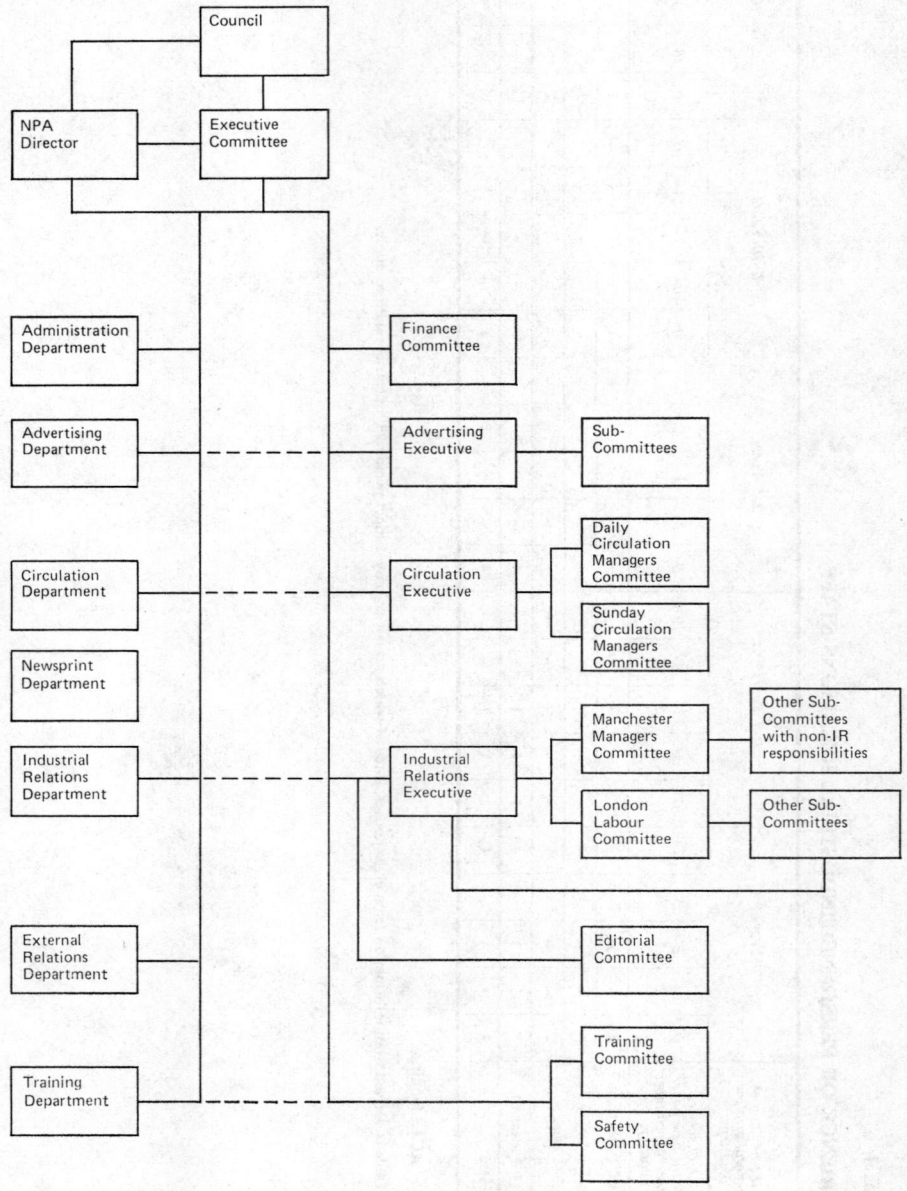

Source: ACAS Inquiries

TABLE 2

APPENDIX 7

DEPARTMENTS AND STAFF OF THE NPA

Department	1976 (April)	1975	1974	1973	1972
Director	2	2	2	3	2
Commercial Director/Sec.	–	–	2	3	2
Administration	7	7	8	8	8
Industrial relations	4	3	3	4	4
Advertising	3	3	3	4	3
Mail Order Fund	4	2	–	–	–
Circulation	6	5	5	6	6
Communicor	–	1	1	–	2
Marketing	2	2	2	1	2
Newsprint	2	2	2	1	–
Training	2	2	2	–	2
Manchester Office	3	3	3	3	3
Total	35	32	33	33	34

Source: ACAS inquiries.

APPENDIX 8(a)

CODE OF PRINCIPLES FOR NATSOPA CHAPEL RULES*

Whereas Chapels of members of this Society are created and exist only under the authority and directions of this Society's rules, being formally recognised and the consistent units of the Society with duties and functions specified, with the rights of notification, nomination, representation and appeal, it is, therefore, resolved and directed as follows:—

1. The word "Natsopa" must form part of the title of any Chapel. There may be added an additional word to designate the Branch, ie, Natsopa "Machine" or Natsopa "Clerical", etc.

2. No Chapel rules shall have any force unless and until endorsed by the Branch Committee, the principles set out hereunder must be covered by such rules.

3. Chapel meetings must be held quarterly for the election or re-election of FOC.† Other officials, if any, may be elected for such period as the Chapel, by its rules, may prescribe. Candidates for Chapel office must be clear of all dues to the Society and Chapel and in benefit at the time of nomination and remain in benefit during their term of office.

The FOC must be the responsible Chapel Official. The Chairman's responsibility is restricted to his duty as Chairman. A Chapel Secretary or Clerk may be appointed to assist the FOC, but all correspondence must bear the signature of the FOC. (NOTE—the reference to FOC is to include the deputy FOC or other member acting as FOC with the authority of the Chapel.)

4. Chapels must direct the time, day, or days, in each week when Society contributions must be paid to the FOC or other person appointed by the Chapel to assist the FOC in collecting Society and Chapel dues.

5 The Chapel fund must require a minimum contribution to pay the FOC for his services and cover the necessary expense of calling and holding Chapel meetings, and cost of correspondence, and may also cover the purchase of the "Natsopa Journal" for all Chapel members.

6. At the regular quarterly Chapel meeting preceding the Branch Delegate Meeting, or at a special Chapel meeting called for that purpose, delegates shall be elected to represent the Chapel at such Branch Meeting, or alternatively a rota may be adopted whereby all members of the Chapel take their turn as delegates.

No motion to be moved or seconded at a Delegate Meeting on behalf of any Chapel, unless it has been submitted, considered and adopted in accordance with the rules, but this shall not apply to formal motions, such as "Next Business", "Previous Question" and "Closure".

7. Provision must be made for the investigation of complaints against any member before any complaint against such member is lodged at the Branch office.

8. Chapels may establish funds for the purpose of Sickness, Death, Holiday Pay, making of grants to Hospitals and to other organisations or for any other object approved by the Branch Committee, and may levy contributions, collectively or separately, for any such purpose, in addition to the administrative contribution set out in Section 5. The funds referred to in this Clause and the regulations for collection and payments shall be Part 2 of the Chapel Rules and must cover all administrative details.

---

*Extract from the rules of the National Society of Operative Printers Graphical and Media Personnel.
†Changed to annual election in February, 1976.

9 The funds of any Chapel where contributions other than administrative are collected shall be held in the name of two Trustees.

10. The accounts of Chapels with funds under Part 2 shall be audited quarterly or at such other periods not exceeding one year at the discretion of the Chapel. An audit service established by the Society will be available if required by any Chapel in the larger Branches.

11. Chapels may only make grants from the Chapel funds to such objects as set out in Section 8, provided that such grants are voted at a Chapel meeting called by due notice and that the suggested grant has been stated in the notice convening the meeting. Authority may be given to a Chapel Committee to make grants for such purposes up to a limited figure. In small Chapels where meetings may be called without written notice, members should be informed of any such proposal together with the full agenda for the meeting.

12. As Chapels owe their existence to the fact that they are created under the rules of the Society and all members of the Chapel must be members of the Society, no Chapel can be affiliated to, associated with, or subscribe to any movement of any kind that is not recognised by the Society.

13. Every member of the Chapel must be provided with a copy of the Chapel Rules.

14. The Society will offer at a nominal charge, Chapel Rules and Chapel Contribution Cards for all Chapels whose rules follow the model set issued and approved by the Executive Council.

15. Chapel Rules shall not be altered in any way except upon due notice given at a quarterly Chapel meeting for discussion at the next following quarterly Chapel meeting. In no circumstances can there be any departure from or variation of the principles set out in the approved code. When a Chapel has satisfied a Branch Committee that it is expedient to make a change in the rules relating to the internal administration of the Chapel, permission may be given for the giving of not less than seven days' notice of a Chapel meeting for that purpose, provided the proposed alteration is set out in the notice convening the meeting.

16. Chapel Rules must contain a provision whereby an agreed number or percentage of members shall have the right to call a Chapel meeting by signing a request to the FOC stating the purpose of such meeting. Any such requested Chapel meeting must be called as early as possible and not later than seven days from the date of handling the requisition to the FOC. The number of signatures required for calling such meeting shall be such number as the Chapel may decide to insert in the rules. Special Chapel meetings shall be called (a) at any time when directed by the Branch Secretary or Executive official of the Society and (b) by the FOC or Chapel Committee at such notice as may be expedient in the circumstances.

17. AUTHORITY OF THE SOCIETY'S RULES—In no circumstances can Chapel Rules override or take precedence over the Society's Rules.

APPENDIX 8

TABLE 1

NATIONAL NEWSPAPERS (LONDON)—LENGTH OF TIME FOCs IN POST*

Union	Chapel	Average length of time (years) FOC in post	Shortest time (years) FOC in post	Longest time (years) FOC in post	Number of chapels in sample
NGA	Imperial	6·7	1·0	16·0	14
	Machine Managers	5·1	0·75	15·0	12
	Stereo	4·5	1·0	10·0	11
NATSOPA	RIRMA	5·2	0·75	20·0 (2)	23
	Clerical	3·0	0·5	10·0	12
	Machine	4·7	0·25	14·0	18
SLADE	Process	5·5	1·0	20·0	11
SOGAT	Publishing	9·4	2·0	30·0	5
	Pressmen	8·0	0·25	20·0	8
NUJ	Editorial	1·8	0·25	3·0	13

Source: ACAS inquiries.
*At December 1975.

272

TABLE 2
M/FOC ELECTIONS*

APPENDIX 8

Union	Chapel	Number of FOC/MOC elections in most recent four held that were:—		Number of elections held	Number of chapels in sample
		contested	unopposed		
NGA	Imperial	21·2%	78·8%	52	13
	Machine Managers	20·5%	79·5%	44	11
	Stereo	25·0%	75·0%	36	9
NATSOPA	RIRMA	1·2%	98·8%	84	21
	Clerical	7·5%	92·5%	40	10
	Machine	28·9%	71·1%	76	19
SLADE	Process	31·8%	68·2%	44	11
SOGAT	Publishing	40·0%	60·0%	20	5
	Pressmen	14·3%	85·7%	28	7
NUJ	Editorial	23·1%	76·9%	52	13

Source: ACAS inquiries.
*At December 1975.

APPENDIX 8

TABLE 3 CHAPEL SIZE AND FACILITIES IN DUAL (OR MULTI) TITLE HOUSES (6)

Union/Chapel	Number of chapels in sample*	Number of chapels with at least one official spending nearly all his/her time on chapel business†	Number of chapels with at least one official spending more than half his/her time on chapel business	Number of chapels‡ without at least one official spending half his/her time on chapel business	Number of chapels with office facilities	Total working in chapel area	Average number of employees in each chapel	Membership of smallest chapel in sample	Membership of largest chapel in sample
NGA Imperial Composing	14	8	5	1	12	2,154	154	63	306
NGA Stereo§	10	2	3	5	4	544	54	5	98
NGA Machine Managers	10	7	2	1	9	459	46	8	126
NGA T & E§	3	–	–	3	–	54	18	9	24
NATSOPA Clerical	8	7	1	–	8	3,838	480	252	671
NATSOPA Machine	17	16	1	–	15	5,157	303	56	778
NATSOPA RIRMA	55	8	7	40	19	2,339	43	3	230
SOGAT Publishing	21	15	–	6	14	5,012	239	9	585
SOGAT Circulation Representatives	4	–	1	3	1	267	67	14	198
SOGAT Pressmen Process Provers	17	–	3	14	2	173	10	1	33
SLADE	11	1	3	7	1	336	31	4	60
EETPU	6	1	1	4	4	499	83	14	146
AUEW	7	4	–	3	6	505	72	17	135
NUJ	15	–	3	12	4	2,344	156	18	340
Total	198	69	30	99	99	23,679	120	1	778

Source: ACAS inquiries.

*The sample does not include all chapels in national newspaper houses, complete information being unobtainable from 2 dual (or multi) title houses, and 2 single title houses.
†In the sample taken, the range of each officials is from one to seven (not including other officials or chapel members spending more than half their time on chapel business).
‡This nevertheless includes many chapels whose officials may spent at least part of their working time on chapel affairs.
§Some Imperial chapels include either or both stereotypers and T & E local chapels in their membership.

APPENDIX 8

TABLE 4
CHAPEL SIZE AND FACILITIES IN SINGLE TITLE HOUSES (5)

Union/Chapel	Number of chapels in sample*	Number of chapels with at least one official spending nearly all his/her time on chapel business†	Number of chapels with at least one official spending more than half his/her time on chapel business	Number of chapels‡ without at least one official spending half his/her time on chapel business	Number of chapels with office facilities	Total working in chapel area	Average number of employees in each chapel	Membership of smallest chapel in sample	Membership of largest chapel in sample
NGA Imperial Composing	5	1	2	2	3	413	83	34	185
NGA Stereo§	3	–	–	3	–	54	18	6	30
NGA T & E§	1	–	–	1	–	4	–	–	–
NGA Machine Managers	5	1	–	4	1	64	13	3	22
NATSOPA Clerical	4	1	–	3	1	454	114	16	260
NATSOPA Machine	6	3	–	3	3	340	57	8	120
NATSOPA RIRMA	18	–	–	18	7	258	14	3	46
SOGAT Publishing	8	1	–	7	4	334	42	7	168
SOGAT Pressmen, Process Provers	7	–	–	7	3	19	3	1	7
SOGAT Circulation Representatives	2	–	–	2	–	26	13	11	15
SLADE	5	–	–	5	1	34	7	3	13
EETPU	2	–	–	2	1	47	24	14	33
AUEW	4	–	–	4	2	43	11	7	18
NUJ	5	–	1	4	–	446	89	27	195
Total	75	7	3	65	26	2,536	34	1	260

Source: ACAS inquiries.
*See notes to Appendix 8, Table 3.
†In the sample taken, the range of each officials is from one to seven (not including other officials or chapel members spending more than half their time on chapel business).
‡This nevertheless includes many chapels whose officials may spend at least part of their working time on chapel affairs.
§Some Imperial chapels include either or both stereotypers and T & E local chapels in their membership.

APPENDIX 8

TABLE 5

CHAPEL DISCIPLINE AND FINES FOR MISCONDUCT: PROVISIONS OF CHAPEL RULE BOOKS*

Offence	Up to 25p	26p–50p	51p–75p	76p–£1·00	£1·01–£2·00	Over £2·00	Suspension of chapel benefit and participation	Dealt with by Chapel Committee or Branch	Not specified	Total no. of rule books with relevant provisions
Non-attendance, lateness or early departure from chapel meeting	8	10	–	3	1	–	–	–	–	22
Absence from two consecutive chapel meetings	–	1	–	2	3	–	–	6	–	12
Absence from three or more consecutive chapel meetings	–	–	–	–	3	2	–	5	–	10
Non-attendance at special chapel meeting	3	2	–	1	2	–	–	–	–	8
Frivolous calling of special chapel meetings	2	2	1	–	–	–	–	2	5	12
Non-attendance by delegates appointed by the chapel	1	3	–	–	–	–	–	1	–	5
Interviewing or contacting management on any matters without the FOC's presence or approval	–	1	–	–	–	–	–	2	15	18
Arrears of contributions (generally 2 weeks or more)	1	–	–	–	–	–	6	2	–	9
Imperilling a member's situation or the chapel's interests, or divulging chapel business without authority	–	1	–	–	–	–	–	8	4	13
Refusing to vote	1	–	–	–	–	–	–	–	–	1
Defacing notice paper	1	1	–	–	–	–	–	–	–	2
Striking another chapel member	2	1	–	–	–	–	–	–	–	3
Refusing to pay fine	–	–	–	–	–	–	–	4	–	4
Falsifying overtime dockets	–	1	–	–	–	–	–	–	–	1
Non-inspection of cards by FOC	1	–	–	–	–	–	–	1	–	2

Source: ACAS inquiries.
*Based on a sample of 22 production and clerical chapel rule books.

TABLE 6
SIZE OF CHAPELS IN SINGLE TITLE AND DUAL (OR MULTI) TITLE LONDON NATIONAL NEWSPAPER HOUSES

Union/Chapel	Number of chapels in sample*	Size of chapels in dual or multi-title houses (6)							Number of chapels in sample*	Size of chapels in single title houses (5)						
		Under 10	11–19	20–49	50–99	100–199	200–499	Over 500		Under 10	11–19	20–49	50–99	100–199	200–499	Over 500
NGA Imperial composing†	14	–	–	1	2	7	4	–	5	–	–	2	1	2	–	–
NGA Stereo	10	1	1	2	6	–	–	–	3	–	1	2	–	–	–	–
NGA T & E	3	1	–	2	–	–	–	–	1	1	–	–	–	–	–	–
NGA Machine Managers	10	1	1	4	3	1	–	–	5	2	2	1	–	–	–	–
NATSOPA Machine	17	–	–	1	2	5	4	5	6	1	1	–	3	1	–	–
NATSOPA RIRMA	55	10	11	18	11	4	1	–	18	7	7	3	1	–	–	–
NATSOPA Clerical	8	–	–	–	–	–	4	4	4	–	1	–	2	–	1	–
SOGAT Publishing	21	2	1	2	1	4	8	3	8	3	1	1	2	1	–	–
SOGAT Pressmen, Process Provers, Monocasters	17	11	3	3	–	–	–	–	7	7	–	–	–	–	–	–
SOGAT Circulation Representatives	4	1	1	1	–	1	–	–	2	–	2	–	–	–	–	–
SLADE Process, Publicity Artists	11	4	–	4	3	–	–	–	5	4	1	–	–	–	–	–
EETPU	6	–	1	1	2	2	–	–	2	–	1	1	–	–	–	–
AUEW	7	–	1	2	2	2	–	–	4	2	2	–	–	–	–	–
NUJ	15	–	1	2	1	5	6	–	5	–	–	2	1	2	–	–
Others	9	2	1	5	1	–	–	–	–	–	–	–	–	–	–	–
Total	207	33	22	48	34	31	27	12	75	27	19	12	10	6	1	–

Source: ACAS inquiries.
*See notes to Appendix 8, Table 3.
†Of the total of 19 Imperial chapels, all include the local chapels of piece case, time hands, linotype operators and readers, 4 include the local T & E chapels, 6 include the local stereo chapels, and one includes both local stereo and T & E chapels.

TABLE 7
ANNUAL SALARIES PAID TO CHAPEL OFFICIALS

APPENDIX 8

Title	Annual Salary					Not specified	Total*
	Under £10·00	£10·00– £19·19	£20·00– £34·99	£35·00– £59·99	£60·00 and over		
FOC or Imperial FOC	1	1	–	7	5	8	22
Deputy FOC …	1	2	7	2	1	8	21
Financial Secretary/ Treasurer …	1	–	3	1	–	2	7
Clerk … …	1	2	1	1	3	5	13
Committee Member/ Local FOC…	6	1	–	–	–	13	20

Source: ACAS inquiries.

TABLE 8
WEEKLY CHAPEL SUBSCRIPTIONS

Up to 10p	11– 15p	16– 20p	21– 25p	26– 35p	36– 50p	Over 50p	Not specified	Total*
13	1	2	–	3	–	1	2	22

Source: ACAS inquiries.

*Total from sample of 22 production and clerical chapel rule books.

APPENDIX 9(a)

ABBREVIATED ACCOUNT OF TRADE UNION DEVELOPMENT IN THE INDUSTRY

1. The earliest recorded evidence of the existence of a formal trade union in the printing industry dates from 1786. In that year a group of bookbinders formed three lodges in London and they were followed soon afterwards by compositors and paperworkers. Outside London local societies, founded by groups of local chapels, were formed in the major urban concentrations, the first recorded being the Manchester (Typo) Graphical Society in 1797.* A National Typographical Union was formed in 1845 by merger between the Northern Typographical Union (NTU) and the London, Scottish and Irish Societies. The NTU collapsed three years later, largely through the cost to the union of unemployment and dispute benefits during the 1846–48 recession. A number of separate societies were formed following the collapse of the NTU, these being the London Society of Compositors (LSC), the Typographical Association (TA) and the Scottish Typographical Association (STA).

2. In 1880 the Amalgamated Society of Lithographic Printers was formed, and in 1885 the Amalgamated Society of Lithographic Artists was established†, (the forerunner to SLADE), both of these unions developing on a national basis with the introduction of new printing processes (including the replacement of manual composition by mechanised typesetting equipment). It was at this point that unions for semi- and unskilled workers began to develop, and in 1889 the Printing Labourers' Union, (the forerunner to NATSOPA) came into being as a result of a strike of printers' labourers at Spottiswoode's plant in London. By the end of the nineteenth century the printing industry craft unions had attained a high level of organisation and membership density, a situation which quickly developed in the non-craft unions and was largely complete by the end of the First World War, NATSOPA being joined by clerks and ink and roller makers in London a few years later.

3. Until the formation of the NGA in 1964 the bulk of craftsmen were organised into the London societies on the one hand, and the regional and national societies on the other. Together with the LSC in London (organising readers, compositors, and their apprentices in a 15-mile radius of Charing Cross) there existed the Printing Machine Managers' Trade Society (PMMTS), the Association of Correctors of the Press (ACP), and the National Union of Press Telegraphists (NUPT), (the bulk of whose members worked in London). The number of unions in London resulted from both its location as a communications centre, the number of printing shops and in consequence, the large numbers employed in the printing industry which facilitated contact and encouraged the development of collective identity.

4. The wide distribution of the industry in the provinces, and its concentration in London, played a major part in the forms of structure and constitution that the unions adopted, particularly in regard to the autonomy given to individual branches and regions of the trade unions and associations. This devolution of control and responsibility (particularly in those printing unions established in the early part of the

---

*This society was one of the members of the Manchester and Salford Trades Council instrumental in establishing the first Trades Union Congress in Manchester in 1868.
†Formed initially by lithographic artists, designers and writers, and copperplate and wood engravers, SLADE now caters for "those who produce the pictorial image and illustrative design, whatever the method or particular process of printing may be".

nineteenth century) resulted from a complex interaction of factors, including the local customs and issues particular to each branch, the difficulties of communication between branches and the ever-present possibility of secession from existing associations* remains an important and distinctive feature of their present structure. Amalgamation of local societies into trade unions did not result in their separate identities being submerged they retained their titles in branches of the unions (eg Manchester Graphical Society, Glasgow Typographical Society, etc), a consciousness of independent development and certain freedoms of action.

5. The period from 1880 to 1925 was marked by the formation and growth of the non-craft unions, and by amalgamation of a number of them stimulated by a desire to avoid conflict over demarcation and membership organisation questions†. Chief amongst these were NATSOPA, the National Union of Paper Mill Workers, and the National Amalgamated Society of Printers' Warehousemen and Cutters. In 1914 the latter two unions amalgamated to form the National Union of Printing and Paper Workers (NUP&PW). There was at the same time a strong possibility that NATSOPA would merge with the organisation, which was seen by some as a vehicle by which an industrial union for the printing industry might be achieved. NATSOPA did not, however, amalgamate with the NUP&PW, in spite of a vote by their society of four to one in favour. (The law regarding trade union amalgamation at the time required a majority of at least two-thirds of the membership in favour for any amalgamation to be successful.) NATSOPA, did however, form a "defensive alliance" with the NUP&PW, thus forming in effect a power bloc *vis-a-vis* that of the craft unions.

6. In 1921, after three years of talks, the National Union of Bookbinders and Machine Rulers (formed in 1911 from three London unions and one national union) amalgamated with the NUP&PW to form the National Union of Printing, Bookbinding, Machine Ruling and Paper Workers (NUPBMR&PW), with over 100,000 members. The merger evolved out of increasing demarcation and membership recruitment difficulties between the bookbinders, the NUP&PW and NATSOPA, the latter two unions having been expanding their memberships both in London and the provinces, particularly in recruiting female workers in the industry. The bookbinders, like the other craft unions, had developed and organised most of the craft workers in their jurisdiction, and were being faced at the time with the growing militancy and size of the "new unions". The eventual amalgamation of the craft-based NUB&MR was achieved through the initial help of the Parliamentary Committee of the TUC.

7. The amalgamation was one of great significance, in that it signalled the dilution of the previously rigid craft and non-craft division of the unions in the printing industry. The method of amalgamation allowed the new members protection of their craft by provisions for sectional control and trade administration in the union structure. This pattern was developed by the fusion of the Platen Machine Minders' Society into the NUPBMR&PW in 1924 as the Printing Machine Branch, who were joined in 1925 by the Amalgamated Association of Pressmen (AAP), another highly skilled craft society. The AAP had been under pressure from other unions whose members were, as the technology of the industry developed, increasingly encroaching on their juris-

---

*eg in 1872 the Edinburgh Press and Machinemen's Society withdrew from the STA. At the fourth meeting of the National Printing and Kindred Trades' Federation (NPKTF) in 1892 the Edinburgh Society argued that while wishing to be on amicable terms with the parent society, they had been a separate society for 20 years and would not relinquish their separate existence.
†In London the unions had established fairly well defined jurisdictional areas, but semi-skilled workers in the provinces were not organised and presented an attraction in terms of membership growth, particularly for those with the goal of industrial unionism. This to a large extent explains the organisational anomalies touched on in Chapter 9 paragraphs 318 and 321.

dictional areas which included the pulling of proofs and work at press. In the same year the London Society of Machine Rulers merged with the NUPBMR&PW, thus completing the major amalgamations of printing trade unions until 1955.

8. The period was also one of consolidation of membership growth, and while fluctuations in numbers did occur, this applied in the greatest degree to the Paperworkers, the craft unions maintaining a stable membership. By 1939, the three largest unions—the NUPB&PW, TA and NATSOPA—accounted for roughly three-quarters of the total of organised workers in the printing trades. One of the most prolonged disputes of the inter-war years concerned NATSOPA's claim to organise clerical workers, a matter that was resisted by employers (the Newspaper Society and Federation of Master Printers) in the Joint Industrial Council until 1938, when NATSOPA was recognised.

APPENDIX 9
TABLE 1
PRINTING TRADE UNION AMALGAMATIONS: 1945–1976

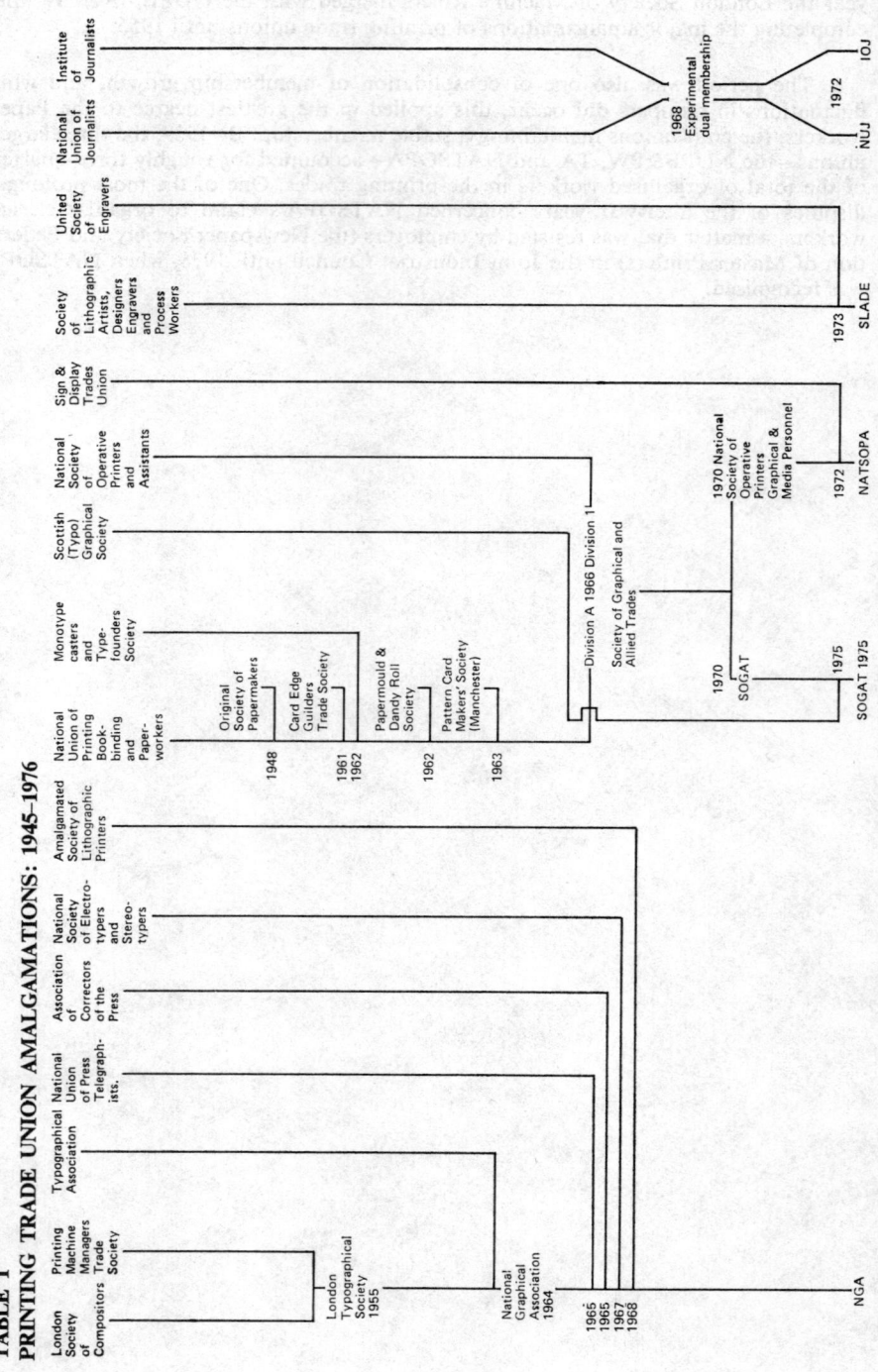

Source: ACAS Inquiries

APPENDIX 9

TABLE 2
TRADE UNIONS: NATIONAL MEMBERSHIP, 1964–1974 (YEARS ENDING 31ST DECEMBER)

Union \ Year ending	1964	1965	1966	1967	1968	1969	1970	1971	1972	1973	1974
SGA	7,279	7,125	7,130	6,985	7,221	7,050	6,906	6,987	6,697	6,702	6,418
SOGAT	172,165	177,511	224,452	228,902	229,089	235,927	192,920	183,276	183,990	187,580	193,804
NATSOPA	46,351	47,535					50,981	50,587	55,691	56,146	55,992
SDTU*	3,355	3,518	3,333	3,306	3,413	3,618	3,919	4,157			
SLADE	15,523	15,523	16,032	16,014	15,963	16,148	16,519	15,541	16,741	16,600	16,925
NGA	84,615	84,975	85,805	92,021	106,783	106,236	107,360	108,036	107,374	107,510	107,670
NSES†	5,183	5,056	5,056								
ASLP‡	11,744	12,419	12,987	13,216							
NUJ	17,933	18,762	19,613	20,271	21,290	22,404	24,503	26,742	27,587	28,082	29,433
IOJ	N/A	N/A	2,104	2,015	1,955	1,922	1,804	1,658	1,826	2,017	2,282
Total	364,148	372,424	376,512	382,730	385,714	393,305	404,912	397,984	399,906	404,637	412,524

Source: ACAS inquiries.
* Sign and Display Trade Union.
† National Society of Electrotypers and Stereotypers.
‡ Amalgamated Society of Lithographic Printers.

TABLE 3   APPENDIX 9

PRINTING TRADE UNIONS: BRANCHES WITH MEMBERSHIPS WORKING IN NATIONAL NEWSPAPERS

Union	Branch (or Region)	Membership										Working membership of the Branch employed in 1975 in national newspapers	Number of full-time officers	Number of administrative staff	Chapels in National press	Chapels in Elsewhere	Number of members per full-time officer
		1966	1967	1968	1969	1970	1971	1972	1973	1974	1975						
NGA	London Region	21,835	21,999	23,003	25,731	26,431	26,014	25,052	24,366	24,298	23,633	20·25% (1974)	9	30	46	1,100	2,626
	Manchester Graphical Society (Branch)	N/A	N/A	N/A	N/A	N/A	5,160	5,022	4,980	4,921	4,873	35·09%	2	7	32	188	2,437
	London Machine	9,194	8,969	8,874	8,694	8,598	8,426	8,425	8,395	8,373	8,161	48·89%	2	29	24	200	4,080[1]
	London RIRMA	N/A	N/A	N/A	7,262	6,977	7,292	7,243	7,127	7,034	6,678	50·89%	1		N/A	N/A	7,791
NATSOPA	London CA & E (Clerical)	N/A	N/A	N/A	4,756	4,630	11,063	11,847	11,869	11,133	10,450	42·36%	2		14	80	5,225
	Manchester	4,998	4,910	4,827	4,756	4,630	4,564	4,509	4,446	4,484	4,424	95·41%	2	11	63	22	2,212
SLADE	London	6,378	6,323	6,089	6,021	5,983	5,751	5,474	4,994	5,000	4,907	7·41%	5	11	11	N/A	981
	Manchester	1,209	1,194	1,190	1,231	1,357	1,380	1,360	1,905[2]	1,984	1,949	17·09%	3	4	5	N/A	650
SOGAT[3]	London Central	26,518	25,746	24,945	24,421	23,474	22,647	21,938	21,686	21,399	21,160	c30·00%	6	20	24	c1,000	3,527
	Printing Machine	4,665	4,653	4,551	4,414	4,374	4,285	4,238	3,656	3,517	3,420	5·61%	2	3	24	427	1,710
	Circulation Representatives	1,707	1,698	1,692	1,686	1,699	1,699	1,546	1,538	1,549	1,517	51·42%	1	2	13	21	1,517
	Manchester	7,888	7,658	7,667	7,984	8,790	8,956	9,109	9,659	10,190	9,883	c8·60%	2	1	7	N/A	4,942
	London Evening Papers	311	314	329	334	353	363	370	380	390	399	91·57%	0	0	2	3	N/A
NUJ	Central London[4]	3,267	3,432	N/A	3,794	3,834	N/A	3,849	3,853	3,920	3,509	96·58%	1	2	16	N/A	3,509
	London Freelance	726	808	879	1,021	1,079	1,220	1,332	1,463	1,573	1,701	N/A	0	3	0	0	N/A
	Manchester	1,019	N/A	984	1,032	1,040	1,084	1,038	1,068	1,112	1,106	c73·00%	0	2	10	0	N/A
IOJ	London (District)	N/A	N/A	N/A	807	763	693	767	831	907	948	c16·25%	0	0	7	9	N/A
	Manchester (District)	N/A	N/A	N/A	34	28	32	27	26	22	48	N/A	0	0	0	7	N/A
AUEW	Fleet Street	N/A	720	N/A	N/A	N/A	N/A	N/A	N/A	N/A	1,018	62·87%	0	0	21	N/A	N/A
	Manchester Press	N/A	N/A	N/A	N/A	N/A	N/A	N/A	N/A	N/A	N/A	N/A	0	0	N/A	N/A	N/A
EETPU[5]	Fleet Street	N/A	N/A	N/A	N/A	N/A	N/A	N/A	N/A	N/A	967	82·94%	0	0	N/A	N/A	N/A
	Manchester Press	N/A	N/A	N/A	N/A	N/A	N/A	N/A	N/A	N/A	153	85·62%	0	0	N/A	N/A	N/A

Source: ACAS inquiries.
[1] In 1976 the membership increased to 7,791, largely as a result of the inclusion of Sign and Display Section members.
[2] On 1 April 1973 the United Society of Engravers amalgamated with SLADE, the greater proportion of its c400 members working in the Manchester area.
[3] The Monotype Casters, Filmsetters and Typefounders Branch (not included on the Table) has 8 members working in national newspapers.
[4] In 1975 the Branch membership working overseas and for news agencies formed a separate News Agencies Branch, which has some 400 members.
[5] The total national newspaper membership of the EETPU is 952, which includes 47 members of its white collar section, the Electrical Engineering Staffs Association, not accounted for in the Table above.

APPENDIX 9
TABLE 4
NATIONAL GRAPHICAL ASSOCIATION: ORGANISATION

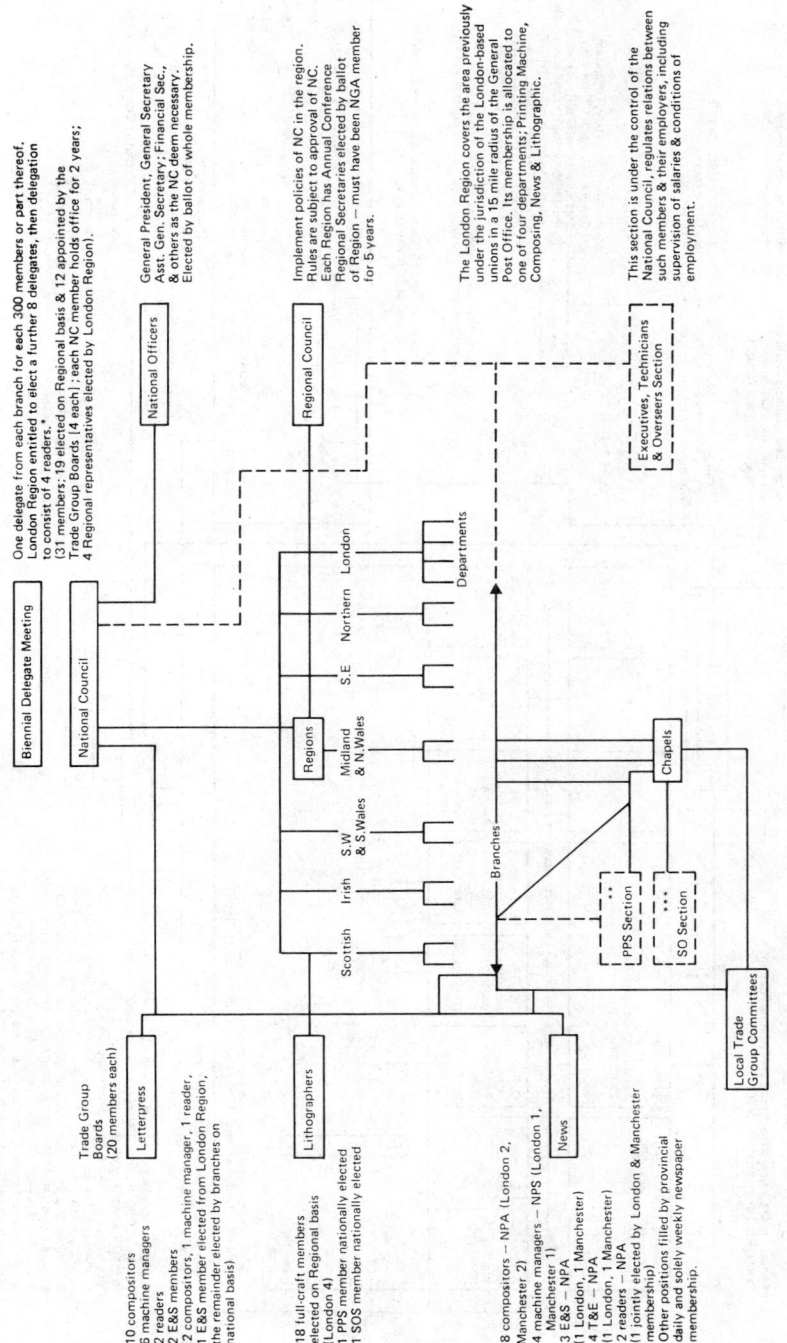

*There is also trade representation on the basis of one for every 300 members for the following sections: Telecommunications & Electronics, Electrotypers & Stereotypers, and Lithographers.

** Plate Preparers, Metal Varnishers & Metal Decorators.

*** Small Offset Section — Where area membership exceeds 50, these may meet separately as an SOS Consultative Committee under own Chairman, & Secretary of the parent branch.

Source: ACAS *Inquiries*

APPENDIX 9
TABLE 5
SOCIETY OF GRAPHICAL AND ALLIED TRADES ORGANISATION

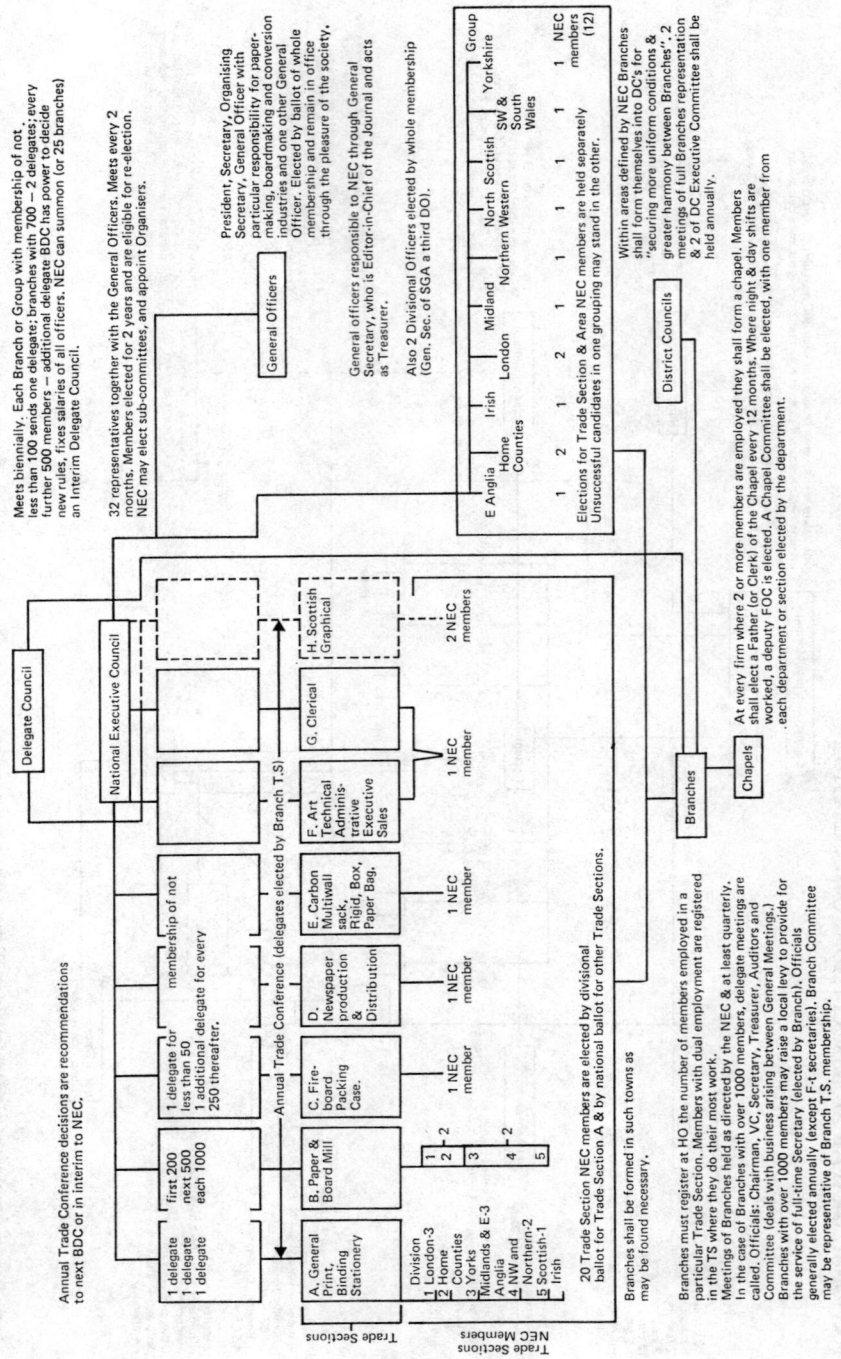

Source: ACAS Inquiries

APPENDIX 9
TABLE 6
SLADE: ORGANISATION*

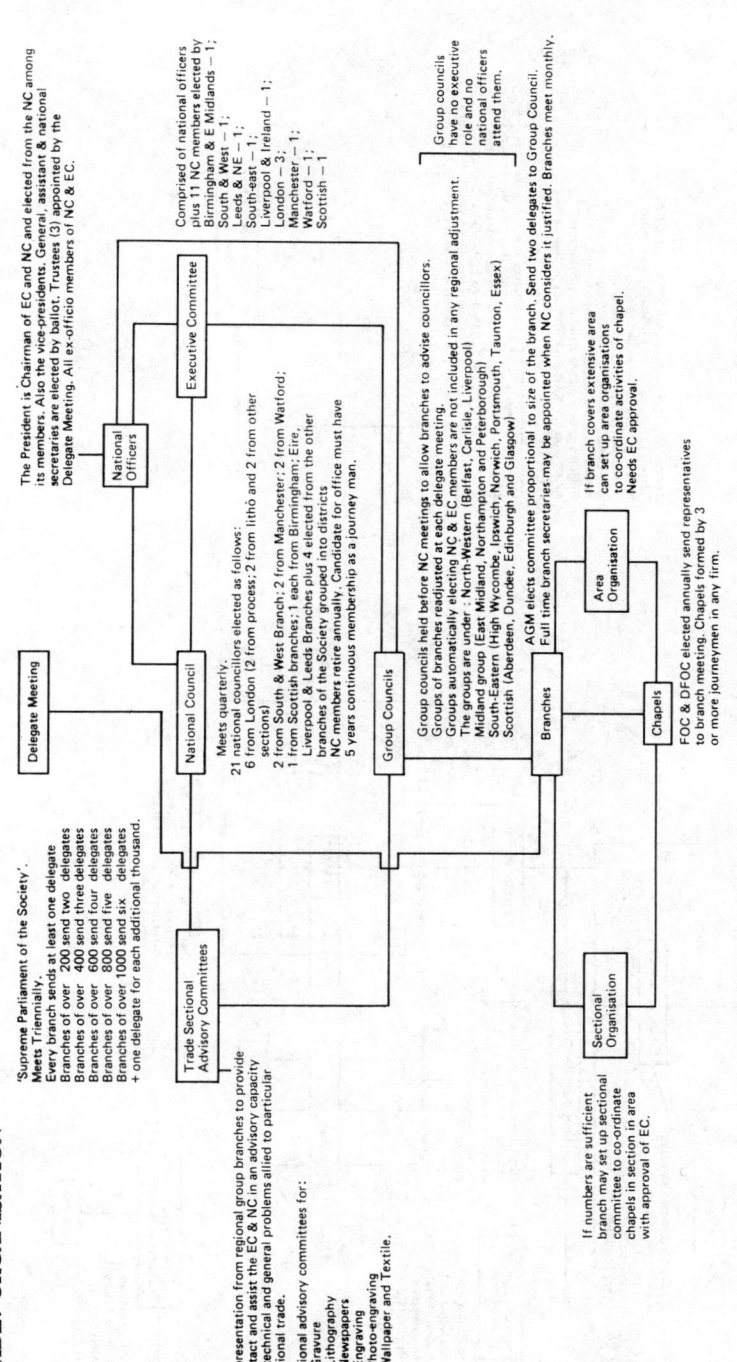

Source: ACAS Inquiries

* The SLADE Art Union was created in 1974 and caters for members engaged in preparing and producing art and photographic material. The Section is responsible for formulating and adopting any rules applying to its membership.

An **Auxiliary Section** caters for members who are engaged in production and preparatory processes whose qualifications are limited to operations not requiring apprenticeship — handymen; rulers and varnishers; painters; lithographic negative spotter.

A **Wallpaper and Textile Engraving Section** caters for members engaged in the artistic engraving and embossing processes preparatory to the printing and production of wallpaper, textiles and plastics.

APPENDIX 9
TABLE 7
NATSOPA: ORGANISATION

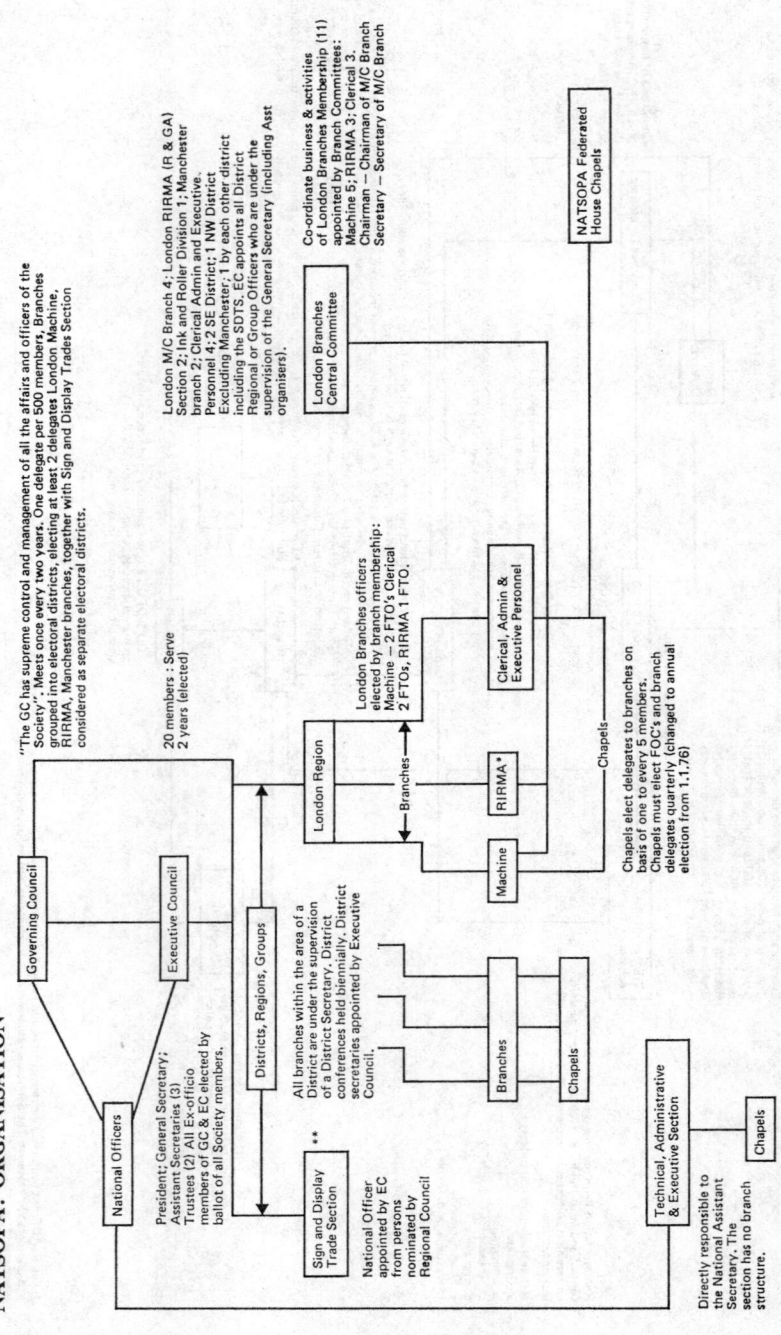

Source: ACAS *Inquiries*

APPENDIX 9
TABLE 8
NATIONAL UNION OF JOURNALISTS: ORGANISATION

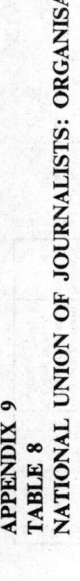

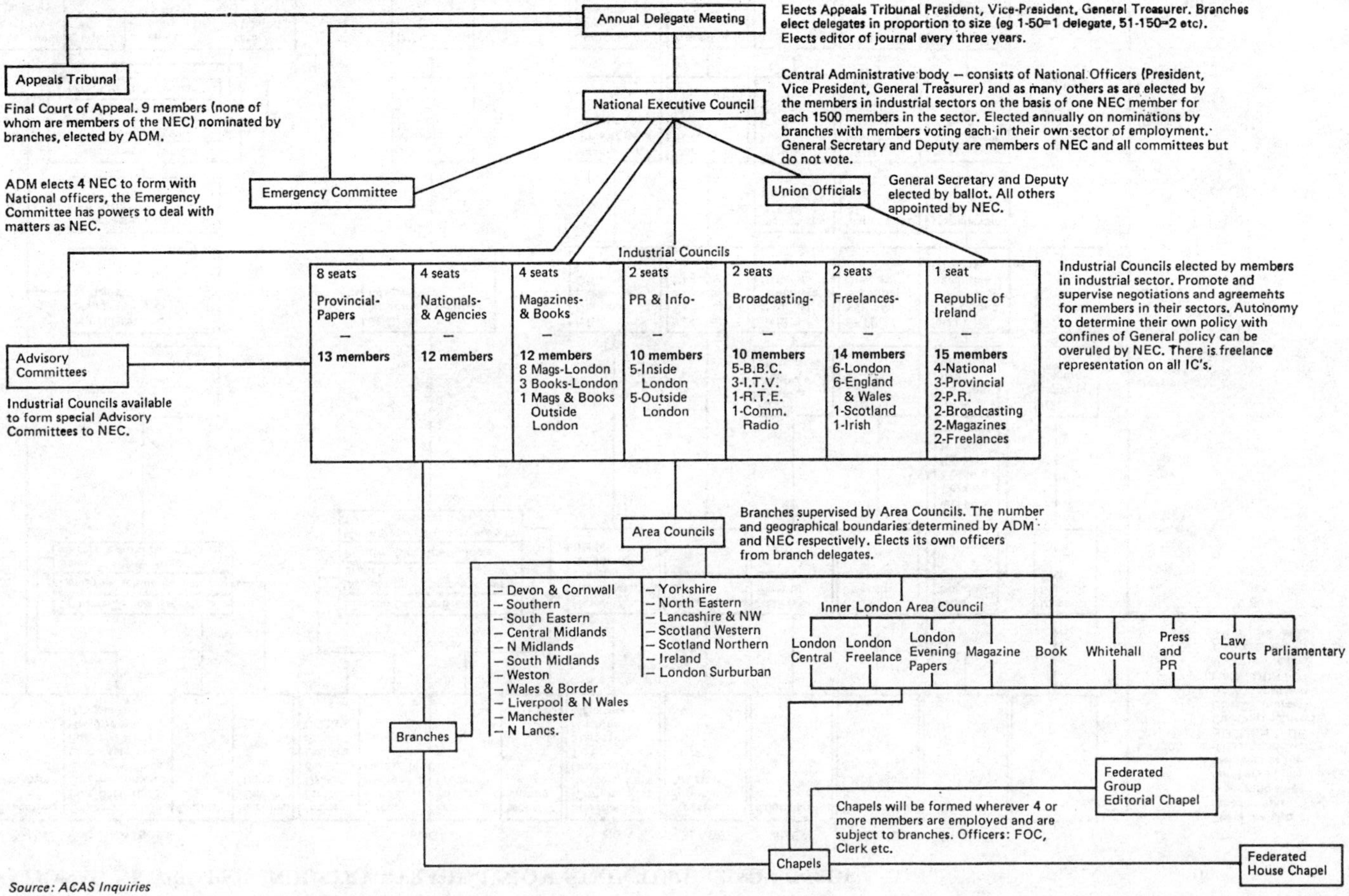

Source: ACAS Inquiries

APPENDIX 9
TABLE 9
NATIONAL NEWSPAPER INDUSTRY—TRADE UNION STRUCTURE (SIMPLIFIED)

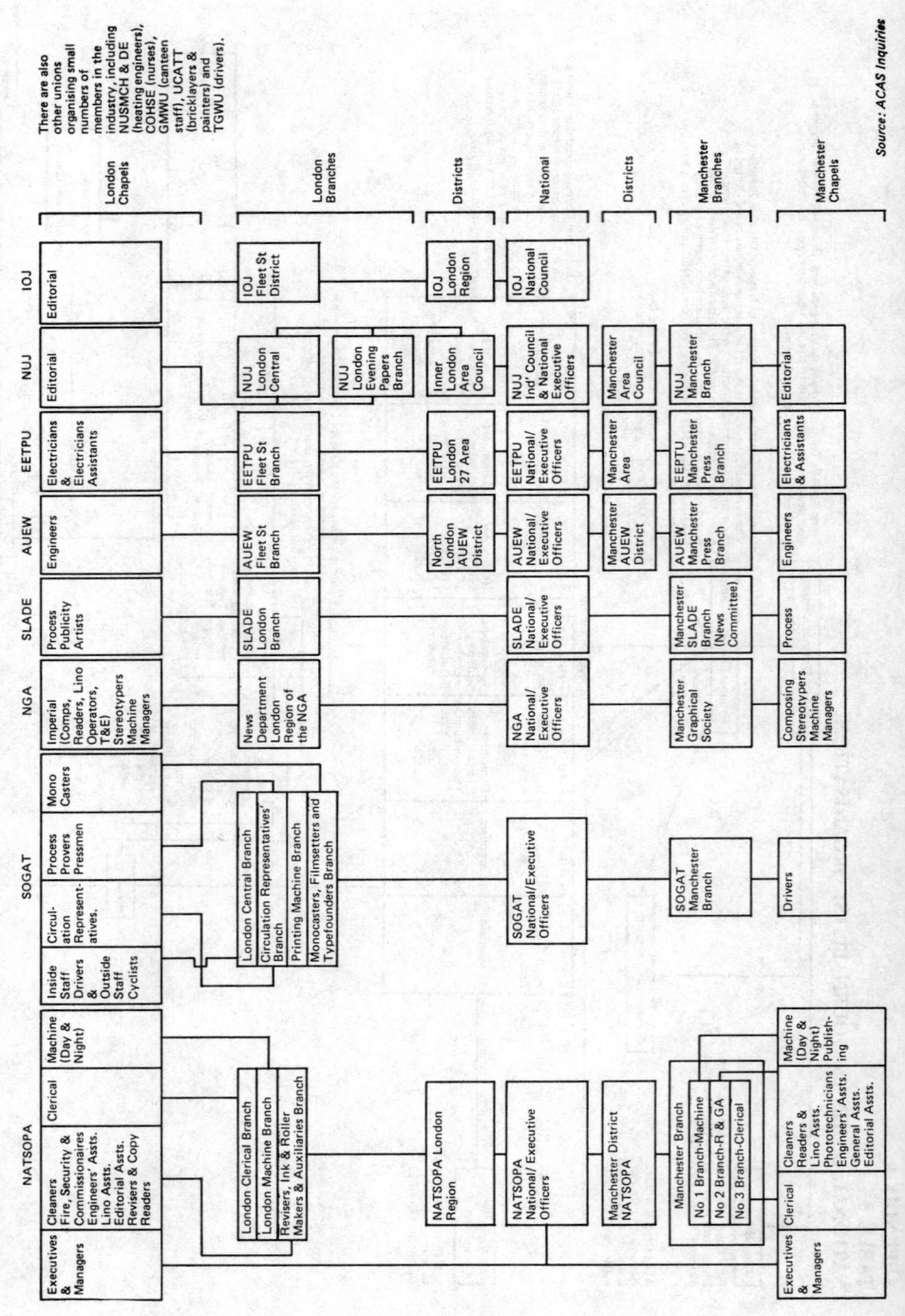

Source: ACAS Inquiries

APPENDIX 9
TABLE 10
NGA LONDON REGION: ORGANISATION

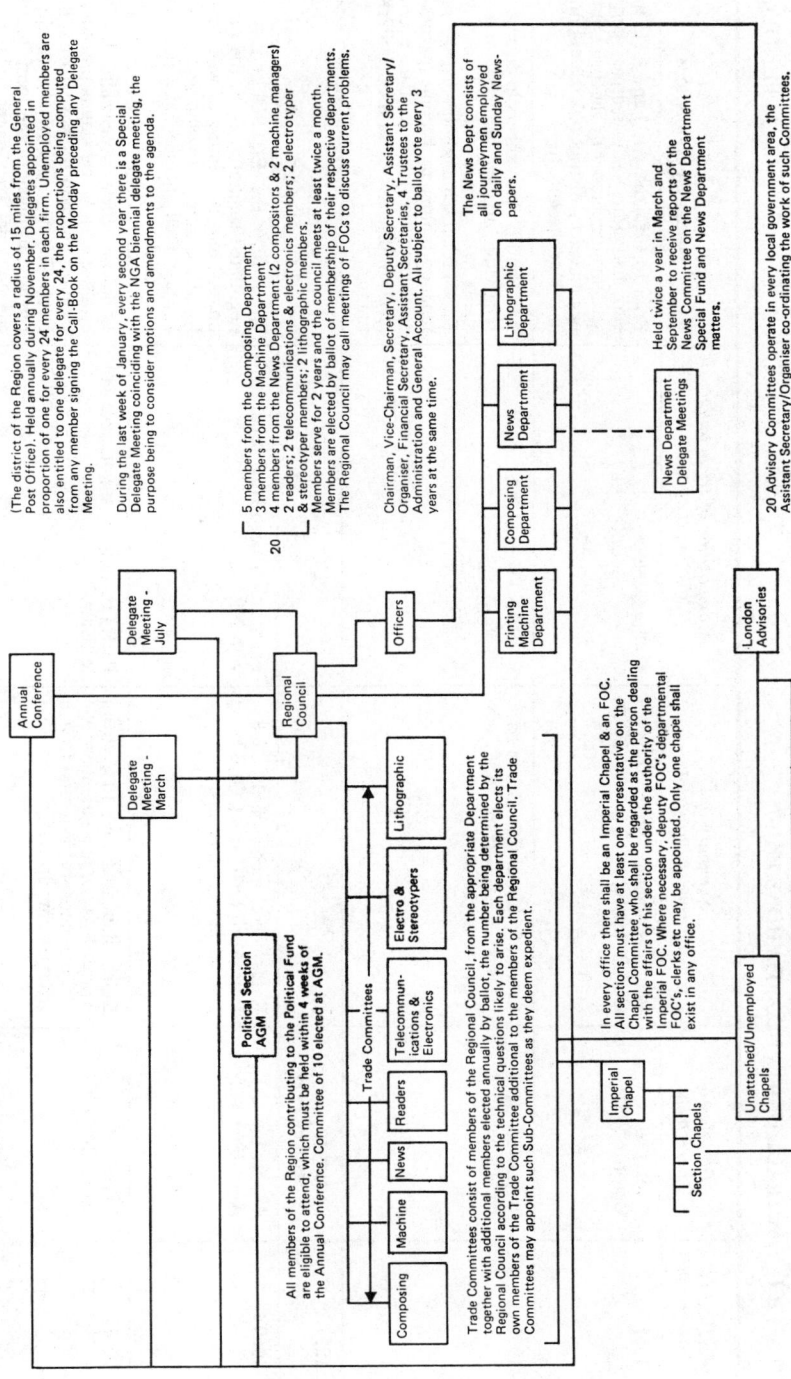

Source: ACAS Inquiries

APPENDIX 10

TABLE 1: NPA/TRADE UNION NEGOTIATIONS 1951-75

Date of agreement	Duration of agreement	Summary of agreements/provisions	Composition of trade union side in negotiations	Notes on negotiations
1951	3 years to October 1954	Wages stabilised, apart from COLB* changes.	Printing unions.	Prior to 1955 the AEU and ETU members had rates adjusted as per the settlement achieved by the print unions negotiated by district officials in London and Manchester.
1955	2 years to November 1957	Consolidation of COLB into basic rates, 12½% increase, and new COL arrangements.	9 P&KTF unions, but LSC separate.	AEU and ETU members in dispute over relativities of their members, and over rights to negotiate with the employers; P&KTF subsequently invited the maintenance unions to become parties (by representation at national executive level) to discussions with other P&KTF unions.
1957	2 years to November 1959			
1960	4 years to April 1964	Rates were increased by 7-8% from April 1960, with COLB being paid at agreed intervals.	Each union negotiated separately with NPA.	Until 1970 the EETPU and AUEW negotiated separately from the printing unions, and the timing of wage awards for them were not coincidental, mainly because their members did not receive the COLB.
1964	3 years to September 1967	Rates increased by 10% from April 1964 (and in September 1964 for maintenance workers) COLB arrangements applied.	P&KTF unions negotiated collectively.	Following their conclusion the NPA established a house claims procedure to monitor and control wage drift at house level. The negotiations also resulted in the establishment of the Joint Board for the National Newspaper Industry.

292

1968	2 years to 1970	COLB arrangements continued from 1964 agreement. In September 1968 previous COLB was absorbed together with basic rate increases of 3% and 2% in 1969.	Separate negotiations with each union.	Working party established of union general secretaries and NPA's Labour Executive to decide on allocation of savings from productivity bargaining; SLADE members, who were opposed to abolition of COLB and method study, engaged in go-slow followed by a six-week lockout.
1970	2 years to 1972	Extra week's holiday; 5% increase on earnings or 10% on basic rate, whichever was the greater.	Collective negotiations involving AUEW and EETPU for first time.	SOGAT in dispute over claim for 20-25% increase with no strings attached. National Newspaper Steering Group established.
1972	2 years to 31.1.74	Two stages, with 8% increase in October 1972, 8% increase in October 1973.	Collective negotiations.	During currency of the agreements, the Conservative Government's pay policy intervened, preventing the agreement being renegotiated, as agreed, on 1.2.74 (as result of inflation increase).
1974	1 year from October to October 1975	5% increase in October 1974 and 2% increase in April 1975. Payment of threshold of £2.80 became a house payment, and was removed from the arena of industry rates for all time.	NGA, although initially with EETPU, negotiated apart from the other unions.	Minimum increase guarantees given to all earning under £55 per week. NGA in dispute over reduction of house differentials by 35p (12½% of the £2.80 threshold); their particular concern applied to the machine areas and readers' departments.
1975	1 year	£6 per week increase to all employees, payable as a supplement (apart from those earning £8,500 plus p.a.).	AUEW negotiated separately.	Difficulties encountered over the application of the £6 to casual workers.

Source: NPA and ACAS inquiries.
*Cost of Living Bonus.

TABLE 2

REVIEW OF AGREEMENTS IN FOUR MULTI-TITLE HOUSES

Union	Chapel	Regular annual review	Regular review more frequent than annually	Review on an ad hoc basis	Total
NGA	Composing* and reading	8	3	10	21
	Stereo	3	—	6	9
	T & E	2	—	1	3
	Machine managers	—	2	7	9
NATSOPA	Machine	1	3	11	15
	RIRMA	21	5	23	49
	Clerical	2	—	3	5
SOGAT	Publishing	—	5	17	22
	Provers and Process	1	2	8	11
	Circulation reps.	1	—	3	4
SLADE	Process and Publicity	1	2	6	9
AUEW	Engineers	5	—	2	7
EEPTU	Electricians	4	—	2	6
Total	Number	49	22	99	170
	Per cent	29	13	58	100

Source: ACAS inquiries.
*Excludes 18 piece case and linotype chapels whose members are paid on a piece work basis.

APPENDIX 11

TABLE 1
DEPARTMENT OF EMPLOYMENT RECORD OF STOPPAGES OF WORK 1970–1975

	1970				1971				1972				1973				1974				1975			
	No. of stoppages (1)	Days lost '000 (2)	Days lost per stoppage (3)	Days lost per 1,000 employees (4)	1	2	3	4	1	2	3	4	1	2	3	4	1	2	3	4	1	2	3	4‡
All Manufacturing Industries ...	3,906	10,908	2,793	475	2,228	13,589	6,099	600	2,497	23,909	9,575	1,050	2,873	7,197	2,505	325	2,922	14,750	5,047	650	2,282	6,012	2,634	371
Paper, Printing and Publishing* ...	33	120	3,636	275	12	36	3,000	90	13	24	1,846	60	23	42	1,826	25	30	134	4,466	375	23	46	2,000	140
National Newspaper Industry*† ...	2	1·7	863	47	2	·7	364	20	2	·5	263	14	2	2·13	1,068	58	5	28·2	5,641	773	4	16·4	4,102	449
Motor Vehicles ...	336	1,105	3,288	2,150	241	3,100	12,863	6,150	217	1,355	6,244	2,750	297	2,082	7,010	4,100	223	1,755	7,869	3,550	150	829	5,526	1,040

Source: Department of Employment.
*Including the national newspaper industry.
†Figures for days lost and number of stoppages provided separately by DE. The number of employees used to calculate incidence is a current figure thus marginally overstating the days lost per 1,000 employees between 1970 and 1974.
‡The employment figure for April 1975 was used in this case.

295

APPENDIX 11

TABLE 2

RECORDED INDUSTRIAL ACTION IN NINE NATIONAL NEWSPAPER HOUSES DURING 1975*

Type of Action	Issue Involved	Annual Review	Differentials	Other pay questions	Physical conditions of work	Work organisation manning, etc	All other matters	Totals
Stoppage of work		6	—	2	1	5	2	16
Unauthorised meetings in working hours		1	—	1	—	6	1	9
Restrictions of output		1	2	2	—	5	—	10
Others and combinations of action		—	1	1	1	—	—	3
Totals		8	3	6	2	16	3	38

Source: ACAS inquiries.
*Excluding section involving all houses.

TABLE 3

APPENDIX 11

INDUSTRIAL ACTION: DURATION AND WARNING 1975

Duration of industrial action	Time between the date the issue was first raised and the beginning of industrial action					Total
	24 hours or less	Over 24 hours to 7 days	8 days to 28 days	29 or more days	Not available	
Part of one shift ...	5	1	1	1	1	9
One shift or more up to 24 hours	2	1	—	3	—	6
More than 24 hours ...	4	4	2	1	2	13
Not available ...	—	—	—	—	10	10
Total	11	6	3	5	13	38

Source: ACAS Survey of Houses.

APPENDIX 11

TABLE 4
VARIATIONS IN BASIC DISPUTES PROCEDURES

Union	Section	1	2	3	4	5	6
NGA	Press Telegraphists (London)	Yes	(a)	Yes	No	Yes	Yes
NGA	Readers (London)	Yes	(b)	Yes	Yes	"no stoppage or threat of stoppage by the Association or any branch or Chapel".	Yes
NGA	Stereotypers	Yes	—	—	Pending (1) no interruption of work in any office.	"no stoppage of threat of stoppage by the Society or any branch or chapel".	Yes
NGA	Machine Managers (London)	Yes	(b) If Joint Committee fails to agree on appointment of referee Minister of Labour shall be invited to appoint an arbitrator whose decision shall be final.	Yes	Yes	"no stoppage or that re of stoppage by the Association or any branch or chapel".	Yes
NGA	London Typographical Society	See Clause 1* below Committee of Arbitration: 5 nominees LTS 5 nominees NPA	Appeal Committee of three 1. Independent Chairman 2. Representative of LTS 3. Representative of NPA	Recommendation for settlement.	—	"no stoppage or threat of stoppage by the Society or any branch or chapel".	Yes See Clause 5* below.
SLADE	Process Workers Publicity Artists (London and Manchester)	Yes	(b)	Yes	Yes	Yes	House Agreements only.

			(b)			
SLADE	Process Workers (London)	Yes		Yes	Yes	Yes, but Saturday working (not Saturday night working).
NATSOPA	Machine RIRMA Clerical	Yes	Failing agreement by Joint Committee unless mutually agreed to proceed to 'c' below referred to Conciliation Committee: equal number of representatives of NPA and Union, and (if mutually agreed), independent Chairman as conciliator who shall make a finding not necessarily binding on parties.	—	'd' column 2: "no hostile action by either side during the 14 days following the breakdown".	Yes
NATSOPA	Machine RIRMA Clerical	—	Failing agreement by Conciliation Committee or acceptance of Chairman's findings: (c) Referred to NPA council and National Executive of Union. Failing agreement: (d) See Column 4 (e) In event of hostile action during 14 days matter referred to arbitration for settlement. (f) During period of 14 days either party, or parties jointly, free to report situation to P&KTF and Ministry of Labour.	—	—	—

TABLE 4: VARIATIONS IN BASIC DISPUTES PROCEDURES (*continued*)

Union	Section	1	2	3	4	5	6
AEU & ETU	Electricians and Engineers (London)	Yes	(a)	Yes	Yes	Yes	Yes
SOGAT	Div A (London) PMB	Yes	(b)	Yes	Yes	Yes	Yes, but Saturday working (not Saturday night working).
SOGAT	Paper Workers London Central Branch	Yes	(b) If Joint Committee fails to agree on appointment of referee: (1) Minister of Labour shall be invited to appoint a conciliator. (2) Failing agreement, Minister of Labour shall be invited to appoint sole arbitrator, whose decision shall be final.	Yes	Yes	Yes	Yes
SOGAT	Paper Workers Circulation Representatives	Yes	(b) If Joint Committee fails to agree on appointment of referee: (1) Minister of Labour shall be invited to appoint a conciliator. (2) Failing agreement, Minister of Labour shall be invited to appoint sole arbitrator whose decision shall be final.	Yes	Yes	Yes	

Source: ACAS inquiries.

Key to Table 4

1. Joint Committee: three NPA nominees, three union nominees.
2. (a) Joint Committee has power to resolve disputes and appoints referee if it fails to do so.
   (b) Joint Committee appoints referee.
3. Referee's decision final.
4. No hostile action to be taken on either side pending reference and decision.
5. No stoppage or threat of stoppage by any union, branch or chapel without recourse to disputes machinery.
6. Applies to house agreements, collective agreements, and Saturday night working.

NGA London Typographical Society

Clause 1* In the event of any question arising on which the Agreement is silent or not clearly defined, such question shall be governed by the custom of the trade (if any), or decided by mutual agreement; it being understood that for work of an exceptional character the compositor is entitled to receive such special rates as will adequately remunerate him for the time occupied on the work.

Clause 5* Withholding of payment of a charge which has been supported by the News Department shall be justification for either the NPA or the Society to make immediate application for the invoking of the disputes machinery.

APPENDIX 16

TABLE 1

TYPICAL ORGANISATION OF THE EDITORIAL DEPARTMENTS OF A NATIONAL NEWSPAPER

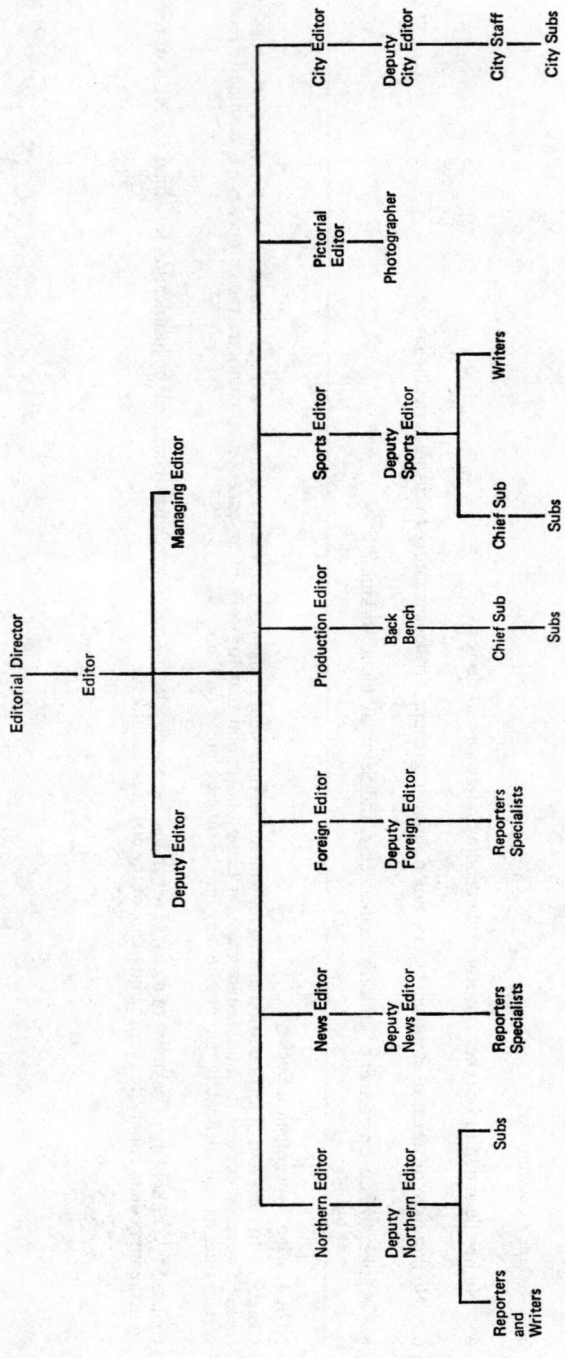

Source: ACAS Inquiries

APPENDIX 16

TABLE 2
FULL-TIME EDITORIAL STAFF EMPLOYED BY NATIONAL NEWSPAPERS IN OCTOBER 1975

Category Location		Senior Editorial*	Sub-editors	Reporters and Correspondents	Photographers	Other Editorial†	Totals	
							number	per cent
LONDON		569	611	936	120	351	2,587	71·0
MANCHESTER		147	227	205	55	147	781	21·0
Elsewhere in UK and overseas		0	0	231	35	10	276	7·8
Totals	number	716	838	1,372	210	508	3,644	—
	%	19·7	23·0	37·7	5·8	14·0	—	100

Source: Labour Survey.

* Includes editors and their deputies.
† Includes such staff as those permanently employed on work of a statistical nature in City offices.

TABLE 3

AGREEMENTS BETWEEN MULTI-TITLED HOUSES AND THEIR LONDON NUJ CHAPELS

Company	Newspapers produced in London	NUJ London Chapels	Agreements covering chapels
Associated Newspaper Group Ltd	1 Daily Mail 2 Evening News	(1) Daily Mail (2) Evening News	(1) Daily Mail and Evening News
Beaverbrook Newspapers Ltd	1 Daily Express 2 Sunday Express 3 Evening Standard	(1) Daily and Sunday Express (2) Evening Standard	(1) Daily and Sunday Express (2) Evening Standard
The Daily Telegraph Ltd	1 Daily Telegraph 2 Sunday Telegraph	(1) Daily and Sunday Telegraph	(1) Daily and Sunday Telegraph
Mirror Group Newspapers Ltd	1 Daily Mirror 2 Sunday Mirror 3 Sunday People	(1) Daily Mirror (2) Sunday Mirror (2) Sunday People	(1) Daily Mirror (2) Sunday Mirror (3) Sunday People
News Group Newspapers Ltd	1 Sun 2 News of the World	(1) Sun (2) News of the World	(1) Sun (2) News of the World
Times Newspapers Ltd	1 Times 2 Sunday Times	(1) Times (2) Sunday Times	(1) Times (2) Sunday Times

Source: ACAS inquiries.

APPENDIX 17(a)

PREVIOUS INQUIRIES INTO INDUSTRIAL RELATIONS IN FLEET STREET
The 1947–1949 Royal Commission on the Press

1. The 1947–1949 Royal Commission on the Press was set up amidst fears that the increasing concentration of ownership of the newspapers was becoming a threat to freedom of information by limiting the number of alternative outlets for such information. The Commission made no specific examination of industrial relations, having been charged with inquiring into "the control, management and ownership of the newspaper and periodical Press and the news agencies, including the financial structure and the monopolistic tendencies in control". However, evidence to the Commission complained of restrictive labour practices inflating production costs. The Commission did not consider it to be within the scope of its inquiry to investigate these allegations, but felt that a separate inquiry into the question might be necessary.

The 1961–1962 Royal Commission on the Press

2. The Royal Commission's terms of reference were "to examine the economic and financial factors affecting the production and role of newspapers, magazines and other periodicals in the United Kingdom, including:—

(*a*) Manufacturing, printing, distribution and other costs;

(*b*) Efficiency of production; and

(*c*) Advertising and other revenue, including any revenue derived from interests in television;

to consider whether these factors tend to diminish diversity of ownership and control or the number or variety of such publications, having regard to the importance, in the public interest, of the accurate presentation of news and the free expression of opinion". The 1949 Royal Commission had concluded "any further decrease in the number of national newspapers would be a serious loss" and since 1949 a further seventeen daily and Sunday newspapers had ceased publication in London and the Provinces and the ownership of those that remained was concentrated in fewer hands. Essentially, this Commission was set up for the same motives as the earlier one but the emphasis of its terms of reference on the economic efficiency of newspapers meant that industrial relations became relevant to its deliberations.

3. The Commission's findings were that technical innovations involving a reduction in manning were hampered by the lack of comprehensive schemes allowing for the transfer of pension rights, redundancy compensation, or retraining. It urged fuller consultation on management plans to bring in labour-saving techniques and recommended that there should be a joint standing body of employers and unions "charged with the oversight of planning and development over the whole field of national newspaper production". This body would attempt to facilitate developments in machinery and techniques and plan for long term manpower and training requirements. It could also develop a scheme for adequate transferable pension rights, and "fair methods of mitigating the consequences of redundancy". The unions were urged to agree to a fixed retirement age, to take a more flexible approach to new techniques and develop more power to the PKTF.

4. On manning standards the Commission supported the findings of Personnel Administration Ltd, the Management Consultants engaged by the Commission to examine the efficiency of the National newspapers, that in the four offices covered a saving of the order of 34% could be achieved in the manpower employed on production and distribution. The tendency in productivity was also found to be a

downward one. Many "extras" were found to be "anachronistic and fictitious". Particular reference was made to "ghost" payments. There was, in the Commission's view, a need for a complete recasting of the industry's wages system to relate basic rates realistically to actual normal earnings. Reference was made to the trade union branches acting as "employment exchanges". While acknowledging that such control seemed satisfactory to both sides of the industry, the Commission felt that it might be open to abuse because, for example, a union could dictate to a member where he might work.

5. The Royal Commission found a number of reasons for the inefficiency it identified. It was felt that the multiplicity of unions, and especially of chapels, undermined agreements between the NPA and the unions at national level. House agreements between individual chapels and managements led to a general upward drift of earnings on comparability grounds that were suspect. The Commission did not accept as the complete explanation of the "ineffectiveness of the employers' collective organisation" the "traditional management defence" in the industry that the ephemeral character of a newspaper makes it especially vulnerable.

6. The Commission, on the premise that "the similarities between newspapers are more important than their differences", urged "better and more authoritative negotiating and consultative machinery". In reconstituting the machinery the industry was urged to attempt to reach agreement on the sanctity of the disputes procedure, leaving production unhindered until the procedure was exhausted. The machinery, in the Commission's view, had to be capable of achieving:—

(*a*) Central agreement on manning standards, as far as this was possible;
(*b*) Realistic future revisions of manning standards;
(*c*) Reductions in casual labour, by encouraging regular manning levels for average or normal production requirements with built-in flexibility to avoid discharging or engaging casuals;
(*d*) The elimination of "extras" and their absorption in normal wages;
(*e*) The rewarding of special skill or experience with "merit money";
(*f*) The joint central ratification, before implementation, of house agreements.

7. The Commission also felt that the NPA should be strengthened, and that, in particular, majority decisions should prevail when the collective interest was involved; that management should be represented more during the night, the main production period; and that "a more constructive spirit" was needed together with a real desire to see the revamped negotiating machinery work properly.

8. Despite discovering so many examples of wasted manpower resources, low productivity and weak management in the industry the Commission concluded that the salvation of the industry could not be found in the large potential savings on labour costs which seemed possible. Rather, the Commission found that the fatal casualties of the industry had received their wounds from the competition of their rivals, and had failed on a commercial basis in not selling enough newspapers or advertising space.

The Economist Intelligence Unit Survey: 1966

9. The 1962 Royal Commission's suggestion of a "joint standing committee" for the industry bore some fruit in the setting up, in 1964, of the Joint Board for the National Newspaper Industry, JBNNI, whose aim was to increase the efficiency in the publication and production of national newspapers. The JBNNI was set up after an NPA initiative, and the unions agreed to it after they had managed to get a 10%

increase on basic rates. The Board quickly decided that it needed a comprehensive factual survey and established three committees, each with its own set of problems. The Economist Intelligence Unit was then commissioned to carry out a comprehensive factual survey of the publication and production of national newspapers with the intention of making recommendations to the NPA and the unions which would lead to increased efficiency. The main findings and recommendations of the EIU are summarised below.

10. **Management.** The EIU found that the industry, with some exceptions, was dominated by a small group of proprietors whose power was such as to mould the whole managerial philosophy. Some adopted a commercial approach to newspaper publishing and managed accordingly, whereas others had "little interest in modern management methods and techniques". The management structure in companies differed, but it was felt that insufficient lines of communication prevented unanimity of approach by managers at different levels. Management quality varied, but in general there was a need for more professional and management training.

11. **Production.** Under this heading the EIU felt that:—

   (*a*) The production departments had an "insular" atmosphere, with very little knowledge of what went on in other industries;

   (*b*) Earnings did not bear a direct relationship to the work content of the job, nor to the skill and effort necessary; the strength and militancy of the union or chapel were the decisive factors affecting earnings. The payments system, with extras forming a large and constantly negotiable part of earnings, was a main weakness of the industry;

   (*c*) There was a lack of knowledge of normal engineering practice, and little preparation of employees for inevitable technological innovations by either managements or unions;

   (*d*) The apprenticeship form of training for the industry was dated; a broader-based training designed for the current and potential needs of the industry should replace it;

   (*e*) More effective and authoritative night management was necessary. Chapels had complained that managements allowed minor problems to escalate, and only responded to militancy;

   (*f*) Complaints also arose from the inequities caused by inconsistent manning levels which resulted in different effort/pay relationships for men working virtually side-by-side;

   (*g*) Manning levels could be reduced. The EIU produced detailed suggestions of possible savings in individual departments if manning levels were reduced. Unlike PA Consultants, who in their work for the 1962 Royal Commission used manning levels in regional and provincial newspapers as a comparison the EIU produced their own "manning standards" for the various departments and computed possible savings from these.

12. **Trade Unions.** As far as trade union organisation was concerned the EIU thought that:—

   (*a*) There was a gap in communications between branch and chapel;

   (*b*) There were variations in the power and "quality" of FOCs. Union officials took "little or no interest" in the election of chapel officials and should become more involved;

(c) Restrictive practices were not as bad as some had claimed;

(d) Inter-union relations had improved, although those between senior FOCs were often found to be bad. The inter-branch relationships were aided by the regular meetings of the London P&KTF;

(e) Many branch secretaries and even general secretaries received less pay than those they represented;

(f) There were large variations in London Branch organisation of the unions in relation to FTOs/members ratios. For example, the R&GA branch of SOGAT Division 1 had one full-time officer per 6,375 members, whereas the NSES (now part of the NGA) had one FTO per 925 members.

13. **Finance.** A substantial proportion of the industry was found to be working at a loss; only three of the eight national dailies (excluding the *Financial Times*) were making a profit, the remainder being heavily subsidised by other interests. However, the EIU did not feel that its gloomy forecasts for the industry would be remedied by reductions in costs alone. Like the 1962 Royal Commission they felt that even the substantial savings in costs, especially labour costs, they saw as possible, would not on their own make the industry financially viable. They saw the crucial problem as one of revenue, decreasing circulation, growing price resistance, and an increasing dependence on advertising revenue with little potential for growth.

14. In general terms the EIU called for the business efficiency of the minority of the industry to be extended to the majority. It called for a rational approach to technological innovations, and for a reform of the payments system. The "horse-trading" approach to manning should end, helped by better pension schemes and, in certain cases, redundancy would have to be financed from sources outside the industry. The proliferation of chapels on the production floor was a cause of friction as was the chapel/branch gap in communication. The training needs of the industry were no longer satisfied by the traditional apprenticeship system, which should be re-evaluated.

Reports of the National Board for Prices and Incomes

15. The Board reported three times on the National Newspaper Industry*. Reports 43 (1967) and 141 (1970) both examined "Cost and Revenue of National Newspapers" and were a result of proposed rises in cover prices. Report 43 recommended that there be no price increase, and that the industry should improve its productivity, especially in relation to manning levels (*Daily Mirror* manning was examined). The Government should help to finance a redundancy programme, but not if the industry evaded its problems by raising prices. Report No. 141, which was based on a survey of five main production areas in a sample of seven newspapers, found that the industry had moved a little towards realistic manning levels in the period 1967 to 1969.

16. In production departments, manning had been reduced by 5% on average, mainly through the increasing number of comprehensive agreements. Productivity had also increased by an average of 9%, but average production wage costs had increased by 12%. The Board felt there was still much room for improvement; manning levels should be based on objective work standards and work study. The Board remarked on the fragmented bargaining in the industry, and found that union amalgamation had not reduced the number of chapels. One newspaper company had concluded productivity agreements with 44 chapels. Comment was also made on the fact that the most inefficient areas had the most to gain from productivity deals and that savings shared on a departmental or chapel basis led to a distortion of relativities

*Report No. 2 "Wages, Cost and Prices in the Printing Industry" examined the provincial press and general printing.

within the office, and consequent claims to restore differentials. The Board felt that the benefits of such agreements should be distributed on an office-wide basis, noting that an NPA/PKTF agreement allowed such sharing but had not been implemented. Like the EIU and the 1962 Royal Commission, the Board made the point that "the economic problems of the national newspaper industry do not arise solely, or even principally, from labour costs or trade union resistance to technical innovation", but also said that savings in wage costs might be the marginal factor which would save a newspaper from extinction. Obstructive union attitudes, bad inter-union relationships combined with weak management to give a fragmented structure. The increase in local productivity agreements had made national agreements even less relevant; the Board felt that there was a case for national negotiations on pay ceasing altogether. National negotiations, it was thought, should provide a basis for manning negotiations at office level. The NBPI suggested a joint committee be set up in each newspaper company to convert nationally-agreed policy into practice; it acknowledged, however, that such committees could only function if prior national agreement were reached between the NPA (which then of course represented all the national newspapers) and the PKTF (which when it existed could negotiate, but not conclude, agreements on behalf of its constituent unions). Short of such agreements, the NPA was urged to draw up productivity guidelines for individual managements and to use its collective strength to facilitate adherence to them. The Board felt that Federated House Chapels should be given a more prominent role by management and unions.

17. NBPI Report Number 115 on Journalists' Pay (June 1969) resulted from a pay settlement between the NPA and the NUJ. The Board felt "compelled to comment" on negotiating procedures. A radical restructuring of wage scales, career structures, and negotiating procedures was thought necessary. The NPA and the NUJ were urged to form a standing joint committee for negotiating minimum salaries, establishing guidelines and for vetting house agreements.

The 1967 Court of Inquiry into the problems caused by the introduction of web-offset machines in the printing industry

18. This inquiry was initiated under the Industrial Courts Act as a result of disputes at Southwark Offset Ltd and the Co-operative Press Ltd, Manchester. The inquiry concentrated on the provincial press and general printing (represented on the employers' side by the Newspaper Society and the BFMP), although the NPA gave evidence of the difficulties experienced by the *Morning Advertiser* when it introduced web-offset machines. One of the Court's recommendations was that the NPA, The Newspaper Society and the BFMP give consideration to a possible merger. The Court had felt, despite evidence to the contrary from the three organisations, that they had enough common interest to warrant such a merger. The Court also recommended one union for the industry, an objective of which the NGA had said "the sooner . . . (it) is attained the better for all concerned". The Court recommended a new JIC for the industry as well as a national disputes procedure. The employers were urged to establish what objective methods existed to determine the manning of new machinery and processes, and to discuss their findings with the unions.

APPENDIX 17(b): JOINT STANDING COMMITTEE FOR THE NATIONAL NEWSPAPER INDUSTRY: CONSTITUTION

Name

1. The name of the Committee shall be the Joint Standing Committee for the National Newspaper Industry (hereinafter called "the Committee").

Objectives

2. The Objectives of the Committee shall be:

   (*a*) To secure the joint action of management, trades unions and employees to a common aim—the viability of the national newspaper industry.

   (*b*) To maintain levels of employment compatible with each company's long-term viability, with career opportunity and job security for all staff.

   (*c*) To develop policies essential to the future well-being of the industry and to provide a forum for dealing with problems of immediate urgency.

   (*d*) To consider the implications of annual company manpower and technology planning proposals and the co-ordination and development of training and staff requirements.

   (*e*) To devise and establish a policy framework and procedures:

   — to enable staff to volunteer to leave the industry or retire before normal age;

   — to enable women over 60 and men over 65 to retire from employment in the industry;

   — to regularise all employment and ensure a wholly regular work force committed to full normal working week or single shift appearance;

   — to establish minimum common scales of pension benefits;

   — to consider the implications of the introduction of new technology, and the co-ordination of plans for its introduction.

   (*f*) To represent the industry in discussions with Government and other authorities, where appropriate and mutually agreed.

   (*g*) To devise and monitor comprehensive procedures for the settlement of disputes.

   (*h*) To raise funds for, set up, monitor and ensure the completion of any training activity associated with the introduction of new technology and any retraining which may be necessary for people leaving the industry.

   (*i*) To provide resources to advise staff leaving the industry on the use of financial benefits and on alternative employment possibilities. In co-ordination with the Department of Employment and Manpower Services Commission, to advise on retraining.

   (*j*) To examine demarcation issues arising from current production methods and new technology.

   (*k*) To do all such things as are incidental or conducive to the attainment of the above objects or any of them.

Membership

3. The Parties to the Agreement to which this Constitution forms a schedule and such other persons as shall be admitted to membership in accordance with this Constitution, and no others, shall be members of the Committee and shall be entered in the register of members accordingly.

4. Membership of the Committee shall be open to National Newspaper Employers (hereinafter called "Employer Members") and to Trades Union representing the employees of the above members (hereinafter called "Trade Union Members").

5. Any person desiring to become a member of the Committee must apply to the Joint Secretaries at the Office of the Committee by instrument in writing in such form as the Committee may prescribe. The Committee shall have full and absolute power and authority to refuse any such application for membership.

6. If elected by the Committee each applicant shall be so notified by the Joint Secretaries and shall, on signing an undertaking to observe the Constitution and the regulations of the Committee, and on paying or undertaking to pay the amount of any levy payable in accordance with the Constitution, become a member of the Committee.

7. A register shall be kept by the Committee containing the names and addresses of all the members.

8. Any member may, at any time, resign his membership by written notice sent to the Joint Secretaries at the Office of the Committee. Unless the Committee otherwise resolves a notice of resignation shall not be valid unless all moneys due to the Committee from such members shall have been paid.

9. Membership shall also cease if:

   (i) the member ceases to be qualified to be a member;

   (ii) it is resolved by all members other than that member that it is undesirable in the interest of the Committee that such member, should remain a member.

Upon ceasing to be a member, whether by registration pursuant to Article 8 or pursuant to this Article 9 a member shall forfeit all rights and claims whatsoever against the funds and property of the Committee.

Government

10. The Committee shall have a Chairman and a Vice-Chairman who shall each hold office for one year. The appointment to Chairman and Vice-Chairman shall be made in such a way as to ensure that one of these positions is held by a representative of a Trades Union Member and the other by a representative of an Employer Member. The first Chairman of the Committee shall be the Chairman of the Printing Industry Committee of the Trade Union Congress, and the first Vice-Chairman shall be the Vice-Chairman of the Newspaper Publishers Association.

11. The Committee shall appoint Joint Secretaries, one of whom shall be nominated by the Trade Union Members and one of whom shall be nominated by the Employer Members. The address of the Office of the Committee shall be 6, Bouverie Street, London EC4Y 8AY.

12. The Committee shall appoint Auditors and approve their remuneration. The first Auditors shall be Messrs. Hard, Dowdy, Watson, Collins & Co. of Transport House, Smith Square, London SW1.

13. The Committee shall hold an Annual General Meeting, the first of which shall take place in 1977 and succeeding Annual General Meetings shall take place not less than 12 months and not more than 15 months after the preceding Annual General Meeting. The Annual General Meeting shall:

    (i) receive and consider the Annual Report and Accounts;

    (ii) appoint a Chairman and Vice-Chairman;

    (iii) appoint Auditors and approve their remuneration;

    (iv) take in such other business as has been notified in writing to the Joint Secretaries by any member not less than 21 days before the meeting.

14. At least 28 days' notice shall be given of an Annual General Meeting followed by an Agenda at least 14 days before the meeting specifying the business to be transacted thereat.

15. The Committee shall meet such number of times in the course of each year as it shall think fit. Not less than 7 days' notice in writing of meetings of the Committee shall be given to the members of the Committee except when in the opinion of the Chairman and Vice-Chairman, it is desirable to convene a meeting at shorter notice and all members of the Committee consent to such shorter notice.

16. A resolution signed by or on behalf of all members of the Committee shall be considered to be a resolution of the Committee notwithstanding that it was not passed at an actual meeting.

17. Each member shall be entitled to be represented at meetings of the Committee by such person as that member shall have notified in writing to the Joint Secretaries as its representative and may at any time upon notice in writing to the Joint Secretaries change its representative.

18. Each person attending a meeting of the Committee as a member or as a representative of a member shall be entitled to one vote. In normal circumstances decisions shall be reached by a simple majority of those attending the Committee. Notwithstanding this, if 20 per cent or more of the members of the Committee, or three or more of those members attending a meeting of the Committee deem a matter under discussion to be one of major principle, then any decision shall be reached only by unanimous vote.

19. Votes may be given either personally or by proxy. A proxy must be a member or a representative of a member. The instrument appointing a proxy shall be in writing under the hand of the appointor or under the hand of an officer of the appointor so authorised.

20. The Committee shall have power to form sub-committees and working parties either on an *ad hoc* or permanent basis, to determine the composition of such sub-committees and working parties and to delegate to them such powers as it shall think fit.

21. The Committee shall cause Minutes to be made in books provided for the purpose of:

    (i) The names of the members of the Committee present at every meeting, and

    (ii) all resolutions and proceedings at all meetings.

Every member of the Committee present at any meeting of the Committee shall sign his name in a book to be kept for the purpose.

Finance

22. The Committee shall have the power to raise finance:

(i) by such levy upon its members as it shall think fit, which levy may be calculated upon different bases with respect to trade union members and publisher members, and/or,

(ii) from other sources.

23. The Joint Secretaries shall have power to open a Bank Account in the name of the Committee and to operate upon that Account.

24. The Committee shall have power to appoint Trustees upon such terms as it thinks fit, and the property of the Committee, including such moneys as are raised pursuant to Article 22 above (other than such cash for day-to-day purposes as shall have been placed under the control of the Joint Secretaries) shall be vested in them and shall be dealt with by them as the Committee shall from time to time direct by resolution (of which an entry in the Minute Book shall be conclusive evidence).

25. The Committee shall cause true accounts to be kept. The books of account shall be kept at the Office of the Committee or at such other place as the Committee may determine, and (subject to any reasonable restrictions as to the time and manner of inspecting the same that may be imposed by the Committee) such books of account shall be open to the inspection of the members at all times during usual business hours.

26. The Committee shall cause the Joint Secretaries to prepare annually accounts covering the period from 31 March to 1st April except in the first year the period shall commence on the 26 March.

27. A copy of every Balance Sheet and Income and Expenditure Account which is to be laid before the Annual General Meeting accompanied by a report upon the general state of the Committee and the Auditors' Report shall not less than 21 days before the date of the Annual General Meeting be sent to every member.

28. If a Proposal is made in writing to the Joint Secretaries by any member at any time the Joint Secretaries shall immediately send to each member a copy of the Proposal and shall convene a meeting of the Committee as soon as possible for the purpose of considering the Proposal. Unless all members of the Committee agree in writing to shorter notice, at least 21 days shall be given to each member of such meeting. A resolution to dissolve and wind up the Committee shall be adopted and shall be effective only if it receives the votes of:

(i) All Employer Members or all Trade Union Members, or

(ii) More than 50 per cent of all Employer Members and more than 50 per cent of all Trade Union Members.

29. In the event of a resolution to dissolve and wind up the Committee being adopted the Committee will stay in being until such time as all the funds which have been placed within its control have been appropriately utilised or returned to the sources from which they were received.

APPENDIX 18(a)

FINANCIAL TIMES PROPOSAL ON JOINT UNION ORGANISATION

1. All staff currently working in areas directly affected by new technology shall, irrespective of the union of which they are members, become represented by a new "joint technology section" of all the National Newspaper unions with members in areas affected by the new technology in the Company.

2. As technology develops and its impact extends, employees in more areas will become directly affected and so become covered by the "joint technology section" rather than their individual unions—so the new section will tend to grow within the context of a shrinking total staff.

3. The "joint technology section" would co-exist with the unions which constitute it. Every union involved would receive union subscriptions as if all employees in the total joint technology areas were members of that union, but employees in the area would only pay the subscription, via the joint technology section, which they paid to the union of which they were originally members. All other subscriptions on behalf of each employee would be paid by the Company as long as the experiment continued. (Provided the rate of subscription was on a par with that paid by normal members of each union.)

"The Joint Technology Section" would have three main functions:—
(a) To negotiate with the Company and implement jointly, the best acceptable scheme for allocating existing employees covered by the section to jobs defined in the new technology. It is suggested that allocation be on the basis of the objectively assessed suitability of the individual for each defined job within the new technology area. In particular, the allocation should be without regard to the traditional territorial concepts which any union would otherwise advance when extending into the areas of new technology.
(b) To negotiate a mutually acceptable logical salary structure as part of a total remuneration package for all employees represented by the "joint technology section". It is suggested that remuneration be based solely on the relative skill, responsibility and effort content of each function within the new technology area, irrespective of the background of the individual objectively allocated to that function.
(c) To arrange jointly with the Company, or-going programmes of training for those employees represented by the "joint technology section" who are ultimately involved in using the new technology as it is introduced, so that they are equipped to fulfil their allocated functions irrespective of background.

Such a section would also be well placed to negotiate and organise jointly with the Company, retraining, necessary financial compensation and redeployment outside (a) the joint technology section, and (b) outside the Company, for those employees initially within the joint technology areas who will no longer be required within those areas as the technology is progressively implemented.

Although this concept, so far explained, leaves unanswered a number of questions concerned with (a) other newspapers' policies, (b) replacement in new technology areas, and (c) staffing for expansion in new technology areas, the concept aims to answer the unions' main problems in providing, without conflict:—

(i) Each affected union with a complete, but not exclusive, influence in all areas of new technology.

(ii) Each affected union with the subscription income due to it by virtue of all staff in new technology areas being its members.

(iii) An equitable allocation of jobs, incomes, retraining prospects and social policy provisions among all individuals affected by the new technology.

Index

Index references relate to paragraph numbers except in the case of appendices and footnotes where references are to page numbers.

A-pressens, app 219
Absenteeism, 109,178
Accounting staff, 63
Administrative staff, *see* Managers
Advertisement shift, 46
Advertisement staff, 63, 348, 367, 459; Manchester, 551
Advertisements, 27, 222, 621, app 217
Advertising Reps, 518, app 240
Advisory Conciliation and Arbitration Service, 678
Aftonbladet, app 219
Age, average, 102, 103; casuals, 122
Agreements, 668
   Comprehensive, 139–145, 170, 171, 209, 224, 270, 271, 302, 414–5, 425, 457, 643; Manchester, 545, 547
   Disclosure of, 753, 754
   House, 243, 245, 302, 393, 578, 648–50, app 306; on disciplinary procedures, **475**; of journalists, 588–90, 593, 600–601, 605, 607, app 304
   National, 390, 393, 402, 403; of journalists, 596–600, 602–606; Netherlands, app 224; Sweden, app 220–221
   Negotiating, *see* Negotiations
   Review periods, app 294
Aitken, Sir Max, app 230
Algemene Nederlandse Graphische Bond, app 223–224
Allowances, 590
Amalgamated Association of Pressmen, app 280
Amalgamated Society of Lithographic Printers, 322, 335, app 279, app 282, app 283
Amalgamated Union of Engineering Workers, 388
   Branch organisations, 297
   Chapels, 281, 282, app 274–275, app 277; Fathers, 372
   Disputes, 456
   Fleet Street Branch, 371–2
   House agreements, app 294
   Job entry qualifications, 100
   MGN agreement, 411
   Manchester Press Branch, 373
   Membership, app 78
   NPA negotiations, 398, 408, app 293
   Occupations, 44, 53, 68, 199, 316
   Organisation, app 289
   Pay rates, 401, app 249
   Relations with EETPU, 392
   Relations with NATSOPA, 644
Ancillary workers, 150, 281, 316, app 249, app 262
Appraisal of staff, 600
Apprentices, app 104; journalists, 580; qualifications, 98; termination of recruitment, 40; union membership, 332; wages, 385
Apprenticeship schemes, 370
Arbitration, 232–3, 386, 443, 445, 447, 456, app 298–299
Artists, *see* Publicity Artists
Associated Newspaper Group, 3, 25, 34, 58, 534, app 230; demarcation dispute, fn 178
Association of Correctors of the Press, 322, app 232, app 282

Bank Holiday working, 406
Bargaining, *see* Negotiations

Beaverbrook Newspapers Ltd, app 230
   Casual work, 116
   Chapels, 560
   Consultation and disclosure, 458–7, 568
   Disputes, 233, 433
   Glasgow closure, 32, 534
   Manchester, 34, 534, 549
   New technology, fn 18, 58, 62, 66, 536
   Proprietors, 25, app 230–231
   Training programme, 522, 532
Bench Room staff, 49, 159, app 255
Berry family, app 230
Biffing, 277, 278
Blockmaking, 369
Blow system, 175–8, 458, 643, 677
Board of Directors: industrial relations function, 189–92, 215, 450, 452, 454, 486, 495, 549, 592, 703–4, 749, app 265; organisation, app 263; union membership, 316, 357
Bonus payments, 546–7, app 221, app 251
Bookbinding staff, 360
Book publishing staff, 360, 364; training, 511
Brake Hands, 50, fn 53, app 254, app 256, app 259–261; differentials, 158, 159
Breakdown payments, 148, 271
Bricklayers, 53, 316
Briefing groups, 701
British Federation of Master Printers, 216, 241, app 309
British Rail, 221
Broadcasting staff, 378
Broom hands, 117, fn 53
Budgetary controls, 200, 206–213
Bundesverband Deutscher Zeitungsverleger, app 227–228
Bundesverband Druck, app 227–228

Call book, 93, 112
Call card, 111
Call clerk, 464
Calls offices, 107, 109, 111, 115, 540; staffing, 113
Camera operators, 159
Canteen, *see* Catering
Car allowance, 590
Card agreements, 362, fn 105
Card Edge Guilders Trade Society, app 282
Carpenters, 53, 316
Carr family, app 231
Cartoonists, 573
Cashiers, 459
Casters, operatives, 318; tape-driven line, fn 18
Casual workers, 80, 86–96
   Administration, 107–113, 270, 460; costs, 113
   Age levels, 122
   Agreements on, 579
   Calls, app 236–237, app 240; offices, *see* Calls offices
   Casual casuals, 95, 121, 575, 579, app 238–239
   Chapels, 280
   Decasualisation, 123–5, 698, 788; Working Party, 56
   Discipline of, 278

Joint working party, 123–4, 631, 698
  Journalists, *see* Journalists, Casuals
  Manchester, 539–44, 726; pool system, 540, 542, 562
  Manning agreements, effect of, 108
  Motivation, 105, 121
  Negotiating for, 416
  Pagination, effect of, 109, 110
  Pay, 117, 118, 578, 606
  Problems of, 114–125, 643
  Registers, 109
  Rules, app 241–247
  Shift statistics, app 235
  Sick pay, 163
  Stand-by, 115
  Statistics, 87, 88, 89, 93, 94, 95
  Union co-operation, 544
  Union membership, 350, 356
Catering staff, 53, 316; committees, 497, 568
Chapels, 742
  Agreements, 301, 393, 419, 583; reviews of, 414, 417–8 (*see also* Agreements, House)
  Casuals, 280
  Clerical, *see* Clerical staff, Chapels
  Discipline and fines, 276–8, app 276
  Disputes procedures, 440, 448–50
  Effect on industrial relations, 18
  Effect on working relations, 313
  Facilities, 293–6, app 274, app 275, app 277
  Finance, 290–2
  Functions, 260–278, 337; administrative, 109, 110, 111, 113, fn 53, 196, 267, 270, 271–3, 275–8, 479–80, 636, 643; blow-time, 177; discipline, 474; overtime, 174; promotion, 467–8; recruitment, 460–66; work allocation, 457–9.
  History, 259
  Inter-relations, 307–313, 559, 560, 629, 648, 676, 766, 767 (*see also* Federated House Chapels)
  Journalists, *see* Journalists Chapels
  Manchester, 559–61; joint negotiations, 563, 568, 609–10; organisation, 727
  Membership, 279–285
  Negotiating practices, 152, 158, 166, 303, 413–423, 428, 440, 592, 649–652; strategy, 422–3; union control, 424–7
  Officials, 262–73; emoluments, 290, app 278; Fathers *see* Fathers of the Chapel; non-working, 293
  Organisation, 279–85, 287–92, 629, 719–22
  Pay comparisons, 423
  Pay pools, 133, fn 44
  Relations with management, 199, 480–1, 642
  Rules, 260, 261
  Sizes, app 274–275, 71
  Subscriptions, app 278
  Traditionalism, 657
  Union control, 297–303; Code of Principles, app 270–271
Check-off, 296, 377; Manchester, 561
Christelijk National Vakverbond, app 223
Circulars, 701
Circulation, app 230–231; decline, 621; effect on costs, 27, 31; effect on industrial relations, 197; Netherlands, app 222
Circulation manager, fn 130; union membership, 364

Circulation reps, 318, 404, app 240, app 300; union membership, app 284
Claims
    Co-ordination, 399–400, 408
    Extra, 440
    Procedures, 279, 299, 303, 385, 388, 399, 400, 427, 612, app 292; Manchester, 551, 555; Sweden, app 221–222
Cleaners, 53, 350, app 255
Cleaning tasks, 440
Clegg, Prof. H. A., fn 52
Clerical employees, app 240, 126
    Chapels, 274–5, 282, 286, 288
    Characteristics, 79
    Disciplinary procedures, 475
    Flexible hours, 184
    Induction, 475
    Job evaluation, 204
    Joint house committees, 686
    Manchester, 551
    New technology jobs, 63
    Pay, 159, 180–4, 725, 790
    Productivity agreement, 184
    Promotion, 473
    Recruitment, 464–5
    Union membership, 338, 346, 348, 628, app 219–220
    Work allocation, 459
Closed shop, 9, 314, 348, 593; Netherlands, app 218
Closures, 32, 363, 534, app 234
Collective bargaining, see Negotiations
Colour pay, 148, 159
Commissionaires, 53
Communauté d'Associations d'Editeurs des Journaux de la CEE, 241
Communications, 482–506, 643; of management policy, 701–4; training for, 516, 525
Competition, effect on industrial relations, 16, 31–33, 434, 668; influence of costs, 31
Composing room staff, 318
    Casual shifts, app 235
    Chapels, 271, 307, 559; Imperial, 648
    Hours of work, 167
    MGN, 60
    Manchester, 547, 551, 552, 559, 566
    Pay, 146–50, 152, 212, 547, 727, app 249
    Piecework, 643
    Recruitment, 463
    Work allocation, 457
Composition methods, 42–47; photocomposition, see Photocomposition
Compositors, for 114, 463, app 253
Computerised systems, 53, 62, 63–9, 535, app 225, app 229
Confederation of British Industry, 241
Confederation of Health Services Employees, 316
Conciliation, 444, 456; Government service, 447
Consultation, 499–506, 643, 671, 668, 755, app 305, app 306
    Committees, 485–6, 491, 495–7, 568
    Councils, 491
    In-house, 484–506
    Informal, 482–4
    Journalists, 618–9
    National, 483

Netherlands, app 224
Continuity shift, *see* Dog watch
Contract printing, fn 178 (*see also* Production: Shared facilities)
Co-operative Press Ltd, app 309
Co-operative Wholesale Society, 333
Copyholders, app 254, app 256, app 260, app 261, app 262
Copyreaders, 47, 68, 130, 152, 155, 159, app 248, app 250, app 251
Copytakers, 551
Cost of living pay, 136, 403, fn 14, app 292, 293
Costs, 27, 31, 210–11, 564, app 217; analysis, app 266; reduction, 206–9
Court of Inquiry (1967), app 309
Cowdray, Lord, app 230
Craft unions, 319–21, 331–3, 645, app 281
Craft differentials, fn 114
Craft status, 333
Cushion Trust Ltd, app 231
Custom and practice, 168–70
Cut and paste, 65

Daily Dispatch, fn 12
Daily Express, fn 10, 116, 485, 609, app 230; Manchester, 534
Daily Mail, fn 10, app 230; Manchester, 534, 554, 556
Daily Mail and General Trust Ltd, app 230
Daily Mirror, fn 10, fn 51, 604, 610, app 230; Manchester, 534, 550, 551, fn 178
Daily Sketch, fn 10, fn 12, 397, 621
Daily Telegraph, app 230; colour supplement, 32; Manchester, 70, fn 178, 534, 550, 551, 553, 565; new technology, 63, 66, 537, 565, 570; ownership, 25; profitability, fn 10; shared facilities, 35, 57
Daily Telegraph Ltd, app 230
Day shift, 46, app 254
Death benefit, 290
Decasualisation (*see under* Casuals)
Demarcation, 644–5, 739
    Disputes, 333–4, fn 178; procedures, 717, 764
    Effect of new technology, 58–9, 64–5, 67–9, 72–3
    Effect on production, 643
    Machine room, 159, fn 53
    Union attitudes, 78
Demonstrators, 332
Department of Employment conciliation services, 447
Departmental heads, 463, 469, 567
Depot man, fn 130
Deutsche Angestellten-Gewerkschaft, app 227
Deutsche Journalisten-verband, app 227
Devlin, Lord, 395
Differentials, 132, 150–9, 184, 186, 398, 406, 408, 415, 421, 643, 674, 20.5; craft, fn 114; disputes, app 296; inter-office, 426; inter-union, fn 117; journalists, 599; Manchester, 546; Sweden, app 222
Disciplinary procedures, 158, 474–6; union, 276–8, app 276
Disclosure of information, 485, 486, 490, 494, 498–9, 501, 619, 672, 678–81, 753–5; Code of Practice, 678, 681; Germany, app 218; Netherlands, app 225–6; Sweden, app 218, 222
Dismissal, 434, 475–6
Disputes, 15, 642–3
    Daily Telegraph, 157

    Demarcation, 717
    Economic effects, 16
    Industrial action, *see* Industrial action
    Inter-union, 385–6, 717
    Manchester, 565–6
    Potential, 41
    Statistics, 435–441, 565–6
    Sunday People (Manchester–555)
    Sweden, app 9
    Trends, 624
  Disputes procedures, 264, 623, 682–4, 695–7, 784–787, app 224, app 228–229
    Branch, 299–300
    Communications, 499
    Committees, 443–4
    Domestic procedures, 448–50, 451–6, 601
    Journalists, 601, 613–7
    Liaison procedure, 431
    Manchester, 238, 567
    National procedures, 227, 229, 232, 438, 442–7, 455–6
    Table of procedures, app 298–300
    Time limits, 126, 446–7
  Distribution, 217, 221, 416, app 223, app 226
  Distribution staff, 366, app 219
  Dog watch, 46
  Double-set working, 173, fn 58
  Drivers, 159, 318, 366, fn 130, app 255, app 262; assistants, fn 130
  Drunkenness, 476
  Dual membership, 341
  Duty free quota, 224

Economic situation, 27, 200; effect on unions, for 114 (*see also* Financial situation (Publishers))
Economic Intelligence Unit, survey, 180, 190, 396, app 306–307
Edinburgh Press and Machinemen's Society, app 280
Edition shift, 46
Editorial control, 641
Editorial input, 58, 64
Editorial staff (*see also* Journalists)
    Characteristics, 79
    Definition, 573
    Employment, app 303
    Management, 202, 591–3
    New technology, 75
    Organisation, app 302
    Pay costs, 208, app 266
    Union membership, 593
    Work allocation, 459
Editors, 573, app 302, app 303; assistants, 584; negotiating role, 592; pay, 586
Electrical, Electronic, Telecommunications and Plumbing Union, 388
    AUEW relationships, 392
    Apprenticeship schemes, 370
    Branch structure, 370
    Chapels, 282, app 68, app 69, app 277
    Fleet Street Branch, 370
    Agreement review periods, app 294

Job entry qualifications, 100
MGN agreement, 411
Manchester Press Branch, 370
Membership, app 284
NPA negotiations, 398, app 292
Occupations, 53, 199, 316
Organisation, app 291
Pay, 401, app 249
Electrical engineers, 370
Electricians: apprentices, 101; assistants, app 248, app 250, app 255, app 262; Manchester, 563; overtime, 174; pay, 130, 150, 157, app 248, app 250, app 255, app 256, app 260–262; union membership, 316, 370
Electronics engineers, 357
Electrotypers, 93, 356
Empire News, 13
Employers' Associations, 216, 240–41 (*see also* Newspaper Publishers' Association
Employers' Joint Liaison Committee, 241
Employment figures, 78, app 232–233 (*see also under* Manning)
Employment and Training Act 1973, 511–12
Employment Protection Act, 678, 681, 707, 753
Engineers, 53, 68; assistants, 152, 350, app 248, app 250; chapels, 281, 563; dispute, 233; overtime, 174; pay, 150, 152, 157, app 248, app 250, app 255, app 256, app 260–262; union membership, 316, 350, 371
Engravers, 337
Estimators, 357
Etchers, 48, 159
European Economic Community, 241
Evening Citizen, 32
Evening News, fn 10, app 230
Evening newspapers, 26, 29, 132, 375, app 254, app 255
Evening Standard, 32, fn 10, 116, 485, app 230
Examinations, readers, 159, fn 54
Expenses, 590
Extra pay (*see under* Pay)

Facsimile, 70, fn 24, 537
Fathers of the Chapel, 94, 95, 107, 110–11, 262, 264–8 278, 361, 453–4, 469–70, 486, 494–5, 498, 501, 503–4, app 270, app 272–273, app 307-308
 Elections, 265
 Functions, 264, 267–8, 271, 273; administrative, 480; branch, 297; disciplinary, 476
 Manchester, 561
 Training, 488, 510, 514, 524–6, 532, 707
 Salaries, app 278
Federated House Chapels, 304–6, 307–10, 313, 493–4, 570, 673–4; Manchester, 560
Federation International d'Editeurs des Journaux, 240
Finance courses, 516
Financial control, *see* Budgetary control
Financial reporting, 210–11
Financial situation (Publishers), 621–22, 658, app 308
Financial Times, 35, app 230
 Consultation, 492
 Development plan, 55
 Joint supervisory board, 492
 New technology, 58, 63, 66, 570; joint organisation proposals, 69, 72, 715, app 314
 Ownership, 25

Profitability, fn 10
Shared facilities, 57
Financial Times Ltd, app 230
Fines, *see* Chapels: Discipline
Finishers, 48, 159
Firemen, 53
Flyhands, 50, 51, fn 53, 158
Flat-bed houses, 371
Foundry workers, 49, 173, 176, 463, app 26, app 249
Freelance agencies, 576
Freelance journalists (*see under* Journalists)
Fringe benefits, 426, 564, 588–90
Full page composition, 59

General and Municipal Workers Union, 53, 316
General managers, 189
Germany, West, app 216, app 217, app 226–229
    Costs, app 14
    Distribution and circulation, app 226
    Disputes procedures, app 228–229
    Employers' Associations, app 218, app 227
    Legislation, app 226–227
    Negotiating procedures, app 22–229
    Technological change, app 217, app 218, app 229
    Trade Unions, app 218, app 226–229
    Works councils, app 226–228
Ghosting, fn 38
Glasgow Typographic Society, app 280
Go-slows, 433
Government Actuary, 164–5
Government loans, 55
Grafiska Fackforbundet, app 219, app 220
Grants, chapel, 261
Graphic Reproduction Federation, for 124
Graphische Bond NKV, app 223, app 224
Grass hands, 93
Gravure workers, 337
Grievance procedure, 448, 614
Guardian, 25, 34–6, fn 10, app 230; Manchester, 70, 534, 535, 554, 556, 560; new technology, 58, 535; shared facilities, fn 178

Haley, Sir William, 252, fn 77
Harmsworth family, app 230
Head printer, 457
Health and safety, 388; committees, 496, 568; training, 516, 529
Heat engineers, 316
HMSO, 360
Holiday framehands, 463
Holidays, 406; annual, 179; casual cover, 125, 574; journalists, 574, 589; negotiations, 564; overseers, 187; public, 589; rotas, 109, 457
Hot metal composition, 42, 65
Hours of work, 406; agreements, 589; blow-time, *see* blow system; flexible, 589

negotiations, 564;
production staff, 166–74;
shorter, 408, 425, 589
House journals, 490, 495, 701

Imperial chapels, 152, 263–4, 284, 307, 420
Imperial Fathers of the Chapel, 264, 268, 309; functions, 264, 271, 648; salaries, app 278
Incomes policy, 425, 427
Induction training, 475, 512, 529; managerial, 531
Industrial action, 428, 453
    Consequences, 433, 434
    Journalists, 613
    NUJ/IPC, 601
    Statistics, 435–8, app 295–297; Manchester, 565
    Stoppages, *see* Stoppages
    Union regulations, 303
    Unofficial, 303
    Warning periods, 437, app 297
Industrial Courts Act, app 309
Industrial development, 395
Industrial relations; characteristics, 13–14; functions, app 265; managers of, 200–203, 549, 625, app 267; policies, 192, 214, 246, 251; staff, app 267; training, 507–33
Industriegewerkschaft Druck und Papier, app 227, app 227, app 228
Inflation, *see* Economic situation
Information services, in-house, 489–90, 495
Injury schemes, 160, 161
Institute of Journalists, 315
    London District, 380; membership, app 284
    Manchester District membership, app 284
    Membership, 573, app 283, app 284
    NUJ relationship, 341, 730, 795–796, app 282
    National agreements, 404
    Negotiating rights, 593
    Organisation, 380, app 290
Institute of Supervisory Management, 517
International Graphical Federation, 382
International organisations, 382
International Publishing Corp., 25, 333, 601–4 (*see also* Mirror Group)
Interviewing, 470; training, 525

Job entry restrictions, 542
Job evaluation, 182–3, 204, 724–5, 790
Job grading, 158–9, 584–7
Job satisfaction clause, 572, fn 160
Jobbers, 95, 174
Joint Board for the National Newspaper Industry, 395–6, 630, app 306
Joint house committees, 674–6, 685–6, 689–90, 693, 697, 722, 748, 789, 782, 786–7, 789
Joint Pressroom Agreement, fn 50, fn 51, 675
Joint Standing Committee, 227, 394, 478, 519, 570, 630–1, 646, 660, 674, 687–90, 695–6, 711, 717, 768–9, 785–6, 789; constitution, app 310–311, demarcation machinery, 717; members of, app 310; new technology, 55, 57; Training, Education and Counselling Sub-Committee, 519
Joint supervisory board, 492

Journalists, 9, 570–619, 729–33, 795–9
    Apprenticeship, 580
    Casuals, 96, 574, 575, 577, 578, 579, 606
    Chapels, 583, 594
    Consultation procedures, 618–9
    Disputes, 572, 613–7; IPC, 601–4; procedures, 601
    Employment figures, app 303
    Freelance, 375, 574, 576, 578
    Germany, app 226–7, app 227
    House agreements, 578, 588–90, 593, 600, 601, 605, 607
    House negotiations, 609–12, fn 114
    Job entry rules, 580–83
    Job grading, 584–7, 601
    Job satisfaction, 572, fn 160
    Manchester, 551
    Merit payment, 600
    National agreements, 404, 596–600, 602–6
    Negotiations procedures, 592, 596–9, 609–12
    Netherlands, app 224
    Nightworkers, 589
    Organisation, app 302
    Pay and conditions, 243, 584–90, 581; differentials, 599, 601; negotiations, 596–9, 601–5, 609–12; structure, 733
    Recruitment, 581–2
    Star, 586, 600
    Sweden, app 222
    Training, 580
    Unemployed, 575
    Union membership, 329, 374, 375, 583, 593, app 283–4; Sweden, app 219–220

Koninklijk Nederlands Verband Drukkerijem, app 223

Labour costs, 564
Labour party proposals, 663
Labour Research Department, fn 12
Lay-off agreements, 434
Law Courts journalists, 375
Legislation, app 3; training for, 525–6, 528, 532–3
Library staff, 551
Linotype assistants, 44, 45, app 248, app 250, app 254
Linotype engineers, 152, 316
Linotype keyboard, 90 key, 60
Linotype operators, 44, 45, 60, 65; casual, 93; chapels, 263, 307; pay, 130, 131, 132, app 248, app 250; piecework, 146
Lithographic equipment and methods, 40, 369
Lithographic staff, 337, 368
Local government staff, 378
London evening papers, 29, fn 130, 375
London Joint Union Committee, 718, 721, 732, 765, 766, 798
London Piece Scale, 146–7, 212, 723
London Master Printers' Association, 216
London Society of Compositors, 216, 320, app 279, app 281
London Society of Machine Rulers, app 280
London Typographical Society, 320, 321, app 282, app 298, app 301

Machine assistants, 50, fn 53; casual, 94, pay, 150–1, 158, app 248, app 250
Machine managers, 68, 50, 51, fn 65; casual, 356; disputes procedure, app 2 8; pay, 130 152,156, app 248, app 250, app 251, app 253, app 256, app 260–262; union membership, 317, Machine minders, casual, 93, pay 151, 159 union membership, fn 96
Machine operators (publishing), 159
Machine room staff, 50, 51
   Blow-time, 176
   Casual, 87, 93, 94, 117, 356, app 235
   Chapels' 121, 282, 307, 312, 563
   Manning agreements, 468
   Overtime, 172
   Pay: agreements, 402 differentials, 152, 158, fn 127; figures, app 249, app 243
   Recruitment, 463
   Replacement agreements, 358
   Rest periods, 178
   Union membership, 353
Magazine hands, 50, fn 53, 158, app 254
Magnesium platemaking, 535, 537
Maintenance staff, 53, 68, 316, 401, 404, app 249
Management:
   Communications, 214–5
   Control, 640–1
   Negotiations strategies, 421
   Organisation, 188–215, 548–57, 591–2, app 264, app 307
   Policy, 699–707, 741, 744, 752
   Relations with chapel, 642
   Sanctions, 434
   Sectionalism, 653–5
Management consultants, 625
Managers, 126, app 240
   Associations, 187, 289
   Chapels, 288
   Industrial relations: awareness, 654 functions, 639, app 265; training, 194, 507–523, 531–3, 705–6, 750–752
   Joint house committees, 685
   Length of service, app 267
   Pay, 185–7, app 266
   Promotion, 467
   Recruitment, 472
   Union membership, 288, 316, 357, 370, 716, 763
Managing editor, 592
Manchester, 8, 34, 534–569, 726–8, 791–794
   Casuals, fn 34, 539–44, 562, 726
   Chapels, organisation of, 727
   Disputes, 445, 565–7, 601
   Journalist employment figures, app 303
   Management organisation, 548–557
   Negotiation procedures, 562–568, 728, 794
   Recruitment, 470
   Technological change, 70, 535–7, 565
   Terms and conditions, 545–7, 562
   Trade union organisation, 318, 558–61, 727; branches, 358, 359, 366, 370, 378, 563; membership, 329
Manchester and Salford Trades Council, app 279
Manchester Evening News, 353, 534, 554, 556, 560, app 2 30; new technology, 535
Manchester Graphical Society (*see under* National Graphical Association)

Manning levels, 12, 657, 665–6, 738, app 306, app 307–308; agreements, 108, 139, 411, 468; NPA survey, 227; reductions, 116, 124, 125, 139, 142, 158, 397, 406, 412, 478
Manpower Services Commission, 511
Manufacturing industries pay comparisons, 137
Marketing staff, 223, 348
Maternity leave, 588, 590
Meetings, unauthorised, 434, 436, app 296
Merit payments, 159, 182, 183, 585, 600, 733, 799
Messengers, 53
Method study, 142, 143, fn 48, 184
Mirror Group Newspapers, 3, 6, 7, 218, app 231
   Chapels, 312
   Collective agreements, 411
   Consultation procedures, 488–91
   Disputes, 243, 447
   Manchester, 70, 534, 551, 553; collective agreement, 562
   NGA agreement, 411
   NPA relationships, 242–4, 250–4, 562, 626, 653, 688, 709
   NUJ agreement, 610
   Negotiations, 411–412, 692; joint union, 421; procedures, 673
   New technology, 58–61, 65–6, 537, 565
   Ownership, 25
   Pay differentials, fn 51; rates, 411
   Shared facilities, 57, 60
   Training, 488, 522, 580
Mirror Group News, 490
Misconduct, 277–8, 476
Monotype casters, 33, 318, 334, app 254
Monotype Casters and Typefounders Society, 321, app 282
Morning Advertiser, 7, 218, 484, 631; new technology, 58, app 309; ownership, 25; production staff, fn 29
Morning Star, 6, 7, 631, app 231; communications, 484; negotiations, 410; production staff, fn 29
Morning Star Co-operative Society Ltd, 218
Moulding Department, 49
Murdoch, K R, app 231

National Amalgamated Society of Printers, Warehousemen and Cutters, app 280
National Association of Journalists, 341
National Board for Prices and Incomes, 584, 599, 600, 673, app 308–309
National Council for the Training of Journalists, 580
National Examination Board in Supervisory Studies, 516
National Graphical Association, 315
   Amalgamations, 335, 633, app 282
   Branch organisation, 297, 354–8
   Call books, 110
   Casuals, 87, 93, 112, 280, 356, app 241–244
   Chapels, 260, 263, 264, 268, 279–80, 282, 284, 307, 312, app 274, 275, 277; casuals, 356
   Imperial, 420
   Demarcation disputes, 333, 334
   Entry conditions, 356
   Examinations, 159, fn 54
   Executives, Technicians and Overseers Section, 357
   History, 134, 321, 322, app 279
   House agreements, app 294

Imperial Father of the Chapel, 264
Job entry conditions, 98
London Region, 40, 312, 328, 389, fn 117, 463, 720; membership, app 283; organisation, 354–6, app 291; News Department, 343, 354–5; overtime, 174; redundancies, app 234; unemployment, fn 183
London Typographical Society, *see* London Typographical Society
MGN agreement
Machine managers section, app 298
Manchester Graphical Society, 318, 358, app 279–80; casuals, 541, 544; joint negotiations, 563; membership, 329, app 284; News Compositors Consultative Committee, 358; pay agreements, 547; pay dispute, fn 182; stoppages, 565
Membership, 332, 362, 713, app 283–4
NATSOPA negotiations, 358, 644
NPA negotiations, 398, app 88
National structure, 335, 337, app 285, app 290
New Technology, 72, 634
Occupations, 43–5, 47, 49, 50, 53, 63, 65, 68, fn 53, 199, 317–8, 471
Overtime rules, 174
Pay: differentials, 150-2, 159; figures, app 249, app 251
Press Telegraphists Section, app 298
Readers Section, app 298
SOGAT, relations with, 362, 391, fn 105
SLADE agreements, 67
Stereotypers Section, app 298
Stoppages regulations, 303
TUC affiliation, fn 112
Trade groups: boards, 297, 335, app 285; committees, app 291; Letterpress, 335; News, 355
Training, Educational and Research Committee, 56, 328, 524
Training programme, 56, 524–6
Unemployed, 541, app 234
National Newspaper Industry, fn 12, app 308
National Newspaper Steering Group, 397, 630
National Press Finance Corporation, 663
National Printing Corporation, 663
National Society of Electrotypers and Stereotypers, 322, app 282, app 283
National Society of Operative Printers and Assistants, app 282
National Society of Operative Printers, Graphical and Media Personnel, 315, 321, 323, 324, 325, app 310
Amalgamations, 633, 713, app 282
Branch structure, 308, 345–53
Calls offices, 89, 90, 110, 111, 113, 239, 275, 349, 461, 540, app 236
Casuals, 87, 91, 94, 112, 117, 118, 125, fn 38, fn 39, 280, 350, app 236, app 237, app 238–240, app 244–245
Chapels, 260, 263, 268, 278, 279, 280, 282, 283, 288, 293, 296, 312; Code of Principles, app 270–1; federated house, 308; negotiations, 425; officials, 265, 266, 270; statistics, app 270–1; federated house, 308; negotiations, 425; officials, 265, 266, 270; statistics, app 274–5, app 277
Disciplinary policy, 474
Disputes, 456; demarcation, 333; procedures, fn 126, 444, app 289–299; regulations, 303; federations, 420
Finances, fn 100
General Secretary, fn 99, 388
History, app 279–281
House agreement review periods, app 294

Job entry qualifications, 99
Joint arbitration committee, app 298–300
London Clerical Branch, 275, 345, 346–8, 349, 473; calls office, 464; job recruitment, 464–5; NPA negotiations, fn 112
London Machine Branch, 283, 312, 345, 349, 350, app 288, app 290; calls office, 111, 119; casuals, 89, 94, app 245; job entry qualifications, 99; membership, app 284; redundancies, app 234; unemployed, 15
Manchester Branch; casuals, 539, 540, 541, 542–4; Central Committee, 353, 540; chapels, 559; joint negotiations, 563; membership, 329, app 78; structure, 352–3
Membership figures, app 283–284
National Executive, 444
NGA agreements, 358
NPA agreements, 139
Occupations, fn 53, 43, 44, 47, 50, 53, 63, 68, 126, fn 84, 317, 318, 338
Officials, 351
Organisation, 338, app 288, app 290
Overseers, 471
Overtime rules, 174
Pay: differentials, 151, 152, fn 52, 159; figures, app 249, app 251
Recruitment, 461
RIRMA, 94, 325, 330, 345, app 288, 290; calls office, 113; chapels, fn 84, 263, 281, 293, 300; claims, 405; membership, app 284; occupations, 350, fn 84; pay figures, app 248, app 250
SOGAT merger, 713
Sign and Display Section merger, 350
Stoppages regulations, 303
TA and E, 316, 345, 347
Training activities, 528
National Typographical Union, app 279
National Union of Bookbinders and Machine Rulers, app 280
National Union of Journalists, 315, 795–8, app 310
    Amalgamations, 578–9
    Branch structure, 374–9, 595
    Central London 4, app 284
    Chapels, 260, 282, 376, 292, 295, 301, 559, 577, 579, 592, 594, 607–12, 731, 795, 797, app 274, app 275, app 277, app 304
    Fathers, 267, 374; federated editorial, 310; joint negotiations, 570
    Claims procedure, 612
    Disputes procedure, 456
    Finance, 377
    Freelance Branch, 329, 357, 577, 578, app 284
    General Secretary, 388
    IOJ, relationship, 341, 730, 795–6, app 282
    IPC agreement, 601–4
    Industrial action, 613
    Industrial councils, 339, 379, app 289
    Inner London Area Council, 377
    London Central Branch, 330, 374, 595
    London Evening Papers Branch, app 284
    London News Agency Branch, 374
    London No. 1 Branch, 375, 595
    MGN dispute, 243
    Manchester Branch, 378, 595; membership, app 284; stoppages, 565
    Membership, 327, 329, 339, 573, 593, app 283–4
    NPA agreement, 602; memorandum, 580–3; working parties, 598–9, 606
    National agreements, 404

National Executive Committee, 339, 612
National structure, 339–41, 379, app 289–290
Negotiations; house, 376, 592, 607, 609–12; national, 578
Occupations, 63, 573, 576
Pay; agreements, 584–87; rates, 581, 596–8, 602–6
Relations with other unions, 392, 570, 732, 20.61
Technological change, 75, 76
Wages Committed, 301

National Union of Paper Mill Workers, app 280
National Union of Press Telegraphists, 322, app 279, app 282
National Union of Printers, Bookbinders and Paper Workers, 285, 321, 323, 336, 338, fn 178; formation, app 280–1
National Union of Printers, Bookbinders, Machine Rulers and Paper Workers, app 280
National Union of Printing, Bookbinding and Paperworkers, app 280
National Union of Sheetmetal Workers, Coppersmiths, Heating and Domestic Engineers, 53, 316

Nationalisation, 663
Natural wastage, 411, 412
Nederlandse Christelijke Graphische Bedriftsbond, app 223, app 224
Nederlandse Dagbladbers, app 223, app 224
Nederlandse Vereniging van Journalisten, app 224
Nederlans Katholick Vakverbond, app 223
Nederlans Verbond van Vakvereinigen, app 223
Negotiations: (*see also under* subject)
    Chapel: *see* Chapel: Negotiating procedures
    Collective, 671
    Departmental, 674–7, 781–3
    House, 376, fn 114, 411–427, 564, 592, 607, 609–12, 648, 699, 671, 679, 742; fragmentation, 649–52; Germany, app 228; procedures, 673–86, 741, 743, 774–6, Sweden, app 221
    Joint, 385, 390, 394–401, 671, 674
    Management strategies, 421
    National, 255–7, 394–409, 578, 596–9, 601–7; procedures, 687–698, 770–3, Germany, app 228; Netherlands, app 224–5; Sweden, app 220–1; table of, app 292–3
    Overseers role, 197
    Senior management involvement, 203
    Union sanctions, 428
Netherlands, app 216, app 217, app 222–6
    Advertisements, app 217
    Closed shop, app 218
    Costs, app 217
    Disclosure, app 225
    Disputes procedure, app 224
    Employers' associations, app 218, app 219, app 223–4
    Joint procedures, app 224
    Journalists, app 224
    Negotiating procedures, app 224–5
    Newspaper industry organisation, app 222–3
    Pay structure, app 225
    Redundancy procedure, app 226
    Technological change, app 217–8, app 225–6
    Trade unions, app 223, app 224
News agencies, 579; journalists, 374
News and pictures department, 43

News Chronicle, fn 12
News Group Newspapers, 58, 159, fn 53, 312, 610, app 231; agreements, 675
News International Ltd, 25, app 231
News of the World, fn 10, fn 16, fn 53, 317, 539, app 231; Manchester, 534, 539, 550, fn 178
News room staff, app 249
Newspaper Publishers' Association, 6, 23, 216–258, 626, 756–9, app 306, app 307, app 309
  Advertising Executive, 222
  Agreements, 390, 393, 402 ,403; blow-time, 175; casuals' pay, fn 40; disputes, 442–7; hours, 167; on negotiations, 139; overtime, fn 58, pay (*see under* Pay)
  Circulation Managers' Committee, 217, 221
  Claims procedures, 229; house, 427
  Commercial functions, 253
  Council, 220, 231, 233, 248, 444, 445
  Criticisms, 708
  Director, app 310
  Disputes procedures, 227, 232, 455–6, 615–7
  Effectiveness, 245–58
  Executive Committee, 220, 231, 248, 251, app 268
  Finance, 219
  Formation, 216–7
  Industrial Relations Department and Executive, 226–231, 232, 245–9, 711, app 271
  Joint Copy Committee, 222
  Joint NUJ Memorandum 377, 580–3
  London Labour Committee, 226–7, 230, 245, 711, app 271
  London News Committee, 634
  London Region, fn 114
  Manchester, 234; agreements, 562; calls office, 540; disputes procedure, 567; Managers' Committee, 234–9, 445
  Marketing and External Relations Department, 223
  Membership, 218
  NUJ agreements, 580–3, 602; working party 598–9, 606
  Negotiations: policy, 406, 407; procedures, 385, 400, 578, app 292–3; with AUEW, 398; with EETPU, 398; with NATSOPA, fn 112; with NGA, 398
  Objectives, 217
  Organisation, 218–225, 226–239, 708–11, 758–9, app 270–1; staffing, app 269
  Pay rates (*see under* Pay)
  Pay Survey, 129–33
  Relations with MGN, 242–4, 250–4, 658, 709
  Relations with NATSOPA, 348
  Relations with SOGAT, 361
  Strategy Group, 246
  Trade union views, 255–8
  Training role, 515–9, 705; Committee, 204, 519; Department, 225, app 268
Newspaper Society, 241, 708; app 309
Newsprint costs, 27, 206; rationing, 33
Night work, 406, app 255
Non-automatic replacement, 411, 412, 692
Non-co-operation, 433–4
Northern Typographical Union, app 279
Northprint, 534, 535, 554, 565, 727
Notice periods, 406; protective, 434
Nursing staff, 316

Observer, 16, 25, 36, app 231; colour supplement, 32; consultative procedures, 494; financial crisis, 494; profitability, fn 10; owner, app 310; relocation, 34; staff reductions, 32, 93; technological change, 58
Oilers, 50, fn 53; pay, 158, app 254
Original input system, 62, 63–9
Original Society of Papermakers, app 282
Overseers, 126, 628, 642, app 242
    Associations, 289
    Definition, fn 65
    Fringe benefits, 187
    Functions, 210–11, 479, 486, 495; industrial relations, 196–199, 416, 450, 557, 567 685
    Junior, 469, 481
    Manchester, 557, 567
    Pay, 185, 187
    Recruitment, 469, 471–2
    Relations with chapels, 480–1
    Training, 509–510, 515–7, 706, 751–2
    Union membership, 287, 357, 370, 20.29
Overtime, 145
    Administration, 271, 457
    Extent of, 172
    Guaranteed, 173
    Limitation, 174; agreement, 139, fn 58, 625
    Manchester, 546
    Pay, 134, 148, 169–172, 406, 416; examples, app 251

PA Management Consultants Ltd, 188, app 307
Page make-up, electronic, 65
Page size, 33
Pagination; effect on casual work, 108, 109, 110; effect on pay, 136, 145, 159, 546, app 45; effect on overtime, 173
Painters, 53, 316
Paper industry, 324
Papermould and Dandy Roll Society, app 282
Part-time staff, 83–5, app 235
Pattern Card Makers' Society, app 282
Pattern plates, 59, 61, 66–7
Pay, 657, app 307
    Average weekly, 42–4, 49–54
    Basic rates 770–1; joint assessment, 723–5; MGN rates, 411; NPA rates, 134–7, 155–7, 171, 183, 249, 393, 398, 402, 403, 578, 584, 596–8, 691–4, app 251–5, app 292–3
    Comparisons, 679, app 260–2; disclosure, 789; house, 131–3; inter-chapel, 423; joint, 723–5; with manufacturing, app 257–9
    Components, 134–8, app 251
    Costs, 207–8, app 266
    Differentials: *see* Differentials
    Disclosure, 498
    Disputes, app 276
    Effect of new technology, 149
    Effect of pagination, 136, 145, 159, 546, app 251
    Effect on job entry controls, 97
    Extra, 148, 271, 414, 416, 440, app 251; Manchester, 546–7, 564, 584
    Growth rates, 136–8, app 257–9
    Incremental, 584–7

Indices, app 257–259
National negotiations (*see also* Negotiations), 228, 393, 691–4, 770, app 224–5
Pools, 133, fn 44, 139, 142
Rationalisation, 425, 472
Records, 204
Relative movements, 17
Restraint, 398
Survey, 227
Pearson and Son, 3, app 230
Pearson Longman, 25, app 230
Pensions, 74, 103, app 305; joint committees, 497; negotiations, 406; overseers, 187; production workers, 164–5; working party, 56, 631
People's Press Printing Society, fn 10, app 231
Periodicals publishing, 364
Permit holders, 94
Perscombinatie, app 223
Personnel Department; 204–5; staff service, app 267
Personnel Director, 486
Personnel records, 204
Photocomposition, 20–1, 29, 535–6, 570, 634, 638, 643, 659; dispute, 565; systems, 58–62, 363
Photo-engraving staff, 40, fn 106, 337, 368
Photographers, 573
Photopolymer plates, 66–7
Photoprinters, 43, app 262
Photo-reproduction equipment, 369
Phototechnicians, 350, app 248, app 250
Physical conditions, 416, 440, app 296
Piece case hands, 45, 132, 146, 263, 307, app 248, app 250
Piecework, 140, 146–9, 547, 643; budgetary control, 212; rates, fn 57; trackers, 212
Planographic process, 29
Plate-founding, 334
Platen Machine Minders' Society, app 280
Popular newspapers, 82, 88, app 232, app 240, app 250; profitability, 26, 28, 29
Press Council, 341
Press telegraphists, *see* Telegraphists
Printed waste hand, fn 53
Printers on metal, 48, 159
Printing and Kindred Trades Federation, 328, fn 94, 342, 383–8, 399, 400, app 305; Administrative Council, 386; disputes machinery, 717; negotiations, 399–401, app 292; summer schools, 527; survey, fn 12
Printing and Publishing Industry Training Board, 23, 204, 225, 511–14, 580, 705
Printing facilities, shared, 11, 35, 36
Printing Labourers' Union, app 279
Printing Machine Managers' Trade Society, 320, app 279, app 282
Process department, 48; MGN, 61; manager, fn 65; overseers, 471
Process employees: casual shifts, app 26; chapels, 311; differentials 152, 156, 159; disputes procedures, app 298–9; pay figures, app 248–50, app 254, app 256, app 260–2; payagreements, 402; redundancies, 363; unemployment, 368; union membership, 367
Process operators, 48
Process provers, *see* Proof pullers
Product market, 16, 17, 657, 658
Production: cycle, 16; disruption, 433–4; integration, 554; loss, 436, 565; management, 193–5, 203, 549, 639, app 264; output control, 641; shared facilities, 11, 35, 36; union control, 13

Production employees, 9, 79, fn 27, 82–5
　Annual holiday, 179
　Age problems, 102–3
　Casual, 86–96
　Chapels, 270, 271, 290, 294
　Dismissal, 476
　Germany, app 228
　Hours of work, 166–74
　Manchester, 538–44, 551
　Manning levels, 108
　Part-time, 83–5, app 235
　Pay, app 306; costs, 207, 209, app 266; figures, app 248–55; patterns, 129–159; Sweden, app 221
　Pensions, 164–5
　Promotion, 467–72
　Recruitment, 460, 461
　Shift-work, 166–78
　Sick benefit, 160–3
　Statistics, 82, 87
　Unions: membership, 318, 327; Sweden, app 219
Production Director, 549
Production managers, 193–5, 203
Production supervisors, 196
Productivity, app 308; agreements, 140, 141, 184, 649; bargaining, 415, fn 114, 20.7; pay, 134, app 251
Profitability, 26, 28, 30, 206, app 308
Promotion, 467–73, 510, fn 130; barrier, 159; temporary, 468, 481
Proof pullers, 45, 48; pay, 152, 159, app 248, app 250, app 254; union membership, 318, 325, 362, fn 96
Proprietors, influence on industrial relations, 190, 191, 192, 252, app 305
Provincial newspaper industry compared, 3–5; technology, 72, 77
Public relations staff, 378
Publicity artists, 311, 367, 404
Publishing department staff, 52
　Blow-time, 176, 177
　Casual, 87, 117, 539, app 235
　Chapels, 563
　Entry age, 103
　Manchester, 539, 563
　Manning agreements, 468
　Pay, 130, 150; agreements, 402; differentials, 157, 159; figures, app 248–51, app 256 app 60–61
　Recruitment, 461
　Union membership, 318, 338, 353

Quality newspapers: casual staff, 88; costs, 21; employment figures, app 232, app 240; pay figures, app 250; profitability, 26, 28
QWERTY, 46, 60

Radio Times, 350
Readers, 47
　Assistants, fn 52
　Casuals, 93, 94
　Chapels, 263, 307

Disputes procedures, app 298
Examinations, 159, fn 54
Pay, 130, 152, app 248, app 250–1, app 256, app 260–2; agreements, 402; differentials, fn 52, 155, 156, 157, 159
Union membership, 353
Reading room staff, 152, 159, 563, app 235, app 249
Recruitment, 204, 580–3, 643; joint activities, 392
Red toppers, 94, 110
Redundancy, 40, fn 97, 363, app 234; compensation, app 305; negotiations, 494; new technology agreement, 56; procedures, 477–8, app 226; voluntary, 56, 74, fn 38, 477, 631
Reed International, 25, app 231
Reel supply hand, fn 53
Relations at Work, 514
Relocations, 32, 34, 36, 37
Replacement agreements, 358
Reporters, 573, app 265, app 269
Researchers, 573; union membership, 328, 332
Rest periods, 176, 178
Restrictive practices, 665
Retail prices, 621
Retirement, early, 477
Retouchers, 159
Reveille, 7, 65, app 231
Revenue forecasts, 209
Revisers, 47, 130, 152, 155, 159, 350, 358, app 248, app 250, app 254
Revisers, Ink and Roller Makers Auxiliaries, *see under* National Society of Operative Printers, Graphical and Media Personnel
Rotary letterpress, 358
Round boys, fn 130
Royal Commission on the Press, (1947–9), app 305; (1961–2), 16, 394, 395, app 305–6; (1976) Interim Report, 14, fn 10, 54, 55, 81; (1976) Labour Survey, 23, fn 43
Ruskin College, 526

Sabbaticals, 588, 590
Sabotage, 433
Safety, *see* Health and safety
Saltsjobaden Agreement, app 220
Saturday night work, 83–8, 90, 95, fn 35, 122, 406; Manchester, 539–41, 543; pay rates, 159
Scotland: unions, 326
Scott family
Scottish Daily Express, 32, 34, 485, 534
Scottish Daily Newspaper Society, 241
Scottish Daily Record, 604
Scottish Graphical Association, 326, 331, 336, 388, fn 99
Scottish Newspaper Publishers Association, 241
Scottish Sunday Express, 534
Scottish Typographical Association, app 276
Scottish (Typo) Graphical Society, app 282
Secretarial staff, 126, app 240
Sectionalism, 644–56, 672, 741
Service increments, 183, 584, 587
Shared production facilities, 11, 35, 36

Shift work, 46, 83–5, 89, 166–78, 406; limitation, 40; Manchester, 539; pay, app 221, app 251, app 255; rotas, 457
Shorter working week (*see under* Hours)
Sickness pay, 406; administration, 109; chapel role, 261, 290; joint committees, 497; overseers, 187; schemes, 160–3, 261
Sign and Display Trades Union, 350, app 282, app 283
Sisson Keith, fn 6
Skilled status, 333
Slip editions, 148
Society of Graphical and Allied Trades, 315, 326, app 310
    Administrative, Executive, and Sales Branch, 392
    Age statistics, 103
    Amalgamations, 633, app 282
    Calls office, 90, 95, 110, 113
    Casuals, 87, 95, 118, 280, app 230–40; Manchester, 539, 541, 544
    Chapels, 260, 268, 279, 280, 283, 293, app 274, app 275, app 277; combined, 309; Manchester, 559; officials, 270
    Circulation Representatives' Branch, 359, 364, 473, app 78
    Demarcation disputes, 334, fn 178
    Disputes procedures, 95–6
    Finances, fn 100
    Formation, 323
    General Print, Process and Typesetting Section, 362
    General Secretary, 388
    House agreements reviews, app 294
    Job entry qualifications, 99
    Job recruitment, 461, 473
    Joint arbitration committee, app 300
    Liaison groups, 420
    London branches, 359–65, 647; District Committee, 365
    London Central Branch, 36, 40–1, 95, 359, 360, app 257–9, app 284
    London Women's Branch, 365
    MGN agreement, 411
    Manchester Branch, 366, app 284
    Membership, app 283, 78
    Monotype Casters, Filmsetters and Typefounders Branch, 318, 334, 336, 359, app 284, app 289
    NATSOPA merger, 711
    National agreements, 404
    National organisation, 335, 336, 337, 338, app 286, app 290
    Newspaper Section, 360, 362
    New technology, views on, 74
    Occupations, 45, 48, 52, 318
    Pay: differentials, 152, 159; figures, app 249, app 251
    Printing Machine Branch, 283, 325, 362, 363, 462, 468, fn 105; occupations, 68, app 284
    Redundancies, fn 100
    Relations with other bodies, 311, 361, 387, 391, 392
    Research Department, 328
    Ruling, Manufacturing and Stationery Branch, 365
    Scottish Graphical Division, 326, 331, 334
    SGA merger, 331, 334, 336, fn 99
    Trade sections, 336, app 80
    Training activities, 527
Society of Licensed Victuallers, 25, 218, app 231
Society of Lithographic Artists, Designers Engravers and Process Workers, 57, 315, 330, 631, app 282

Art Union, 332
Auxiliary Section, 332
Casuals, 96
Chapels, 260, 279, 282; Manchester, 544, 559; statistics, app 274–5, app 7
Demarcation disputes, 334
Differentials, 405
Disputes procedures, app 298
Formation, app 279, app 282
Fathers of the Chapel, 367
Job entry qualifications, 98
Job recruitment, 462
Joint arbitration committee, app 298–9
London Branch, 367, app 284
Manchester Branch, 369, app 78
Membership, 332, app 283, app 284; levy, 368
Occupations, 48, 65, 66, 79, 199, 318, 471
Organisation, 297, 335, app 287, 84
Overtime rules, 174
Pay, app 249; differentials, 152
Relationships with JSC, 688
Relationships with SOGAT, 311, 362
Stoppages, regulations, 303
Unemployment, 40, 73
South West London College, 516
Southwark Offset Ltd, 333, 620, app 309
Special editions, 416
Sporting Chronicle, 534, app 231
Sporting Life, 7, app 231
Staff hands, 469
Staff reductions, 32
Star, fn 12
Statisticians, 573
Status quo concept, 18
Stereotypers, 93, 263, app 298; pay, fn 51, 130, 135, 156, 402, app 248, app 250, app 250, app 256, app 260–2; union membership, 334, 356 (*see also* Foundry workers)
Sterling devaluation, 27
Stoppages, 432–3, 436–8, 565, 624, app 221, app 295–6
Stripping hand, fn 53
Sub-contracted services, 35
Sub-editors, 575, 584, app 302, 99
Subscriptions, 291, app 217, app 278
Sun, app 231; casuals, fn 39; chapels, 312; machine room staff, fn 16, fn 53, 317; profitability, fn 10
Sunday Chronicle, fn 12
Sunday Citizen, 621, fn 12
Sunday Dispatch, fn 12, fn 149
Sunday Express, 485, app 230; casuals, 116, 539; Manchester, 534, 539; NUJ house agreement, 609; profitability, fn 10; relocation, 32, 34
Sunday Graphic, fn 12
Sunday Mirror, 312, app 231; casuals, 539; Manchester, 534, 539, 550, fn 128; pay differentials, fn 51; profitability, fn 10
Sunday newspapers: casuals, 88, 93, 575, 578; NGA rates, app 254; pay comparisons, 132; production staff, 82; profitability, 26
Sunday People, app 231; demarcation dispute, fn 209; Manchester, 534, 539, 555, 584; profitability, fn 10
Sunday Telegraph, 25, 32, fn 10, app 230

Sunday Times, fn 10, app 231; colour magazine, 32
Superintendents, 357
Supervisors, app 240; pay, 105–7; promotion, 467; training, 515–8; union membership, 332, 346, app 220 (*see also* Overseers)
Svenska Arbestgivare Foreningen, app 220, app 221
Svenska Journalist-Forbundet, app 219
Sweden, app 216, app 219–222
    Disclosure, app 220
    Disputes, app 221
    Employers' associations, app 220–221
    Negotiating practices, app 220–221
    Newspaper industry structure, app 219
    Pay, app 221
    Social Democratic Party, app 219
    Technological change, app 217–8, app 219, app 222
    Unions, app 219–221; Federation, app 216, app 219, app 220–2; Organisation, app 217, app 219
Syndication staff, app 217, app 219

Task bargaining, 440
Taxation, casuals, fn 40
Technicians, 332, app 219
Technological change, 638, app 305, app 307
    Consultation, 487, 492, 495, 502–3, 643
    Demarcation, 58–9, 64, 65, 67–9, 72–3
    Editorial staff, 75
    Effect on unemployment, 40, 60
    Effect on industrial relations, 20, 54–77, 633–4, 638, 659
    Effect on pay, 17, 149
    Effect on trade unions, 41, 71–7, 319, 322, 333, 334, 342, 360, 363, 369; chapels, 271; NGA, 72; SLADE, 73
    Manchester, 70, 535, 551, 565
    Negotiations on, 536
    No redundancy agreement, 56
    Staff functions, 570
    Training, 69, 509, 528
Technology: present methods, 42–53
Tele-ad sales staff, 348
Telegraaf, De, app 223
Telegraphists, app 248, app 250, app 257, app 260
Telephone allowances, 590
Telephone information services, 489, 495
Telephone reporters, 459
Telephoto operators, 43
Teletype setting, 44
Theft, 476
Thomson, Lord, app 231
Thomson Organisation, 3, app 231
Thomson Regional Newspapers Ltd, 553
Thomson Scottish Associates Ltd, app 231
Thomson Withy Grove, 534, 537, 550–3
Threshold pay, *see* Cost of living
Tidningarnas Arbets Givareforening, app 220
Time hands, 45, 65; chapels, 263, 307; pay, 130, 157, app 248, app 250, app 256, app 258–60
Time-keeping, 476
Time-served craftsmen, 100

Times, 34, 36, 58, fn 94, 495, 570, app 231; profitability, fn 10
Times Educational Supplement, 7, app 231
Times Higher Educational Supplement, 7, app 231
Times Literary Supplement, 7, app 231
Times Newspapers Ltd, 7, 25, 35, 57, 63,
Tobymen, 405
Trade agreements, 261
Trade unions:
  Administrative staff, 330
  Amalgamations, 320–6, 331, 334–5, 336, 342, 387, 442, 633, 645–6, 712–4, 206, fn 178, app 280–1, app 282
  Branches: functions, 277; inter-relations, 647, 718; officials, 330, 524–6, 528; membership, app 284; organisation, 628; relations with chapels, 13, 297–301, 424–6, 455
  Chapels, *see* Chapels
  Discipline, app 276
  Executive Committees, 445
  Facilities, 293–6
  Finances, 338, fn 100
  Germany, app 218, app 226
  History, 320–6, app 279
  Inter-relations, 304–6, 311–3, 342, 381–7, 558, 644–52, 712–2, app 308
  Manchester, *see* Manchester
  Membership, 13, 327–30, 331–3, 713, app 283, app 284; length of, 98, 99, 100; transfer, 473
  National Executives, 303
  Netherlands, app 217, app 222
  Officials, 299–300, 450, 452, 455, 499, 707, app 307
  Organisation, 331–42, 343–80, 627–8, 715–7, app 289, app 308; joint, 715–7, 204, app 314
  Overtime regulations, 174
  Subscriptions, 291, app 216, app 278
  Sweden, app 217, app 218
  Training, 518, 524–8
  Views on NPA, 255–8
TUC Printing Industries Committee, 388–9, 399, 431, 492, 570, 646, 712, 206, app 310
Training, app 307
  Administration, 204, 225
  Costs, 511
  For industrial relations, 507–33, 705–7
  For new technology, 69, 509, 528
  Grants, 526
  House programmes, 488, 520–3, 529–33
  Joint courses, 707
  Leave, 590
  Levy, 512, 519, 520, 529
  Management, 350–2
  Packages, 514
  Retraining, app 101
Training Managers, 523, 530
Training officers, 523
Training Services Agency, 511
Transfer of Jobs, 106
Typefounders, 334
Typesetting, computerised, 535
Typographical Association, 320, 321, app 279, app 281, app 282

Unemployment, 71, 73, 356, 368, 397, 657
Unemployed, recruitment of, 462
Union of Construction, Allied Trades and Technicians, 53, 316
United Kingdom Newsprint Users' Committee, 224
United Society of Engravers, app 282

Vacancy book, 100
Van loaders, 318
Verband Deutscher Zeitschriftenverleger, app 227
Video display units, 63, 76

Wage drift, 200, 564, 600, app 306
Wages, *see* Pay
Wallpaper Workers' Union, 383, 388
Waste end differentials, 159
Waste hand, fn 53
Waste reduction, 206
Web-offset, fn 3, 50, 333; inquiry, 241, app 309
Weekly Handicap, 534
Welfare schemes, 497
Wholesalers, 360
Winsbury, Rex, app 216
Wireroom employees, 43, 551, app 248, app 250
Women, union members, 349
Work allocation, 271, 272, 275, 457–59, 640, 643, 677
Work organisation, app 296
Work study, 142, 143, fn 48; courses, 518
Working parties, joint, 631
Workers' Educational Association, 526
Works Councils, app 227–8
Works managers, 357
Works rules, 475
Wrapper hands, 159; casuals, 117
Writers, special, 584